LETTERS TO OUR SONS

A COLLECTION OF LETTERS BY PRISONERS & EX-PRISONERS
TO STOP MASS INCARCERATION OF OUR YOUTH

DAWN SIMMONS, MSSW, MA
HERU MOSSIAH MAAT

www.imperial-imprint.com

ART & LITERATURE ™

ISBN-13:978-0-9863903-9-5 (Paperback Edition)
ISBN-13:978-0-9863903-2-6 (Hardcover Edition)
ISBN-13:978-0-9863903-0-2 (E-book)

Library of Congress Control Number: 2018945661

Infographics by The Sentencing Project, Community Coalition, "In the Public Interest" & Hearts for Inmates reprinted by permission.
Credits for illustrations by Kobe Carter, Andre Cannon & Michael Moore
Credits for cover design and images Ernest Kumi Osae
Credits and permissions by ThomsonReuters for "Civil Asset Forfeiture" and additional credits and permissions are listed on pages 525-536 (Bibliography) and are considered a continuation of the copyright page.

Printed and bound in the United States of America
First Printing October 2018

Published by Imperial Imprint LLC
New York, NY

Please contact us at:
PO Box 6180
Bronx, New York, 10451
info@imperial-imprint.com

Visit www.imperial-imprint.com

This book is dedicated to those who lost their lives behind the fences, the 7 ~~prisoners~~ martyrs from Lee Correctional Institution during the riot and all corrections officers, law enforcement and criminal justice professionals who do not abuse their power but do their jobs to make the world a better place to be, both inside and outside of the prison walls.

Table of Contents

PREFACE

When my business partner/big sister from another mother presented me with the idea for the "Save the Children" project in December 2013, I knew automatically that it was something that I wanted to be a part of. Having been incarcerated for the past 10 years and noticing that the faces are getting younger and younger, I knew something had to be done to stop it.

At first I thought it would be an easy task to get guys to participate, thinking that everyone would feel the same passion I felt when first hearing about the project. Little did I know that the grip of ignorance was stronger than I had anticipated. I handwrote a memorandum detailing the project for every dorm. There are four dorms with two sides in each one so I wrote out eight memos and had someone I knew post them up in the bulletin boards on each dorm.

I also spread the word myself and explained what the project was about.

A few guys felt the way I did and wrote their letters immediately. Some gave me some B.S. excuses talking about they did not have the time, while others were honest and told me flat out NO, some people made false promises and never came through.

I couldn't believe that dudes wouldn't take 30 minutes away from the card table, chess/checker boards, televisions and other frivolous activities to sit down and write a letter that may one day be read by a troubled youth and may touch him or her to the point that they may change their lives.

I even received resistance from some of my so-called brothers in the struggle who are supposed to be on the path of righteousness. After three weeks, I only had taken up about 20 letters. I had put an eight week deadline on the project so I guess guys felt they had time to get them done.

During the final week, the letters started to trickle in. Not as many as I expected but enough to get the project done.

If it were not for the C.B.U. (Character Base Unit) at Perry Correctional Institution in South Carolina, which is only one dorm, I would not have received nowhere near enough participation. So I would like to give special thanks and shout out to the guys over there that came through for me. I would also like to thank all of my comrades in the struggle that also came through in the clutch.

1

For the guys who passed up on the opportunity, it was your loss. I just pray that our efforts were not in vain and if our letters affect the life of just one person, then it was a job well done.

Sincerely, Heru Mossiah Maat

****

"Letters to Our Sons" Why not "Letters to Our Daughters," "Letters to the Children?" Why not? Because young males are going to prison by the truckloads. We have issues with young ladies, but for this particular book we are focusing more on males, although some of the men have also written letters to females.

This book came about as my partner/younger brother, from other parents, Heru Mossiah Maat and I did a project with some of the inmates at Perry Correctional Institution, where they kept a journal during the month of October in 2013. The project was requested by a friend of mine, Ronaldo Clement, who advised that people were fascinated with what goes on in prison. People always think they know what happens in prison. However, we were able to get 14 willing/unwilling participants to chronicle their lives for that month. Personally, I did not find anything fascinating or exciting about it. What goes on there was downright upsetting, hurtful, frustrating and kind of disrespectful.

The work was so compelling and moving that we thought, *'let's really make a difference and give prisoners the chance to make a difference in the world and take responsibility in helping others stay OUT of prison. Just because these men are locked up, they are still human beings despite some of the heinous crimes, and that does not mean that they do not have wisdom or words of value to help others.'* In about two or three letters, you will be able to tell that the stress of prison has affected their minds. It was difficult getting people to participate. Some of the men were eager and willing to assist, while others were thinking *'What am I getting out of this?'* or *'What are you getting out of this and cheating me out of?'* Heru asked his Character Building classmates to assist and many of them did. Some of the men, he did not even know personally. However they wanted to give their advice and lend their knowledge so that they would not see any more young/males coming into prison to live with them in the near future or ever. Because the work was compelling, we also asked people from other prisons and previously incarcerated men to assist. Current and former correction officers and police officers gave the book balance to ensure that BOTH SIDES are told. I also asked politicians, well-known criminal justice reform activists and those working with the incarcerated. Some people jumped to assist and others never even responded.

Although this book can be considered an educational or empirical study on incarceration and its causes and effects on the inmate, as this book is actually targeted towards EVERYONE. It is written in a language that everyone can understand and in all actuality it is just a self-help guide. This book does not speak to one group of people specifically, as it does not matter what your race, color, creed, socio-economic status, religion, etc.; because the men who wrote letters are of different races, backgrounds, socio-economic classes and two-parent homes. Hence the message is: *ANYONE can go to prison!* ANYONE can get caught up in drugs, greed, peer-pressure, accidental killing /assault, being in the wrong place at the wrong time (innocent) or have no sense of direction/hopelessness in their lives. When any of these situations come up (sans wrong place, wrong time) think about what these men are telling you. And then think TWICE before acting.

Remember, if we just save ONE person from prison, we are saving about 10 people from pain and despair. If we stop just ONE murder, we save TWO lives the victim and the perpetrator, not to mention all of the loved ones that are affected.

This book is not to excuse anyone of their past crimes or behavior. This book is not to disrespect people who work in law enforcement and corrections. It is simply a tool to stop the next person from committing a crime, and going to prison. We and the authors herein, hope to stimulate positive choices in life so that our home, community and world are a better place to live in.

Peace and good luck to you all,
Dawn Simmons

INTRODUCTION

There is a growing epidemic in this country and it is called mass incarceration. "Mass incarceration is defined by extreme rates of imprisonment and by the concentration of incarceration among the most marginalized."[1] (Garland, 2001) While mass incarceration is a global phenomenon, it occurs in epic proportion in the United States. For example, according to the Sentencing Project's Incarceration webpage, "2.2 million people are now incarcerated in the U.S. – a rate of incarceration far higher than that of any other industrialized nation, and unprecedented in U.S. history."[2] (The Sentencing Project) Today, the U.S. is 5% of the World population and has 25% of world prisoners[3] (NAACP, 2016) In addition, according to a Policy memo prepared for the Organization for Economic Co-Operation and Developmental (OECD) countries, the United States has more per people per capita incarcerated than in any other country in the world with a rate 710 per 100,000 people. (Kearney, Harris, Jacome, & Parker, 2014)[4] Chile has the next highest per capita incarceration with a rate of 266 per 100,000,[5] and it is noted that "the U.S. incarceration rate is more than six times that of the typical OECD nation."[6]

MASS INCARCERATION AN EPIDEMIC

Mass incarceration is not new, however it has become an epidemic as everyone is once again talking and writing on the subject. A recent article in the *New York Times* highlighted that 1.5 million African American men are missing in this country[7] as most are incarcerated. Hillary Clinton speaking at the David N. Dinkins Leadership and Public Policy Forum at Columbia University on April 29, 2015, stated that we must make effort "to end an era of Mass Incarceration."[8] [9] President Trump and President Obama recognized that importance of this needed change and gave pardons and have made criminal justice/prison reform part of their platforms.

Michelle Alexander's cutting edge book, *The New Jim Crow*, famous rappers, Criminal Justice advocates/activists Van Jones and President Trump's son-in law Jared Kushner, Mark Holman and the Koch Brothers, Republican politicians such as US Senator Tim Scott (R-SC) and Charles Grassley (R-IA), Democratic politicians such as State Assemblyman Walter T. Mosley (D-NY) and US Senator Adriano Espaillat (D-NY) as well as a bi-partisan alliance with US congressmen Rep. Hakeem Jeffries (D-NY) and Rep. Doug Collins (R-GA) who together created the FIRST STEP Act[10], and even reality show celebrities turned activist Kim Kardashian as well as conservative Christian businessman agree that prison reform is needed[11]. President Trump and President Obama made criminal justice and prison reform a top priority to help our country and to give compassion to those who need it most.

There are also countless other books, articles, speeches, social groups, etc.,[12] such as The Vera Institute Policy Book, 'Play Book for Change? States reconsider mandatory sentences'[13] that all agree that mass incarceration in the United States is an issue and that prison reform is needed. What is missing however from this dialogue are the personal accounts of the inmates, sharing their experiences and their victimization both inside and outside of prison and the pitfalls our youth can avoid so as not to become a statistic.

To keep things simple, the trends in United States incarceration rates over the years are as per the graph below.[14]

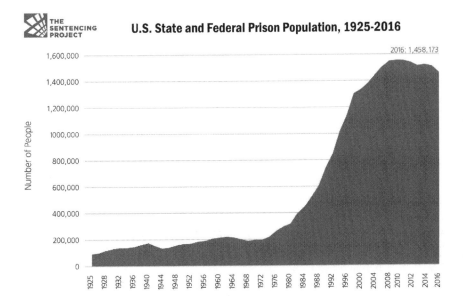

Imperial Imprint LLC received permission to use the above 'Trends in US Corrections' infographic from the Sentencing Project. www.sentencingproject.org (https://www.sentencingproject.org/wp-content/uploads/2018/07/u.s.-state-and-federal-prison-population-1925-2016.png)

The above graph illustrates that the incarceration rate has more than tripled from 1980 to 2016. As of 2016 there were 1,458,173 people in prison as per the Bureau of Justice Statistics Prisoners Series.[15]

To break this down along racial lines, by race African Americans have the highest number of people incarcerated, followed by Latinos, then Caucasians As noted by the PrisonPolicy.org

In 2010, for every 100,000 men by race in prison, the numbers are shown in the below table. Information retrieved from the prisonpolicy.org, where the statistics came from the Bureau of Justice Statistics in an article by Peter Wagner. Race within the prison population are as follows:[16] [17]

Men in Prison by Race and Age in 2010 (Number of men in U.S. prisons per 100,000 by race)			
	Black	**White**	**Latino**
Ages 25-29	8,932	1,437	3,892
All Ages	4,347	678	1,775

(Created with information from prisonpolicy.org/Bureau of Justice Statistics, Correctional Population in the United States in 2010, Appendix Table 3)

****

As per the Bureau of Federal Prisons, the racial breakdown for current incarceration in the United States is as follows: [18]

Inmates in the Bureau of Prisons as of September 29, 2018		
Race	**# of Inmates**	**% of Inmates**
White	105,497	58.2%
Black	69,020	38.1%
Native American	4,073	2.2%
Asian	2,712	1.5%
Total	**181,302**	**100.00%**

For full prison population (Federal & State) see DID YOU KNOW???Racial Disparities

Below are a few facts about race and disparity within the criminal justice system.

- As per Michelle Alexander, "African Americans make up 13.6 percent of the U.S. population according to census data, but black men reportedly make up 40.2 percent of all prison inmates."[19]

In the Criminal Report Sheet by the NAACP, it states:

- "More than 846,000 black men were incarcerated in 2008, according to U.S. Bureau of Justice estimates reported by NewsOne."[20]

- "One in six black men had been incarcerated as of 2001. If current trends continue, one in three black males born today can expect to spend time in prison during his lifetime"[21]

- "In comparison, 1 in 100 African American women are in prison."[22]

REASONS FOR INCREASED INCARCERATION

"The first federal criminal statute, signed into law on April 30, 1790, includes only a handful of offenses: treason, counterfeiting, piracy, and murder, maiming and robbery in federal jurisdictions."[23] By the 21th century it was estimated to be 3,000.[24] And as of 2013 there about 4,850 offenses with approximately 10,000 to 300,000 that can be enforced criminally, as per Matt Vespa's article on internet site Townhall.com "How Many Federal Laws are There Again?"[25] With the War on Drugs, which has imprisoned thousands of people for non-violent crimes with extremely long sentences, and sometimes even LIFE in prison, President Clinton's three strikes law, where one's third felony can result in 25 years to LIFE imprisonment, and the Truth in Sentencing Law, (where one must serve a *minimum* of 85% of their sentence) incarceration rates have soared. As per a *Wall Street Journal* article, "With the growing number of federal crimes, the number of people sentenced to federal prison has risen nearly threefold over the past 30 years to 83,000 annually."[26] "Many of the new federal laws also set a lower bar for conviction than in the past: Prosecutors don't necessarily need to show that the defendant had criminal intent."[27]

PRISON THE INSTITUTION & THE ECONOMICS OF PENOLOGY

It has been well researched historically that mass incarceration is an institution. "An institution that extends beyond the prison walls to other systems of social control[28], such as the parole system.[29]"[30] Also noted is that "Whether called mass incarceration, mass imprisonment, the prison boom, the carceral state, or hyper incarceration, this phenomenon refers to the current American experiment in incarceration, which is defined by comparatively and historically extreme rates of imprisonment and by the concentration of imprisonment among young, African American men living in neighborhoods of concentrated disadvantage."[31]

Examples of this prison system are the private companies such as, GEO Group, Management and Training Corporation and Core Civic (formerly Corrections Corporation of America "CCA"), which is a publicly traded company (ticker: NYSE: CXW). These companies own prisons and are making money off of increased incarceration rates. Core Civic makes money when beds are filled, i.e. people are in prison. "This is a massively profitable operation for CCA who recorded $1.64 billion in revenue, $883.1 million of which came from state governments in 2012."[32] "CCA has made profits from, and at times contributed to, the expansion of tough-on-crime and anti-immigrant policies that have driven prison expansion."[33] The article written by Joe Weisenthal, "This Investor Presentation For A Private Prison Is One Of The Creepiest Presentations We've Ever Seen"[34], which is in BusinessInsider.org, an internet business magazine, shows how a company put together a PowerPoint presentation to encourage investors to invest in private prison.

In general although private prisons in 2017 made about USD $4 billion in revenues (for immigration and non-immigration detention)[35] and in 2016 they housed 128,063, approximately 8.5% prisoners of the Federal & State prison population.[36] Most private prisons are moving towards detaining and making money off of undocumented immigrants. While Core Civic is one example, there are various companies using prison labor where prisoners receive less than minimum wage and in some states such as South Carolina, most prisoner labor is free. Using prison labor is the equivalent to slavery. A person can be considered insubordinate and punished (sent to lock up/jail within prison or receive an extended prison term) if they refuse to work as some prisoners do not receive good time nor are their sentences reduced when working without pay. "If prisoners don't work, they serve longer sentences, lose privileges, and risk solitary confinement."[37] *(For a background history on private prisons, see Mother Jones article by Shane Bauer. https://www.motherjones.com/crime-justice/2018/09/corecivic-private-prison-shane-bauer-book/)*

One may say, *"So what?"* as this is punishment for the crime. Perhaps justifiably so; however, if money is being made off of free to low-cost labor, similar to slavery or to the current national phenomenon of U.S. companies outsourcing labor and jobs offshore to other countries such as India to have reduced labor costs, how does the average law abiding American support themselves? "Proponents of the practice claim prison labor is a low-cost alternative to offshore outsourcing, but critics say it takes jobs away from law-abiding U.S. citizens."**[38]**

SOLUTIONS

What is needed, in my opinion is to provide intervention and *educate* our young men and women about the consequences of a career in crime... Education, such as a high school diploma, in general, reduces rates of incarceration. The Hamilton Report writes that those black men in their mid-thirties without a high school diploma have a 70% chance of being sent to prison.[39] The Prison Policy shows that "social intervention"[40] is very effective. This book, *Letters to Our Sons* is meant to be an educational guide; similar to a guide that provides information on various career paths and the pro/cons of a particular profession. In this instance "Crime" is the profession similar to that of one who chooses a career path in Accounting, Law, Medicine, etc. The goal however in "Letters to our Sons" is to avert the number of African American youth in particular from choosing this particular path.

For example, with Accounting, one will have to obtain a college degree, study and pass the CPA exam to receive licensure, and then ultimately have an opportunity to obtain a good job, thus living a decent lifestyle. However choosing a career or even "part time/consulting job" in criminal activity, will lead one to some initial benefits such as illegally obtaining money, illegally earned goods and services through violence and/or non-violence, enjoyment of using/selling/abusing drugs or a host of other illegal activities. Of course, prison *or an untimely death* shall be the ultimate result of this "Criminal" profession, thus the pinnacle of a career in criminality. This book provides insight on what will happen when one receives forced retirement benefits (arrest and imprisonment) which can occur at the beginning, middle or end of a criminal career.

Most of the following letters show the reader the 'retirement benefits' of choosing a life of crime, as these men were in forced retirement (prison). You will hear from incarcerated men about their lives before prison, and they will discuss what it is like living inside of prison, the emotions one deals with, the loneliness, the abandonment of loved ones, dehumanization, constant fear of violence or extended prison sentences, basic stress and trying to keep one's sanity. You will also hear from law enforcement, loved ones and short research/informational essays and Factoids.

So please kindly turn the page so that you may receive an education in criminal activity retirement benefits, i.e. prison.

Please note: This book is for ALL races, socio-economic groups (rich/poor), however since more people of color are being incarcerated the book will tend to focus on the black men at some points. But please know that people of different races and ethnicities have contributed written work to this book therefore this book is intended for ALL.

Some of the writing will show spelling errors and the sentence structures may be grammatically incorrect, however the edits were not done to correct this on purpose in order to keep the authenticity of the letters.

(The views, opinions and experiences are those of each writer, Imperial Imprint LLC takes no responsibility for the writer's comments.)

This book is packed with information. However, if you want to see raw accounts of what Prison Life is like proceed straight to Sections "Realities of Prison Life" and/or "Prison in General."

"My worst day out here is better than my best day in there."
Steve-O Lawyer

PRISON by LUMUMBA K. INCUMAA

Existing within a world designed to destroy my mind,
A world in which I have been physically chained and confined,
A world that is the reality of living hell,
Because it is the domain in which all the characteristics of the real devil dwell.

Within this world I struggle from day to day to maintain my sanity,
And not lose my grip on life and fall from civilized humanity
This is not an easy struggle because this not a world
In which civilized humanity exists.

It is a world in which all that is evil rises from the darkness of the abyss.
And contaminates the hearts and corrupts the soul of all manner of men,
Who are unfortunate to find themselves confined,
Within this world of the devil's den?

Surrounded by this evil and wickedness each and every day,
I must remain mentally and physically strong and not become its prey.
And fall victim to a world that has no pity or remorse,
A world that will consume your entire being if give that choice.

This world that I speak of is the reality of prison,
Which seeks to remove you from civilized humanity and limit your vision?
To the confines of these concrete walls,
Where only the strong survive and the weak always falls.

Prison is a world that is a desert of sin,
Where all the evils of Sodom and Gomorrah are found within.
It is a world where you can live or die,
Kill or be killed without any reason why.

A world that is the incubator of all things wrong,
Destroying the soul of the youth tricking them to believe,
that this hell is where they belong.

Where each Prisoner is a commodity of free labor,
from which a profit can be made,
By greedy politicians, Judges, business men and police,
who all profit from our imprisonment and conditional release.

Currently serving a LIFE sentence

*(This poem was written for the book in 2015 during his 19th year in Solitary
Confinement. Mr. Luumba was released back into general population in 2016)*

FACTOID: STRIP SEARCH

One of the most humiliating, degrading and downright disrespectful things you have to experience in prison are the strip searches. What happens in a strip search is that they take off ALL of your clothes, including your undershirt and underwear, then they tell you to lift your nuts and turn around and spread your ass cheeks and cough, while they watch you, inspecting the inside of your ass.

The reason for these strip searches is to catch prisoners with contraband. Especially homemade keys to un-lock handcuffs and other restraints, door keys, cell phones, drugs, and homemade weapons... but your visitor can be subjected to this when they come to visit you as well. Visitors are given a choice to either- no, first let me say this, if a metal detector keeps going off, they will tell your visitor to either consent to a strip search, or leave. But if they suspect, or have been tipped off that your visitor is bringing in contraband, they will wait until the visitors has made it into the building then escort them to a room and let them know they have reasons to believe they've brought in contraband and they "must" search them. ("Most of this information you can get off the web.")

Anytime a prisoner receives a visit he must allow a male officer to strip search him. Sometimes you get lucky and there is a heterosexual male conducting the searches who may tell you to hand him your clothes but will allow you to keep your boxers on because he does not want to see your ass and nuts just as much as you do not want to show it to him.

Another option after strip searching is Dry Cell. (Look under Section "Prison in General") This is a method of making a Prisoner be in a room with no running water or anything and swallow a pill, or drink that will make them use the restroom, so that they have a bowel movement in a bucket and the correctional officer can look in the bucket every so many hours to see if the prisoner has swallowed contraband, or stuck it up his anus to hide it...

Then you have officers who are suspect... probably just perverts, or some prisoners call homosexuals, who go overboard and make you strip down and take their time inspecting your naked anus and testicles. The reason the prisoners view these types of officers as homosexuals is because any straight man with an ounce of self-respect would never feel comfortable looking at another man's genitals and rectum, as a part of their job description. But again, they are just probably perverts.

For your wife, or girl to know that an Officer, or a few officers violate you like this is something that a new Prisoner deals with, Prisoners who've been down six months or more do not talk or think about it. For some people, reading about it in this book will be the first time it's been brought to their attention, because the Prisoner is too ashamed to talk about it especially to their male friends, sons, nephews, cousins, uncles or brothers.

Below is a letter which provides you with an example of this practice of which feels dehumanizing to any person and makes one feel sexually violated, yet this practice is legal and you have no control of this practice happening at any time.

****

Dear Future, I want to continue this letter by sharing one of the many dehumanizing situations that I've personally experienced in prison. Today is June 2, 2015 and I had an order to report (O.T.R.) to medical. Anytime that a prison/inmate leaves the dormitories (dungeons) he has to have a pass or O.T.R. from the correctional officer (C.O.) who is working in the dorm. There is a locked gate that separates the dorms and the operation, education and medical buildings. Anytime that one has to go beyond the dorms, he has to be frisked/patted down. Normally there are male officers that do the frisking, however today they had a female. (Sargent X) doing the frisking.

Due to the fact that I am a Muslim, (and Muslims are not supposed to let females other than their wives touch them), I asked the Sargent to get a male officer to pat me down; which is in accordance with the Department of Corrections Religious policy which basically states that whenever possible shakedown (including frisking) should be always be done by an officer of the same sex as the inmate. Being that I quoted the policy, Sargent X called Captain X (who was nearby and a male) and asked him to frisk me. Captain X told me that if I didn't want Sargent X to frisk me, then I could return to the dorm. I quoted the policy once again and Captain X them told me that if I wanted to go to medical then I'd have to be stripped searched and not frisked. I told him to do what he wished, but I had to go to medical.

I was then escorted to the operations building where I saw the Major (Major X) coming out of operations and attempted to explain the situation to him, but he was dismissive in his manner, showing absolutely no concern. Then Captain X made the comment "You gone make me put my hands on you." I then told him that if he did then there would be immediate repercussions. He humbled himself a little, realizing that he was a small white guy talking to a six foot three inch, two hundred plus black guy.

I was taken to a holding cell by Captain X and Lieutenant X. I was ordered to strip down to nothing (while standing on a cold filthy floor); then told to lift my testicles and penis up. Then turn around, bend over and spread my butt cheeks. All the while, with the two of them standing there smiling. All of this was done because I attempted to assert my religious right to be frisked by an officer of the same sex.

15

Upon leaving the operations area, I encountered the Major again, along with the Warden. I attempted to tell both of them the situation that had just transpired, but the warden was very disrespectful; the warden told me that he did not care what the policy said and that I was in prison and if I did not want a female officer to frisk me, then I needed to change my religion...

Dear Future, NO ONE knows better than me that I am in prison because there is not one single day that goes by wherein I don't psychologically and emotionally torture myself for allowing myself to end up in prison. Each and every day, I wish that I could kick my own ass for being so stupid. On any given day, prisoners face numerous situations where they are disrespected, humiliated and violated in the most inhumane, unethical, and illegal ways; and even a six foot three inches 200-plus pound angry black man is powerless in most of these situations.

Please Future, learn through my example, learn from my pain and torment so that my humiliation will never become yours. The system neither honors nor respects any part of our lives. And the sad truth of the matter is that it's a good possibility that I will have to endure these types of dehumanizing humiliations for the rest of my life, because I have LIFE in prison.

Gerald Brown #174505

POLITICS AS USUAL

KIMJARO PRESLEY - PRISON PARADISE

The U.S. Government can't thank you foolish youth enough for your relentless dedication to keep our prisons overcrowded. Another year you have made history by raising the incarceration rate of young blacks to an all-time high! That's right, "The Land of the Free" has the highest incarceration rate in the world, and four out of every 10 Black men in their twenties are in prison, jail, on probation, or on parole. Just read the 13th Amendmentof the United States Constitution and you'll see that the "prison correctional system" is simply freed constitution of slavery. From the 1860's (the time of the Emancipation Proclamation, which supposedly freed the slaves) with the 1890's, the prison population rate of white stayed constant while the Black Prison population increased by 900%! In 2012, there are more black men in prison, jail, on probation, or on parole than there were slaves in America in 1850!

The privatization of prisons has generated immense profits for the US Government and has coincided with Black imprisonment campaigns with names such as the "Three Strikes Law", "Tough on crime", and my personal favorite, "Truth in Sentencing" which is better known as the 85% law. This law means that you can never receive parole or good time. So if the judge sentences you to 10 years in prison under the 85% law, then you must do at least $8^1/_2$ years before being released. But if you choose to violate the prison rules while incarcerated, you'll end up doing the entire 10 years sentence. This law includes not only "Violent Offenses" but also drug charges and even petty larceny or shoplifting offenses.

This is even better than the old days of chattel slavery when we had to whip and kill numerous men, women and children in order to get the others to comply. Nowadays all we have to do is to tell you that you are a criminal and must "pay" for your crime by serving time (see the 13th Amendment of the United States Constitution). We thank you, not only because we get paid for you being incarcerated but we are also getting paid for your free labor in prison. I bet you didn't even know that we sell prisoners (as credit) for stocks and bonds with private corporations on the stock market exchange. But that's not all. Many major corporations profit from prison labor including IBM, Texas Instruments, Dell, Motorola, Compaq, Microsoft, Revlon, Chevron, Macy's, and Target Stores just to name a few[41].

Let's thank the innocent black labor force victims for building America's roads, bridges, dams, and railroads. Now fast forward to today as inmates are contracted out to private industries to do agriculture, manufacturing of goods, telemarketing and even bill collecting at slave wages. You people are so devoted to assisting us in oppressing you all that it is almost beyond belief.

However, prison life is not "that bad." Just consider all of the luxuries that you'll receive. I mean, no, there aren't any video games to play, you are away from your family and friends, but you don't have to worry about not having anyone to keep you company. You are **never** alone in prison. Not even when you try to cover the window on your door; therefore anyone can look in and watch you while you sit on the toilet. This is especially good for homosexuals and weirdoes because they get free peeks. And some female CO's tell you to leave the window open so that they can 'check' to ensure you are not doing something wrong.

Speaking of free perks, correctional officers are allowed to strip search you at any time and for whatever reason. They simply order you to get "buck-naked," turn around and bend forward at the waist so that they can inspect your cavities (inside of your anus).

Oh, and for all you gangbangers, you have so many "brothers" back here who would love for you to help them do their time. They are always in need of young strong bodies to take stab wounds for them and even sacrifice their lives, all for a prison reputation. Just think, if you are killed in prison behind gang violence then you will become a legend. Well, not really, but at least it'll be considered cool.

For those of you who are naturally tough guys/girls, you can always show and prove strength in prison. There are plenty of violent individuals in prison who would love to "test your gangster," or try to harm you, if for no other reason than to receive a reputation or to be initiated into a prison gang or organization. And even if you do happen to win the fight, you may still be cut, stabbed, or have hot boiling oil thrown into your face simply because your opponent is unable to accept a loss.

That's why we offer a 24-hour medical facility, in case you need attention. Whether you are physically hurt, poisoned by contaminated food, or mentally exhausted due to abnormal conditions of the prison environment, we can provide what little knowledge we have and possibly help (or hurt) you. We have mental health counselors and psychiatrists who will only see you for 15 minutes per month despite the fact that you are dealing with a mental crisis and are eager to prescribe you the latest medications, which may help ease or worsen any stress-related psychological issue that you may experience, especially since we have pharmaceutical companies paying us to experiment with these new drugs in prisons before they place them on the insurance to receive benefits! It's the least that we can offer, since we will be using you all as "guinea pigs" to test out the effect of the latest generic drugs. PRISON has always been a cheap laboratory for testing experimental drugs, and we intend to continue the tradition.

Come and feel larger than life in the tiny cells where you can touch both walls by simply extending your arms to the side. Get the latest prison trends, including "crocs" which will be the only footwear provided, compliments of the State. Wear our stylish jackets that are much too thin to protect you from cold weather, but at least you can look cool, right? Since we know how much you all cherish being "fresh to death" we figured we would help.

Allow us to serve you gourmet meals three times per day, except on the weekends when you'll only receive two meals per day, free of charge. Unless you are not cleanly shaved, shoes are unlaced in those fashionable ways that young people usually wear, your shirt is untucked (even partially), you don't have your ID card, your pants are sagging, you don't walk in a straight line, you are talking too loud, or simply because an officer doesn't like you, then you will be able to eat our complimentary food in the "Mess Hall" (Cafeteria).

Even when you are placed on lockdown (which could last for months at a time), you will be treated like a king/queen and have your "bag meals" (one piece of bread and one piece of meat or boiled egg) delivered to your cell at no cost. You won't be able to shower, but the sink always has running water, even if it's cold. Also, you can't make any phone calls on lockdown yet you have all day and night to write letters with no distractions (with the 4 sheets of paper and two envelopes they allow you each month when on lock down).

So come hangout at a place where you don't have to worry about life's surprises because everything in prison remains the same, day in and day out. This is a vacation of a lifetime and I promise that you'll leave prison a new person, *__if you ever leave at all.__* If you don't believe me, just ask those repeat offenders who can't stay away and continue to come back over and just to experience prison again. There are so many more amenities that can be received in prison that I can't list them all in this short letter. But don't take my word for it. Come experience prison life for yourself and I guarantee that you won't be disappointed. All you have to do is continue to disrespect and ignore your parents, teachers, and all other authoritative figures, because hey, what do they know anyway? "Keep it one hundred" by running the streets and doing whatever you want. Keep thinking like Kanye West taught you to think when he rapped, *"You can't tell me nothing!"* Keep chasing the lifestyle of 'gangsta' rappers and entertainers, and we will continue to lock you all up by the truckload. Like our motto says, "Come in as a young adult with infinite potential and leave as an old fool with only lost hopes and dreams".

Sincerely,
Your Local Government,
Kimjaro Presley - shipped to a private prison in Mississippi.

(The views and opinions are those of the writer, Imperial Imprint takes no responsibility to errors in comments.)

LEONARD "PETEY" ROLLOCK- SMART PEOPLE LEARN FROM THEIR MISTAKES

Smart People learn from their mistakes
Smarter People Learn from other's mistakes!
~~~~~Unknown

In the past week or so 10-10 WINS, a New York based 24 hours news station, repeated the NYPD Police Commissioner Bill Bratton, was quoted as saying "It was hard to hire African American men because so many have criminal records" ..."and the Police Department simply cannot hire people with criminal records." Another source nationalized that Stop and Frisk had unfairly targeted men of color resulting in a lot of low level marijuana arrest which was partially responsible for the disqualification. Police Commissioner contested his reported statement was taken out of content from another discussion misrepresenting his and the department's position.

The point here is not whether it is true but more so why it is believable. There is a lot of evidence that our sons are at war... a war for our minds and their bodies. The mind and body count is high, too high. Michelle Alexander the author of the critically acclaimed best seller "The New Jim Crow," calls it "Drug War Racism." She concretely points out this war is exclusively held in poor neighborhoods, despite the facts Blacks and people of color, do not use or sell any more drugs than white...the activity is rampart in both communities but fought in only one. The facts are criminal convictions disenfranchise people from many civilian rights forever.

Too many grandfathers, fathers, uncles, brothers, sons, and grandsons, have been, are, or are going to be victims of this lop sided scheme in order to quill this attack in our communities. We first have to share information and insight to master the distortion.

Whether or not the culprit is exposable by name, the parent culture aka influences of society are exerting their power in our community... over us. Power, in this sense, is the ability to create reality and have others respond to that reality if it were their own.

One of the oldest most profound pearls of wisdom handed down through the ages etched in the oldest stone buildings standing on the earth states as a warming and sense of direction is:

"Know thyself: Self-Knowledge is the basis of all hue knowledge"

This statement is found in the Walls at the Temple at Karnack in the Valley of the Kings in Egypt (Kemet)

When we scrutinize the educational system in place, conscious minds understand the parent culture sets the standards in our education. A focal point is missing and that is essential it's the whole history and our rightful place in it. We as a people are functioning as a subculture when in fact we are descendants of the authentic parent culture – one that raises the expectation of ourselves hence our creative energy. As a people under attack we are suffering from the severe condition of amnesia. The therapy is to research our history.

All men who became great critical thinkers had a chief hand in their own education. The public school systems in our neighborhoods do not provide true historical perspectives so when we look in the mirror we cannot see our true potential as a group. A few years back CNN reported that the State of Texas Educational Department had decided to take the wording "the Slave Trade" out of the public school's depiction of our experience in this country to smooth it over as being now mentioned as "the triangular trade." Our education is constantly being shaped to distort reality... creating a people with amnesia.

To put this in a clearer overall context, just imagine...How good a decision maker you would be in the ways of this world, at the age of 12, 13, 14, 15? If, the first 10 years of your life you could not remember? Would you be confident? Could you be practical? Would you be motivated enthusiastic? Or Frustrated? This is not hard to rationalize and until we understand our responsibility at this point we will remain angry with each other, untrusting and short tempered.

One of the greatest scholars who is a must study...self-taught... Dr. John Honrik Clarke (1915-1998) received his doctorate status after he taught and proved his superiority his-self. He eloquently explains the importance of having this foundation of Knowledge:

"History is not everything, but it is a starting point...he goes on to explain

Dr. Clarke's word on History

"History is a clock that people use to tell their political and cultural time of day. It is also a compass that people use to find themselves on the map of human geography. History tells people where they have been and what they have been, where they are and what they are. Most important, history tells a people where they still must go, what they still must be. The relationship of history to the people is the same as the relationship of a mother to her child."

Everyone whom I see that took time to really study their history became more serious on how they would spend their time... approach subject matters with more zeal and confidence and critical thought, and in our case become more ready to give someone who looks like you a pass. Meaning we will value ourselves more as a group and individuals.

24

The movie "Malcom X" has a great example of what study can produce when it's done independent of the parent culture in America' tutelage. It has been observed that intellectuals move to solve problems while geniuses prevent them. This ideal readily translates into brothers recognizing their sense of misdirection from the street and moving to correct it in prison educating themselves. However, we should come home as intellectuals to have our youth (geniuses) prevent what has been set up for them from taking place some or all of their lives in prison!

Until him write their own history,
The tale of the hunt will always fortify the hunter
~~~African proverb

When there is no enemy with the enemy without can do us no harm!
~~~African proverb

My experience with the prison system came from 30 years of total incarceration. In 1977 I went to trial with Nicky Barnes when known as Mr. Untouchable. I was convicted receiving two (2) 15 year sentences to run concurrent. I did 54 months before I was released on parole.

Then, in July 19, 1988, I was arrested after being tried in Absentia and sentenced to three (3) 50 year sentences concurrent after conviction by a jury trial where I was charged as a co-conspirator with the Gambino crime family members and associates. I was not released on parole until May 6, 2014.

My son Peter Rollock aka Pistol Pete is serving life in federal prison – he has been incarcerated since June 1995.

Peace and Blessings to Everyone!

TORRANCE MCCRAE - SECTION 1. SLAVERY PROHIBITED

66"Neither slavery nor involuntary servitude except as a punishment for crime whereof the party shall have been duly convicted shall exist within the United States, or any place subject to their jurisdiction."

The primary objective of Thirteenth Amendment was to end a barbaric and vicious period in American history of chattel slavery, peonage, and involuntary servitude. But they never ended anything they just change the language of the words. The plain intent was to abolish slavery of whatever name or form, and all badges and incident, to render impossible any state of bondage, to make labor free, by prohibiting that control by which is the essence of involuntary servitude. Prisoners are forced to work 12 to 16 hours a day of free labor and if we don't, we are punished by being thrown into the hole, so if that ain't slavery, then what is?

Slavery and involuntary servitude were institutionalized in the prison system. As stated by the U.S. Supreme Court in its long standing precedent in Ruffin v. Commonwealth, 62, Va. (21 Gratt.) 790-796 (1871), states as per below:

"(A prisoner) "has, as a consequence of his crime, not only forfeited his liberty, but all his personal rights except those which the law in its humanity accords to him. He is for the time being the slave of the state.""[42]

[This was/is also known as the "hands-off doctrine" whereby government did not interfere with the treatment and the goings on in the prison until the 1960s. (However being a slave of the state still stands) When Wolf v. McDonnell, 418, U.S. 539, 555-56 (1974) and Procunier v. Martinez, 416 U.S. 396, 405-06 (1974) became case law, it was determined that if the prisoner's constitutional rights were violated, then the court would have to allow the prisoner to apply for due process.][43]

It has been this way for some time, but when will we stop it? See there is no adequate or substantial debate on mass incarceration that fails to begin with this understanding of the law. In essence, the US Constitution sanctifies the very vestige and foundation of the inhumane treatment of US prisoners. The fact of the matter is that the Black, Brown and Red men of America is being targeted to pillage and conquer for profits, collusion of government, military, and business interests has turned inward, and now the enemy is us. It's the poor, it's the immigrants of color, and is the disenfranchised.

When will peace break out in our communities like war has? It is like genocide was unleashed in the past 15 years. Of course, conflicts of gangs vary from state to state, but certain characteristics mark them all. This is where my interest lies, in the hoods in the slums, in the home of laughter mixed with misery that permeates the flavor of free Africans in peace, here in American and abroad. The words written upon these pages are aimed to illuminate human tragedy in a way that shows how such tragedies may be easier to avoid in our communities and beyond in the future.

I look at my people to balance the remarkable good between the intense evil, but today shows me that there is a battle between the forces of light and darkness because as it is as if evil is also extraordinary. Brothers, how long will the blood of our people have to flow in this country before we stand together to stop it? What do we gain for allowing these cops, gangs and uneducated brothers to continue killing and shedding the blood of our people?

My journeys in life didn't start out as such, and the time in this prison cell certainly did not. Since I been here I have seen brothers get murdered, I have seen brothers commit suicide, I have seen brothers get raped and I have had friends that died from HIV and AIDS behind these prison bars. Prison is not a place for any man, woman or child. These walls have broken men mentally, emotionally and physically. Brothers are selling their soul and their bodies jut to have something different to eat. To be faced with these kinds of acts can harden the heart of a man. And to see a man eating out of the trash can like a homeless man in society is painful. Picture yourself faced with a homemade knife used to stop other men beating on you and ripping your clothes off to rape you. Picture yourself fighting for your manhood, your shoes, your food or your life. This is not how a man should to be forced to live. This is hell, this is real, this is do or die, and this is why I fight so hard to correct the minds of the young generation. My writings bring on profound changes in my thoughts because my thoughts are like notebook paper, ruled with perfect thin blue lines that imposed order on my unruly handwriting. These written pages and un-mailed letters have been trapped inside the belly of this beast pockets. For they leave no room in my thoughts for anything else, but the truth of my heart. The whole universal truth lacking which any story ephemeral and doom-love, honor, pity, pride compassion and sacrifice. So until this is done, my labor is behind these bars.

Yet, there is still so much to be learned. The world is beginning to be smaller place, and ignorance is no longer a valid argument for inaction, when presented with evidence of the crime for which they claim we done. This government has never done away with slavery and I see and feel it every day behind these walls. See the Thirteenth Amendment of the US Constitution reads as follows:

America prison system is nothing but a business system; they wish to grow the prison industrial complex, creating a profit-motive foundation for mass incarceration. The US has grown to the distinction of holding more citizens imprisoned than any other industrialized nation. Wake up my people, hear me through these words, feel me through these words of course news today is live and instantaneous. With satellite technology, there is nowhere we can't be and no place where television cannot report. However I am not out there to use the media. These bars of prison are holding me tight. The power of the media must be used to shape our collective consciousness and attitudes. So I ask what does it do to provoke action? Our children being killed by the white oppressors in law enforcement, the same law enforcement system that is supposed to serve and protect. If hate has any measure, then you would agree with this analysis:

"Africans were killed as a people, and not just one single person, hence this has affected both rich and poor Africans."

These words I write show how Africans have not recent inevitable. I hope these words give you better understanding of Africans itself. They averted of much suffering. These conflicts do not arise out of some uniquely "African" weakness. Instead, they have often been made worse by wrong-headed uneducated brothers with something to prove. Learning the reason why a Black Officer will allow a White Officer to kill a black brother or learning the lessons of these gangs will be critical to understanding the conflicts in our communities and how the people, ourselves failed our children and will continue to fail if we don't stand together to bring forth peace.

Cursed by the fact that there has been no defining moment to force closure to the gang crisis we are faced with day to day, inside and outside these prison walls. Brothers on both sides of this fight have fallen into a chronic rhythm of conflict virtually impenetrable from the outside. But locking them up has not stopped this crisis, cause they are behind these walls killing each other. Why are these white racist cops on the outside killing off the rest of our race? The times are different, yet still the same. Here the signs of preparation for genocide are clear enough for anybody who cared to see. Yet I have the sense that no one cares enough to stand against these savage white pigs, and uneducated brothers who think they are a gangster 'cause they can kill their own race.

Revealing these crimes of our people against our people reminded me of the injustices of us against this wicked government, and how so little has been done as if a decision has been made, somewhere, that Africans are not worthy of justice.

Fascinating as these entrenched killings are, they are so ingrained that they are largely stale. To obtain a grasp of true African hatred, you have to dig deeper and plumb histories that are as myth-ridden and prejudiced as these days are. Real hand to hand combat must be carried out today. But except in the rarest cases, you yourself can engage in these battles if you would just come together as one people like our ancestors done.

Being in this place has been difficult and writing and studying has been a lot like traveling to the Mother Land Africa. No day and no part of it has come easily in this place, but there have been moments for me of epiphany and triumph as well as those of great despair. I have written a lot of my work in isolation. The act of my writing has partly expunged those memories, shedding light on my past life, leaning them, boiling them down to moment of essential emotion and value. Mysteries remain, of course. For despite the scale of life, I have only two eyes and as much as these eyes may have seen, there is so, so much more to being a African then that is being taught in the homes, schools and the communities of today!

Africa is the cradle of civilization, the place where life first began. With this letter I am concerned here only with African life and history. The failures of one people should serve as a warning of what to avoid, and not as a justification for similar failures by another.

GRAVE DOORS

Chrome chains, handcuffs and cold rain, death have come to collect another man... they have buried him beneath a body of bricks and steel, buried in a field, where none can see...

Blood dripping from his teeth, raw as the meat he eats...

Stones at his feet, for this is the place which he sleeps...water sour, from the dead bodies in the creek, bodies smelling from the bitter heat...

Dry air is being shared in this grave... oh, how the night grows cold... as he gathers his thoughts together to warm his soul, as they covered the hole to his freedom, death lies and waits, to seal his fate...

For the sun never shines his way, only the fear of his brothers he feel, just as the wild winds blow

Opening another grave door...

Cries of the night rise even more, for the soul begins to praise the Lord even more to let them go...

But he cries at night when none will know, for death waits, for the wild winds to blow open his door...

He gather as much stones his hand could hold, for his heart is now cold, blood ice cold, for if the grave doors should open he shall fight, the one he feared, his life is replace with the faith he now faces, death has come to collect, collect another man lost to the system of Uncle Sam...

Torrance McCray #293580
Ridgeland Correctional Institution, GB-0049-B
P.O. Box 2039, 5 Correctional Road
Ridgeland, SC 29936

RONNIE JORDAN aka MUGABE ATIBA KUFERE - WHAT YOU CAN BE

As I sit here I thank you for allowing me to be an intricate part of your life decision-making process. It behooves me to give you the best of myself. In all earnest as you read this, always remember life is all about living. Living is all about growing. Growing is all about learning. Learning is all about trial and error. You make good and bad decisions, you learn from those experiences, grow in knowledge, and live on to the next stage in life. You never maintain your existence or your experience by trying to redo, or relive you past. You can never move forward successfully by looking through your rear view mirror. It only leads to low self-esteem, distrust, and makes you an extreme pessimist. Living today trying to make up for yesterday is no fun at all. Why? Because you are always behind, never will you be able to catch up. Since you are chasing something that has moved on. You cannot change one iota of yesterday or what took place five minutes ago. The Creator of this Universe made it so that you cannot change or tamper with time and space. It was designed to experience creation for an amount of time, and to learn all you can about God, yourself, your family and friends, and to learn all you can about LIFE.

Depending on your nationality, where you were raised, and what status of birth you were born into, entails the type of life experience you will have. For me, life has been eventful yet borderline crippling because of my decision making process. I was born an African in America and a male—both a target by my government. This area of the world called North America is an Anglo-Saxon cultured society perpetuating that they are chosen by their God to be in a position of rule over me. So every waking moment of my life has been war. By design I have been told what to act like, how to dress, what to play, who to play with, what to listen to, what to read, what to learn. I have been told who to act out on, who to respect, who to fear, what to buy, what to eat, where to go. It always seems to be someone somewhere telling me what to do and ready to punish me when I chose not to.

There has to be structure in society, and laws in place to protect you and yours. Standards have to be set that help exemplify the best in man and woman. But when you tell me that Black is ugly and you should be shunned from a point of reference where beauty is in question, there is a problem. When I am learning in class that Blacks were savages and slaves incurred by our own hands and God's anger, there is a problem. When I cannot afford to wear Jordan shoes or name brand clothes to school every day so I am not a worthy friend to have, there is a problem. When I come home with some homework from school and no one at home can help me with problems, then I get into trouble at school for failure to complete assignments, there is a problem. When I get home from school and no one is at home and there is no food in the house. It's getting late and school is tomorrow and no one is still not home in the morning when I awake, there is a problem. If someone older than me touches me and takes advantage of me and I feel so scared, so alone because I don't know who to tell or I don't know what to do so I do nothing, there is a problem. When you are feeling that you are left with no other choice in life except to sell drugs, sell your body, or rob and take someone else's property, there is a problem. When you have given up on happiness at age 13 or so because you never had good things happen to you so you live life mad at everyone because you really don't want to live throughout the day, there is a problem.

If you are poor, living a poverty-stricken lifestyle, afraid to live because you really don't know how because you were never given the chance, I feel you, I know you. If you are middle class, yet abused mentally and sexually, parents don't understand how to relate to you, know that you are not alone. I went through the same things. If you are financially able to do what you want, when you want, how you want because you can, yet, you feel unhappy, feel used, been abused, feel lonely, detached from the world, I understand what you are going through. Money cannot buy you everything including the things that matters most to human beings.

We must remember that everything I just describe to you are problems. They are circumstance that we have to exist within. However, they are problems that can be resolved. (All problems have some workable solution to fix them.) Never did I say life is fair, because there are some cruel, evil people in this world that benefit and profit from our misery and our discomfort. The people that gains from our problems do not want them to disappear. If you are reading this and you are one of many who are going through something that you feel you don't have to, "Pat yourself on the back," because you are a survivor. You have been through the fire and made it out alive. You have wounds and scars to show for it but you made it.

Now you have two choices that will either make you or break you. You can choose to get out of your victim state of mind, brush yourself off and get back to living life, becoming something of value and worth. You do this by not allowing your problems, your aggressor, your attacker, or your provoker to win. Because you got knocked down don't mean you stay down. You get back up remembering how you got knocked down in the first place. Then you try to prevent it from happening again. If you go down again you get back up with the knowledge you learned every time till you will not be knock down again. However, please be one of those people who remember what it feels like to be oppressed and suppressed against your will so that when you overcome your particular struggle you don't give rise to that same behaviour or attitude towards others. Never turn into your worst enemy by redirecting the same mentality on someone else.

31

You know the Creator gave Hue-man beings the one command above all else, "Go out and replenish the earth," procreate. So giving birth is a testament to the Creator and a blessing to us. However it saddens me to know that even in 2014 the color of my skin alone places creation, "BLACKS," in opposition of the pursuit of happiness. We have an African American President, and African Americans are in many seats of influence and power in Americans society. The problem lies in the fact that none of those in positions of power and influence sense the interest of Africans in America. The Middle Class is under direct attack by the rich because of the black populace. The poverty rate is a staggering 31% for blacks in the USA; incarceration rate is 56% nationwide. The under development in the public school as loathsome as the teen dropout ratio. The single teen pregnancy rate is too high, yet the #1 killer for Africans in America is "abortion." We are the richest people on earth yet blacks have the top five spots for unemployment, homelessness, poverty, incarceration. There are countries around the world that don't even know what a diet is, yet we throwaway 40% more food than many countries produce. And to think that people are starving in the USA, children go to school every day hungry. So under the circumstances it is a blessing and a curse to have children.

If you were born and raised in a position in life where very little was pointed toward progress, nine out of 10 times you fell into the societal snares arid traps to fail. You became a part of the needed chaos, the status quo, a statistic. George Jackson said, *"Discipline is the training that makes punishment unnecessary."*

Regardless of the odds, no matter how unbearable things may seem, the last thing a person loses before it's all over is hope. As long as you are allowed to see tomorrow you have the opportunity to do something about your situation/circumstances.

It took me coming to prison, to have everything I thought meant something to me taken away, to be existing as subhuman to understand what hope really was. To understand that all the things, objects, material possessions I was aspiring towards were nothing of worth true worth. I had to become a man inside these oppressive fences and, I may never get the chance to be of value in society. Do I like my predicament? No! Do I wish things were different? Absolutely! But time waits on no one and my space on earth is limited.

Now the question becomes, what are you going to do with what you have? When I started to see myself as a survivor and not the victim I began to find purpose. I started seeing a reason to get up every morning and make a difference. The more I started doing the more reasons I found for living and it gave me hope. To help someone else through or out of situations and problems enriches my life and it defines my role on this earth. I hope this life we live will give us reasons to go on, give us moments where we can smile and enjoy the simple things in life. I hope this life gives us a moment to breathe, time to heal, and reasons to forgive.

I encourage you to learn all you can from wherever you can so that you can equip yourself with enough knowledge to arm yourself enough to see your way through all the bullshit that is out there to make you stumble and fall and try to keep you down. I hope you draw on the example of my Africans ancestors as an example of resilience and an unyielding approach to defeat. All that we have suffered we are still here, still fighting, still forgiving, and still moving forward. Nothing or no one except yourself can stop you from achieving your goals. Fight till you have nothing left, pray until no more words come out; cry until your tears are gone. Once you are fed up and through, get up and keep on moving on for tomorrow is promised to those who best prepare for it today.

Until We Struggle No More,
Mugabe Atiba Kufere,
#240874, July 12, 2015

(Do you want to hear more from Atiba and visit him for a month in prison via his journal? See our next book in this series: "<u>Blindside Diaries, Life behind the Fences</u>" coming soon in Winter 2019)

KENNETH RIVERA – LOYALITY & RISKS

Peace My Kings and Young Princes,

Revolutionary Greetings! A fellow comrade informed me about Letters To My Sons and ask "Will I be interested in sending my thought to you."

It is an honor to be able to be a part of this project; we all need that positive guidance to lead us in the right direction. We as Black Men must do everything we can to be better Fathers and role models to our Sons and Youth in our communities,

I can relate to the young brothers pain, emotions, and state of minds. In today's time they are being misguided due to the lack of education, unity, and role models. In the Urban communities across the nation young brothers including us older ones are being exterminated on many levels.

Take a look around you and tell yourselves what do you see? You will see: "Black on Black crime, homes and families destroyed due to the drugs, young boys standing on corners when you should be in school. Pigs (Police) controlling our communities waiting to brutalize another, man, woman, and child. Young brothers robbing, killing, snitching on each other for the love of their so called gang."

My brothers it's time to change the way we think and live. You will notice this imperialist Government don't give two pennies about us. I know your pain, trust me I been in your shoes; however we must learn from our mistakes and experiences. There is no future in gang banging, selling drugs, and disrespecting women. It may seem cool to throw rocks at Prisons; however, you don't want to feel this oppression.

I am serving a fifteen (15) year sentence for arm robbery and gun charges. You want to gang bang so peep this. I am held hostage against my will in the Restricted Housing Unit. This means that I am segregated from General population. I am locked in a cage under a wrongful validation called "Security Threat Group." I am a co-leader of the South Carolina Chapter of the United Blood Nation.

This is due to the ignorant life style I once lived. That set you think is loyal to you is not. Your homies will tell on you and leave you in time of war; will not hold you down when you need them the most. Back here in these death traps there is no peace nothing but hard dicks and Pigs plotting on your life. You will be denied human rights, told when to do things and how to do things. Trust me oppression is no game young brother.

I care about you even though we have never met. I know what you are going through. The important of education I stress to our communities. Education gives us the ability to be productive, make wise decisions, and have respect for ourselves. Without education we are lost and will forever be depended on the slave master. Education my brother is the key to unlock the golden door to freedom.

"Whatever the mind of man can conceive and believe, it can achieve." As quoted by Napoleon Hill. Never allow your situation, conditions, circumstances dictate your future. Allow what you are going through be your motivation to succeed in life. As you know the way we are living gets us nowhere. I don't want to be sounding like a Preacher; however, we must end this cycle of lost dreams and empty lives.

Let's pull together so that we as a nation can be unified for freedom, justice, and equality. If we don't unite as people, educate one another, love ourselves and others we will forever be divided, ruled, and controlled. The only solution to our problem is Unity, education, and standing together for a common cause. I am loyal to all of you; your struggle is my struggle. On a closing note, without struggle there is no progress. Peace, Unity and Freedom...

PS You have permission to print this in your Newsletter

Live from Segregation, I am Comrade Syncere Bullmaster
AKA
Kenneth Rivera #318979, MO-0187-A
Broad River Correctional Institution
4460 Broad RiverRoad, Columbia, SC 29210
(Now currently located. He was moved from segregation in 2016)

GROWTH & DEVELOPMENT

GROWTH & DEVELOPMENT - *Table of Contents*

JULIAN FERGUSON AKA WALI ABDUR RAHIM – THE REAL DEAL

TO My Beloved Children, Cashya, Isaiah, Treazure, and Sincere
And all the other young men and women

"All praise is Due to Allah Lord of the World"

My name is Julian Ferguson #298672 aka Wali Abdur Rahim. I'm currently serving two (2) LIFE sentences and sixty-five years, for two counts of murder, armed robbery and kidnapping.

Once before I would have said that 'thuggin' was the way to do things. If a nigga disrespected you, you handled your BI (business). And if you had to clap (shoot) them then so be it. I would say get money by any means. Slinging, robbing, etc. I would have said the "G-code" was the only code to live by. I would say snitches get shallow graves. Why? Because in the 'hood this is what you see, are taught, and want to be. Nobody wants to be poor, laughed at, or picked on. But what we don't realize or choose not to see is that this destructive path leads only to jail or graveyard. How many homeboys or homegirls have we lost to the streets? From violence? Or being out at the wrong place? How many sisters, brothers, mothers, fathers, etc. have we lost to drugs that we sold to them? How many families have we destroyed by taking one of their people's lives? How many black communities are in total chaos from these things? And how many of us care? Do we care when our life is taken? Or when the judge hits that gavel? Or when we lose someone close to us? And what about those we deem weak? We step on them and abuse them mentally and emotionally. It can be a girl or boy. We call them ugly, fat, stupid, uncool, whatever and the end result is still the same. We feel better by making another feel bad.

But in truth we are the ones broken mentally and emotionally. The actions we take make us feel better about ourselves. When in reality we are part of the problem. But at that time we are blind to that.

I remember when I had the attitude that jail would miss me, death would miss me. That is a lie a false sense of security given to us by what we think we're getting away with while our hands were really bringing forth our own destruction. I had the attitude that nobody couldn't tell me shit. My unwillingness to listen to reason was the beginning of my end. And because of this I have left those I love behind.

PRISON LIFE

The life of a prisoner is one I wouldn't wish on my worst enemy. For the last twelve years of my life, I've had to experience being stripped searched, locked down, and placed in solitary confinement. I have been in wars, stabbings and being stabbed. I've had to deal with racist officers, gay ones and ones I've had to put hands my hands on. Your manhood is constantly tested by these pigs and other niggas. I've seen grown man reduced to crying bitches. Cats being raped, extorted, and stabbed to death. Prison life is what you make of it. One thing I learned early on in prison life is that you couldn't show any weakness. I used to carry two knives with me when I went to bed. I slept with a knife. When I went shower, you went with a knife and had a man stand watch for me. When I had beef, it was beef. Is that the kind of life you want to live? The food you eat ain't shit. If you ain't got nobody on the outside to help you out, then you got to rely on the state and SCDC (South Carolina Department of Corrections) don't give a fuck about you. Have you ever been in a hostage situation? Where the National Guard had to come in? Our administration was so corrupt where the FEDs had to come in and take over. All this shit has gone on. Are you willing to give up your freedom for all of this? Think long and hard about it.

SOLUTION

The answer to this is simple if you are willing to listen and stay in school for starters. An education will open a multitude of doors for you. Separate yourself from those that only think and do negative. It doesn't matter if they think you are down or not, because you'll suffer your own consequences. Find positive afterschool programs. Listen to those who have your best interest at heart. Give respect to your parents, even if you think they don't deserve it. Respect will take you a long way (It took me a long time to realize that). No matter how bad things may look, keep pushing forward. There is a light at the end of the tunnel. And keep faith in your God. Through Him all thing are possible. Because of Him, I have kept my "sanity". I hope those words will give you young people something to think about because most people don't get, second chances.

"The life of crime leads to a life of time or worse Death!"
Remember!!

Wali Abdur Rahim
–"Peace to all my people in the struggle" – "Keep Hope Alive"

(Do you want to hear more from Wali and visit him for a month in prison via his journal? See our next book in this series: "Blindside Diaries, Life Behind the Fences" coming soon in Winter 2019 & Read his new book "2Faces: The Saga" at https://www.amazon.com/dp/1721938095)

TERRIEL MACK AKA ZAM ZAM - REFLECTION: SON, WHAT YOU CAN BE

TO THE BLACK YOUTH WHO IS ALSO THE FUTURE OF OUR GREAT AFRICAN LEGACY

At this very moment 10:13 pm Dec. 31, 2013, I sit inside this prison cell with thoughts rapidly running through my head. One of my thoughts is it's going to be the first day of a New Year. The next thought that comes after that is I'm only 27 and I've spent the last 10 years of my life incarcerated for mistakes I made as a child. Some may consider 17 as being a grown man. But in all reality, "Age ain't nothing but a number." What defines your manhood/womanhood is your conscious state of mind, not your age. At times I sit back and reflect on my childhood and I ask myself this question: "How could I call myself a grown man when I had no idea of what being a man was all about because there was none there to show me how to be a man?" When I say show me how to be a man I'm not speaking about being able to use your sexual organs to make babies. I'm speaking, on the morals and values a real man holds close to his heart or what are the responsibilities of a real man/woman.

I look at the reality of the situation and realize that although there were different individuals that played roles in my life they never showed me how to be a real man because they didn't <u>know</u> what a real man was themselves. As you can see I have '<u>know</u>' underlined. That's because know is the root word of <u>Knowledge</u>. Knowledge is the key to get us where we need to go. If you're reading this letter you may be asking "Knowledge" of what? The answer is to have knowledge of who you really are and knowledge of the lineage of great leaders, real men and women, kings and queens, princes and princesses, warriors, architects, scientists, musicians, doctors that you come from. You come from a lineage of Africans that built great countries such as Egypt and Ethiopia. These black men and women built monuments such as the Pyramid and the Sphinx. These black Africans performed the first brain and open heart surgery. Our ancestors created math, astrology, and science. Those things are what real men and women do.

The Honorable Marcus Garvey said, "Man is the individual who is able to shape his own character, master his own will, directs his own life and shape his own ends." So if you want to be who you really are, then be a man/woman and the world will be changed by you. Nelson Mandela said "It always seems impossible until it's done." I say to you, "It's not gonna be done until <u>you do it</u>." The only way you gonna know what to do to be a real man/woman and change the world to make it better for those people coming after you is to first know who you are. You find that out by seeking knowledge. <u>Knowledge is a powerful key that unlocks the door that keeps boys/girls from crossing that threshold and becoming the men/women needed to carry on our African legacy.</u>

Peace,

ZAM ZAM - Terriel Mack,

SCDC #312070 - January 1, 2014 12:03am

TYRONE D. TISDALE - FROM YOUNG BOY TO BEAST TO ENLIGHTENED MAN

Dear My Beloved Youth:

Many of you that are reading this letter do not know me personally but I assure you that I AM YOU and YOU ARE ME! There is a known statistic that says that one out of every three black males born in the United States are destined to go to prison. Does that revelation make you think, '*What the fuck?*' It should! And it should also make you want to contribute to a better and brighter future, but I know that statistic is not enough to detour your mind away from the foolishness that your mind has been trained to glorify.

As I pen this letter from the depths of this cold and lonely cell, my heart and mind are burdened. I am burdened by the lack of knowledge that we face as a people to successfully and righteously reach you so that your next turn in life is not like my last. Point blank, period, prison life is fucked up and no one that is here will be the same upon release if you make it that far.

When I arrived at Lee Correctional Prison, one of South Carolina's worst, at the young age of 18, I was thrown into a world I knew absolutely nothing about. And with a 20 year sentence, I was about to learn a lot, but ultimately became involved in much more. Things that I never thought I'd get involved in became my norm. Lee Correctional is known as 'Gangland,' and gang violence was at an all-time high. You either 'banged' or got 'banged on'! Coming from a fatherless background, naturally I wanted to be accepted by those I looked up to, so I ended up being initiated into the GKB Blood Gang. They were now my family providing everything I could want from shoes, drugs, cigarettes, and assistance at war time, but none of that came without sacrifice.

I was given my first mission which was to stab someone during a gang riot. I was uneasy about it being that this would have been my first time stabbing a person with intent to kill them. I sought guidance from older bloods about what and how to handle my first mission only to be told that everybody was nervous their first time, but would be a piece of cake every time thereafter. That could not have been the furthest thing from the truth I'd ever heard. I completed my mission with flying colors in the eyes of the OG's, I felt every bit of fucked up about it, which was how any compassionate human being should have felt but I convinced myself that I did what I had to do even though my victim posed no threat to me. Hell, he didn't even see me coming. From that moment on, I became distant from values, principles, and morals taught to me by my mom and grandmother. I became the beast that society said I was. Loyalty.

Years passed with virtually the same cycle of events repeating themselves. I went to war with correctional officers because they were doing their jobs. I went to war with Crips because I was taught to hate the color blue. I went to war with Gangster Disciples because they chose to break a barrier by allowing "white boys" to get down. Every reason I used to justify what I was doing was plain stupidity and fruitless.

When you go to war about anything isn't something supposed to change? Nothing changed, not even my way of thinking. I struggled so much because I couldn't identify myself. I didn't know who I was anymore and couldn't remember who I had been prior.

By the time I was 22 years old, I thought I was still the best thing that ever happened to a woman since the tampon. I had lots of pen-pals and girls to call when I needed to be lied to or get some stress off, but when those letters stopped coming and the phone numbers changed I was faced with a brand new dilemma. It was then that I realized why homosexuals had it easier in prison. A lot of guys before me experienced the same thing but fell victim to their own carnal desires and lust. There are two ways to break down the homosexual lifestyle in prison. You have those that engage and those that don't. Now it is not my mission to bash homosexuals but the major issue of genocide is still relevant. How do we reproduce within a race that is already dying by consciously engaging in sex with the same sex? It's impossible. There is a crisis going on here and we must end it; first with proper education. There are some things in life we must learn constraint in at all cost.

At 29 years old I have a daughter who is 11 years old in which I've never seen, nor held and that is all due to unconscious decisions I made prior to her birth. It was my dream of getting out and become a great father that propelled me to want more and seek more for my life. I started by changing the way I thought about life in general; and I'm asking you to do the same. This is real talk from one black man to another!

Peace and Love,

Tyrone Tisdale,

(Mr. Tisdale was released in 2017)

EUGENE THOMAS - THE EFFECTS OF PEER PRESSURE

Dear Youth,

I write this word to you with nothing but love. It really doesn't matter to me if you are black, white, purple, or orange: All that matters to me is that somehow or someway these words and knowledge I am passing unto you in this letter reaches as many of young people as possible. My name is Eugene Thomas, a Florida native, and I have been in and out of prison since I was 18 years old and now I am 52. I am here to tell you that being in here is nothing pretty. The bottom line is, "Don't Break the Law". Be smart and make the law work for you and not against you.

Believe me when I say peer-pressure is a young person's worst enemy. I have witness thousands of young males that come into this prison system strictly from peer pressure. They come into this system not knowing anything, and then leaving the system worse than they came in. Why? Because once they are in, they are influenced once again with peer pressure. They are forced to join gangs, and then they leave the system with gang mentality.

If you are capable of understanding anything, then please understand this: if you are in prison, you can't help or be with your love ones out in the free world. You must start with yourself first, when it comes to help. Realize the mistakes people have made. Those mistakes are real, young people. As I write this letter, I am experiencing a hurt so deep that I cry out to God day and night pleading and begging for another chance to prove that, if given another chance I would live my life differently.

So my young people please understand what I'm saying. Do not throw away your life behind peer pressure and be like me, sitting here with LIFE without the possibility of parole.

– Gene

Eugene Thomas
SCDC# 222351- December 11, 2013

JERMAINE MILES AKA LORD INFINITE - THIS IS WHERE GREED WILL GET YOU

WISE WORDS TO THE YOUTH -- Peace to all youth.

My name is Jermaine Demetrius Miles age 37. I'm also known as Lord Infinite. I'm currently housed at Perry Correctional Institution. I've been locked-up for 18-and-half years. I have about two years and a couple of months left to make out my 25 year bid. I would like to share a little with the youth, to show you where I went wrong and how you can avoid the same mistake I've made plus plenty of others who are incarcerated.

My life growing up was real ragged. When I was nine, 10, 11 years old I started hanging out in the streets, drinking, and smoking cigs and weed. I was introduced to the dope game when I was 12 years old. A dude gave me 10 baggies of pure cocaine. Told me to sell each one for $20, bring him back $175, I keep $25 for myself. Back then at 12 years old $25 was a lot of money. As I got used to the game the money got a little better. Life seemed much easier. I didn't care about school. Life in the street was school is what I thought. The dude who put me on the dope game had me chilling and going to clubs. He used to take me to the mall and buy me clothes and shoes. I started thinking of him as a father figure because my real dad been in prison since I was like two or three years old. At the age of 14 years old, I caught my first criminal charge. I shot a bouncer at a club for kicking me out. After it was over I ran home. The next day the police came, got me, and took me to the Juvenile Detention Center in Greenville County. I was then sent to RPE Center in Colombia.

Before I was to be released back into society, I was adopted by someone, because DSS and DYS said my mom was not fit to take care of us meaning me and my brother. We were too wild, and my mom could not handle us, me and my brother wound up getting adopted. We got adopted by my Aunt and Uncle.

By the time I was 15 years old. I was doing good playing basketball for school, my grades were good. I was even going to church. My aunt was kinda strict, especially in education. Then we moved to a bad neighborhood and that brought out all the bad in me back on the surface. I started back hanging out late, smoking and drinking again. Having sex with girls without protection, skipping school, selling dope.

Now that I was older and $25 to $60 wasn't nothing. I started making $250 to $600 easy. When I turned 16 years old, I was already making over a $1000 a week. But I was not saving it. I was blowing it quick as I made it on clothes, shoes, weed, drinks, club, girls, food, hotels, etc. You name it. I felt like this was the life for me, not hurting for nothing. I moved out of my auntie's house into the house with my grandmother and granddad. I was also making sure they were ok with their bills and food.

One day coming from Georgia, me and my man got pulled over and jumped out the car and ran with the dope and guns. When they caught me, they found two hand guns and some weed I still had in my pocket. They never found the crack, but they sent me back to the juvenile detention center, I just knew I was going to get committed and do a lot of time down the road at John G or Berthwood, but little did I know they continued to hold me in jail since I turned 17 years old in September. When I turned 17 years, they tried me as an adult and gave me Y.O.A. (youth offender authority) sentence, one to six years.

I was scared as hell. I was going to the big house with all the stories you hear about prison. Don't drop your soap, protect your bottom. People will steal and rob canteen from you. People will test your manhood to see if you are solid, I was supposed to do six months, but I ended up doing 13 months for getting into all kinds of trouble.

When I got out I had just turned 18 years old. My main man came and scooped me up. We went to the mall. He told me whatever I want to get it. He saw me as a real ass nigga, because I took a charge for both of us.

I bought about $5,000 worth of stuff. We went out to eat and then he took me to a woman's house to get laid. I felt I was back to business and even doing it bigger. My man hit me off with a big eight (that's 4½ ounces (oz) of crack). He said from that point on any time I need to cop, to cop dope from him. I couldn't believe he just gave me 4½ oz for myself and I don't owe him nothing. I got on my grind and had people selling dope for me. I was soon coping a quarter brick for myself. I bought two cars, a motorcycle, and was paying a few of my relative's bills. I had money in my loved one's account for a rainy day.

I wasn't missing anything until I got pulled over in a rental car. We had just come back from Georgia; we were all high and shit. Me and one of my workers went to jail. They charge him with possession of weed, and charged me with possession of crack cocaine. Now remember, I'm already out on YOA Parole. I got a crack charge to go with it. I called my sister to get me a lawyer and bonds men. Within a week, I was out on bond and in my lawyer's office. He told me he could get my YOA reinstated and I wouldn't have to go down the road, but it will cost a little money. It's funny what money will do. It cost me a lot of money to not go back to jail.

Back on the scene, I took a big hit with the court shit, but I was still free. Later on that year my man got knocked in Florida. So I had to start dealing with people I wouldn't have dealt with if my man was here. I had to pay more for my dope. I got shitted out of my dope. I was spending more money than I was making. I tried to sell weed but 'Wind up smoking more than I was selling. Money started to decline. My PO officer on my back about getting a job. I got one to keep the pigs off me. I had to get one of my workers out of jail, paid his bond, got him a lawyer. Money was constantly slipping out of my hand, until one of my homeboys had a lick that could put us back on track. Well the lick fell through and it turned into a shooting spree. That left one of the guys in the car shot up, and we went on the run. I went to GA until everything cool down in South Carolina. I stayed down there for three months and came back. The same guys I was hanging out with did some dumb shit, and the police came from everywhere, saw me, and then arrested me. I was in the city jail on assault and battery with intent to kill, attempted armed robbery, criminal conspiracy, and accessory after the fact. I was facing like 55 to 60 years in prison. I stayed in the county about eight months before pleading out to 25 years.

I said all that to say that it took me coming to prison and gain knowledge of self to realize all the chances were given to me and I blew them. I could have killed someone or could have been killed. In a lot ways prison has really taught me not to take life for granted. I've lost my loved ones that I will never see again because of my incarceration. My son and daughter have grown up without me in their life. A lot of things I wish I could take back and do it again. If I could I would have listened to a lot of people in my family. This is why I'm speaking to you, the youth, about all the signs I had to get myself together. It took me doing almost 19 years in prison to finally realize that. Now that I'm a conscious brother, I want to enlighten you on that lifestyle verses the real life, especially the black youth.

I'm not racist or nothing, but black youth are more targeted than any other race, and that's a fact. Those at risk are those living in these types of conditions: one parent home, home in drug neighborhood, parents on welfare, kids kicked out on the streets, etc. These are some of the signs society sees as failure, and are more targeted to black youth, to see them in prison getting free labor off them. They use them as modern day slaves. This is how the system is set up for minority people, poor people, and uneducated people alike. I do a lot of reading and studying the system from when I came in till now, and the result is the youth are dominating the system nowadays. Guys who just turn 17 years old got 30 to 50 years in prison plus 85% of it, and most of them are black males. This is sad but it is true. No one wants to really express that truth to the black youth. They want to sugar coat it to please the system.

I'm gonna give it to you raw and uncut. I love all of you, even though I might not physically know you, but mentally I'm striving to get there with you. You are what I missed growing up. I had to grow up in prison. Having to be told what to do, what to wear, when to eat, stand in line, don't talk, etc. This is the type of stuff you go through in prison. Not to mention the homosexuality, fighting, stabbing, robbing and killing each other. I prayed every day that my kids don't go through what I went through.

I met my dad in prison. I did about three to four years with him. He maxed out (completed his full sentence). It's a whole other world back here. My duty as a civilized person is to give knowledge, wisdom, and understanding so understanding can be understood clearly and fully. A lot of people kinda know about prison but lack wisdom and understanding of prison. This is why they are not complete within self-awareness. When you are young we are naive and don't really grasp understanding until you become a statistic in prison. To the system you are nothing but money and a number they use to keep you here. That's why an education is very important to us, because if you do not know where you are, how can you know where you are going? You are a blind person who cannot see or hear. These are the triple stages of darkness that we often lack (blind, deaf, dumb) to the reality of life. Again, I speak these wise words to the youth because I see them as a reflection of me. Choose a different path, choose a righteous path. That way you are setting a role for the next generation. This is why I'm reaching out to those who were just like me growing up. These are wise words spoken by a wise person, who learned the hard way in what life is really about. I regret a lot of dumb things I did in my young life. Especially having kids and not being able to hold them when they cry or helping them with their homework. Just actually being in their lives physically. It really hurts me a lot to see me and many others go down the same road knowing what it leads to. When are we gonna learn, and stop the madness that keeps us in this mental and physical slavery?

I pray and hope I touch at least one person, because I was once like you and have made an 180 degree turnaround on the righteous path and I pray you do the same. I leave you with these jewels of thought. If you want to be successful in your journey, you must first crawl before you can walk. Don't always be ready to run before you walk. Always take one step at a time. The results will be difficult and your life will be easier.

Peace,

Proper **E**ducation **A**lways **C**orrects **E**rror

Lord Infinite aka Jermaine Miles, (Released)

(Do you want to hear more from Lord Infinite and visit him for a month in prison via his journal? See our next book in this series: "Blindside Diaries, Life Behind the Fences" coming soon in Winter 2019)

DEMETRIUS BLANDING - THE STREETS DON'T CARE ABOUT ANYONE

12/16/2013 - Greetings lil bruh. Man, It's been a while since I had a real good build with you. Mostly it's my fault because I was caught up in seeking knowledge, wisdom and understanding for myself. But the most important lesson I learned was 'The highest elevation of knowing is doing.' So I'm taking this time out to give you the understanding of the knowledge that I received.

First thing is know thyself! You must understand yourself and know who you are in order to know what you want. The world can mislead you into thinking that you want something and when you receive it you regret that you wanted and asked for it in the first place. You must find something that you not only like but love to do. I don't care if you love to wash cars, take that and add dynamics.

Take what you want and add what you love. Say you like all the hot flashy things of the world today but again you love to clean cars. Put it together and focus your mind on it and with a little education you can start a detail stop. You get to wash and clean the cars plus add your own art and style into the detail. Not to mention you making more money off one car or truck than your friend did on the block selling drugs for a whole month. Now look at what you've made! Money to stabilize yourself and your family, a job for others who might have the same passion as you, plus you set an example for others to see that they can do what they love and get what they want too, and still have fun doing it. By doing this you dodged the 'circumstance' that many in today's society falls victim to and that 'circumstance' is called prison!

Man, lil bruh, it's terrible back here. We use to come back here and get smarter, continue school, high school, even take college courses and obtain a degree. But now they're taking that from us. _The system doesn't want us to get smarter because they know that if we do then we will start businesses and never come back to prison._ You see prison is a corporation that makes thousands of dollars off of each employee a month. The employees used are not the ones who work here but the _prisoners_ who are kept here. They make $2,500 for each inmate a month and you have 28 prisons in this state alone housing from 100 to 1,200 inmates a prison. So you do the math. They need us, so the only way to keep us (their money) is to keep us ignorant and stagnate. By doing this we come back and forth to prison. We must educate ourselves to break this cycle, if not we, as well as our love ones, will strive and die without us. Second, you must go for what you want in life.

You may tell yourself that you want the best things in life but instead you settle for the least or you set yourself up to receive the least. It's like looking for a woman to marry. Someone you would love for the rest of your life. You say that she must be smart, diverse, independent and want more out of life than just sex, money, and jewellery. But you go looking for this woman in the club, in the hood or at the hood mall. If you want smart, she got to go to school or have finished it. You want diverse, she has to have been to college so she can converse on any level no matter what it is, even teach you something from time to time. You want independent, then you too must be independent. You must be smart and diverse because you are only going to get what you put out. You walk, talk and act hood then that's what you are going to get. But if your personality and everyday walk show and proves that you are educated, that you want more out of life and that you will most importantly not settle for less, then you will get all that and more in return.

Now let me show you what the, *gotta get it fast because I want it now* life will get you. I was a kid, notice I said 'kid' because there comes a time when we think were a man because were either on our own or because we're having sex and making money. Well that's far from what a real man is bruh. Trust me I know. Anyways man, dude kicked me out the house because I took my home boy's word over.my moms. (Never do that!).

I needed money to get a hotel because all the girls I was dealing with stayed with their parents and they definitely wasn't about to let me stay with them. So I started robbing people. Money was good while it lasted but I got cocky started letting more people come with me on the robberies and then I got locked up. Don't get me wrong I did have fun once I got the money that is; well at least I thought it was fun. Travelling to different states with a lot of money in my pockets, jewellery in my mouth, on my wrist, hands and two chains around my neck...yeah I was something, I was in Atlanta, GA, Jacksonville, Fla., Miami, Fla., Dolthan, Shoreport, and Montgomery, Alabama.

Man, I was doing it up real good, then I met this girl who I could see myself just laying down with. Man, I was willing to give up the streets, the robberies and the homeboys for her. So I told myself just one more robbery just to get up a lot of money to settle down and last me a while. ***The truth about the street—you don't let it go, it lets you go.*** You must know one thing about the streets when you start playing the streets game, you never get to decide when to quit only the streets decide when to let you go. I got caught on that last robbery and two, not all, but only two guys that were with me told on me and about the other robberies. That was in March 2005.

I was denied a bond and was labelled a menace to society. I sat in that county jail until I went to court 14 months later.

While I was in the county jail the girl who I was willing to give everything up for never wrote, when I called and told her I was locked up she said, "Too bad" and hung up the phone.

It's a cold world lil bruh and love ones are a safe commodity when you are in the street. My homeboy never sent me any money not even a letter. The streets don't care about anyone always remember that. I end up catching 15 years, 85% and was sent to Lee Correctional Institution, the state's worst prison at the age of 18. I had to be standing at my door with my shoes on at four am every morning, even Saturday and Sunday, not because they made you, but because you might have some homosexual to try you or your homeboys, meaning wherever you are from in this case Colombia a.k.a the Metro.

If they had some beef with some other person and they will get at you the best way they can. In your room while you sleep, while you're in the shower, while you're eating in the chow hall or even in church. They don't care. War is war and you better be ready. Respect is a must back here. Either you give it or it will be taken....the hard way!

But you can make it only if you want to. I do by maintaining on growth plus development. A constant prayer keeps you on elevation. I've learned a lot back here about who I am and what I actually want. But you can do the same a lot faster than it took *me,* if you start applying yourself now. Educate yourself and do some reading. Find out what you want to do in your life then make preparations to get it done. Never give up, keep fighting and stay focused on your goal. Remember what I said in the beginning of this letter "The highest elevation of knowing is doing." Learn! Then do it! Whenever you meet someone who says *'You can't do that'* then buckle down and prove them wrong, but prove them wrong in a smart way. I don't care how long it takes as long as you prove them wrong. Time waits on no one, that's so true but time is at your advantage when you have a plan and know how to manage it. Most of all, time is your most deadliest weapon when you have patience. Never rush to do anything. I don't care if it's getting a girl because as the saying goes, 'Everything that comes fast doesn't last long!" Keep your head up lil bruh always strive for growth plus development and never settle for less.

Love You Always,
Regardless! Demetrius Blanding SCDC #315632

STANLEY BRADLEY - ASK FOR GUIDANCE

To the Youth,

Grace and Peace from the "Father of our Lord Jesus Christ." May your lives be prosperous even in times of tribulation, meaning that your shortcomings make you a better person instead of becoming bitter. The outcome of a bitter attitude is always negative. So learn from your mistakes and ask God to guide you through whatever storms come your way. You must understand that we all have a purpose in this life not only to our immediate life, not only to our immediate family and friends, but to our community, country as well as the world as a whole. We must break down barriers of hatred towards our fellow man, and be responsible for the choices we make, good and bad. So that you can know not to repeat the ones that were detrimental to an outcome you did not desire. Keep an open mind, because a closed one is stagnated. Know that you are fearfully and wonderfully made in the eyes of God the Creator, of all things. One last thing, "Be strong in the Lord and the power of His might" *Ephesian 6:10...*

God Bless,
Stanley Bradley #307864

MICHAEL L. ELMORE - DELAYED OBEDIENCE IS REALLY DISOBEDIENCE

Dec. 9, 2013 - Shalom,

I've been in captivity for the past twenty seven years and let me tell you, this life I wouldn't wish on my worst enemy. You do not have control over yourself or your being, they tell you when to eat, sleep, exercise, shower, and watch entertainment. Being in prison makes you regret the things that you had took for granted when you had your freedom—going to the refrigerator, being outside at night listening to the insects, or looking at the stars and moon, having intimate conversation with a female, being around your family or friends. But this could be taken away from you because of one bad decision, and you will be controlled by an individual who gets paid to make your life misery.

If I would have explored and enhanced my sense of social and cultural identity, I would have been telling you this face-to-face instead of putting it on ink and paper, but as an Hebrew Israelite it's my duty to tell you about our Heavenly Father Yahweh 613 Laws. Yahweh can provide us purity, character, righteousness, and wisdom. You will have new strength and character, and righteousness, and purity. Everyone should know that when you are given something to do *that delayed obedience is really disobedience.* Understanding can wait, but obedience can't, instant obedience will teach you more about character, obedience unlocks understanding! Character is the inward qualities that determine a person's responses, regardless of the circumstances. Character affects your attitudes, words, and actions. Good character is the inward motivation to do what is right, even when you think no one is watching. Your character determines your attitudes, thoughts, feelings, and decisions. Building character is a lifelong process. Do not make excuses. Tough situations reveal your character and provide opportunities to adjust your attitudes and thinking.

Whatever your past, tomorrow will reflect the choices you make today. It is assumed that you harbor feelings of anger, frustration, and negative self-regard. These feelings and attitudes are often unconscious but they affect the individual's behavior and interactions with other people (family members, friends, the community, and the larger society). Because an individual's sense of self and positive regard are shaped and affected by his social and cultural experiences, sent mean you cannot overcome negative it's around them. Enhance your self-esteem, sense of social competence, awareness and understanding of your social and cultural identity. We have more brothers incarcerated then in college. Let's start with you making it to college and being successful. Shalom!

Michael Elmore #138418, Q4B-0216-B, PCI 430 Oaklawn Rd, Pelzer, SC 29669

TIME WAITS ON NO ONE

THE SENTENCING PROJECT

LIFE SENTENCES

The number of people serving life sentences continues to grow even while serious, violent crime has been declining for the past 20 years and little public safety benefit has been demonstrated to correlate with increasingly lengthy sentences. The lifer population has nearly quintupled since 1984. One in nine people in prison is now serving a life sentence and nearly a third of lifers have been sentenced to life without parole.

Number of People Serving Life Without Parole Sentences, 1992-2016

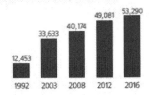

Number of People Serving Life Sentences, 1984-2016

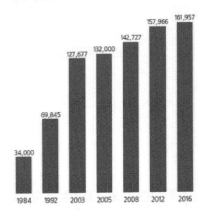

Imperial Imprint LLC received permission to use the above "Life Sentences" infographic from The Sentencing Project. www.sentencingproject.org[44]

Receiving a LIFE sentence was not an easy thing to accept. Losing everything—family, friends, possessions, freedom—was enough, yet to know, and understand, that you will be locked away for the rest of your life definitely changes your paradigm on a lot of things. All the people I loved, all the relationships I had built, all of the activities I enjoyed—all of it flashed before me, because I did not know if my future included any of it.

When I was sentenced, the thought I dwelt on the most on was of my children. I wondered how my oldest daughter would react. My relationship with her had been strained from my divorce of her mother and from my remarrying; I didn't get to see her as often as I wanted. But during the seven months that I was out on bond, we had cultivated the father/daughter relationship that I had always wanted with her. Now, 18 years later, she has nothing to do with me.

I thought of my son. Because I knew I would be lost without him in my life, I assumed he, too, would be lost without my presence. He was my little buddy, my fishing partner, and my reason for wanting to be a good father. I rarely did anything without him by my side. Now, 18 years later, he, too, has nothing to do with me.

I then thought of my youngest daughter, my princess. Her mother would still take her shopping; of that I was sure. But there were other things I wasn't so sure about. Would she end up calling someone else "Big Daddy"? Would she continue to suck her thumb just because she was told to stop? Because she liked to take naps on my chest, would she stop taking naps now that I wasn't there? Now, 18 years later, she, too, has nothing to do with me.

My ex-wife, someone who believed in the innocence I proclaimed at the time of my arrest, came to hate me for putting myself in this position. I can't blame her for that, because had I been at home where I should have been, I would not be writing this missive. Even though she was someone I loved with all my heart, she ultimately became just another character in the tragedy that is my life.

I had plenty of friends at the time of my incarceration, yet none of them visit, none of them ask for me to call, and none of them pose questions to my family concerning my well-being. I used to be someone who thought the world revolved around me. I obviously got that one wrong.

Socrates said, "The unexamined life is not worth living." I have examined my life and have come up wanting. Even though I may never see the outside world again, I remain positive in the hope that I will one day be set free. Even if that never happens, I will never lose hope. Either way, until then, I will strive to be the best person I can be for those around me.

--Richard K. Patterson, August 2018

JAMES MACPHEE - "TO THE SON I NEVER HAD" (MUSINGS FROM A PRISONER'S FORTIETH (40th) CHRISTMAS)

December 25, 2013-Today I again sit alone in a cold, gray 8 by 10 foot cell as the Christmas songs murmur in the distance, the laughter of loved ones whispers a world away, and the realization of forty Christmas' in prison resound in my head. The many years of seeing, hearing, feeling and enduring all, while being locked away from the real experiences of life, have left their scars, the visible and invisible. I know however that the too many fierce· battles I've fought have culminated in the qualities that make the man.

We understand that for some of us the greatest challenge in life is mere survival. Survival is their heroic act. But a life story is written each moment, each day, as the pages turn into chapters and one's life progresses through months, years and decades.

I entered the maddening, chaotic hell of prison in the youthful spring of my life, walked amidst the rage and violence of caged men through learning summer, survived to an insightful, knowing autumn. As the beard turns gray as the walls that surround me, and the years of hardship carve in my face, the recognition of fading dreams and unrealized goals aches in my bones as arthritis in the dead of winter. Strange how I desperately yearn for my once youthful spring yet paradoxically relish the confidence and maturity of autumn. Now I must share what I've accumulated with the generation that follows me.

I'm achingly aware that my pinnacle nears, for the tortuous trek up the high, steep mountain has been long and arduous. The vital years of productivity and fruitfulness will soon begin to wane. I know that the passing seasons cannot be retrieved nor the cold stillness of winter be denied. Every day I push harder down the path that I hope will lead to some semblance of accomplishment, or acknowledgement I've somehow made a difference in all of this. I strive each day for merit in life while the energy, enthusiasm, and desire are still alive. I have to wonder how deep those emotional reserves are as I survey the lost souls that surround me each day.

Every step this LIFER takes while still confined to prison's excruciating aloneness is another step towards chilling, barren winter. I do not fear reaching winter, only arriving there with no past, no legacy and no pride in accomplishment.

How many of us wish we could start anew, rewind it all and begin again? But I know there can never be a fresh start, for each man is everything he's ever done, said, or even failed to do. The experiences are layered on his being over time, adding to what's already there, amending the whole.

At this milestone fortieth Christmas I celebrate life and recognize the need for each of us to share it.

TO THE SON I NEVER HAD: As you travel on this journey called life, please understand that all of us are born with potential, but we are not supposed to die with it. We must learn to utilize the resources we have been gifted with: Talents, Intellect, Abilities, and Passions. Be resourceful and pull out the stuff God has placed inside of you and draw on the creativity and experience stored in to develop your unique self, and then contribute it to our world. Always stay true to you, know who you are, and who you want to be but never violate that on your journey. You must know what is at your core, the principles you base your values on. If you don't know what's truly important. You'll treat everything the same. You must know what your non-negotiables are that you will stand on these principles regardless of the situation and circumstances. Son, know what is at your core, don't be like a coconut, hard on the outside, hollow in the center, this is how we can easily rise above our circumstances and never surrender to them. Loyalty, honor and faith are paramount.

Son, please be good. Follow instructions, be teachable and remember that we all have the ability to make a difference. It is not enough to just be good, we must also do good. To live your life at your highest level allows you to give your life for the greatest good. Don't die with that potential. You'll only reach your full talents when you learn how your gifts can help others. Everything we gain in life is not for us, but others, so seek opportunities to reach out to the ones you can help. That's what love is, being the part of them that needs nurturing that is missing. Sadly, some of us have denied ourselves many of these opportunities. Please son, don't (by your choices), be one of the denied.

Merry Christmas Son!

Jimmy MacPhee,
SCDC #92234

TOIQUAN EADY - LETTER TO MOM (SON IN PRISON WHEN MOTHER PASSED AWAY)

From: Toiquan Eady #348383
430 Oak Lawn Road
Pelzer, SC 29669

Jan 1 2014

To: Tammie Eady
1 NA, 1000,000 Lane
Heaven 2014
To the realest woman on the planet ever!

Dear Momma AKA Ma dukes:

This is the letter that you never got the opportunity to read you are always with me and you feel what's on my heart, so you don't have to be here physically to read this.

First and foremost, I apologize for not keeping my word. I promised you that I was done with the street life and that I was gonna try the straight and narrow. As you can see, I made some more bad decisions that again cost me my freedom. They say, "You never miss a good thing until it's gone," and truth be told now that you are gone, I miss you more than ever. My heart cries out daily.

I remember the last time I heard your voice, our last conversation. You made me promise that I would at least get some type of trade so that I could legitimately provide for my little ones. We even argued because you wanted to talk to me and didn't want to three-way my girl for me. If I knew then what I know now, I would have cherished moments like that. Would you believe that the money that you put on your phone is still there since my punk ass sister never paid the bill? Now some college girl has your old number. I don't know what to say about that. Regardless of what has and will happen, you always have been and always will be my backbone.

Even though pops was in and out of my life, somehow you taught me how to make it on my own. They say a woman can't teach a boy to be a man but I truly beg to differ.

Sometimes I wonder if you know how much I miss you, and how much it hurts that I can't pick up the phone and call you. I smile to myself at times when I think about how you always used to tell me that no matter how old I get I'll always be your baby.

I want you to know that your baby boy got his head out his ass for a change. I finally got that trade. Tell granddaddy I'm laying bricks now. And nah I ain't talking about no dope. I did something decent with the prison time they gave me and learned brick masonry. So if everything doesn't work out at the shot I've got something else to fall back on. Speaking of which I want to say thanks. I didn't know that when I got out of prison that I had a little insurance money waiting for me. I did something smart with it, unlike somebody (Day Day) I bought a house off Montague and I opened up a paint and body shop. Believe it or not Daddy is helping run it now so that the bills at home are still taken care of. He has really stepped it up since you and I have been gone and Lord knows I appreciate it. You taught me a lot in life and now I strive to be everything in life that Pops wasn't to me. He was not there but I'm trying to-No 'a try is a failure.' I'm striving to be there. There as in emotionally, mentally and eventually physically to support my kids.

You see how big they done got? And can you believe your baby boy is a grandpa? Yep Sunny has a lil girl on February 13th this year. She didn't find out she was pregnant till November. Somehow she still had her girly thing going on (cycle) throughout the whole pregnancy. When I found out I wanted to kill her but what could I say when I had my first at 13. She's 18 now and I'm glad to say that it didn't slow her down a bit. You'd be proud to know that your first granddaughter is currently a student at Strayer University, going for her Associate in Criminal Justice. It makes me feel like her mother and I did something right.

I wish that I could see you smile 'cause I know your smiling right now. You only get one momma and I wish I would have done right by you. I just pray that you will forgive me for my mistakes they say that life goes on and I'm doing my best to live on. I wrote you a poem as well. It's just about the best way I can express how I feel.

Every day is a battle. It seems that it may never end, but be that as it may, the days come and they go. I pray since I know pain won't last forever! But then maybe it will, because God made it his will when the rib of a man, Eve ate from the tree. She was cursed to bear you and to carry me therefore there would forever be pain in child birth. Does that make each child cursed? Or just the first and what's worse is when she hurt, so may be or this pain will last forever. But then they say that joy and pain are like sunshine and rain which takes me back to the days of Abel and Cain. The beginning at man 40 days the rain cover the land and just as long before you'd see sand but when Noah emerged from the ark with lamb, rabbits, ducks, horse and goats. We now saw all that God has to show with every color in the rainbow to let us know that the word would never flood below. The cloud submerge the trees like the seas and what I think that really mean is sunshine may be this pain won't last forever. Speaking of sunshine you are just that, my sunshine. So divine it could only be destiny which is why I hurt without you next to me, which takes me, I am back to praying knowing, wishing and hoping that this pain won't last forever.

You left me in this world to deal with the good and the bad. [The Department of Corrections would NOT even let me attend your funeral] and everyday it hurts but I know that when I finally make you proud the pain may just go away. I know you are smiling down on me from heaven just to let me know, I miss you and even though I didn't have to tell you, because you already know, I'll always love you. I will see you in the next life.

Love always and forever,

Your baby boy,

Toi

L.A. BERNSTEN–MINDSET & FEELINGS CHANGE WHILE IN PRISON

Dear Child,

I am writing this message from the past for the future, *your future*. You who are reading this may be my biological child or children or perhaps metaphorically children.

This letter is coming from a plant that produced or is capable of manufacturing many different types of emotions, but essentially produces just one, hatred.

None of us wakes up one morning and says I think I will go to prison or will spend most of my life incarcerated. We start small by stealing from the corner store or from a neighbor's home or somewhere like school. Then we graduate to robbing, raping, and killing. We generally come to these factories for a small stretch 2-3 years the first time. We get a short indoctrination with disliking people who don't look like us, don't talk like us or even all people who are working to keep us locked-up.

Your heart becomes like a rock and not in a good way. You will watch a man be beat to death or stabbed or hit with a weapon and your only concern will be 'how long?' or 'if we will be locked down'. You become immune to feelings to emotions and only self-gratification is what makes you happy. One day you wake up and if asked to describe your philosophy your answer will be HATE. Your time will go by and you will not receive any mail or phone calls, why? Because you have driven everyone away with your hate and using of them. *(People may try to* **come** *into your life and show you love but you are always thinking how can I use them? What's in it for* **me?)**

Your whole entire life will revolve around your cellblock and the rec yard. You will fight to your death or someone else's for a perceived slight to your manhood, to your clique. Speaking of cliques, everybody is trying to use everybody and everyone is making moves to get to the top spot. You will spend years on lock up or lock down because you are in a clique.

If you are fortunate you will one day have a light bulb go off in your head, an epiphany, and you will understand that some of the decisions you made in your past were not very good. Then you will begin to understand that you can change your cognition, your thought patterns, how and what you think about, what becomes important to you.

Little Brother or Little Sister, if you are blessed, you will still have a few years to affect a good change in your environment, your neighborhood city, state and nation.

How do you avoid all this first off, find a mentor in your home, barrio, church, mosque, city, Police department, fire house. Anywhere! Ask an elder to help you with any and all problems you are experiencing new or in the future. Then after a few years you become a mentor. If you want to keep it you must give it away. Be cool and stay in school. Get an education; understand how to use money and the power of using or not using it. Always be involved with something positive.

It took me *more than two decades to understand that doing the right thing is the right thing to do.* I have spent more than 35 years in prison, I am 58 years old. You can do the math.

L. A. Berntsen

(Released in 2014)

(Do you like what Mr. Berntsen has to say? Would you like to hear more from him? Come and see his life for one month when he was in prison via his journal, "BlindSide Diaries, Life behind the Fences", coming soon...thankfully he is home enjoying his life and doing the right things...also see his interview in Section "Coming Home and Healing")

ROBERT DIEHL - IF I COULD DO ONE THING

Robert Diehl- SCDC# 301189

If I could do one thing ---- If I could do one thing, anything, can you guess what it would be? Make myself rich? Free myself from this prison that separates me from the ones I love? No, it wouldn't be either of those. If I could do one thing, something that's currently not possible, it would make me rich in ways that money couldn't. It would make the ink fade from this very page, and erase wounds that penetrate far deeper than flesh.

The one thing I speak of is a letter to myself. I would write the most important letter of my life, a letter in which everything hangs in the balance. There would be no lies, no faking, no acting tough, just truth. I would mail it to myself at about the age of 13. If I could convince me then that it was truly from me at the age of 36, then I know the younger me would listen. I know that at 13 years old, the only person that could get through to me, would be me.

Why would I write the letter, and what would it say? The "Why" is easy. At that age, I was lost, totally. My mother passed away from cancer about seven years prior, so at six, it was only my father and me By 13, I was very rebellious, had no discipline, and basically did anything I wanted to. I vandalized, I stole, I skipped school, I ran away, and all of this, I did repeatedly. I went to counselling, and it did no good, none at all. I was suspended from school, expelled, time after time, again and again. Eventually, I was charged with felony crimes and sent to a juvenile detention center for three months. It was awful, and I just wanted to go home. Eventually, home I went, but only to begin living the same way as before. I ended up going to juvenile detention centers over the next couple of years, putting myself and my family through unimaginable heartache and pain.

Eventually, I became an adult, and my selfish and ignorant ways led me to prison. I served six years, day for day, and then I was released. I rebuilt my life over the next two years, was on the verge of getting married and had a great job, my own car, and a cool motorcycle. For the first time my father and I had a relationship and was friends again. For the first time in my life, I thought I had it right. I was happy, I was making others happy, and then, it happened. The happy life I had created, shattered. I experimented with drugs, and they consumed my life, and left me with nothing. I destroyed everything good in my life, and rock bottom wasn't as far as I would go. I ended up back in prison, this time serving 12 years and nine months off of a 15 year sentence. My life seemed over, and the sweet taste of success and happiness I had only ended up leaving me broken and bitter.

After being locked up for less than a year, I escaped from the top maximum security prison in my state. I was shot at, cut up by the razor wire, but still managed to get away. I was the first inmate to do so in over a decade. I ended up getting caught, and seven more years was added onto my sentence, leaving me with 22 years. All I can say is it surely went from bad to worse. I have been in here for over 10 years now. That's more than a decade gone. I can honestly tell you, these 10 years have not been easy, and I've seen a lot of bad things. The majority of my life has been pain, sadness, and regret. So, that's why.

If I could send myself a letter, imagine how different things could be today? Had I, at 13 years old, straightened my life out, where would I be? Surely not here! That gets us to be the big letter, one shot, and one chance to convince myself to wake up, to change everything. I guess that I could say to another child, teenager, or young man who is going through a struggle. Any young person who is facing trouble, who feels alone or who feels like no one understands you, I will show you that there's more going on than you're aware of at this point in your life. Pay attention, please, I am about to give you the most important words that you've ever heard, just trust me. I've been where you are, and I remember it like it was yesterday. Let me tell you what I wish I had known at your age.

Letter to Rob (me) at 13,

*H*ey there little man. Have I got a big surprise for you? You're probably wondering who this letter is from, but I know you won't believe me when I tell you. So first off, let me tell you this, I know you cried on the way home after mom died. I know you were balled up in the back of the car, and it was dark out. I know about the bad dreams you had, and I know there's more to them than anyone would believe. I know you were scared when you stepped on that snake when Dad sat you down on the other side of the fence to look for golf balls in the backyard. Ever wondered where your best friend Richard is today? And by the way, that Dynovfr bike was the coolest Christmas present ever, 0.5mm frame, way cool dude.*

So, pretty curious who this is right? It's me. Well, I mean you, Rob, yourself. I know you don't believe it, but I was given one thing, one thing I could do that was not possible, in the year 2014. That thing was this letter. Still don't believe? How could I know those things from different years, different states? Dad? Ok, Dad doesn't know about the 380 chrome pistol you stole out of a boat, and he surely doesn't know about your girlfriend Dee at the skating rink, or about the Poo-nanny crew, or how about Mr. Weaver, "Gargamel", your teacher? Now believe me? Listen up I could have made myself a millionaire, I could have gotten a get out of jail free card, yes I'm in jail or anything else I wanted, instead, I'm about to give you, me, something worth far more than money, and that's advice. If you don't listen to and follow these truths, then when you find yourself serving a 22 year prison sentence, separated from dad, him 80 years old, alone, with no one in sight, don't say I didn't tell you. I know that you've seen counselors, lived with our sister, and at the end of the day, you listen to no one. I figured, you'd listen to me, and you better, this is your only shot to fix our mistakes.

First off, quit thinking that you know everything, you don't know half what you think you do, honest. Listen to the adults who try to tell you things, they know more than you, and they really do want the best for you. I know you think they just want to stop you from having fun, and that their way is boring, but their way will keep you out of trouble, and out of jail. Remember when Dad told you, "Boy, one day you're gonna wish you'd have listened to Ole Dad"? Well, he was right, and you had better start, because you'll be in jail soon, a first of many. And stay away from Steve and Louis. Trust me, they are nothing but trouble. Find friends who do not do bad things, if they do, stay away from them. Right now, that is the smartest thing you can do, live by this. A real friend wants you to do good, to be happy. A real friend would never let you do bad or do bad with you. Pick your friends wisely, so that means ditch the ones that you do have now.

Next up, respect Dad, and respect everyone else, cussing at people and being disrespectful is not cool, and it is not funny. When you get older, you will look back and be ashamed at the way you acted and treated people. Remember this; you get more with sugar than you do with you know what. Respect will get you far so make people want to associate with you because you are a good kid, a kid well-liked. What will dictate the way people view you and treat you is your attitude, bottom line. So, be nice to people, respect them, and treat everyone the way you want them to treat you.

Next, your education. Now I know you hate school. You hate the kids, and homework is out of the question. I get it, I'm you remember? But newsflash, the life you have when you are older is determined on what kind of education you get. If you do bad in school or don't finish it, you get jobs that suck, and they don't pay you much of anything. When you get older do you want a nice car, a nice place of your own? Do you wanna get paid good money and go to a job that's fun and that pays you enough to take care of the people who depend on you? Well, you have to get a good education, because companies and businesses want to hire smart people who know what they're doing. So, get the good grades, get the education, and at all cost, go to college. You see, college isn't just education, money and a cool job when you graduate, its parties and hot chicks all the time. So don't miss it for the world, I did. This is your chance, you can do all the cool things that I missed, you can fix my mistakes, you can be anything you want, just trust me, I wouldn't tell you all this if It weren't so, so get with it today. Well Robert, I've tried to give you the best advice I can, and if you follow what I've told you, these basic things, then you'll be alright.

I decided to save the best for last. I often wondered why life turned out like it did, and why me, why, why, why? I must tell you, I figured that out too. Now don't think I'm nuts, but hear me out. You know you've been in and out of jail growing up, but only because you had to go. Well, funny thing, now you go because you want to. I've learned something that you haven't gotten around to yet, too busy being all wild and crazy, I know you, I did all you are doing already, here's the thing, God is real, and he has been with me the entire time, and he's with you now, you just have to look. He's with you, me, and everyone else who seeks him, truth.

A while back, things got really bad for me, I was at the lowest point in all these 36 years, and I couldn't do it any longer, I just couldn't. God waits on us, He waits for the stubborn, He waits for the selfish, and I was both of those. I eventually cried out to God, and I asked for Him to help me. I told Him I was weak, that I couldn't go on, and that I was tired. I told Him that if He would deliver me from my chains, my spiritual chains, my mental chains, and my emotional chains, even my physical chains, that I would give my life to him. I promised I would truly live for Him, not just in word, but in actions, and so far so good.

I prayed to God and asked Him to forgive me for all the bad things I've done, for all the sins I had committed. I asked Him to take away all of my guilt and shame, my fears and regrets. I asked Him to do these things, and most importantly, I accepted His son, Jesus Christ, as my Lord and Saviour. I acknowledged that He died for my sins, and I accepted His gift of forgiveness.

I can tell you, from that point; things have never been the same, although still in prison, for the first time in my life, I'm truly free. I'm happy, I have joy, I have peace, and most important, I have love. I have forgiven anyone who's ever done or said anything bad to me, and I love everyone, not of myself, but of Christ Jesus who lives in me. Always remember this, in life there will be things you can't do, things you can't change or fix, or can't make right, but through God, He will give you the strength to overcome anything. When you deal with God, you deal with love, you deal with truth, and you deal with trust and faith. When you don't understand something, you just have to trust that God will do what He says, that's faith. So, our problem has been, we weren't living for God, we didn't trust, and we had no faith. Well, once you put God first, stop being selfish, start living to serve Him, and doing what's good, pure, and true, the good things start to happen. Your life will never be the same, I promise, this will be the best thing to ever happen to you, just trust me!

Well Robert, that about ends my letter. I gave up a lot of cool things in order to get this to you. I could have had anything, keep that in mind. See how I put you first; think of others more highly than yourself. I think of good things, do good things, and show love and compassion to all, even to those who do wrong to you. Don't ever let anyone tell you that you can't, or that you're not good enough. Always strive for perfection, but always realize you're not perfect. Set goals, dream dreams, and always remember you can achieve them. The words you've just read are priceless; they are your road map, your game plan. They are your keys to success, if you apply them, and I know you will, then not only will you have a wonderful life, but you will be able to bless others, of which there is no greater privilege of this earth. Good Luck.

Sincerely
"Yourself at 36"

HENRY MITCHELL - DON'T BREAK THE LAW

12-3-2013 - To the young,

I am a 52-year-old black male who has been incarcerated since January 20, 1986. Almost 28 years in Prison. I am writing you because I do not want to see your years spent as I have spent so many of mine, behind prison bars and razor wire fences.

I am speaking as one who has firsthand experience in this matter. There is nothing glamorous here. Here you will find bad food, horrible and cramped living areas, constant lockdown, an uncaring staff and fellow inmates whose main agenda is what they can get. Not all is bad, but not very much is good in prison. Eat when I say eat, sleep when I say sleep, wash when I say wash, visit when I say visit, and suffer when I say suffer, even if only few have broken the rules, many times all will be punished.

Two things I want you to consider. The first being how years spent in prison will affect you and the second being how they will affect your love ones. No matter how tough you are, you will hurt, even if you hide it well and your loved ones will hurt. Many survive and some even prosper after years in prison but no one comes out unchanged. While we are in prison the world keeps moving. When I came to prison the internet was still a dream.

The best way to not end up in prison is simple: **don't break the law**. I don't say that to judge or criticize but because it's just that simple, I know that many times many young people are faced with tempting situations for whatever reason but always remember that good decisions usually lead to a good life. Learn to make good decision while you are young. Decisions that will keep you out of prison.

Life is precious and so is freedom, both are to be respected and cherished. May God bless you with a good life and may you never know what it means to lose your freedom.

Henry Mitchell - SCDC# 134563

RODERQUIZ COOK - LETTER OF ENCOURAGEMENT TO OUR SONS

Peace Young Brother,

December 19, 2013 - As I sit down to write this letter, I envision it being read by a very intelligent young man that simply needs motivation. I too was that same young man at one point of time where you are now. The only difference is I wish I would have taken the opportunity to focus and analyse life differently from another perspective before it was too late.

Young brother, it's my hope and aspiration that this brief letter awakens the power that is embedded in your DNA. Young brother you are more than just a minority, you are more than just another prison number, you are more than just another chalk line drawn out in the streets. What you are is ROYALTY. You are an inventor. You are an educator. You are an astronaut. You are any and everything you set your mind to be. You were born with a purpose and believe you me; it's not to be sitting in a 10 x 5 foot prison cell where I am currently at, with a prison sentence longer that the time I have spent on this earth. Young brother, I beg you to stop and analyse your life and take the time to find your purpose. Motivate yourself to become more than just another member of the minority that becomes a part of the prison system majority.

Young brother, YOU ARE THE FUTURE. Become what you already are: Greatness!

In closing, I leave you with this...

Adversity introduces a man into his true self. So find yourself and never deny yourself. I pray that this has planted a seed of motivation in you, our future BLACK MAN!

Peace,

Roderquiz Cook SCDC# *261587*, bka Preacher

REALITIES OF PRISON LIFE

FACTOID: HUNGER

Have you ever been in a situation where you have not eaten in over 12 hours and there is nothing or no way to get food? Ravenously hungry with your stomach hurting, making all kinds of growling noises demanding that you feed it and there is nothing you can do about it? Well, Welcome to prison!

Being a free man living in society, hunger is not really an option, unless you are really broke, homeless or burned all of your bridges to the point that no one wants to deal with you. But of course, you can always beg on the street. As far as being a person incarcerated, you have very little power of how, how much and when you can eat. The prison has rules and policies that they follow and control movement is the main one. So they have you on a time schedule when they feed you unlike at home when you or your parents may cook a meal when ready.

You are allowed 10 minutes to eat from the time you sit down. At least that's what it is supposed to be, but really they give you about 6 minutes. At the institution where I'm housed at there are 96 prisoners on each side. There are 2 sides so that's 192 prisoners in each dorm when the dorms are full. When they call you to eat the officers yell out "chow time" not breakfast, lunch or dinner time but chow time like we're a pack of animals or something. Then as we file out of the dorm they want us to walk in a single file line one behind the other and will stop the line and make us wait if we aren't lined up. Once inside the cafeteria you have two small windows that they serve you through. There's a tall stainless steel wall separating you and the kitchen workers so you can't see them and they can't see you. Back in the days this wall wasn't there so you could see who is serving your food, but the Department had the walls erected so the workers couldn't see who they were serving just in case the prisoner might be cool with the person and want to look out for them with extra food, and also so that people won't see whose responsible for putting such small portions of unidentifiable food on the tray. Anyway you have 192 people divided up into two lines being served through a wall. One by one we receive our trays. Picture an elementary school cafeteria with the portion sizes on an elementary school tray. However the people being fed are not 8, 9, 10 year olds, they are grown ass men. (And when you are in lock up, it is half the portion size)

You have to get your drinks before you sit down at the table with 4 other Prisoners. There are no switching tables; and most of the time you cannot choose where to sit. Imagine going down a line like in a restaurant, except in a prison food line there's a stainless steel wall that divides the Prisoners eating chow, from the working Prisoners serving chow. Imagine there being at least 7 guards in the dinner room area either at a post watching you, or walking between tables looking over our shoulders like Nazis at concentration camps for the Jews. As you are sitting down to eat you have a prison guard standing over your shoulder yelling you have 5 minutes to eat. Most of the time, you don't even have enough time to finish your food. Then upon leaving you are stopped and are pat down searched before you leave the dinner hall. You go through this 3 times a day once at 5:00 a.m. then at 11:00 a.m. and the last meal is fed at 5:00 p.m. Just imagine how hungry you are by 10:00 p.m. It starts to feel like your stomach is touching your back and the only thing you can do is drink some water to stave off the hunger until the next morning.

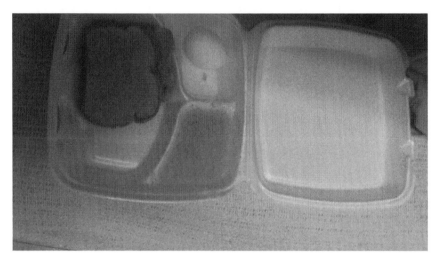

Example of a tray given to inmates when on lock down... 7 a.m. breakfast, after not eating since 5 p.m. the night before.

The Department of Corrections also has ways you can support yourself to survive and that is the "Canteen". They have packaged food, which is basically high sodium, high carb and very expensive, [As a side note, they also have boots and tennis shoes that you can buy, (because the state only provides you with one pair of crocs to wear for the year, rubber sandals with holes in them).] But if you do not have anyone sending you money you cannot get anything from the store/canteen. If you are on restriction punishment for a prison rule then you cannot go to the store to buy food, only hygiene. And so what does that mean? That means that you are ravenously hungry every day. This is also the case if you have no family sending you money. So what is implied is that punishment in prison also consists of refusing people food hence starving the inmate (via the lack of canteen) when an inmate is accused of committing an infraction where the punishment is loss of canteen privileges. (This can be ANY infraction the prison administration chooses)

There is an article which references Frederick Douglass and explaining h how hunger was used by how slave masters as a way to control their slaves.[45] Is that humane? By not allowing inmates commissary to eat and allow them to remain ravenously hunger where there are NO OTHER options for getting food other than stealing or violating the rules to get food, is that humane? Furthermore, in some states, if one has committed a drug related felony, they are not allowed to received food stamps or any benefits upon release permanently. This basically means if you sold drugs to have food, upon release from prison, you will go hungry because the state government will not help to give you food. And just recently a bill was passed in the US House of Representatives, H.R. 2, AGRICULTURE AND NUTRITION ACT OF 2018 which would basically will cut SNAP (Food stamps) benefits for those who do not work or get 20 hours per week of employment.[46] [47] (And we know how difficult it is for an ex-convict to get employment upon release).

If you can't go to the store because you do not have anyone on the outside helping you (or have loss your canteen privileges) and you are very, very hungry you take the risk in hustling or robbing other inmates just to survive and eat. Just like in society, when you are broke and you feel your back is against the wall, you resort to selling drugs, robbery, committing all types of crime just to keep from going hungry. This is not an excuse for this behavior when you are on the street because you can always go to the food pantry or get help somewhere, but in prison there are **NO OTHER OPTIONS** to solve your hunger and the COs don't care. Worst case scenario, some people have to sell their souls, allowing others to have sex with them, doing other people's dirty work or be their "boy" so that you can just survive.

Which leads you right into a life of crime *inside* the prison, and you are back to the same MO (modus operandi). Also the toughest thing about being incarcerated is that you can only go to the store whenever they allow you to go. The prices on food compared to prices in the outside world are highway robbery and not really justified. The DOC is a billion dollar industry and they feed you nasty food where on the boxes in some cases it says "not fit for human consumption". They provide food that they would not feed to their family or eat themselves. What is worse is that the staff could care less if you eat it or not. The food is sometime cold and the meat is the lowest grade that you would not buy on the outside, which makes the food unhealthy. The most common food bought off the canteen is ramen noodles, otherwise known as "crackhead soup" because it is cheap and filling, however it is not nutritious.

Also fresh fruits and vegetables are NOT given because they claim that the prisoners are going to make wine with it.

Everything in the canteen is expensive especially when the state provides you with no means of making your own money and you have to rely on your family to send you money over and over again. They also sell hygiene in the canteen like toothpaste, soap, shampoo, lotion and hair grease, and all at exorbitant prices (way over priced!)

Sometimes the COs come and take an inventory of your items, tell you have too much and will take your property, including your food. If they feel you have too much food or hygiene they can take it from you. Imagine that?! Stealing you and your family's hard earned money. Sometimes prisoners have extra food because at any time the prison can be short staffed or some knuckle head decides he wants to stab someone up and disrupt the dorm. When this happens the WHOLE dorm (everyone) goes on lock down and this can be for days or weeks at a time. During this time, they will bring the food to the inmates on trays, but the food is much less than what one would receive if they go to chow/the cafeteria. Given that you are being given less food, you need something to supplement it, but when on lock down you cannot go to the canteen, so what do you have to eat when the food you are given is not enough? (Remember Lock Down–where YOU and the other prisoners have done nothing wrong (as it is not considered punishment) can go on for days or weeks at a time)

So again, when on lock down they bring your food on Styrofoam trays. These are times when you feel it the most cause the portions are about half of what you normally receive. So you have to eat and lie down and try not to even pass gas or else your food will be gone just like that.

****

(Below is an excerpt by from a journal by L.A. Berntsen from our next book "Blindside Diaries, Life Behind the Fences" (coming in Winter 2019) that will convey the importance of food.

October 9, 7:00pm

Man, this food in the mess hall, now for breakfast, we get eggs, grits & biscuits, lunch might be anything supper we get rice & something else. Tonight we had some kind of "jambalaya" with sausage, last night we had chicken casserole. Now people listen to me in prison, chicken especially fried chicken is a big deal...So now let me get back to chicken, fried chicken. It was summer, maybe July. I was at a different institution. We had fried chicken for supper. Man I will never forget the hush that fell over the mess hall when this one guy just took Red's piece of chicken, "Man fuck you I took that!" a hush fell over the room and Man, I didn't know 1,500 guys could be that quiet.

83

Well Red just put his tray down on the table and walked out the back door of the mess hall. The other man just kept on talking smack, giving dab, laughing. "Man I took his chicken."

Well Red had a piece of pipe buried on the back yard that few knew about, so he got his 3 foot piece of pipe and just waited for the guy that took the chicken. When that guy came out the mess hall talking smack about he took Red's chicken and now he was going to take "all" of Red. Red didn't say anything as he and his boys walked by, but when Red swung that pipe. He was like 'Hammering Hank' and he swung for the fence. The chicken thief's head popped like a ripe cantaloupe.

Red kept hitting the chicken thief and it wasn't long before half the yard is going at it. Guys stabbing each other, taking sides, Red standing over-like he was chopping wood, blood and brains going everywhere. As the blood spilled out of the head it just pooled up right around Red's feet. The body holds a lot of blood and like water it finds the path of least resistance. So as Red beat the chicken thief to death and beyond, the blood spilled around his feet in fact, after the killing you could see the outlines of two feet where the blood had been. It lasted for a long time despite repeated rains and washings.

Meanwhile, lots of guys were getting their frustration out on each other. The "goon squad" finally made an appearance, as things cooled down guys was throwing knives down, trying to edge away from where they've been busy at. Goon squad hollering "Get down!" Well, most guys are lying down but you got a couple of "psychos" hollering "Get the pigs!"

Well the pigs were the ones getting other people this day, in just a few minutes the "goons" had control of the yard. (This wasn't their first big job) Everybody but Red was on the ground, he was standing over the chicken thief, surrounded by his blood with the pipe in his hand, just looking at the dead body.

Well Red got about 5 years for manslaughter, and the next few months after that, Chicken Day was very calm.

****

Below is another excerpt by James Sigler from our next book "Blindside Diaries, Life Behind the Fences" (coming in Winter 2019)

October 1, 5:30 A.M. Reflections. Day One.

I awoke a little too late due to the fact my roommate snores all night and real loud. So by the time I awoke the officer was not unlocking the cell doors for chow instead they were being lock since they had already been open 15 minutes (All cell doors are only open 15 minutes after they are opened then relocked. *So you are either in or out. Sometimes this wouldn't be a problem because some officers have a little understanding, but this particular officer was a straight Jackass!) Not only was he a Jackass but it seem to most that he hates blacks and inmate was something he scrape off the bottom of his boots. I just got out of lock up (The hole) Sept 13. So I was in the process of trying to regain my weight back. I went from 155lb to 130lb by the time of 6 months lock up time was completed so missing chow today was not in my plans.* "Open da door C.O.!" *I shouted pointing on the door trying to get the officer attention. Since the officer refuse to acknowledge me I got a fellow inmate to let the C.O. know I was trying to go to chow. As the inmates started filing out the door heading to breakfast the C.O. finally made his way to my door.*

"Me and my roommate trying to go to eat we overslept," *I responded trying not to sound too aggressive.*

"Too bad for you and your roommate," *the officer told me with a smirk on his face.*

"Come on man we just got off lockup we don't have nothing in our lockers and we are hungry." *My roommate shouted behind me.*

"You better drink some water and hope it lasts until lunch." *The C.O. told my roommate then walked off like there was nothing left to be said.* "BOOM, BOOM, BOOM!!!" *That was the sound of my roommate kicking on the door because he was mad as a grizzly bear. I know he was as hungry as a hostage because my stomach was touching my back!*

"Fall back roommate before he call backup down here, you know he soft as hell! And you know how they roll I ain't gone let them do you nothing. We gone get it on the flo' and ain't no need to go back to lock up, we at least gotta last a month on da yard." *I told my roommate finally getting him to calm down. We both downed two cups of water and jump back into bed hoping the two cups would hold us until lunch.*

****

October 23 - 4:30 P.M.

I got turnaround from dinner because the officer said I had to get my "water" when I got my tray. I couldn't sit my tray down then get back up and get my water because I might be trying to sneak in and get an extra cup of water. Water? It can't even be that serious! These officers are so miserable at home that they just have to come here and find something to pick about. This shit is crazy!

****

10:30 A.M.

85

We have been on lock down all the way until they called lunch. They released us to lunch just to get one apple and a pack of peanut butter! They don't even feed us enough to fill a ten year old!!

****

3:50 P.M.

They released us again after locking us back in our cells after lunch to go to dinner. Now dinner was a little better they serve chicken! The way inmates were trying to steal extra pieces of chicken you would think they were dying of starvation! Even though it's true they really didn't feed us anything really today every chicken day is the same! One inmate even got sent to solitary confinement for taking his chicken out the kitchen trying to get it back to the dorm. He tried to explain to the officer that he was hungry and that was the only reason he was trying to get his chicken back but the officer wasn't trying to hear none of that! It's crazy because these officers act like they are not human and can't understand why a man who gets nothing from home and only have what the state (Department of Corrections) gives him (which is nothing!) would try to take what he can't eat in the kitchen back with him to eat later. They only allow us ten minutes to eat so it may not even be his fault he couldn't eat all his dinner. It may take five minutes to go through the line get tray and sit down! I just shake my head and am thankful a couple people on the street still love me, because it gets real hard sometimes!

(Mr. Sigler was released in 2018)

(Would you like to hear more from James "Yuk" Sigler and his former life in prison? Come and visit him for a month in prison via his journal, see our next book in this series: "Blindside Diaries, Life behind the Fences" In addition, Mr. Sigler is also a talented writer. See his e-book "Twisted Loyalty" published by Imperial Imprint LLC currently for sale on Amazon: https://www.amazon.com/dp/B01M9BYL6O and "Susie Q" (A gangster deeply in love and would do anything for his an HIV+ female childhood friend) coming out Winter 2019.)

LETTERS TO OUR SONS

FACTOID – SOLITARY CONFINEMENT/LOCK UP /THE HOLE/CLOSED CELL RESTRICTION

P risoners say that prison is a world of its own so in that regard you have to envision the prison itself as being the city and lock up being the city jail. (Lock Up, Solitary Confinement The Hole, Closed Cell Restriction ("CCR") all the same thing) Yeah, that a perfect similarity because in lock up your movements are under more scrutiny than being in a cell block in jail. If you leave your cell in lock up you will be handcuffed everywhere you go and in a few lock ups you will wear what we call "prison jewelry" which are chains wrapped around your waist with a lock and handcuffs with a chain around your ankle even when you are going to the shower in which you only get 10 minutes to do that. And even worse, in some camps they further demean you by making you strip all of your clothes off, bend over and spread your butt cheeks so that the male CO can look in the crack of your ass and inside your anus for a shank (weapon), like someone would actually put a knife up their butt knowing they will have no opportunity to get it out and use it.

Just to give you a little history on HOW you get into solitary confinement/lock up: "Individuals receive terms in solitary based on charges that are levied, adjudicated, and enforced by prison officials with little or no outside oversight. Many prison systems have a hearing process, but these are seldom more than perfunctory. Prison officials serve as prosecutors, judges, and juries, and prisoners are rarely permitted representation by defense attorneys. Unsurprisingly, in most prison systems, they are nearly always found guilty."[48] (http://solitarywatch.com/facts/faq/) In addition, one can go to lock up for any reason such as cursing (using profanity), a CO saying that they "disrespected them" even if the CO disrespected them first, for contraband such as drugs, tobacco, cell phone, using social media, or having something that is not necessarily illegal, but not allowed, for refusing to obey an order such as cutting their hair (as some Rastafarians have found themselves) or taking food back to the dorm since they did not have enough time to eat it during chow, or for protective custody, for being a homosexual, being a gang member which may be considered a "Security Threat Group" (STG), such as the Black Panther Party, or just because they say you had too much food/property. The prison administration may want to put you in there because they don't like you, for fighting, threatening or hurting staff or other prisoners, because the administration says they need to "investigate you" and the list goes on and on. To learn more about Solitary ConfinementLock Up check out http://solitarywatch.com/facts/faq/. The website is very enlightening and informative.

I've sadly been doing time ever since 1988 off and on and the part about lock up that messes with me is the other prisoners you have to deal with. It's a place of loneliness even though there are about thirty other prisoners in here

87

with you, however most of the time they are not in the same room with you and you do not see their faces. The loneliness starts once they become bored, because a lot of them do not know how to deal with boredom. Their education is low to none and therefore their ability to be creative is low. Think about it, when you are bored you watch TV (but no TV or radio in lock up) or read a book...what if you don't know how to read? Then what does one do??

For the younger ones, conversation, rapping and urban novels are all that they have (if they can read), but when those options become tiresome it's back to boredom. That's when fellow prisoners begin to bang on the doors to get attention from the police because they have become stressed out, or they start arguing with the next prisoner over the smallest, dumbest shit like what rappers have the hottest music, or the most money or what females in the industry look the best or what they was or wasn't doing on the bricks (on the streets outside of prison) or over cars. Never anything of any real importance. All because they are bored and truly lonely. Some get to stuffing toilet paper or clothes in their toilet to stop it up so they can start flushing it repeatedly and flood their cell so they can get out of the cell for a while – for a change of scenery. This may be an act at the police or prisoner worker [Side note, run around.... (A run-around is a prisoner who is in general population that is given a job in lockup to clean the empty cells and what we call the rock (the general area) because everything is concrete and metal.] Sometimes prisoners get crazy because the CO or the run-around won't pass things for him (such as food or a book) or acknowledge him when he calls him. Boredom turns some of us to acting like spoiled brats. But it can eventually evolve into mental illness or suicide...due to a nervous breakdown from the stress of being in there.

Then there's the fucked up food that they serve. It is bad enough that the food is nasty, but they do not serve you enough food. Imagine going from eating barely one plate of nasty food per meal, which is what one gets when in population. Now image getting half that amount, not even enough to fill up a dogs bowl. When you come to lock up I have seen fellow inmates who were 250 pounds on the yard, but when they come off of lock up, they are weighing 140 pounds in less than 90 days. Imagine going to bed every night ravenously hungry like a homeless person and looking out your back window of you cell and seeing kitchen workers throwing away trash bags full of food. They don't care because they are going back to the yard where they may have their canteen to eat when getting back to their cells. In lock up, you only eat the 3 plates of food that are given to you because you don't have access to anything else.

Now imagine having to deal with all of this when you are in a cell with another prisoner. If y'all are compatible, have similar interests and can respectfully get along, it helps you cope with being in lock up a lot better.

That is someone to talk to, trade food with and hook you up with one of his girlfriend's girls (they give them their peoples addresses and they write them.) But if it is the opposite --- then you have a real problem. The cells were not designed to house two individuals. The prison officials just decided they would save time and money by forcing us to live together like sardines in a can. In some of the cells there is an iron desk top with four legs that's connected to a short iron bench. But if you are in a room that does not have a desk seat then there exists a few problems. The desk seat is bolted to the concrete floor in the back of the cell by the window and close to the iron bunk beds. If there is no desk seat then both prisoners have to sit on their bunks or the stall of the toilet to read or write. The prisoner on the top bunk has to jump up to his bunk bed because now there is nothing for him to use as a step ladder. And if the prisoner on the bottom bunk does not allow his cell mate to sit on his bunk, then the other must sit on the toilet to eat his meals. (Remember this can be for weeks, months and years at a time)

Then what if you have a cell mate who is a loud mouth all day while you are trying to read a novel, do your legal work or sleep? Then there are the cellmates who display all loss of home training, dropping food on the floor, leaving piss on the toilet bowl and floor, forgetting to flush the toilet after pissing or defecating...or just letting the feces marinate in the toilet and stink up the room when they are on the toilet. Or not wanting to do his part in cleaning up the cell when the officers pass out cleaning supplies, or only taking a shower one out of the three times per week that we are given a shower. (Some don't even take a shower because they do not want to be stripped searched before going into the shower. Imagine the smell of living in a 6x8 cell 24 hours a day/7 days per week with someone who has not taken a shower in over 3 months with little to NO deodorant?)

Then there are the ones who snore louder than a lawn mower and passes gas constantly. Straight foul character. It's bad enough that we have no privacy to piss and shit, but on top of that he lives like a savage. Before long, the arguments will start which will lead into a fight. If you're in a room with someone twice your size and you can't come to an understanding with him then you can wait until the officer is at the door and you hook off on him and hope they come and assist you before he recovers and gets your ass.

On the rare occasions where a person may attempt to enforce their will on you and rape you, you better scratch, bite, knee, scream, hope and pray that the officer hears you and comes to your aid before you're violated too badly... And this can become fatal because you may have a cell mate who is a person who plots on his foes, so he may not fight you head up. Every time you leave the cell, you must be handcuffed, but they do not handcuff you both at the same time. You turn around and stick both of your hands behind your back under the bars where there is a section cut out to receive your food tray. So that you will be handcuffed while your body is facing your cellmate. And once he hears the handcuffs click, you are his victim because you are defenseless. You will be lucky if he only uses his hand and feet to attack you. Worse case is he stabs you up with a pen or a homemade shank he somehow snuck into the cell.

And there are the CO's (prison guards) who treat you like shit because you can't get to them since you are locked behind the cell doors. They take their time feeding you by letting the food sit out in the hallway for hours, and if you beat on the door to complain, they will refuse to feed you at all. Now you gotta go all out just to get something to eat (Going all out means beating on the door, screaming and yelling or even flooding your cell by stuffing the toilet with tissues and continuously flushing.)

And it's the same with the shower, phones, visits, books, US mail and recreation. (Recreation on lock up is being handcuffed and placed in a small chain linked fence cage to walk around in circles for about an hour.) They may put you in the shower after making you wait an hour, but rush you out in less than ten minutes. They don't allow you to wear watches on lock up, but they have clock's hanging on the walls outside the cells that you can see the time. Or they will forget about you while you are in the shower with the water still running because only they can turn it off and on. They take all day to pass out your mail and you may not see it until three, four days to weeks after it comes. And if you are allowed visits they make your visitor sit in the waiting room waiting 30 minutes or more for you (visits are only 4 hours, really 3.5) , if you can even get a visit on lock up, because usually you can't.

They mess with you so bad that some prisoners have killed themselves just to escape the mental torment. If you make a threat to kill yourself they'll rush in your cell hand cuff you and place you in another cell with no clothes on and no linen for your mattress. They keep you in there for 24 hours butt ass naked while counselors come observe and speak with you for fifteen minutes or less with little to no empathy. Sometimes individuals who choose to take this path get placed on psychiatric medication and truly go insane. They get no true psychiatric or mental health counseling, just psychotropic medication and if they act out too much, they get strapped in the chair... (See Section "Prison in General"- 'The Infamous Chair')

This is the mental health/suicide prevention that prisoners receive...no one deserves this. Also there are times when prisoners need to get out of the cell because they feel that the walls are closing in or about to have a nervous breakdown. Often times the COs ignore their pleas only to find the inmate dead in his/her cell the next morning...because the inmate committed suicide.

Tearing up your cell entails stripping all of the linen off your mattress, throwing your mail all on the floor for the most part you don't have much on lock up so they can't tear it up but so much.

Imagine going to bed at night with everything in tact in your cell and then waking up and stepping in a pool of water with all of your legal work floating in it because a few prisoners flooded their cells, or being awakened at night coughing because the CO's have over sprayed a prisoner with gas/mace. Not to mention them randomly running into your cell to shake it down, or better yet, tear it up.

LOCK UP. This is the part that your lawyer, judge, "friends in the street", or the TV show "LOCK UP", did not tell you about. – By Streets (written while on Lock up)

****

Solitary confinement also known as Lock Up, the Bing, SMU (Special management Unit), closed cell restriction where prisoners are place on 23 and 1, which means you are locked up in a cell for 23 hours a day and maybe allowed for one hour if you choose to go out for recreation. Recreation is in a chain linked fence cage to walk around. While in solitary confinement you are only allowed to take 3 showers per week, but must be stripped search before you can take your shower.

There are several reasons why a prisoner is placed on solitary confinement. The most common reason is when a person breaks the rules established by prison officials. The rules can be failing a drug test, fighting, participating in a riot, assaulting a prison official, possession of contraband or something simple as verbally abusing an officer. Remember the excerpt from our next book Blindside Diaries, in the Factoid Hunger, how a prisoner was hungry and tried to take a piece of food back with him to the dorm since he did not have enough time to eat, but the CO did not care, charged him with having contraband and sent him to Solitary Confinement/LOCK UP anyway.

Lock up is used as a means to punish prisoners for so called bad behavior. It is also used as a way to break the more rebellious prisoners who have a problem with being told what to do and when to do it by officers that are at times young enough to be the prisoners child. (Think Malcolm X, refusal to accept his name a prison number)

Lock up is a very lonely place. Just picture yourself in a small cell (the size of a small bathroom) with no one to talk to except yourself for 23 hours per day, for weeks, months or sometimes years on end. I have seen some of the liveliest individuals be placed in lock up and when they return you can see the change in their eyes. Their eyes go from bright and attentive to distant and crazed. I have heard of guys being on lock up so long they start to go insane. They throw their feces on officers and some even eat their feces and drink their own urine.

Some prisoners attempt to kill themselves by slitting their wrist with a razor blade or hanging themselves with their sheets. Some COs and prison administrative staff say that this behavior is just a cry for attention, and that they are just trying to get the prison officials to reduce their lock up time and return them to general population…but what happens when the prisoners cries suicide, the officers disregard the cries, and the prisoner kills himself? (And this happens more often than reported) It has been noted in various publications and reports that…the US has the highest rate of Solitary confinement and it being viewed by as cruel and unusual punishment.[49] [50] In my opinion there is not that much attention in the world that would make me thrown feces on someone, smear it on myself or try to attempt suicide. There obviously is a problem and it just may be what is said, they cannot take the solitary confinement, maybe claustrophobic or due to deprivation of human contact. But as a prisoner you do not have your choice of punishment.

When placed on solitary confinement, the officers treat you with less respect than they do when you are in general population. They speak to you as if you are the lowest creature on the planet, worse than a rabid rat. Every time you want to take a shower the officer does a strip search and as a result most guys refuse showers so they do not have to deal with the humiliation. They take bird baths in their sink until their time is over (which can be weeks, months or years), so you can only imagine what they smell like when they return to general population.

I have seen guys go to lock up with a bronze skin tone and return looking like Casper the Friendly Ghost due to lack of sunlight. Also people return from lock up 15 to 20 pounds lighter than when they went up. The plates have less food on it than in general population, and the prisoners do not have access to canteen or snacks while in Lock up. They only eat what has been given to them on that small tray. Some prisoners need to relearn how to hold their urine and feces and not have a bathroom accident when coming back to general population because they are not used to the toilet so far away, or being told they have to wait to use the toilet, since the toilet was always less than 3 feet away at all times while in Lock up.

We as a people are social beings that rely in interaction with others to live. Being placed in an isolated cell with no one to talk to but yourself will have a damaging effect on anyone. There are guys I know who have spent multiple years behind lock up doors. When you look into their eyes, you can see it. The pain and the loneliness they have endured, as there is truth behind the saying.

Letter to Our Sons readers…please see the following letter of someone on Lock Up for over 20 years at the time of writing…(if you see his latest pictures in 2015 or so, you can see in his eyes how broken he was after all of those years in solitary confinement)

LUMUMBA K. INCUMAA - THE REALITIES THAT NIGHTMARES ARE MADE OF

Peace One

My name is Lumumba Kenyatta Incumaa. This year 2015 marks my 27th straight year of being in prison. I am serving a sentence of double LIFE without parole, plus 50 years for the crimes of armed robbery and murder.

This year 2015 also marks my 21 straight year of being locked in a cell 23-24 hours a day, in what they call administration segregation or lock-up. In April of 1995, as the result of the riot/hostage taking situation at the Broad RiverCorrectional Institution, I was removed from the general prison population and confined to the Maximum Security Unit (MSU). I was criminally charged with the crimes of assault and battery with intent to kill Correctional Officers and hostage taking of SCDC employees, and for these crimes I was convicted and given a sentence of 100 years total. These conviction and sentences have since been overturned and vacated but SCDC Officials treat me like they have not.

The MSU is a concrete and steel building with a total of 50 cells, no windows to the outside and no face to face contact with anyone except the C.O.'s. Each cell has two doors, and outer solid steel door and an inner bar door with a small food flap and covered with steel mesh on its outer side. Some cells have solid metal plates covering all four walls from top to bottom, and a camera in the ceiling, these cells are for those who do not follow the rules of the MSU. You will be gassed with chemical munitions (pepper spray, tear gas, etc....) rolled on by a 6 men or more C.O. cell extraction team, stripped naked and put into one of these cells until you comply with the rules of the MSU. There is no win against this. They will let you suffer and die in these metal cells before they let you break the rules of the MSU.

In the MSU each cell has a shower, some a T.V., and a concrete slab to lay your mattress on. All cells are one man. You eat all meals in the cell, served to you by C.O.s only. No prison worker is allowed in the building, not even to do maintenance work. Every time you leave the cell you are stripped searched by two (2) C.O.'s, who make you lift up and shake your genitalia, bend over at the waist and open your buttocks in the direction of the C.O. so they can look into your anus, then you are made to squat and cough, hold your arms up, lift up your feet so the C.O. can see and rub the bottom of your feet, and you are made to open your mouth and lift up your tongue as you make the sound ahhhhh... All this you are made to do while the C.O.'s search all your clothing and shoes. After you have put your clothes and shoes on, you are then placed in full metal restraints (belly chain with handcuffs attached and leg shackles.) You will go through this humiliating procedure every time you leave the cell in the MSU, and the cell will also be searched every time.

Once you are out the cell, the C.O. will attach a leash to the belly chain in the back and walk behind you holding the leash. The same way you would walk a dog on a leash. If you attempt to pull away or go in a direction you was not told to go, they will snatch the leash jerking you to a stop, and if you even attempt to protest or resist, they will punch the end of the PR-24 (billy-club/baton) attached to the end of the leash being held by them, into your sides, and told to "keep looking forward, don't look back!" One (1) hour of out of cell is for recreation, but in truth it's not recreation because you are still in full metal restraints locked inside a concrete cage. All you can do is stand still or walk with the metal shackles painfully rubbing against your ankles. The only opening in this concrete cage is the metal door and a small triangle shaped hole covered with steel mesh at the back top of the cage. Unless you are transported somewhere outside the MSU building, this is the only time you will see the real sky while confined in the MSU.

The MSU is a tomb in which you are buried alive not just physically, but also mentally. Confinement in the MSU completely disconnects your mind and body from the moving outside world, because it is an artificial world made by prison officials to separate your mind and body from that moving world outside the MSU. You cannot even receive books, magazines, family pictures or newspapers in the MSU. I was forced to spend ten (10) years from April 1995 to June 2005, confined in this artificial world. Ten (10) years of physical and psychological torture which I am still overcoming. Ten (10) years and I am still experiencing thoughts of this physical and psychological torture which I am still overcoming ten (10) years later. This is what the MSU does to you. Everyone who is confined in that building and the longer you are confined within that artificial world the further and further it detaches you from the real world outside the MSU, and as the result it affects your physical and psychological readjustment to the real world outside the MSU once you have been released from the MSU. It is called Post-Traumatic Administrative Segregation Syndrome.

In June 2005 I was released from the MSU to the Special Management Unit (SMU), which is only another form of confinement to a cell 23-24 hours a day but just face to face contact with other Prisoner. Within the SMU I am still subjected to some humiliation strip searches, cell searches at will by the C.O., but now I am also handcuffed behind my back with only a pair of handcuffs with a leash attached to the back, which is held by the C.O. as he walks behind me, like a man walking his dog. The SMU is bigger than the MSU. It has two (2) sides and each side has a total of 48 cells, some of which are two man cells. The cells are filthy and we are rarely given enough cleaning supplies to adequately clean the cells, and the cleaning supplies we are given is too watered down, so it is useless to disinfect anything.

There is no ventilation system in the SMU that works, and as a result thick dust falls 24 hours a day. You can wipe off a surface and less than a minute later that same surface is again covered with a thick layer of dust. We are breathing in this dust daily. The roof has holes in it and water drops from the ceiling every time it rains. We are given a 10-minute shower 3 days a week on Monday, Wednesday and Friday in shower stalls (cages) which are also filthy and rarely cleaned, and when they are cleaned they are half cleaned. I have caught a MRSA infection from the filthy showers and others have also caught staph infection from the shower, but despite these facts which prison officials are aware of, the showers are still not properly disinfected. There have even been times when Prisoners have thrown feces on and at each other while in the shower. The showers are individual stalls (cages) with a bar door covered with steel mesh on the inside, and we are locked in these shower stalls (cages) which makes it hard to breath in some of them because the steam from the hot water becomes trapped in the shower stall (cages) with you.

In the SMU we are served meals in the cells, and we are served smaller portions of food each meal, compared to what's served to the general prison populations. Sometimes we are served cold food, half cooked food, and spoiled food. There have been times when they have run out of food, and this still happens. We are lucky to get one hour of outside recreation a week in the SMU. We are denied all canteen privileges, denied all opportunities to work, denied all educational and vocational opportunities and our personal and legal property is limited to what can fit into a small box. We are essentially warehoused in cages like animals in inhumane conditions, and used as commodities by the state of SC to earn $20,000 dollars a year for each of us from the Federal Government. This money is supposed to be used to provide for our custody, maintenance, health, welfare, education and rehabilitation, but this is not what's happening. Prison is one of the top sources of revenue for the SC Government and this is at the expense of its Prisoner's mental and physical well-being.

I have not been in the general prison population of SCDC in 20 years, ten (10) years in the MSU and now ten (10) years in the SMU. This has not been by choice, but by force. Prison officials have deemed me a threat to the safety and security of the general prison population for something that happened twenty years ago, and because I will not renounce my culture as a member of the Nation of Gods and Earths (Five Percenter – 5%). I have not had a disciplinary charge and/or conviction in 20 years, but prison officials are still punishing me for what happened at the BRCI (Broad River Correctional Institution) in April 1995. This they are doing even despite the fact that my convictions and sentences resulting from that incident was overturned and vacated in 2001. I have not been taken back to court for them.

I remain confined to the SMU daily struggling to maintain my mental and physical sanity and stability under the weight of the persecution of this confinement. I have watched so many become emasculated or completely deteriorate into a psychosis of mental illness from this same confinement, and I know prison officials are hoping I am one day counted amongst these broken ones. They are not satisfied with just locking up our bodies; they want the destruction of our minds also.

PEACE!

Lumumba K. Incumaa, SCDC #155651

(Mr. Incumaa, aka Theodore Harrison was finally released from Lock up/Solitary Confinement in 2016. He readjusted back into general population via a STEP-down program at McCormick Correctional Institution. (A reintegration program for those who were in Solitary for long periods of time). Currently, 2018, he is a STEP-down program facilitator at Perry CI while serving a LIFE sentence.

THE GUY IN THE PICTURE ON THE BOOK COVER- JAMES SIGLER

I'm the guy in the picture. I was about 19 years old, new to a place where they were trying to take the rest of my life away from me. That was the first visit from my family in over two years where they kept me in SuperMax 23½ hours a day, ALONE in a cell. That was the face of a boy who was imprisoned/taken away from his loved ones for almost three years with no idea when he'll be back in society with them again or even moving freely around other prisoners…that is the face of a young man who's every waking and resting thoughts were freedom, who's every minute was spent thinking of his loved ones.

The only thing I could think of on first sight when I saw them was, "This is real! It's all real! My every waking hour, my ending night's thoughts, memories. They are all real! Life before my cell is real!" Then my mind took me further. I saw myself with my mother, chillin' with my brothers, laughing with my cousins—it was like all of my best memories flooded my mind all at once! Everything was there at once!

Picture this: Before that day I hadn't had a visit for 2 ½ years. No communication whatsoever with the outside world. I could only receive mail, outgoing mail was not allowed. The pod I was housed in was called C-pod, and the saying was, once you're in C-pod you'll never see the streets again. Everybody was afraid of C-pod. Some people even assaulted officers trying to get to the telephone to call their loved ones once let out of their cell for their 15 minutes to take a shower. The warden made an announcement stating that if no more officers were assaulted before Christmas, which was 30 days away, then everyone in C-pod would receive a visit. Visitors visiting C-pod was unheard of. There were a couple of people who had been there so long that they could not even remember their family's contact information to let them know they had visits. Some guys hadn't heard from their people in so long that they were just a distant memory to them. Then you had the ones who hadn't heard from their family since forever and they knew life as they once knew it on the streets didn't exist for them anymore. They knew they were either getting LIFE sentences or so much time that it was the same as a LIFE sentence! So they simply did not want a visit.

When Christmas came around that year, it was like I was a kid all over again and every gift under the tree was mine! I had been locked away in my cell for so long that I was starting to forget the "outside world" existed! My whole world was my single man cell (eat, sleep, exercise, all activities, in a dimly lit room, all day, every day with no television, radio, recreation, no one to talk to, no nothing but me, the four walls, bed, sink and toilet) all day trying to keep my sanity. So when they called my name, popped my door open and told me I had a visit. Nothing in the world could compare to that feeling at the time. I was temporarily free and that is why I am smiling in the picture.

D-WEEZ (ROBIN REED) - THEY HAVE CONTROL OF MY BODY...NOW WHAT?

Hi Honey,
I pray by the time you receive this letter that you are in the best of ALLAH's care, as for me I'm good just going through all the jail requirements today they woke me up at 5:00 a.m. to go take tests, blood, urine, and spit, all DNA sample. It reminds me of Yacub history where he only wanted healthy breeders, so he had his Doctors and Nurses examine all his followers, take blood tests to study their DNA (generic coding) only now they are much more advance than Yacub days. After that we came back to the dorm slept until it was time to go to breakfast which is at 7:30 a.m., it is mandatory that we go. This place is like a military base, there are twelve dorms, six ground level houses where each have two dorms. I'm in Dorm C-1, there are sixty beds to a dorm, I'm in bed 46 upper, (meaning on the top bunk) it's kind of warm in the day but at night it cools off, mainly because of the upstate air, there are windows all around the Dorm so at night the air is pretty good. The mattresses are about the same thickness as Rikers (Rikers Island in NYC) but the beds are better because they have a spring bottom instead of flat iron.

After breakfast we went to the infirmary to complete the rest of our physical which was a chest X-ray, which the doctor said mines was borderline, means lay off the salt and seasonings. I weigh 227 lbs. according to the scale yesterday it read 218 lbs., but on my ID card they got 200 lbs. Every test they took I ask questioned about, mainly what was it is for and are there any side effects. When I was on Rikers, the nurse gave me a TB test they checked it a few days later and sent me for check x-ray which came back negative, however because of the redness on my arm you remember that she said I came in contact with TB but I don't have it. A six month treatment to prevent catching it, she said I should have denied the treatment, because I don't have TB and the medicine eventually causes liver problems.

So when this doctor asked me today according to my medical records from Rikers I denied treatment. I told her the Nurse said I didn't have to and I don't need treatment so she gave me the test over and I go back Thursday to check the results. She said she didn't trust Riker Island opinion and I agreed with her. These jails receive a lot of State funding meaning they got to report whatever they do to the government to make sure these program are ran right. Rikers Island is about quotas not really health, but this facility is about the business because they got to qualify you before you could go to Jail population, because if you have any kind of germ or disease they don't want it to affect the population and so I also had taken immunization shots again, they are supposed to get them once as a child and once as an adult, for mumps, measles and chicken pox. The only scary thing about it is when you don't know medicine, you don't know what in the world they are injecting into your body, but according to their medical records my health is good, so if anything develops, I'll be suing the State of New York.

We're getting ready to go to Chow and Counsel visit.

****

We just got back Chow and Counsel visit. They gave us the phone registration list, and we have to write down all the name and number of the people we will be calling and turn the sheet in. If my faith never been tested it is truly being tested now, to be totally honest with you honey, I am so worried not about being harmed but I'm worried about losing the best things in my life. That is you and my family I pray to ALLAH everyday mercifully to protect guide and provide for y'all and I hope with all of my heart he answers my prayer.

The saying is true "you don't know what you have until you lose it" and right now I feel lost being disconnected from my family like this. It feels terrible. I now know what Peanut is feeling. At least on Rikers I could call 4 times a day every day or get a visit once a week. Up here I don't know nobody or nothing. I don't even know if y'all know I'm up here.

It's funny how a person's life could transform so quick, but my faith is in the Lord of the worlds "ALMIGHTY GOD ALLAH." He is renewing my life, he is killing the old me to make the new me, he is cleansing my mind and spirit but the process is not easy, so I am being challenged with difficulties after difficulties, he will apply hell fire on me to burn up all the impurities in my life and make me new again.

Peaches, I miss you so much that it hurts right now. My eyes won't stop tearing and my nose won't stop running. You are the best part of me and I'm cut off from you at the moment. God has made you my protector and comforter, so not being able to see you or hear your voice makes me feel like my blessings have been cut off, but I know "ALLAH" is taking me or allowing me to go through this for a good reason.

My release date is 7/4/2010. If I do not get the program or work release, which 99.9% I'll get "IN SHALLAH" tomorrow I take a test for school, I'm going to take every program they offer me, it is all a part of ALLAH making me new. I pray that you stick it out with me as you have always done.

These are # for Vans that come up this way

Jeff Van 718-940-7477 $45 Door to Door

Knolly's Van 718-893-4074 $55 Door to Door

Flamboyant Van 718—325 7784 Door to Door

Happy Journey 718-856-6692 $45 Door to Door

Visits are every other weekend.

This weekend which is odd# I have a visit Friday or Saturday from 9:00 a.m. til 2:00 p.m. and every other Friday and Saturday after.

If you and Kim or whoever can't make this one, I understand, however give C-Money, NY PB (John) and everybody else my information along with this information.

I need some stamps and envelopes ASAP this is my last one. They give you a couple of free joints. Don't paste the stamp on the envelopes please.

Please write me back, I miss you dearly.

Love your husband,

D-Weez

ANONYMOUS – DEATH & RIOTS IN PRISON

S unday, April 15, 2018 was the final blow that woke the resting giant. Seven (7) prisoners were murdered, slaughtered, and killed at one prison. That was horrible, but even worse was the fact that it all could have been prevented if the prison system had taken actions a long time ago after receiving several warning signs that were ignored.

They say that this riot was gang related. Well first of all, this wasn't a riot. If we go by the media reports, then this was an act of violence with major Casualties, as defined as---One injured or killed, as in battle. This was a small mob of prisoners who set out to kill specific prisoners. This wasn't a massive mob of prisoners who engaged in a large brawl to kill each other on site, nor did the prisoners fight or form a standoff against the guards to prevent them from restoring control of the dorm.

Now the prison officials say that they are going to spend $1.5 million dollars to stop prisoners from being able to have a wireless connection on their cellphones. $1.5 million....WHY??? Just a week earlier before the killings, guards at South Carolina prison, Perry Correctional Institution, intercepted a few foot balls that contained several touch screen and flip phones along with other illegal items that were thrown over the fences in an attempt to get them to other prisoners. To intercept the drop, it did not cost anywhere near $1,500 --- let alone $1.5 million dollars to do this.

Cellphones, weed, nor cigarettes killed those 7 prisoners at Lee Correctional Institution. Shortage of staffing is what played a major part in the deaths of those prisoners. Shortage of staff causes a break down in security, which opens the doors of opportunity for stabbings, escapes, and the flow of illegal contraband. Gang members are not the number one problem in SC prisons, it is the shortage of staffing that creates the opportunity for violent gang activity. When prisoners feel so comfortable that they can walk around the cell block openly filming the violent events as they took place, along with the bloody aftermath, that is a problem.

However if it were not for the contraband cellphones, no one in the outside world would have known about the horrific riot that happened. Although the pictures were graphic and scary, it showed the public what really happened. Also, if it were not for the cellphones, no one from outside of the prison would have known about the slayings of the inmates and the fact that no CO was there to stop things.

Lee County Corrections has always had a bad cloud over it. Over 13 years ago this same camp had a few guards that were assaulted and taken hostage for several hours. This same prison, over 8 years ago, had a supervisor who was shot at his house on his doorstep for finding contraband on prisoners and for allegedly making too many busts which resulted in getting guards fired. And just weeks before the riot which killed the seven men, a guard was taken hostage for several hours and is said to have asked the prisoners to allow him to use a cellphone to talk to his family one last time. That incident should have been the final straw that caused a major change, but instead, within a few days, things returned back to normal operations.

Shortage of staffing also causes the prison to have to be locked down until there are enough guards working to assure the safety of fellow guards and the prisoners. But it also creates lack of opportunities for prisoners to attend programs and recreational activities resulting in them sitting in six by eight foot rooms with another man for days and often without showers.

So now where does all that active energy of these prisoners get channeled towards??? At each other and prison staff, creating high levels of frustration???

At Lieber Corrections prisoners are locked down 85 percent of the time because of staff shortage. Shortage of staffing also causes lack of proper care for prisoners with serious mental health issues, and as a result there's an increase of self-mutilation and suicides. The governor was allegedly quoted as saying that the 7 murders is just the way things are in prison.... It is sad to hear a state's leader think that way. If the governor reduced the amount of emphasis on cellphones and focused it on the real problem;

- Better pay for Correction Officers
- More programs for Inmates
- Small pay and decent food for prisoners, so they will not have to commit more crimes just to have something to eat
- Stop the week/month long lockdowns and keep the programs going
- Provide social, technical & job skills to prepare people for re-entry
- Treat people like human beings
- Don't paint the windows and bolt them shut so prisoners have no access to fresh air and cannot see the sky.
- Leaving people to die in hurricanes and dangerous life threatening conditions

Perhaps the governor would see that the memory of the 7 prisoners that died will one day stop 7 dedicated prison guards from becoming casualties.

CAESAR COVINGTON - PRISON LIFE

4 January, 2014: Dear Son,

I'm writing this letter today because I can't take it anymore! I'm so hungry, cold and scared. This isn't a place where you can relax and just chill, as a matter of fact it sounds and smells like I'm in the middle of hell. The noise level is unbelievable. You can't hear yourself think.

I'm so hungry because the food they give us is a mix of pig's whole body. The meat they put in our spaghetti is the guts from a pig, cow and a chicken mixed together. It's gray and it doesn't matter if you bake, boil, or fry it. It's still gonna be gray and have blood on the inside. So I don't eat it. I just eat the little bread they give us and drink water. Oh-yeah they also gives us old vegetables, I'll eat the ones that aren't spoiled. It's always cold every day, it doesn't matter how much you scream and cry about it, they don't care. They want you to die and they tell us that all the time. That's why I'm scared because I believe they are trying to kill us. If we get sick they don't give us medicine or anything. I've seen so many dudes dying slow, begging for their lives and nobody would help them. I don't ever want you to come back here. I don't want you to have a man tell you to pull down your pant and spread your butt cheeks. You are a man you should never let another man tell you that. These people are very evil; they tell lies and set you up so that you never go home. And most of these dudes are twisted and evil too. **They are always robbing, raping and stabbing each other trying to kill each other for nothing.** *The other day a dude cut this guy throat because the man owed him $1.56, it's crazy.*

But that's just something small. You can control that type of stuff because you don't have to borrow other peoples' stuff. But what you can't control is something like the C.O's putting you in a strapped chair for 18 hours and won't take you out for anything. If you have to use the bathroom you have to do it on yourself. **In some lock up cells they don't have sinks. You have to drink water out of the toilet.** That's why I say I don't want you to ever come here. If I had known that being in prison was like this I never would have been drinking and smoking or selling drugs.

I wish I would have stayed in school and got my education. Because when you don't go to school this is where they send you. Running the streets and partying all the time will get you back here too. I'm not saying don't have fun. What I'm saying is to make better decisions than I made. I'm telling you what it's like in prison so that you will make the right choices in life.

Well Son, I love and hope to see you someday, when I come home, because I don't want to see you back here.

Power up and take care of the family until I get there. You are the man of the family now. So you have to act like it and do the things that a man would do and that's protect, provide, and educate his family. I'm gonna end this letter now but never my love, take it easy son.

Love Your Father,

Caesar Covington

Released in 2017

(Do you want to hear more from Mr. Covington and visit him for a month when he was in prison via his journal? See our next book in this series: "Blindside Diaries, Life Behind the Fences" coming soon in Winter 2019)

KEVIN WHITFIELD - I CLOSE MY EYES AND WAKE UP JUST TO STILL BE HERE IN HELL

I lay on this mattress that's wearing my back out. And all I can think about is how nice it would be to actually lay on a Sealy. Then my reality kicked in and said "Really?" Just as the stress was slowly rolling off my shoulders my grey steel toilet has caught my attention, let alone we are on lock down from a stabbing earlier; both giving off a depressive state of mind. So I close my eyes thinking peaceful thoughts hoping when I open them I would see a colorful setting reminding me of home. But that didn't help because when I looked around I was greeted by the same white paint that covered the concrete block walls making the reality of things more vivid.

The sound of the sliding doors to lock me in my room makes me cringe every time. "I'm not supposed to be here." I yell snapping out of my dreams that consume my every night. So I try sugar coating things by focusing on my health. I thought making money would make me feel better, but damn! I miss the comforts of a woman. So again I try to gain peace as I watch the massive oak trees that seem so serene. But those grey steel bars that I have to look out of have somehow stolen that peace, reminding me of where I am. So I close my eyes, force myself to sleep, praying that when I wake up, things will not appear as they were the day before.

So I'm writing to you Rashad and Byron, to share what I have to go through and I pray you both will never have to go through this demented ordeal. I've been in the 'belly of the beast' (prison) for nine long years. In a place where I never thought I would be; having to witness multiple stabbings, and even a few murders.

I have a question? What man likes going to the shower in his sneakers not knowing who may attack him from behind? Having to peek through the shower curtains to watch your surroundings, because at any given time you can be attacked and beaten in all your naked glory? Having to eat bologna sandwiches for weeks at a time because the yard is on lock down behind a riot for they are short staffed? Or how about drinking water that turns the toilet brown and having someone tell you what to do, when to do it, how to do it ALL THE TIME? The answer is NO MAN.

Every man should have the chance to be successful, have a family he can nurture and provide for. Enjoy his life, the precious gift God had given him. So yes, take advantage of it because it's yours. Because at any given time everything that you worked for, planned for can be taken away from you within the blink of an eye; most of the time from our poor decisions.

So we must stay sober and vigilant so that we don't get caught in the web that was weaved. It is so sad seeing young men your age (late teens/early 20's) come here with forty and fifty years on their backs; smart, intelligent, talented men who have made bad decisions. So stay focused do not stray, stay true to yourself and contemplate the consequences for all your decisions. Keep your eye on the prize, don't slip and stay on top of yourself because once the system gets there hands on you they don't let go, or believe in second chances

Love your father, Kevin...
Kevin Whitfield
#323362 – June 2015

ANTHONY F. MARTIN AKA GHETTO/THE ENCHANTER - "VOICES BEHIND THE WALL"

Written by Anthony T. Martin #242768

This is one of the saddest letters I've ever written, because it's not a letter of caution but a small depiction of how the milk of human wildness has been drained from the souls of people, who were once just like you...when the everyday rudiment of society are snatched away. A different creature emerges. You have no choice but to be barbaric. The things you do to survive will shock the conscience of the average person who lives within the realms of normalcy...imagine having to sleep with someone you don't like as an inmate, waking up around hundreds of strangers whose personalities are a complete opposite to yours. Everything they do is completely against the standards of decency you've been taught, but they push it across to you as normal, and all you can do is feel sorry for their state of captivity. Or maybe you'd like for someone to tell you what you can and can't do, where to go, when you can do this or that. Imagine those small freedoms, you now enjoy are taken.

No more going outside after dark to look up at the stars at night, no walking on the grass, no more causal walks to the corner stores. No getting together with friends in the mall. Everything you do will be to someone else's liking whether you want it to be or not. Even at crazy hours they might decide that they want to come through and strip you naked and search your small belongs just because they can.

So things aren't going so well in your life right now? Big Deal! Get use to the fact that life will not, under any set of circumstances reach out and just hand you what you want, you've got to put it in your mind that you're going to work as long and as hard as it takes for you to get what you want, no matter how many setbacks you encounter along the way, or how hard it seems to achieve what you want...if you don't, you'll end up with someone else making your decisions for you instead of you doing it for yourself. All because you lacked the skills or you were unable to function as a self-sufficient, independent adult capable of dealing with social norms other than negative peer pressure.

Good decision making is a lifelong building process. If you think things are naught now, wait until you have to call home asking for someone to come and see you twice a week except holidays. So, you don't want anybody preaching to you, Ha! *Wisdom is always justified of her children and ignorance is scorned by all.* So tell me young wise one, when was the last time you got up to go to work at dawn to pay bills and put food on the table for your family that depends on you for their survival? It takes someone who's capable of handling responsibility to do those things. Tomorrow's your future. What you're doing today, will somewhat shape the way you'll spend the rest of your life. Even if you just started to throw your future away, you've already began that process slowly, that is what happens to people who commit crimes, they didn't prepare for the future, because they were looking to fail. When failure strikes they find it hard to believe that it's actually happening to them. When you're hard at work doing what it takes to prepare for a future; you will not go out and commit a crime. When you commit crimes are you are tricking yourself into thinking that out of all the hundreds of millions of criminals who came before you, you can or will commit the perfect crime and get away with it, or that you can continuously commit crimes and never get caught.

Of course at some point, when you're not working hard at your future, you'll decide to take a shortcut. But what you don't know is that, the shortcut leads you behind bars, which has some of America's best and brightest minds in storage even as we speak. But don't worry, the voices from behind the wall all across this country can't apply to you, you're smarter, you know better, you look better, you're swifter. They got caught because they didn't know what they were doing. You're much more advanced than any other criminal who's committed a crime before you. If you believe any of those lies, you're on your way here already and the voice you're hearing will take on a face on faces.

Once you are here in prison, you'll see that there's no peace and quiet from sun up to sundown. The lights are always on, nothing goes the way you want it to, because prisons have their own twisted set of rules that govern the conduct of their inhabitants who are forced to survive or die within their shiny walls of bondage. If we never see your face, Good! But if you come through these doors, we're not cool, it's called survival, and only the strong can survive. The courts are handing out stiff sentences for long periods, if you don't like it, stay home and build a future for you and yours.

Anthony F. Martin

A.K.A.

Ghetto my Urban Street novel title

The Enchanter my Science Fiction supernatural novels

Be sure and look for

The Beast Beast I & II

Spawn of the Darkness I

Spawn of the Darkness, the Enchanted Forrest II

Spawn of the Darkness the other world, mid-world, and the Underworld III

All out Magical War IV

The Final Show Down V

Also my favorite for all time *Principalities and Powers of the Air* coming out soon...in the coming times ahead *Spawn of the Darkness* the series will become a web game with lots of prizes, motorcycles, cars, homes, cash, trips to faraway lands, watch closely, our website will be available shortly, when you holla, we will hit you back -12/3/13

(Anthony is a talented writer, you can learn more about him on www.imperial-imprint.com)

BILLY NATHAN LEE - PRISON LIFE

The Facts about the real prison environment.

First, my name is "Nathan," meaning "Gift." Now let me take this opportunity to introduce you to the real prison environment that so many of you young brothers don't have the slightest idea.

Well for one, there isn't any respect of your nationality because once you are in this environment it is all about survival. "Live or Don't Last." Put it this way: your money is well respected.

And you can be whatever you want to be in this environment, or maybe should I say, what this environment makes you out to be, "Live or Don't Last."

No one really cares except what they can get out of you and that's all that matters.

Whatever you had on the "streets" or your "social status," it's all welcome to the men who will take advantage of every penny you have.

You think that you're the man in the free world; well you have to give up a lot to become "the man" in prison.

Take it from a thirty year veteran who has been in and out of prison all of his life. My life began at the age of 16. I come from a two-parent home in Homestead, Florida where my dad was in the military. Trying to fit in with the beach culture crowd from ages 15 thru 18 I got caught up in drugs, first selling and then using. I have been in three different states doing time, and each state is very different. They even give sentences differently. This isn't any fabrication, this life back here is real, "Live or Don't Last."

Don't you know? At any given day, in this environment your life can end with just the wrong word said to another inmate, the way you look at a man, or because of the things you have. Once you get behind these walls you can't have those boyish ways that you had on the streets. Yes, some of you really thought you were men, but this place will make the hardest man cry.

My young brothers, this is only the beginning of the hell you will go through in prison. You could end up being someone's "boy." Crying out to your mothers. But mom won't be able to save you and if you are not strong enough you will end up being taken advantage of by your own homeboys. Young brother, life back here is real. Don't think when you first come in some sick minded man isn't looking at your A-S-S sweet boy! Two ways you can be sweet, "sexually" and 'fresh in the games' of prison life. Sometimes things can get so frightening because you really don't know who your friend is.

The game is a lot different behind these walls than in the streets. Let me explain some of the experiences that you will go through coming into prison that is not something that you are used to. First thing they will do when you come into R&E (Reception Center), is take all of your personal possessions. You are standing there naked, with no clothes on, with other men there standing right behind you. Then you go into see the doctor who will go up your butt hole and manually search your privates to check and see if you have any diseases. Basically treating you like some kind of animal, other men call you names.

Also think about your family not being able to visit you and if you get in trouble, you may not see them for months or years at a time. Neither will you be able to go to the canteen. You won't even be able to call home. There is something I know for a fact, you are not going to listen to the right things in prison. If that was the case, you wouldn't have found your butt in here in the first place. So more than likely you will follow the wrong people in prison as well.

I've seen it 100 times how young men come in looking so righteous, but after a few weeks there are under the wings of the wrong group. In prison, it is all about the mental game and if you are not mentally strong, they will take your food, your television, or anything you have. And if you cannot defend yourself, like you were on the streets, most likely you will get "bet-in, bet-out," Killed or be killed. Now you have a knife, you are a real bad ass! But remember when you get that knife, the game is on, thinking you are that man now, but in reality another knife is out there also thinking that they are that same badass. The only thing that will bring you back to reality is when someone stabs you five times in your back when you are not looking.

Behind this behavior, I have seen young men come in with five years and end up with an additional five/ten years before they can come home, just by trying to live that lifestyle. Trying to be something you are not, knowing you are not really built like that. Think about what I am saying please, making a difference can help your own brothers.

"Making a Difference"

To my brothers and sisters of all races. The first thing that I would like to point out is that I'm sure we can come to some kind of common ground. First, I'm of African descent, with three children of my own. Two daughters and one son. However, the most important impact that I would like to make through this letter is letting you know that I've went through some of the same things you may be facing this very moment in your life. Maybe the difference between us is that I'm in prison and you are not. I have LIFE without ever getting out. But your life, you can have freedom outside for the LIFE without prison.

I came from two different family backgrounds, one family was very conscious of being black, respectable people. And the other family was always in hardship. However neither of them were my reasons for making bad choices in my life.

111

Yes! I have been on welfare, I've seen days where there wasn't much food in the house. I've moved from house to house with my mother, living in a two bedroom, all ten of us. I've been overweight, coming up with kids making fun of me that I didn't have many clothes that I wanted as well. True, there may be factors, but it really didn't contribute to all of the results to my life that I am facing because there was always someone in the community to give some kind of advice.

After reflecting back on my life, the decision to leave home so young was my biggest mistake I could have made. Because at 16 years of age I really wasn't ready for the harsh reality, drugs, violence, use of drugs. Even my own life.

Along the way, there were people I've known who would kill you just for looking at them the wrong way.

Sexual Abusers

The exposure to negative sexual influences like prison can change your life forever, taking you through extreme hardships that you've never had to deal with at home. There have been numerous amounts of times I've nearly lost my life in the streets and in prison. Sometimes without even knowing that death was at my door. From these extreme and harsh experiences, I end up transferring behavior right into my adult life, into my marriage and even my children's lives. Being fatherless. From me not being there for my children most of their lives, they had to experience a point in time in their lives of dealing with negative influences. Today I thank my brother's family for helping them through the ups and downs of life.

The biggest problem was my hyper-masculinity front that I was putting on. Telling myself and the woman of my children that I was ready to be that man in her life. "frontin' isn't it?"

My responsibility was ZERO from using drugs in the streets, not keeping a job, in and out of prison, trying to make money, I thought of only making a name with the police.

Sometimes as I think back on those experiences of that lifestyle, it is hard to face my children on visits. Not that all of my years were bad being around them, but I didn't give enough of being that father. How do I keep moving on from the knowledge of my ancestors? I am now making that difference in their lives.

I pray that this letter will make a very big difference in your life.

I may not be directly your biological father, but having the love within my heart for you. You are still sons and daughters. Being miles apart physically, I'm there in spirit, always thinking about you all.

Just yesterday, I saw one of my sons got gunned down in the streets of Ferguson by the Ferguson police, Michael Brown. His blood came to my room behind these prison walls, feeling the same pain of my ancestors all over again. My children please remember these things:

That you came from greatness! And do not ever let anyone tell you differently. More of your greatness is still to come. So don't let anything stop you from achieving your dreams. Always remember and acknowledge that your greatness came from the beginning of time from God. You are in his image and likeness, spiritually and intelligently. Remember that one day you must also bring to life greatness of your own. "Make the big difference."

To My Beautiful Princesses,

Just as beautiful as the Nile that runs through Egypt, giving life to everything that moves. That is how precious you are to the essence of life—the utmost importance to all living beings. You must be treated as a precious jewel, greatly cherished. I can remember the first time setting eyes on you, admiring everything about you even down to the color of your eyes, knowing that you were from the bloodline of Queens. However somewhere along the path of life, the most important of my life was lost, leaving you unprotected.

My beautiful princesses, I am sorry for not being there. I know there had been nights of hurting emotionally with thoughts of your father. And there have been nights of thoughts of the harm that could have come your way. "I am Sorry!" I know there have been times you needed your father just to talk about the very important things that your mother could not answer. I know this very moment "life isn't right" because your father isn't there. I know there also has been many hardships, school, college, even having children of your own. I am Sorry.

To all my princesses, you're as precious as the Nile, giving life to everything and all living beings.

--Billy Nathan Lee, SCDC# 229707

Nathan Lee is serving a LIFE sentence and is one of our authors for Imperial Imprint LLC; He also ran the 2nd Chance programat McCormick Correctional Institution where (Ret.)Warden Leroy Cartlege & Assistant Warden Scott Lewis (now Warden of Perry Correctional Institution) supported the program as it truly gave inmates a 2nd chance in learning English & Math for their GEDs; which gave both students and inmate mentors increased responsibility with personal & moral conduct and a sense of accomplishment. It was a wonderful and inspiring program for both the inmate instructors and those in the classes.

Currently, Mr. Lee is housed at Lee Correctional Institution, running a mental health and personal empowerment program.

ANDREW LAWRENCE - YOU DO MATTER, YOU ARE IMPORTANT!

Dear Young Ladies and Gentlemen.

Good morning. I doubt there is much I can say about prison life that has not already been said, or you have not already heard. "Don't do this, don't do that." Right. However hearing it is one thing and living it is a whole different story. Obviously you can learn from someone else's loss without incurring your own. In other words, you don't have to stick your head in the fire to know it will burn you. That's even a higher state of wisdom than your personal experience, which is probably the best source. Experience, experience, experience. Try, try and try again.

In order to gain experience you have to invest your time to receive this wisdom. Fortunately or unfortunately, this is your one asset that can't be extended or repeated. Whatever number of heartbeats you've been given by God or Nature, that's it. At least in this lifetime anyway.

For the past 25 years I have lived in a nasty, aggravating, painful fire called prison. It's a total waste of life. You do not need to waste your life like I have wasted mine. Please don't listen to the "tough guy" stories like this is the place to test your metal, etc. That's just hot air. The fights and violence aren't even the worst part. Actually that's the easy part. At least then you are distracted from the constant minute to minute agony of boredom. Stand in line, stand in line all day. Get counted, get counted, get counted all day. Pace the floor, stare at the wall, the constant roar of senseless noise. The silliness, childishness and foolishness of constant mind games by inmates and staff alike. Games, games, games!

You want to know what prison is like? Go into your bathroom, shut the door and stay in there for a couple of years. Have a friend slide some food under the door. Then you will know what it is really like to be a tough guy. (Not to mention all of the things you will miss outside).

You might feel slighted or cheated by life, I know I did. But you see it's like that for everyone. That's just human nature. We are all born with it. The desire to compete, to conquer to be dissatisfied. Guess what? Enough is never enough! There is no end to riches and reputation. You are spinning your wheels pursuing those things. The real values in life are the things that last beyond one's lifetime. The giving of your life to the success of the greater good. Yeah! That's hard to believe, but it is the truth.

Again young folks, "Yeah that is hard to believe." Also you will never believe it until you involve yourself in this process of living for the success of the community over your own personal success. Please try it. "Sounds" like preaching, right? That is because it totally goes against human nature. But you see that's why it works. Human nature, your nature, tell you to "Get me," "Look out for Number One," and "Me first." Self-centered. But thinking that way just pulls you down even further into the quicksand of pain and frustration. Then you're in the pit with me!

Life really is just a never-ending series of choices. Every choice has a consequence. Good choice=good action=good consequence. What we sow, so shall we reap. We don't even need to get religious about it. *"What goes around comes around," "You get what you give," "Do good, get good,"* check out yourself.

Children take, men and women give. Children take, adults give back. Simple really.

Growing up is all about us sharing this life together equally. All people really are all created equal. You do matter. You are important.

Anyway, it's your call to make. I made my choices. They were bad choices, until one day God moved me to join the Perry Correctional Institution - Better Life Academy, a program by Chaplin Whitworth with Mr. Gereal and Mr. Norman who volunteer. It's about God, relationships and sharing.

This great big universe that we share and then a miracle happened. I was granted the privilege of parole.

Life is a gift. We didn't fight our way on to this planet, or think our way on.

I was a "throw away kid" like a lot of you were. When I was a child, my father brought me a movie ticket, and then dropped me off for the show. When I came back out, he was gone. (Another father gone AWOL). There was an old man with no legs shining shoes on a wooden box. He kept me company the rest of the day until the authorities showed up. God is Good!

People in authority aren't always bad, nor are we always good. Life is a mixed bag. It's good and bad at the same time. But in the end, it's ALL all right.

You do know right from wrong. Do the right thing. If you are in a gang, get out. Stay in school or get back in. Join a sports team, join a club, take martial arts, learn a musical instrument, join a church, join a community youth group, just join a positive based group activity. Positive attitude.

Remember, life ain't about me, and it ain't about you, it is about US. All of us!

Praying you good health, and a good future, Andrew

You can contact him at:

Andrew Lawrence, PO Box, 498, Chester Vermont, 05143

(Mr. Lawrence has been released from prison, you can write him at the address above)

BRIAN ATTAWAY, - WHAT PRISON CAN DO TO A PERSON

Fighting to stay in control of myself is a very hard thing to do when you're locked away, because all different types of attitudes and frustration dealing with being locked away comes out in different forms. Prison can only do three things to a person, it can make you a punk, it can harden you until all you got is hate built in you, or change you for the better by knowing how to accept and deal with the condition you are in.

I just came home from prison in 2007 after doing a ten year bid and took myself through a lot before I came home because I was young and wild and even though I wasn't the only wild motherfucker in prison with the "I don't give a fuck" attitude. It was a lot of us who got away from doing LIFE sentences for the crimes we've done. Anyway, I maxed out in 2007 a changed man because I didn't want to come back. I had a nice job paying good money, a child on the way and a good woman who I was planning on spending the rest of my life with. Then all of the suddenly my life took a big turnaround for the worse. The police surrounded me and stated they had a warrant for my arrest and took me in. I wasn't sweating it though because I knew I didn't rob shit after I did all that time. So I went with them without a struggle.

My heart dropped when I looked and saw who they had on film. It wasn't me but somebody close to me who I would die for. My mother came and saw who it was on film as well and asked me what was I gonna do. So I was like, "You know I can't let them go through this, so my best alternative is to try to beat it." So I made my look alike join the army because I refuse to let the system destroy him.

I went to the County Detention Center watching my child grow inside of his mother while dealing with all I had on the table and my world turned dark. I was offered a LIFE sentence over and over so that I would flip. At that time I didn't give a fuck about nothing and didn't even care about living or dying and my baby mother and sister used to come on visits and cry the whole time. All it did was harden me because it's like I stopped caring. That's when I became a danger to me and everyone else around me. It came to the point I would assault other people who joked and played around, especially if I was the center of the joke. I became so dangerous I ended up with 11 charges, all violent. Escape, hostages, I couldn't see the light at all. I ended up getting 20 years and was treated rough by the police because I assaulted an officer and whoever gave me a problem. What made me so dangerous was that I would punch niggas in the throat or jump on niggas chest with all my weight crushing ribs. So I had to get out of population but instead was sent to McCormick Correctional Institution. My first day on the yard I was walking to the dorm I was assigned to and seen a nigga face cut open on the side; all you could see was his teeth and blood. That was nothing to me because my heart was black and my soul wasn't the same. I just didn't give a fuck.

Dudes 18, 19, and up were just babies and in gangs or joining them, trying to stay safe from all these black hearted motherfuckers who would put a blade in them and rob them for whatever they have. And sometimes joining a gang doesn't work for the weak. I seen niggas get raped by dudes. I seen niggas hang themselves because of the pressure to survive. You got to be a man back here even if you must die. What I mean is these niggas ain't too quick to try me because they know I don't give a fuck about dying. Just say if a gang member and I had some beef, they would squash it because I'm stabbing to kill or get killed, I won't sign up for protective custody because I'm a man and I'll die a man.

The reason why I won't kill is because my son can't talk to me if I was in a grave so I'll do my best to talk whatever out. That's what makes this shit hard. But most people see me as being cool because I am neutral. I had to change for my son's sake because I do have a max out (release) date. So I had to want better for myself. Don't get me wrong because I don't play any games, I know how to control my emotions and I am at peace. It's hard for some people to find peace within themselves, because of pride and not knowing what they want out of life. Yeah, I'm cool but I'm always on point because it's always somebody looking to size you up and ain't nothing like a silent enemy.

I sacrificed my freedom because I didn't want my loved one to go through this shit but at the same time, I lost who I was. If I didn't dig deep to find who I was and my purpose in life, I would have been lost to the system and to my son. My son is being raised without me but I am alive and he will be 17 when I max out. Seventeen fucking years without me! That's why I be on these lil nigga backs so hard. If you don't want better and put it into practice, things will only get worse because there are a thousand bad apples in prison and these apples will help you destroy yourself in here. I seen niggas run 10, 15, 20 years up to LIFE sentence out of frustration (add additional years to their original sentence due to bad behavior within prison).

I've seen the police jump on niggas while they're in handcuffs and there was nothing anyone could do about it. My point is that being locked up; you have no rights or freedom period! Who you was on the outside means nothing to the system. I've seen this dude call another dude a 'pussy' and about a week later, the so called 'pussy boy' went to the microwave with a tumbler cup full of baby oil, piss, salt, pepper and hot sauce and put it in the microwave for 15 minutes, then splashed the same dude who called him a pussy boy. Ol' dude beat him with a lock on a drop cord while he was trying to get away. The dude was then rushed to the burn center by chopper (helicopter).

I've seen niggas get murdered and guts cut out and dick cut off because he was a child molester. I seen guys get killed in knife fights. Most of the time dudes will get stabbed in the kitchen because the stabber was afraid or was making sure it's even. Most sign up on protective custody. That's why they do the shit in front of the police (Correction officer) I never been on that 'sneak a nigga' unless I was robbing him or something. I seen niggas hog tied, beat and then stuffed inside of locker. Ain't no such thing as a hard nigga because ANYBODY can get it. Some niggas stab and some are fighters. Most lil niggas do both. I seen a nigga smack a nigga and the nigga he smacked cut his face open with a can lid. It's all about your manhood behind these walls and my mother had a man when she had me because I'm a survivor. I'll never forget all the things I've been through and seen because it becomes a part of you. If you are not careful this system will destroy bonds with family and friends. I put myself in all these situations because I sacrifice but I have not let the system beat me because it's nothing I can't handle. I knew my loved one couldn't have handled this shit here in prison because he ain't done the shit I've done, been where I've been, and seen what I've seen.

My mind used to be confined but now I'm different because of why I made the choices I made. I wouldn't wish this shit on nobody. The system is very fucked up period. I could have told you a lot more about me and the system but this shit ain't easy doing time, unless you got a strong mind and a will to survive...(but sometimes, even that is not enough)...

Peace,

Brian Attaway, SCDC# 242599

KEVIN CANTY - LEARNED MY LESSON

My name is Kevin Canty and my inmate number is 359795. I came to jail July 27, 2011 and I got sentenced to 15 years for two armed robberies, first degree burglary, kidnapping, guns, conspiracy and drugs. Looking at all of the charges I had, I must say that I'm lucky to walk away with 15 years on a 0-8 year plea deal. I was facing 155 years in prison plus a LIFE sentence.

Being locked up has completely changed my whole view of life. As of today, I've been down for 3 ½ years and I am ready to go home. I've actually learned my lesson.

Being incarcerated you have to deal with a lot of nonsense—locked down for things you had nothing to do with but because you are in the same unit everyone goes behind the doors.

The rooms are small, the showers stink, the food is nasty and the environment is not safe at all.

You must protect yourself by all means. All the time, because at any time things can get real ugly.

In the streets you can run and hide or whatever. But in here, everybody lives together. Your worst enemy may lay two doors down from you. There are no guns so people pack knives on a daily basis for protection. Some people in here use them as a weapon to rob another person. Mostly everyone is separated by gangs, organization, religions, etc. We all wear the same color uniform and it's still hard for us to stick together.

The time back here hurts when you are too far to even get a visit from a family member. And even though technology is all over our society we are stuck to writing letters.

We have four TV's that you can't even hear unless you buy a radio for $50 from the canteen.

They want you to shave every day or else they'll turn us around from going to eat. The officers don't give a damn about us. Sometimes I believe that some of the things that go on with the prison system are illegal but hey, people on the outside may never know.

I used to remember how it felt to walk outside whenever you wanted to, but now it's like an old memory. It's crazy when you have people younger than you telling you what to do.

There is absolutely NO PRIVACY in here. If the doors are locked and your roommate has to use the bathroom, you can't walk out the room; you have to smell his shit. If he passes gas, you smell it. If he snores in his sleep, you gotta hear it.

This is a house full of convicts, murderers, rapists, robbers, drug dealers, scam artists, homosexuals and cold blooded killers, to name a few. It can be hard to feel safe around people with 55 years, 70 years, 30 years or a NATURAL LIFE sentence. They might snap at any time because some of them are never going home.

Each day I sit and think about my life before I came to prison. It was hard on the streets but I had a rising career and a talent sent from God. I had money, cars, houses, jewellery and women but you can't have none of that back here so it doesn't even matter.

You gotta depend on family and friends on the outside in order to answer the phone when you call because they can't call you back. They gotta send you money to order extra food or hygienic products, because we don't make money for our hard labor back here.

Most of us actually hand wash our clothes because if you send it out to get washed with the other 1,000 inmates, it doesn't really get cleaned and who really wants their clothes washed with strangers' clothes?

We are issued four uniforms. Two new, two old and they're supposed to last us two years. We are issued one jacket by the state and no tennis shoes. You must buy your own shoes from the canteen at $50. If your family don't send you money, you won't get shoes (you have to wear crocs) and you won't go to the store at all.

I've never depended on another person as much I have now. I'm 29 years old and I'm ready to go home. My projected max out date is April 1, 2024. I am striving for some laws to change or something so I can go home earlier. As of now, violent offenders must serve 85% of their time, nonetheless, with no yearly parole hearings.

This is one of the worst environments a person can live in. This is a very hostile environment. You must be ready for anything to happen at any time.

I hope and pray that this letter touches someone and stops that person from coming to prison. This isn't a place I wish on anybody.

So if you can avoid doing anything wrong, please avoid it for me. I'm blessed to have another chance at society but I have to make it to that point before I can even glorify it.

Thanks for listening to my story. I could tell you much more, but I'm not gonna bore you to death.

Be safe out there...and STAY OUT THERE!

Peace and Love, Illa
Kevin Canty SCDC# 359795

RAPE & SEXUAL ASSAULT

RODNEY ALEXANDER SIMMONS - BLACKMAN'S POVERTY

1-8-2014 - The true root to Blackman's poverty and failure's in society is a broken home: Fatherless, a lack of wisdom, knowledge, and understanding. Sad but yet so true without being taught by a father, the value of wisdom, knowledge, and understanding, is what has lead the young black man down a path of life that leads to bondage, captivity, prison, fear, and death.

To every young black man, that reads this letter **Please listen to every word**. All I hear late in the midnight hour inside the prison walls is young black men, and young white men being extorted, beaten, and raped, forced into such ungodly activity losing their natural affection and manhood in order to escape the fear of death, bondage, and captivity. The taste, and smell of fear and death, day in and day out made a mark in my life that can never be erased. I was slowly but surely losing my mind with the thought will I be next, little did I know that inside my mind I was being raped by fear and death. The sounds of a young man being raped cannot be explained so it traumatized me to the point to where I had to seek professional help. I was diagnosed with beliefs at internalized depression, which caused me to be emotionally disabled. I had become someone else.

The sound of a man being raped had taken total control over my mind. All I could think was kill or be killed. It had total control on my mind. I was being destroyed from within. Young man, this is not a weak mind this is prison life, and the mentality of it, so don't think that it can't happen to you because as you see there is more than one way to be raped. Either way you lose life. So don't gamble with your life, it's a terrible thing to waste. Young black man, listen, wake up, and realize that the court system is against you, they are handing out football numbers to the young black man, 30 years plus and the foundation is 85% in South Carolina. This will trap you inside prison life, and the mentality of it which is destruction for the young black man. Peace.

Respectfully yours,

Rodney Alexander Simmons,

SCDC #343814

STREETS & PAUL – INTERVIEW–Conversation with a prison rape victim

Please note the below has very sexually explicit & disturbing content

1. <u>**What were you convicted of?**</u> Voluntary Manslaughter by a plea for causing the death of my mother. I was living with her and drinking while on my mental medication called Klonepin pills. I have been on some form of this drug since I was 14. I was 34 when I caused my mother's death. She was concerned I was abusing my medication again. She made the decision to take the pills away from me when I was asleep one night. What neither she nor I knew was that you cannot stop taking Klonepin abruptly; you must be tapered down off the drug. I began hearing voices within three days of not having my Klonepin six days later while in a totally delusional state, I accidently broke my mom's neck while struggling over the phone I was trying to call 911 to alert the police of the presence of a man in our house who was made out of rubber, thus invincible, who was going to kill us all. I had not slept for those six days also. The forensic psychiatrist for the State said I had been suffering from Klonopin withdrawal induced psychosis. If I had known I would have gone to the E.R. for help.

2. <u>**What happen March 12, 2011, when you were sexually assaulted?**</u> A few months prior to that day, I had a conflict with a female Officer who would not let me in my cell when she did her rounds, or let me out of my room to go to the pill line on many occasions. I put in a grievance on her, which resulted in her being removed from the dorm. Needless to say that she was very well liked by a lot of Prisoners. I was approached by a Prisoner who asked me to withdraw my grievance and assured me that I would not have any more problems from the female Officer. For three weeks she treated me fair, but then started back treating me the same, because I was a known homosexual. Before too long I filed another grievance and she was removed again, and was only allowed to work the dorm once a month. It was on one of her working days that I was walking past a cell on the top tier, and was pulled into it by four males. I was beaten into submission first, and then told that it was my punishment for being a snitch and putting a grievance on the Officer. Being out of shape, I quickly ran out of breath trying to defend myself. The attackers were the same ones who had assured me that I would be treated fairly. They even allowed me to use their cellphone many times to call my family members. After I was subdued, one individual initiated his assault by forcing his penis in my mouth. He was very rough and caused me to choke several times, while verbally expressing his disgust and hatred for fags, queers, and punks. After he ejaculated, I suffered the same abusive oral acts from two more males, while all the time the fourth individual stood at the door with a cellphone and videotaped the entire

assault. Before they let me go, I was held down while an individual penetrated my rectum with a broom handle repeatedly. This is what tore my intestines and gave me an M.R.S.A. infection. I was told if I snitched on them for this rape they would send the video of the rape to my family. I did not say anything for days, but eventually I had to seek medical care, and was placed on protective custody. I became so broken down by the rape that I lost touch with reality that I became insane. I was transferred from P.C. to the ICS unit at Kirkland When I got there only then did I tell the Doctor about the rape. I had to go through diagnostic test and consult treatment by surgeons, gastroenterologist and infectious disease specialist; I had to undergo a bowel re-section and 4 ft. of small intestine, and different antibiotics for a year. The Office of Inspector General would not substantiate the rape because I would not give the name of the attackers. They don't understand that by doing that I would have had to live my life on protective custody as well as brought harm to my family.

This is Streets (the interviewer), research was conducted to authenticate his claims, and it was discovered that all four males were members of a certain gang. Cats like these shine a false conception on gang life and should not be honored, nor respected in any way. I personal know of a member of the GOD Body Nation who raped Paul. Now where in any gang, GOD Body Nation (Five Percenter (5%). This has not been by choice, but by force. Prison officials have deemed me a threat to the safety and security of the general prison population for something that happened twenty years ago, and because I will not renounce my culture as a member of the Nation of Gods and Earths (Five Percenter), or Rasta Nation will you find them supporting homosexual activity of any kind? If you force, or consensual allow a man to perform oral sex on you, you gay as hell too. And to stand there and video tape it make you a sick minded bastard just as much as the attackers. And you are a coward to hide behind the shield of gang life, faking to the real gang bangers like you bout the same life they are GODs/5%, Rastas, and any other group should feel violated and betrayed by these frauds. To beat someone because you feel they are a rat, or women hater is one thing, but to use that as an excuse to engage in a sick homosexual raping/sexual assault is another.

3. **Were you ever a pill popper who had an abusive habit?** Yes, I've been addicted to benzo's since my first psychiatrist put me on Librium at the age of fourteen. Why? Because it artificially induces false happiness and allows you to be free from fear and anxiety for a little while. When you are deeply emotionally disturbed like I was. That short reprieve becomes longer and longer stretches of drug induced "Peace" you chase.

SEXTING & UNDER 18

This is something that people may not be aware of. If you are under 18 years old and are taking pictures of your sexual organs and/or private parts & sending it via text to another person under 18 years old you can go to Prison and become a convicted a sex offender for child pornography.

This is a very serious crime and although it seems a bit over the top crazy, children who have texted or received text of naked private parts (genitalia, breasts, buttocks, etc.) can get a criminal charge as prosecutors are charging kids like adults.

In addition if you are prosecuted, you sometime have to stop going to school because you are seen as a sex offender, dangerous and predatory to the other kids in your school. If you stay home your parents have to keep an eye out on you ALL THE TIME. Sometimes you are no longer allowed to use electronics so that you can look/play on the internet. And additionally your name will go on a sex offender list for everyone to access and see.

SEXTING...This is a very serious crime.

Once you are 18 years old and have consensual relationship with the other party who is 18 years old/or older, sexting is no longer a crime.

SEX
&
HOMOSEXUALITY

FACTOID - Masturbation

Although this is something that people do not like to talk about, it is still part of reality and being a human being. Masturbation (aka "Choking the Chicken" is something that most men have been doing since they were teenagers, before they were lucky enough to find a young lady to share their intimate parts with them. This was the way they pleasured themselves and release that built up tension. Some even continued to do so after they found a lady if she was not around to take care of his sexual needs.

Well in prison, this is against the rules to masturbate and if you get caught doing it you are sent to solitary confinement. Just think about this for a moment. You are a grown man well out of your adolescent years. You are used to having sex on the regular. Now you are in prison away from women, away from pornography and they tell you if they see you masturbating you are going to lock up. Then to throw fuel to the fire, they hire female officers who walk around in tight assed uniforms showing off their figures. Then you have nurses and case workers who also walk around looking and smelling good.

At one point, with good behavior (staying disciplinary free) and you were married, you would be allowed to have conjugal visits. (Visits where your wife/and children could live together on the prison grounds in a trailer for the whole weekend). You have very few prisons that still allow this. Not only did they do away with conjugal visits, they also made all porn contraband. At first they restricted hard core penetration porn, but then they took away ALL porn. They will not even allow books that have X rated content. All that is left are swimsuit magazine and hopefully they will not take that away as well.

I do not know who makes the rules for the Corrections Department but they have stripped us of all things that we could use to hold on to our masculinity. Or maybe, they just want us to be and think like eunuchs (men with no genitals or testosterone) or monks. After they implemented these rules, dudes just went renegade, pulling out their penises and beating off on themselves masturbating while looking at any woman that was close by. So they implemented the pink suits and started charging guys with sexual misconduct charges if they caught multiple masturbation charges. Then after coming off of lock up for the masturbation charge, you would have to walk around in a pink suit for one year which was one of the most humiliating things that they ever did. Imagine grown men walking around in pink jumpsuits looking like humans flamingos! At the same time for masturbating they were taking away your privileges for canteen, to call your family on the phone or having a television to watch for 6 months to years at a time. (Remember the Department of Corrections says visits and phone calls are not rights, they are privileges that can be taken away at any time, hence the contradiction that prisons try to help keep families together)

134

Someone was smart enough to file a discrimination lawsuit and won. So they stopped putting guys in the pink jumpsuits. All the chronic jackers (masturbators) were doing cartwheels about that.

I try not to judge but some dudes are sick when it come to the jacking game and act straight like animals when women come around. However it is understandable why a red blooded heterosexual grown man would do it, since they have no other release or are not allowed to see partially clothed women. In some instances, a prisoner's visit can be turned away because female visitor's clothes may be considered too tight or too short, when the lady may look totally respectable and wear the same clothes to a professional office or church.

Ultimately because of the lack of females whether it is physically or from a movie, some prisoners turn to other prisoners for sex.

Overall I blame the agency because had they not taken away conjugal visits or porno magazines, things would not have gotten as out of control as they are now.

FACTOID - Homosexuality

Contrary to popular belief you don't have huge cock diesel dudes running around knocking people out and raping them. That's some movie shit. If a dude got down like that he'd be stabbed up so quick it would make his head spin. Although men having sex with other men is a reality. For the most part it's something that takes place on the down low at least at the prison where I'm at.

I have heard stories of dudes holding hands and kissing each other out in the open but I've never witnessed it myself. Most of the time if a person wants to engage in a homosexual act with another man, they will become roommates and do their thing at night in the privacy of their own cell.

At this point homosexuality is still taboo in the prison system. People who partake in this activity try to do it on the sly, but the saying goes what happens in the dark comes to the light eventually. Although the way the world is going I won't be surprised if this behavior will one day be accepted back here as well.

It seems as if that's what the agency who runs the prison system wants the men to be homosexuals anyway. Because anytime you have two men get caught in a sexual act and only go to lock up for a couple of days. Then you have a man get caught masturbating off of a female officer, and go to lock up for months. That's the only conclusion one can come to. I just pray I'm home before it get that far gone cause when it does that's when I may think about committing suicide cause having to see that shit all day will drive me insane.

(The above introduction was written by a 'straight' man who is not "gay for the stay")

PAUL VALDEZ– SHARING THOUGHTS ABOUT HOMOSEXUALITY BY A GAY MAN

This letter is written to you if you are a young man who has been molested, experienced child sexual abuse or rape or who identifies, hidden deep within himself, sexual attraction to other men.

I'm writing to you on this subject because that is my experience and the fall-out, denial confusion, shame and self-hatred led me directly to prison for thirty years.

I've done sixteen out of the thirty and only recently have entertained any hope of ever being a free man out there on the streets again. And the hope of being a free man out there on the streets again. The hope came from recovery, healing overcoming and renewal of the mind; all gifts to me, in answer to prayer after surrendering and submitting my will to God.

The reasons I had no hope were many. First off, I didn't want to live and didn't believe I was worthy of or deserved to live. I sought out death in prison and it fled from me. No, God wouldn't let me off that easy. But I was my own worst enemy because I wouldn't let myself off that easy. I simply could not forgive myself for being gay, for being weak (a victim) especially for my crime.

In short my biography is: I am the youngest child and fifth son out of six children. My oldest brother who has mental illness sadistically, physically, emotionally and sexually abused me and two other siblings. One who took over the sexual abuse until he left when I was fourteen. This abuse during the psychological developmental stages of adolescents and puberty resulted in serious psychiatric illness and I was treated with benzodiazepine drugs which I became addicted to. All these drugs did was cover the emotional pain and artificially induced a state of contentment. They did not heal or cure my mental illness. They did not repair the psychological and emotional wounds that so deeply scared my mind, spirit and soul. These drugs allowed me to suppress the symptoms of my mental illness and hid (or so I thought) my homosexuality. At least until my first night in Prison.

You see on the street I could avoid the presence of men but in prison I could not escape or avoid them and men in prison are experts in psychology and saw through me the moment I stepped on the wing. And I was immediately targeted by the sexual predators to be "turned out." They didn't have to try very hard. I just caught thirty years. My whole family, had abandoned me two years earlier and the identity I had as a man, (I was a father and was also shaken with the loss of my son due to my arrest.) So I felt I had no one else's feelings to worry about but my own and I quickly embraced the gay lifestyle in Prison. It was the most enlighten, educational, fascinating period of personal growth because in my brokenness I finally called out to

God and He heard. He accepted me just as I was, filthy, immoral drug addicted, filled with doubt but empty and completely broken and he put me back together. Cleaned me up. Healed my body, renewal of my mind. Delivered me from thinking negatively of homosexuality, cleansed me of drugs and accepted me as His child. He has loved protected and provided for me and I am constantly aware of how blessed I am to be redeemed. That my heart overflows with gratitude.

I know most people don't want to hear a testimony of a redeemed homosexual sinner. That's not what I want to say to you. That's my personal journey. What I want to say is that if you have been a victim of any kind of abuse in your childhood. Get help! Tell someone. Seek Mental Health Treatment before the secrets you hide manifest themselves in your life and steal your future from you. It wasn't my fault I was abused. But I believed it was. I did not choose to be gay. And I have not been miraculously changed to a heterosexual by God. Rather God gave me the power to control my behavior. I am master over my own body and choose not to give into lust or sexual desire. This is a good healthy choice for me especially here in Prison.

The Prison/Gang culture is not sympathetic to Gay men nor is any division of the Prisons administration. They won't help you. The Prison staff persecutes and discriminates against Gay men in their Prisons more than the Gang members do and that's saying something because gang code is to kill queers. It's ironic though that every sexual assault I've experienced in Prison has been by affiliated brothers. I want to comment on this, I don't fault these men for their deceit or double lives. What choice do they have? They come into the system and are recruited into a Gang or other cultural belief system that forbids homosexuality or penalty of death when they make this vow. This commitment, but they aren't old enough, not mature enough yet to predict that in the future, in Prison they will burn with human sexual desire they can't fulfill, quench or suppress. That as human beings who are separated from their loved ones they would long for companionship, and the normal, natural need to feel human touch. So they commit themselves not anticipating their human need will catch up with them as they grow older and lonelier.

We as human beings need to be more understanding and forgiving for our brothers and we prisoners especially need to stick together and support each other in our struggle against an unjust Government that is trying to kill us. Instead we allow them to play us against each other so we assist them by killing each other back here.

Young men out there don't miss this part of this cautionary tale. Convict/Prisoner and Prison culture is **_not_** progressive and politically correct. You don't have the protections and rights against persecution and discrimination if you're Gay and come to Prison; you will be persecuted, beaten, robbed, abused and likely raped. It's not punks' paradise. No it is the deadliest environment for a Gay man and if you come here you are most likely to leave in a body bag.

Paul K. Valdez #295004
Kershaw CI/SA-0037-B
4848 Gold Mine Hwy
Kershaw, SC 29067

JACOB ALJOE - HOMOSEXUALITY IN PRISON

Coming from an open homosexual male, prison life for us is more difficult than it may seem. First you must understand the stereotypes. Since most of us "punks" are deemed "in the closet" (in hiding) it makes life more difficult for the open homosexuals.

You have five levels of homosexuality (going forward I will use the terminology "gay") The five levels are as follows:

1. **Bottom**: this means that you are a female role only
2. **Versatile Bottom**: You are a female role but every now and then you enjoy playing a male
3. **Versatile**: You enjoy both roles equally
4. **Versatile Top**: You are mostly a male role, but occasionally will play female
5. **Top**: You are all male

Most of your "in the closets" in prison are versatile tops. Coming from my experience, I started as a top and now, in the relationship that I am in, I am a versatile bottom.

Being in a gay relationship in prison is hard. When living in the same dorm, you have an easier time, but you still deal with homophobic gang members, or other gay people that deal in jealousy. We call it "punk drama".

Punk drama is defined as gay people starting drama amongst themselves. For example, this is an issue I just went through personally. I went through a hard break up and after some time, a bottom level homosexual caught my eye. But once my ex found out, he became jealous and started rumors to get him shipped. Now that homosexual that caught my eye is now residing on another yard.

See, life for the gay community is really no different than a normal relationship. In all honesty, at least to me, it is more intense. Both males have the same feelings and emotions, so we tend to bump heads a lot more and have to learn to come to terms with each other. And in doing so, you come to know a deeper love than before.

A lot of people claim you are born gay. I am going to say no to that. It is all in the environment you are raised in. Me, personally, I went through rape at an early age. So I used the relationship I had to overcome my fear of penetration. Now, I can enjoy my life a lot easier. Some experience homosexual activity early on. Experimenting with porn or just sex games, and for some it is a fetish.

Really I'd like to see more bonding in our gay communities in prison. We have no rights back here. The gay marriage laws were just passed, but to this day if we get caught in a relationship, they (the administration) will split us up to different yards. We have no equality back here and judged worse than others.

As to homosexuality in general, as I stated before, to me it is no different than a heterosexual relationship. I still enjoy all the things a male/female relationship enjoys, from being held, cuddling, holding hands and everything else a woman desires.

But since I play both roles, I also enjoy the male side too. I enjoy providing for my lover, making him feel secure and loved and overall spending time with him.

Nowhere did any book or profound speaker proclaim "Love has genders." So why do we (humans) deem it so? When did love start having a mind of its own?

I end with this statement. I have love in my heart. I just choose to give it to the man I am with because he returns my love with his own. And in any relationship, is that not what we all desire?

WIATT WOODS-COMMENTS ABOUT HOMOSEXUALITY IN PRISON

My name is Wiatt Woods I'm age 44. I've been doing time for over 20 years. I'm from Chester, SC. I'm gay. I'm a black male. I've been gay all my life. I was not turned out in Prison. I've always liked men. I'm current in a serious relationship. I'm much in love and I know that he loves me. I have seen so much in prison you can't come to prison and be weak, soft and don't be curious. You are asking to be turn out. Don't ask for anything, that you can't pay back. And don't take nothing from no one. If so, you are asking to be turned out. You have some homosexual inmates that are thugs that will make a straight man give up the "goods." I grew up in prison. I had a mentor and you must watch everything around you at all times

What is it like to be an effeminate male in a man's prison? I know that a lot of peoples think you are having the time of your life because it's so many men around. I would like to dispel that rumour. Too many men means too many problems. Some men are dogs they try to mess with everyone. I'll speak more on that later. The CO's seems to respect the homosexual inmates. The administration respects the homosexual inmates. We often get away with things that the straight men don't. I'm well respected by the inmates. True, some inmates don't like my sexual preferences but they don't make life in prison hard. Yes, straight men do want to have relationship with the homosexual inmates. I believe that those straight men were messing around on the streets. I never have been mistreated by staff. When inmates try to give homosexual inmates a hard time the homosexual inmate come together. You have some inmates who will not allow you to harass the gay population. I'm cool with a lot of real straight men. Yes it's like a fantasy world but I'm not having fun/sex with just anyone. You get a lot of attention/respect from the inmates. It's not a living nightmare. Inmates, who are straight and come to prison with a lot of time, mostly will turn to the homosexual population, because of seeing someone doing it a lot of inmates are curious. Some older cons have "boys" I have seen a lot of inmates turned out in prison. I have seen a lot of inmates turn to homosexuality to survive.

Wiatt Woods

ANONYMOUS – GAY WHITE MAN IN PRISON

Dear Dawn,

I was targeted by an officer who was a Black woman based on her individual and cultural prejudice directed at me because of my sexual orientation but also because I am white. In Southern Black culture African Americans hate white people. And this is the legacy of the discrimination and disenfranchisement they endured here in the South and still do. And although they are over represented in prisons due to the targeting of the Police and Courts, here in S.C. Prisons they rule.

The Prisons in South Carolina are 90% staffed at all levels classification, Psychiatry/Mental Health, Prison Industry, Education, Religious support services, Education, Records, Operations, Security, Programs Administratively and Medicine by African Americans. Why? *Because the State pays inadequate wages.* But the result is that Prison is a Black Man's world (and Black Women) They rule here and have all the power. So they do abuse that power and discriminate against the White Prisoner. I'm not angry about this nor do I return the racism. It is just not my nature to accept, judge or reject someone based on something that was not a choice they made such as skin color but only on their quality of character, are they honest? Do they have honor and integrity? What have they accomplished? That is logical. Accepting or rejecting based on something a person has no control over such as what color they were born doesn't pass the test of logic.

Also to be clear, I am not a women hater. Just because I am gay should not infer that, on the contrary I related better to women. I identify more with women then I do men and I'm not afraid of women as I am of men. Last I'm not looking for anything from you.

About some of the authors of your 'Letters to our Sons' book just for perspective, eight of them participate in Homosexual activity here in Prison. Three are girls or I should say they are the submissive role. Five are Down Low Brothers. I know from personal encounters. Two, I had long term (5½ year) healthy, successful relationships with. I loved them. Still do! The relationships had no drama, never discovered.

143

THE GAME NEVER CHANGES, ONLY THE PLAYERS

(There is nothing new under the sun)

THE GAME NEVER CHANGES, ONLY THE PLAYERS
Table of Contents

ABDULLAH QAWI MUSTAFA FKA PRESTON JOHNSON - ADVICE ON STAYING OUT OF TROUBLE

To The Youth Out There Without Fathers And Some Without Mothers. This picture I'm about to paint can only be heard, so listen closely to every word. Those who maybe struggling with no one to talk to or understand what they may be going through, seek to understand, before you seek to be understood. NEXT STOP PRISON!

I know it's not easy out there without a foundation to maintain. Missing fathers and mothers, this letter is to all out there throwing bricks, making licks, and knocking up chicks, then ending up in prison. Is this where you want to be? I don't think so. In this place called prison, where they tell grown men when to eat, sleep, and wash. There is no more, "What I want to do. It's about what I'm <u>told</u> to do." In a sense, you don't control your life anymore. If you refuse, there's a special place for you, LOCK UP. In lock up, they continually look at a places where you never seen before, your rectum (anus). This is real, for those who throwing bricks, making licks, and doing tricks.

That's why you must change your attitude, we cannot choose our external circumstances, but we can always choose how we respond to them, if we discipline ourselves, and it begins with the mastery of our thoughts. **(If you don't control what you think, you can't control what you do.)** Society is designed to show the big houses, fancy cars, the glitter and glamour. But everybody can't shoot a ball, or run a touchdown, or rap. Education is the key. Practice the skill of listening to those who sit where the grass don't grow...prison!

"Patience," in order to have elevation, there must be separation from those who throw bricks, make licks, and knocking up chicks. Boys and Girls need their Fathers, a woman can't teach a boy how to be a man, girls need their fathers, to show them how the game is played in life, so they won't fall for the brick thrower or lick maker to be left with kids to raise by herself.

In this system where drug dealers get more time than a serial killer, children get tried as an adult before they become one. Being incarcerated, we lose our identities, reputation, our friends, and families. For the first few months or years they are there, but life goes on for them. *(...without us and most leave us behind)*

We are controlled by count time, lockdown called (scheduled) disruption. Then we miss holidays, birthdays, cook outs, and the loss of loved ones. It seems that more parents come to see kids in jail then they do at graduations. That's because the new diploma is parole or probation. Getting back to the third dimension, the most important thing is time, not the thing you have to show. Don't let bitterness, hatred, or anger control your thinking. We have to maximize the moment because time waits for no one. Is seeing and responding to life's situation from a perspective that transcends your current circumstance. Never mistake knowledge for wisdom. One (*knowledge*) helps you make a living; the other (*wisdom*) helps you make a life. Apply what you learn, choose friends carefully, seek good advice, get understanding and learn from the past.

ABDULLAH QAWI MUSTAFA-- FORMERLY KNOWN AS PRESTON JOHNSON -- #268169 – McCormick

RANDY BLYTHE - CHOICES

January 5, 2014

My name is Randy Blythe, known by most people as "Capone." I grew up in a small country spot in South Carolina call Pickens. It's located outside of Greenville, South Carolina, about 30 mins if you drive the way I use to, thinking and feeling that you're in control of everything, feeling you gone live forever and that you can fight and take on the world.

However, life is not like that. And the crucial reality is at a young age no matter how strong you feel you are. That world you're so prepared to fight, is such a big place and it's also too heavy to try to fit on your shoulders to carry. Most things in life are nearly impossible to do alone. That's why it's so important to surround yourself with positive people who will teach you the right way to get them stacks of money that most of you feel can only be obtained by selling drugs, robbing, stealing, extorting, kidnapping or possibly even killing. Real power doesn't come from a gun or by how many people you've done physical harm to. True power comes from the mind, once you have been properly educated and taught to exercise a new way of thinking. So that you may break the cycle of ignorance that continues to keep all of us blind.

There's nothing wrong with wanting the finer things in life. The wrong only comes in when you're willing to break the law to get these things. Putting these material things above the value that you place on your own life or the lives of the people you choose to take these things from. Because no matter how good we think our plan is, the end results are prison. It doesn't take a genius to come to prison. Anybody can spend and waste their life away behind these prison fences. But it does take an intelligent person to know not to travel down the same road of destruction that keeps getting all your friends, family, and people you know taken away for numerous years, half they life, and sometimes for the rest of your life. These are the only results that came from a life of crime or negative thinking.

Those same females you was so anxious to impress and get to know are not gone be around when you make the same mistake as all of us did before you. You may feel like you got a "Rida" ("RYE – DA") someone who is there for you no matter what). But the reality is who don't want to ride when everything good and you on top? The homeboys you were so quick to look out for, bust your guns for, and turn your back on your family when your mom or grandma tell you that they are not really your friends and stop hanging around them. Those are the same friends that will testify and tell on you, be the ones to take that girl away that you were so intent on doing anything to get or be able to hold onto. And not check on your family while you're doing all the years in prison from making a mistake you could have avoided only if you would have listened to all the people who really did care about you and tried to lead you in the right direction. I'm sure each of you are told all the time to pay attention in school, make good grades and learn everything you can. Knowledge really is power.

It's going to take knowledge to get a good position at a job. A lot of hard work and determination is what it takes to do everything in life. Anyone can do anything, but everything is not meant for everybody. Not everyone is meant to be a lawyer and doctor, and it doesn't take a high titled job to define your success. Success is defined by your achievements and good decisions you've made in life. The best thing about doing it the right way is that you will get to enjoy the fruits of your labor.

Everything in life has a price. "The Game," as most of us call it, is really just all types of criminal activities. But with the Game comes death, jail and sorrow. So don't let all the gold, diamonds, women, cars, and fast life fool you. Cause only a fool fails to see that every hustler's reign eventually comes to an end. The lifestyle of a hustler doesn't come with any guarantees of pension plans. You always have to ask yourself, is it really worth it? Yesterday is gone forever, today is all that matters because tomorrow is not promised to any of us. It's time to start making more conscious and productive decisions for ourselves. If not, then you will find yourself spending your life behind bars like so many other people you know and not have anything to show for it but a heart broken family, lost time, and a bunch of regrets.

Each of you has the potential to do or be anything you want to. Our potential is always higher than our expectations. The more you learn then the more you will continue to expect in and out of life. The more you expect out of life, it's going to allow you to achieve more in life.

No one is above making mistakes. We must all learn from our mistakes and move on. But why continue to make the same mistakes continuously if you can avoid it? A man without knowledge is a man without direction and doesn't know where he's going in life. Without order, nothing can exist. Everything in life must have and requires organization. I'm asking and encouraging all of you to organize your lives, organize our thoughts to help better prepare yourself for the future, organize your family, friends and communities, if you fail to listen, then you may just fail to keep your freedom. Three things that are always guaranteed: taxes, death, and prisons. Regardless of the overcrowding, SCDC always has a bed for you. The choice is always going to be yours to decide. We always have a choice. Life or Death. Production or Destruction. Success or Failure. Freedom of your mind and body or captivated and confined in ignorance or behind the fences of a prison. Which choice are you going to make?

Randy Blythe, SCDC #233219

TREVOR MILLER - THE REAL DEAL-STREETS & PRISONS

Nephew,

What's going on with your little family? Ain't much going on my way other than the daily monotony of prison life. But check the business right. Imma cut straight to the chase. Word iz you've decided to run the streets and kick up dust. Well, first and foremost, being as though I am your uncle, it's my duty to put you on real game and give it to you straight. Lil family, I know and understand that from your point of view that the streets iz what's good because we've (black folks) been brainwashed and conditioned to believe so. But take it from someone who has your best interest at heart, someone that loves you, the street life iz "hype" man. All the street life has to offer iz senseless and untimely deaths, and prison opportunities. To sum it up, the street life embodies self-destruction. The street life in its illusion form of "hype" may seem very appealing; however in reality its form is not so appealing. I bear witness to its not so appealing form.

Don't let the media, movies, and rap music fool you with their glamorization of prison into believing that prison is cool. Ain't nothing cool, gangster, or civilized about prison. In fact, I'm going to highlight some realities of prison life to show and prove why ain't nothing cool, gangster or civilized about it. First and foremost, being incarcerated takes away from your manhood, because you no longer have too much control over your own life. If you are a family man, you can't sufficiently provide, protect or care for your family!

Women and children depend on us men for such duties and when we're not performing those duties we can't declare ourselves to be men. As a matter of fact, prisoners become dependents ourselves. If you're fortunate enough to have someone on the outside to look out for you while you're down, then you pretty much become dependent on that person or persons. If you're NOT fortunate enough to have people on the outside you have to depend on the state. Depending on the state makes doing time that much more of a hellish situation because any and all that's state issued or provided is of the lowest quality, be it food, hygiene, shoes, medicine etc. However, either way you're a dependent. Ain't no more going where u wants when you want! Your movement iz completely controlled.

Being deprived of a woman should be the ultimate sin. It's horrible being without the female counterpart. That which makes a man whole. (Feel me?) Picture yourself without being able to really just interact with a female like you want or need to. Picture yourself without the joy that comes with spending time with your girl and just being able to enjoy everything about a girl, that's what prison has to offer. 24 hours a day, seven days a week, 365 days a year, you're surrounded by males. Egotistical males, and if you're not mentally strong you'll succumb to the ill seductions of males that mistakenly think they're females. Yeah, it's plenty of homosexuals in prison. Some come in as homosexuals but a lot of the homos got raped or manipulated or perhaps both raped and manipulated into being homos. And the homos prostitute themselves so that they won't have to depend on the state, and whenever you engage in homosexual activity no matter the form, you've lost your manhood.

Prison is a very ill, sick environment. If an individual doesn't take the initiative to rehabilitate himself, prison isn't designed for rehabilitation despite the propaganda that's falsely put out there. It'll make you worser if you don't initiate the rehabilitation yourself, and that's not always easy because the environment is so negative. You're constantly around a bunch of dudez you can't trust. Mostly everyone has an ulterior motive for why they deal with you. No one hardly ever has our best interest at heart. Everybody's looking for some type of advantage or weakness to exploit. If weakness is shown the wolves are coming. Prison can and will make you a non-trusting, selfish, cold hearted person. It can really taint a person's soul. And another thing, the people you thought was down for you and had love for you when you were on the outside, show you something totally different when you're on the inside doing time.

I'm telling you, nephew, ain't nothing cool about this situation man. And then to add insult to injury, you got these little chumps for COs that try to act tough and talk to you any kind of way. A lot of them are very disrespectful. Most of them more than likely live miserable lives and they come to work trying to take their misery out on those of us that's already miserable! But the only reason they act tough is because the law is in their hands (on the CO's side). Put hands on one of them most likely you'll receive more time. I'm a prime example of that. But these cowards tell us what to do. We have to obey these cowards. Some of these CO's are dudes that wouldn't last a day if they were prisoners. Dudes that wouldn't even go to the projects because they'll be too afraid (feel me)? But these are the cowards that we have to obey. Oh, and a CO is a prison guard, they oversee. Women COs be trying play brothers like chumps! Coming out their mouth sideways and all. Taking their man problems out on us (feel me)? It's crazy, little family. This iz not the life, so don't do dumb stuff that has the potential of placing you back here. Anyone who thinks this life iz cool, gangster, or civilized, is a damn fool. And that's coming from a brother that has done 12 years and counting.

In addition to all of that, know and understand that prisons are designed to be filled up with us. When I say us, I mean blacks. The poor, the minority, they're making millions upon millions of dollars off of us prisoners, or the prison industry. It's so much money involved in our incarceration that the numbers are overwhelming and perhaps unbelievable. And being as though the United States is a capitalistic society (when I say capitalistic society, I'm basically saying a society that they put money before everything – (DID YOU

KNOW??? There are A LOT of People and Industries happy to make money off of you) incarceration isn't so much about breaking the law and purging the streets of criminals as it is about the profits that's being made off of these criminals that they've created intentionally for the purpose of them making money and keeping the black nation in an inferior state of existence. In other words, prison is modern day slavery when you actually look at it. I mean, nephew it's your life to live so I'm not gone try to tell you how to live it but my love for you iz immense so quite naturally I don't want to see you fall victim like I did. So Imma always lend you some positive advice to strive and beat the odds. Strive to do something meaningful with yourself instead of becoming another slave of the state. Another senseless death statistic. Learn what manhood really iz and strive to manifest every aspect of the word because it's only then that your life will begin to have any real meaning. Hold your crown out there and be wise and strong.

Much Love,

Sincerely,

Your Uncle,

Trevor Miller,

SCDC #275851, bka, OSIRIS

MORRIS HICKSON - THE STREET IS NOT YOUR FRIEND

My Children,

Life is important and means a lot. Sometimes it could feel strange and boring. Other times it could be fun and joyful, but we have to look at the bigger picture of life itself. Life's not perfect. It's more boring than anything. We as people look at the things the world have in store for us. Things like education, jobs, and lots of shelter to nurse and raise our future youth which is you. The reason I'm writing this letter because I have been through a lot.

I was raised in an environment full of drugs and violence. Plus I was raised around drug users and sellers so the streets were my role model. At the age of ten I had been cutting school, smoking weed, breaking into cars, and stealing radio systems. I took everything from dirt bikes, four wheelers, car rims, guns, and drugs at a young age. The bad part of me being misled was that I grew up around my childhood friends who grew up without a father figure to teach them as well. So we ended up misleading each other with nonsense and we didn't have the knowledge or understanding to guide ourselves in the right paths. At the age of 12 I slowed down, but became worse in different ways because I had the mindset to be a drug dealer instead of growing and developing a positive mindset. I went from selling weed and crack at the local school to running my own block by the age of 15. All my life I had to take care of myself and siblings. I grew up thinking that I was doing the right things so I brought younger brothers in my circle and misled them in many ways.

I showed them how to use guns, sell drugs, fight, and mess around with this woman and that woman. The same thing the streets showed me for years I want y'all to understand that the streets don't change, only the people in them. Everything that happens on the streets is a repeat and has always been repeated, even before my time. I don't want to mislead my people any more. Instead I want to teach you children what all parents should teach their loved ones and that's unity. Plus we need to learn how to hide our four devils that inside of us, which are "Greed," "Hate," "Lust," and "Envy." Once we can learn about self we can teach one another. I don't want you to think no one loves you, or that the next person is better than you in no way. See I'm 22 years old with four children of my own, but I was not there to help them with their needs due to the fact that I'm in prison serving a 25 year sentence for armed robbery.

I'm telling you this because I don't want you to make the same mistake I did by dropping out of school and having the mindset that the street was my friend.

I hope this letter touched you in many ways, and I hope it helps you make the right choices in life. Prison is not made for us but if we do wrong we will have to pay. I want you to think about the fun things in life that are out there for you. Things like football, basketball, music, poetry and art. You can be all that you can be if you put your head to it and set goals.

- Morris Hickson - #341459

DESMAN JENKINS - DON'T GET CAUGHT UP IN THE MINDLESS HYPE!

Peace Young One,

I know we haven't met before, but I would like to introduce myself to you so as to contribute to changing the tide of the influx of youth offenders. No, I'm not trying to be your daddy. However, I'd like to be recognized by you as a big brother in light of offering guidance and empowerment.

I grew up in a setting where there was plenty of older people but too few, if any, elders, which led to me and too many of my peers walking through life without any guidance or purpose. The life I indulged in was like seeing a strong—vicious dog bound to a tree by a thin-weak chain and me, 110 pounds soaking wet, continuously taunting it with a meaty steak." All the while, not knowing the effect it would have on my mental and physical health, not to mention ego as well if that dog was to break loose and get a hold of me. I and many of my peers, but me specifically, started selling drugs, stealing, committing various crimes in an attempt to get desired materials no one else was willing to get for us. As evident as self-destruction was, and still is, the number of my associates dwindled more by oppressive circumstances inching closer, all I could do is hold true to what I believed in and hope for the best when my time came to either come to prison or die a senseless death.

After being arrested a few times, I now have a clear view of your future if you decide to travel down the same path I have. Being in prison ain't cool by a long shot. Truth be told, most people (not all) that are back here (in prison) for any crime, including murder and selling plenty of drugs, is now either gay or snitching.

The prison environment is far from what some movies show or expose for what it really is. Being confined to a cell small enough to be your bathroom at home with another man or men who can't control or refuse to control their bodily functions, and where your toilet and sink is in arm reach is beyond dehumanizing. The food ain't really food when you are losing weight faster than participants on "The Biggest Loser" show without even working out. You're subjected to be strip-searched at any time of the day or night regardless of how disciplinary-free you are. You can't control the prices of canteen which are steadily rising without any concerns as to how your family or friends are doing (financially) in order to assist in providing your basic need or travel expenses to come see you every so often. Disrespectful officers (most, not all) male and female from any and all ethnic backgrounds bark orders all day, in which you must submit or be denied your already inadequate meals, visits, or canteen and phone privileges, as well as recreational time.

Don't get caught up in the mindless hype. Expand your horizon by joining afterschool or summer programs such as "Upward Bound," "United We

Stand," or one of your big brother/sister divisions near you. You possess the potential to have your name on the next prescription bottle as the founder, not the patient, or the next best "eco-friendly award" recipient of the world. Please grasp the concept and truth that, "A mind is a wonderful thing to invest in, but a terrible thing to waste."

Peace,

Kujichagulia,

Desman Jenkins,

SCDC #333353 – January 4, 2014

ONE BAD DECISION CAN LEAD TO A LIFETIME OF REGRET

ONE BAD DECISION CAN LEAD TO A LIFETIME OF REGRET
Table of Contents

CHARVUS NESBITT - PATH TO DESTRUCTION * PEER PRESSURE (GOOD MAN WHO NEVER TURNED BAD)

To My Peers,

It's a true saying that life truly is what you make of it. In life we all experience what is called rash decisions. We can make rational decisions that can ultimately change our lives for the better or we can make irrational decisions that can be devastating to our lives forever. Just be sure that, "Whatever decision you decide to make has your best interest in heart because at the end of the day you are going to be the one having to live with it whether it's good or bad."

Have any of you ever lived your life to please others rather than to just be yourself? Well, if any of you haven't, I'm here to share with you my experience because I was living my life to please others instead of being who I am. In high school I was in ROTC for two years. During two years I became a staff sergeant and was informed if I took ROTC my junior year in high school I would be eligible for the ROTC College Scholarship. To be honest with you all, I really wanted it.

My mother started off forcing me to take ROTC and then eventually I ended up falling in love with it. One of the main things that made me want to join the service is my father. My father served eight years in the service and one of my brothers served 18 years in the service. I didn't want to join the service only to follow my father and one of my brothers; I wanted to join the service for the experiences. I love adventurous experience except for prison. I _hate_ prison.

What I'm saying to you all is that I never got my ROTC High School Scholarship living to please others! My peers all laughed at my Air Force ROTC uniform that I had to wear every Tuesday. So I fell victim to their criticism and quit ROTC. I'm not faulting anyone for my shortcomings. I'm just using this scenario for example. I should have stayed focused; continued to be my own man decision maker, and care less what they all thought about me or my uniform. We have to learn to endure and make our own decisions regardless what anyone else thinks as long as they are rational decisions.

Another scenario I experienced was about three months before I was arrested for my charges I'm serving time for today. My brother who was in the service and I had a serious man-to-man talk about what I was doing with my life. Truth is at the time it seemed that everything that could be possibly going wrong in my life was going wrong. So I made the decision to join the service. A couple days later I meet up with my fiancée at the restaurant that was just minutes from the recruiting office. She and I discussed my decision to join the service. She was totally against it.

Again, I thought on it some more and I totally put it out of my mind. My brother got back in touch with me. He was not only upset with my decision for not joining, but even more so disappointed. It was some time after that when I was arrested and he was like "I told you so." He was absolutely right. A hard head makes a soft buttock. I was found guilty by ***affiliation.*** (The Hands of one is the Hands of All – a law in South Carolina).

What hurts the most is after I served a couple years in prison my ex-fiancée got married and started a family with a man who's in the service. Therefore, I have to live with the irrational decision that I made for not making the best decision for myself and watch my future fade away. Remember, I'm not faulting anyone for my short comings and failures in life! I'm just sharing the scenario with you all so that you can capitalize off of my mistakes and make better decisions for yourselves. Prison is a no-man's land.

Last and not least, "Birds of a same feather flock together." This is an old saying that has come to haunt me. You have to be aware of your surroundings and be cautious with who you befriend. Everyone isn't your friend. Just because they are family or friends of the family, doesn't mean they're your friend. If the people you are affiliated with aren't doing what you're doing, you need to de-friend them and if you really need friends be-friend people who are compatible with you.

Please take it from my experience. If you're around when something goes down and your name comes up. Guess what? It's every man defending for himself. Don't be affiliated with things that are not a part of you as an individual. Being guilty by affiliation is just as bad as the crime itself. Please start to make wise decisions and if you already are please continue.

Yours truly,
Inspirational Speaker,
Charvus T. Nesbitt,
SCDC #349711

(Just as a side note, Mr. Nesbitt who was not in any previous trouble received a 40 year sentence. He will not be able to come home until 2050)

ROBERT L. WRIGHT - IT'S NOT EASY DOING THE RIGHT THING, BUT IT HAS TO BE DONE

I pray that this letter makes a difference in your life. My name is Robert L. Wright, Inmate #358939. I'm currently serving time at Lieber Correctional Institution which is located in Ridgeville, South Carolina. I would like to begin with the impact crimes have on families of the victim and the families of the person who commits the crime. Sometimes no thought goes into the pain inflicted on loved ones of the victim and the perpetrator.

The heartbreak it causes our Mothers, Fathers, Grandmothers and Spouses is immeasurable. The prison system truly destroys lives. It breaks up relationships; it separates Mothers and Fathers from their kids and siblings. It puts a strain on family members financially to pick up your responsibilities you left behind, not to mention them putting money on your inmate account to help you survive.

There are a lot of misconceptions about coming to prison. Things such as "being real", "being a soldier" or "being a gangster"; well let me tell you that all the types I've just mentioned would give anything to have your freedom. The freedom that we take for granted, prison is not the place to be. Of course there are lessons to be learned here but my advice to you is wise up and learn them while you're free because there are a lot of inmates who won't ever leave this place, no matter what they've learned behind these fences. All the money, women and material things mean nothing back here. Yeah your books (canteen account) might be straight but I guarantee you every inmate on this yard would give up having canteen money for their freedom.

What I ask is that you try your best to make good decisions. I said "try" because no one is perfect and when you feel you don't have the strength to do what seems difficult ask God to give you strength. Also have respect for others. Your mannerism will take you further than money ever will. It will also gain you respect. When trying to do the right thing you will always have obstacles or people who disagree with you but don't let that deter you. Those same people will respect you even if they don't admit it. Don't be a follower, be a leader. Don't let someone who doesn't value their life sink your ship. Make your own mistakes. Don't let someone else's mistake cost you your life or your freedom.

I don't say these things as if they're simple because they're not. Doing the right thing and making sacrifices has always been difficult but hard work truly pays off. Take it from someone who is in prison that this is no place for any man or woman. Don't listen to someone who has never been in here and if they've been here already and haven't made a positive change in their life stay away from them because that person will be coming back!

So experience life you haven't lived until you do and remember trials and tribulation will come, it's not a matter of if but when; and when they do come, pray for the strength, wisdom and focus to overcome them. Remember *all lives matter*! You will make mistakes. Learn from them and the mistakes of others as well. Get your life in order because whether you come to prison or not, we will all be judged by God one day.

Sincerely
Robert L. Wright
#358939

MELVIN STUKES - ADVICE

Dear Youth,
You are the future, and we need great teachers and leaders. Do let me remind you of mistakes we make that can put you in trouble with the law. Bad choices such as "hanging with the wrong crowd, making bad decisions, trying to fit in" often our acting out comes from not getting attention from our parents, or other family members that play a big part in our life and makes us do bad things. The good thing is to learn from your mistake and don't let it hurt you, but let it make you strong…

Hey, youth were the love at? Why you so full of hate? The "Father" created us. He is love.

Youth, don't give up! Remember when that teacher asked you what do you want to be when you grow up? Think about your future, do the right thing!

Peace and Love. You're our future. Up start your future. Teach and study hard to be successful.

-Melvin Stukes,
SCDC# 267991 --12/30/13

AHMED KING - PEER PRESSUREAND ITS EFFECTS

Youth of America take these words of advice before you make any decisions and choices. You better think twice, because it can affect you in the long run if you take the wrong road and put you in situation in which bed you'll make. In the real world you'll definitely tell because my bad choices and decisions landed me in jail.

So take heed to my words, and it will pull you through. Be young and wise don't do what I do. See in life, my choices of friends is what really put me in bad situations, because I always wanted roll with the crowd. Those were bad decisions on my part, because they effected who I was as an individual and I only felt only important when I was around the crowd. Sometimes when people weren't around I found myself being myself and really realizing that I had many talents, but the peer pressure was something that really drove me to be the person that I really didn't like. But I portrayed that in the "circle," because I thought it was cool. However not being who you truly are, people look at you as a fool.

So be the person that you truly are and you'll shine as bright as the North Star. Keep shining on as the world can see, go through life and being all you can be.

Ahmed King - #305316

JOHN ALLEN HAGOOD - PEER PRESSURE

To Anybody's Kid It May Concern- 12/10/13 -- 10:45PM

A word of encouragement, I know you may be going through something right now, but I'm here to let you know you are not alone. I know you may have friends that may tell you a lot of things to make themselves sound cool! Don't let that persuade you into following their lead because God gave you your own mind for you to make your own decisions. I know as a young black man/woman you should never let anyone's word dictate how to think and to live your life. Because trust me when you find yourself in a situation you can't get out of, those so call friends are not there to help you get out that trouble. They are just standing in the background telling you things you already know. But I know you did that to be accepted into their friendship, and the reason why I'm telling you this is because I know, because that was me when I was fifteen years old. If I would have never listened to my friends, I would never have caught 59 years, wasted all of my childhood, all my teenage years and majority of my adult life because I was incarcerated I didn't get out until I was forty two years old!

I'm telling you this because I need you to learn from my mistakes. Listen to your mother and your father, to your grandmother and grandfather or anyone who is trying to tell you positive things to make your life better for a reason. To help guide and help you make it to adulthood. I hope when you read this letter that you will take the time out to think intelligently about the choices in your life.

Thanks for taking the time to listen, and…

P.S You remember it only takes one time to being in trouble yourself, first time to be in trouble now …….First time now!...........First time now!....... First time now!………. Now what are you going to do?

It is up to you!!

Mr. John Allen Hagood # 123067 – One – Good – JAH

JAMES A. OWENS - THE EFFECTS OF NOT LISTENING

I grew up in a loving home, where we learned about God. I knew that God existed. I was introduced to alcohol and drugs shortly after the second grade. Once I started using, I hid from God as my addiction grew. Trouble with the law followed close behind. I received my first arrest at the age of ten. I got out of it, and then I started to run around in the streets with young boys getting in trouble. I started stealing and breaking into places. I got caught breaking and safe cracking. I went to jail and right on into the big prison with a 15-year sentence because I thought that I had all of the sense and no one could see the thing I was doing. But like I said before, I forgot all about God. He sees all things.

I got out again still thought that no one could see me. I had not learned from the 15 years as I only did five years of it. Yes! I still thought that no one could see me because I was so cool and smooth. I went back into the streets started using alcohol and drugs, thinking, *Oh! I can handle it because I've grown up to be an adult. I got it all together.* But quiet as it was kept, I was out of control, robbing drug dealers, and still I had a normal job. One day I ran upon a man and I felt like I had no way out. But the saddest part about it is that I took a human life all because I wanted to do things like I wanted to do it.

Yes! I got a LIFE sentence and was sent right back to the Big House. And I have been in as of today (2013) going on 34 years. My life has been thrown away. Yes! I still had lots of anger inside of me, selling drugs and making homemade wine, getting drunk, fighting and caught in a few stabbings. But one day someone got killed! Yes, the group that I was running with all flipped on ME! Some friends right!?! This awoke me and made me change my way of thinking.

Yes I really had to change or die trying. So I asked God to come in and just take over my way of thinking. Guide my way to righteousness. He did and people don't believe that it's really me. Some will even talk bad about you. But God's got you! So don't be sorry about the talk. Pray for them and keep on doing the right thing and you will be able to set a goal and get it accomplished.

I wish a million times that I would have listened to my parents. I wouldn't have been locked up in prison.

Bare not your soul to everybody nor damage thereby respect for you. Spread not your word among others nor associate yourself with those who bare their heart. Better are those whose knowledge remains inside them than those who talk to their disadvantage. One does not run to reach perfection. And one does not create it in order to destroy it.

James A. Owens, SCDC# *82569*

CHAD WILLIAMS - TO A CHILD IN NEED

Peace be onto you

Whether boy or girl this letter is universal good for all:

First, I want to say that you are loved, a blessing and a gift from above. I'm not going to talk to you about all the wrongs I have done, and pain I caused. There is not enough time or paper. But I will tell instead of coming to prison to realized this, that I should have listened to counsel. I didn't want to hear Instructions both from my parents and neighbors pointing out my faults to help get me right. By me making wrong choices, following negative people I got negative results. Which led to prison not the grave thankfully? I was told that throughout my life, I would go to prison or go to the grave. That was what my mother was telling me. How true it became.

So I tell you to surround yourself with positive people who will help you, and not to see you fail by leading you down a wrong path which ends in prison or the grave. You see your true friends will encourage, motivate, and help you reach your full potential in life. But once you learn to respect your parents biological or spiritual you will then know how to respect yourself which will carry you a long way in life and open doors for you. You should not have to come to prison to get on the right path, change your life. When you have wise counsel out there with you, everywhere and every day have an understanding mind to receive the knowledge that they are telling you. It is either to correct you or instruct you.

Start by getting and having a relationship with your Heavenly Father, then you will have morals and principles for yourself. By being surrounded with positive and respectful people you will never be led astray. You would not be a follower but a leader. You will save yourself and those who listen to you and follow you. Like it is said, "Learn from the wise, receive their knowledge which will instruct you to have an understanding mind and life."

May these words bless you and be helpful to you.

Yours truly,

Chad Williams,

SCDC #303225 -- 12-17-13

170

CHARLES CONNOR - TOE-TAG ENDING

Given up as a very young child and placed in foster care. Seeing my sister being raped by teenage boys and grown men. Finally being adopted only never feeling loved by the woman I was forced to call "mother." Spending my childhood trying to make an emotional bond with a family who picked me, questioning, "Why would you pick a child only to shut him out of your heart?"

Smoking cigarettes to fit in with the "cool kids." Smoking reefer because the "bad girls" liked it. Picking the "bad girls" because they let me go all the way. Playing the "good girls" to turn "bad." Finding out that the older sisters, mothers, and some select teachers like little bad boys as long as they stayed a secret. Getting paid to cut the neighbors grass that her husband had just cut. Acting tough, cold, and bold with a hidden secret that the part I liked best about sex was being held.

Five failed marriages and two daughters later, I sit in prison for the rest of my life. No friends from home, no visits, phone calls or letters. Murder and robbing is my convicted crime, and I am guilty of a whole lot more. I shut people down who tried to love me, because of past hurts. I became my own worst enemy because I didn't really like who I was past or present.

What could have changed the outcome of a toe-tag ending? Speaking up instead of acting out. Changing my future in spite of my past. Not repeating others actions by making victims out of those who tried to love me. Forgiving those who hurt me, asking for forgiveness and finally forgiving myself.

Charles Connor - SCDC# 319090

REGINALD A. CROFT AKA "QADIR" - ROAD TO PRISON WITH A PRIDEFUL/EGO

Mr. Reginald A. Croft - "Qadir" #201256. As a young child, God blessed me with many talents and gift. I was a great youth little league All-Star football player well known throughout Greenville County, I was also about to become sponsored as semi-professional skateboarder, high school wrestler, artist, break dancer, and an acrobat who could do flips as a gymnast with great aspirations in all my talents to become successful. There is even one staff member here at Perry Correctional Institution that can attest to this being true along with several inmates whom know me personally from society outside of these fences from different races and walks of life that can confirm this as well.

As a teenager I took all of my gifts and blessings for granted and started to deal with peer pressure and wanting to fit in while living in two different worlds. So I ended up making bad choices that lead me into jail two times as a Juvenile offender that caused me to spend 16 months of my life locked up for not listening to the people that always had my best interest and knew my talents and potential. But instead, I thought that I knew it all and went from a small time on the corner drug dealer to a big time dealer that led me up to this point. However, on May 3, 1993 I was confronted by a known and respected man throughout the city of Greenville. He did not care a great deal for me and was jealous of my status. But that's neither here nor there. I was in the process of doing a drug deal with a regular customer that wanted quantity instead of a small amount that my victim could only provide. Therefore, me and my partner were playing pool in a local store when the business deal came about, so I told my customer to go to a couple of streets up the block, and wait on me until I get there.

In the meanwhile, I had just been released from my juvenile sentence from the Department of Youth Service (D.Y.S.), but I became a major player/ competitor fast, due to my reputation and association that had a lot of people talking and envying me in my neighborhood. However, when I finally went to approach and complete my business deal I ran into my victim who was the violent, aggressive, and feared man in town that I mentioned earlier, so it really made him very angry and furious at me and the customer that our dealings that did not include him. He said after the customer rejected and refused his business offer that he was tired of guys getting out of jail thinking that they are big timers and things of that nature, so I made the deal final. Then out of nowhere he swung and hit me up side of the head and nearly knocked me out to a dazed state and my uncle caught me before I could hit the ground, and others grabbed my victim to try and stop the altercation. However, as I was putting my shoe back on my foot, the people that was holding him back could not hold him back any longer, so he charged me and threw me into a fence bursting my head, choking me, then my uncle and others tried to pull his hands from around my neck while he was telling his partner to go get the car, so he could go get or retrieve his gun. When I was able to break away from his tight grip as he was holding me, he was focusing in on my uncle saying that we were trying to gang him.

I then broke free and started to walk away. I left the area out of fear, pride, and reputation, I went to get a gun also and I thought he would pursue me knowing my family and where I stayed, so I went back to the area where we first had the confrontation. I then saw him with his hand on his waistband clutching his gun. Out of ignorance, pride, anger, and ego, I ran on him and shot at him four or five times that caused his death and my life as well. That led me to a 20-year-to-Life sentence in the South Carolina Department of correction at the age of 17 years old. That was not worth the pain his family, society, or my family should have had to endure.

Now, as an adult 21 years later, I wish that I could change my past, now at 37 ½ years of age, because of pride, ego, fear, and reputation, I allowed it to lead me into making such a critical and crucial mistake, bad judgment and choice that has affected and changed my and others lives forever.

I wasted and took for granted life, the opportunities, blessings, and talents that could have made me truly successful 21 years ago as well as time, a precious life that can never be reformed, corrected or ever get back. So this is my true reality now and people NEVER MAKE THE SAME MISTAKE...y'all are the future, because I wasted mine and I need y'all to learn from my mistake and become a success...

Peace and ONE Love "REGGIE" – "Qadir"
Mr. Reginald A. Croft, SCDC# 201256

FAMILY SHOULD HAVE ALWAYS BEEN PUT FIRST

FAMILY SHOULD HAVE ALWAYS BEEN PUT FIRST
Table of Contents

FACTOID-Loneliness

No matter how tough or how hard an individual may claim to be, loneliness is an emotion that all prisoners endure. From the moment the judge lowers the gavel and reads off the time you have been sentenced, an emptiness sets in. It is difficult to describe the feeling but trust anyone who has ever been to prison, knows what I am talking about.

It is very hard being torn away from the ones you love, your woman, your children, your family and friends. Not being able to live life freely doing what you want, when you want. Even though people can write you or come visit (which at times makes doing time harder because you have to stay and see them leave, longing to walk out the door and through the gates with them.), you still feel lonely during the visit because you know they will soon be leaving.

As the hours turn to days, the days turn into weeks, the weeks to months and months to years, the feeling grows and grows. Everyone deal with it in their own way. Some read anything they can get their hands on, some watch excessive amounts of television, some play cards and board games, some sleep as much as their bodies will allow them to, while others get high on any drug they can get their hands on.

No matter how we deal with this feeling, it resides in all prisoners. That longing for freedom, being able to do something as simple as driving your children to school, putting on your own clothes, kissing your mother on the cheek, walking across the street, or sitting at the mall watching all of the people including strangers with smiles on their faces walk by, and the fresh air of just getting up to go to the refrigerator to make yourself something to eat.

The pain of loneliness really sets in when a prisoner receives a call from the chaplain that their mother or family member has died.

This place truly drains your life force. Some deal with it better than others, but believe me when I tell you, we all suffer within until the day we return to society free and are able to fly.

They talk about the use of cell phones and how people are committing crimes with them. But in all actuality, people are just reaching out to someone/anyone, just to have someone to talk to. You may say nothing is innocent and it is against policy to speak on a cell phone, but if you have no interaction with the outside world, no one on the outside that is there for you; just a friendly voice of the wrong number is just like a warming of your lonely soul.

If prisoners were given **_monitored_** cell phones or monitored phones in each cell in prison, where there is just the monthly fee to be paid rather than the $2 to $5 per call for fifteen minutes, illegal cell phone use would be cut drastically as there would not be as much loneliness. However according to In

The Public Interest's report "How Private Prisons Companies Increase Recidivism", it states that "Prison telephone companies have helped to pass legislation to ban prisoners from possessing cell phones...In actuality, most prisoners use cell phones to contact their families"[51] and not to commit more crimes or engage in dangerous activity. (See Equal Justice Initiative, "Private Prison Phone Companies Lobbied for the Criminalization of Cell Phones in Prisons" (http://eji.org/news/private-companies-lobbied-to-criminalize-cell-phones-in-prisons) and in addition, the phone companies are making it illegal and making people serve longer sentences, to keep them in prison and so that they can continue to make money off the prisoners by having family have to pay to use their expensive pay phones to speak with their loved ones.[52]

What is most troubling is that information on how dangerous cell phones are is being "researched" and provided by the prison phone companies such as Securus and Global Tel. The research can be construed as a conflict of interest and biased because, when inmates use the cell phones, they are not using these companies' high priced telephone services. Most pre-pay cell phone carriers have a plan of $45 per month for unlimited calls, whereas the Securus and Global Tel can charge upwards of $1.50 (minimum) for 15 minutes, which would only allow someone 30 fifteen minute calls per month or 7.5 calls per week or 1 call per day.

Recently there have been new reports that jails and prisons are combating the phone issue proactively. Instead of banding the cell phones the administration are finding ways to change with the times as the world has become more technology based. In the UK, they have started putting phones in the cells. Having the phone in the cell, the inmate has easier access to the phone and their loved ones, not to mention the calls will still be monitored. In one jail in South Carolina, they are providing cell phones to the prisoners which have all of the same functions as the smartphone WITHOUT the internet, as well as the phone numbers are all monitored.

STEVEN BROWN – POEM: TO MY LITTLE ONE!

Little one I been thinking about you over the years,
I try to hide, but now in here to face all my fears,
It hurts to know that, I left you stranded and all alone,
No true father figure in your life, to help you grow; nor move on,
Thoughts of you push me to remain strong,
So promises I keep to you, until I return home.

My situation will never be forever,
I could identify with your pain and hurt,
When I read your letter;
And it hurts me dearly too my heart,
Knowing that I can't help you grow;
Cause we are so far apart.

If I could rescue you right away,
I wouldn't hesitate to make that happen any day,
Consciousness and aware,
No more lonely days, cause daddy will be there.
No time set! But, things will get better,
Until then my little youth,
Please cherish this letter.

Written by: Steven Brown, *12/18/2013*

LETTER - PAY – CLOSE – ATTENTION

For years throughout my incarceration I've heard brothers speak about unity and how we should and need to unite. Nevertheless, all I've heard was consistent talk; and seen no "true action!" A lot of people speak highly intelligently and the majority seem to have the right intentions, however their ways and actions contradict what they speak. So how do you expect someone to take heed to those things you speak of so profoundly when your everyday walk of life doesn't coincide nor reflect that of which you religiously profess? There's a variety of questions we can ask ourselves:

For Prime example: Who am I?

Have you ever woke up in the morning and faced that split-like image of yours and was more willingly ready to accept that of what you observed? Or did you find yourself trying to hide and/or run from reality of that horrible picture you faced?

Keep in mind; we are not a perfect people, though that should not hinder us from striving at reaching some level of perfection. Even the Creator himself has observed that man will sin, commit errors and mistakes, etc. It was already written. Nevertheless, a man who maketh the same mistakes, commits the same errors and sins, learneth not. But a man who strives to change his ways and living conditions displays great intentions, efforts, and a strong will to overcometh his self-created destruction. I have accepted the fact that I have much room for improvement, there is tremendous, but limited amount of negative qualities that in which dwells inside of me that warranted correction. We should never relinquish the golden opportunity to excel at the things we so desire to achieve. Most individuals are quicker to unify for the wrong cause, but less quick and slower to unite for a true/good cause.

Keep in mind, we can participate in the changing process, but never can we demand nor dictate change within the process.

Never allow someone else's ignorance or stupidness to become a part of your own downfall.

So what a man can't write of, he may can stealth of, and for that alone will keep his head highly above the water and from drowning as a result from his own agony, pain and misery.

PAY CLOSE ATTENTION

Written by Steven Brown, (Released)

TREVEE J. GETHERS – ADVICE TO SON

From the cold and grey confines of this concrete jungle, I sit and pour my wisdom and love through this pen hoping that words can recede some of the pain that I know you must feel. I want to begin by letting you know that I truly love and miss you dearly and I apologize for my abrupt departure. I never meant to abandon you and I pray that one day you can forgive me.

You are my greatest accomplishment and most prized possession. My first son and my best friend, there are so many things that I have to teach you. Like how to interact and communicate with females and how to manage your finances. I named you after me so you carry on my legacy and also build your own. I see me in you in so many ways. I just want you to learn from my mistakes and blossom into a successful and productive man. Although physically I may be absent spiritually and mentally I will always be here for you. I have a lot of plans for us and hopefully the Lord blesses us and gives us the chance to grow a true father and son bond outside of these prison walls.

Until my return I need you to be strong and hold down the fort. Know that everything in life isn't easy. There will be numerous stumbling blocks put in your path on this journey that we call life. But as long as you put the Highest first and have faith you will be able to overcome all adversaries. I love you son and until next time peace!

Love,
Your Daddy -- Trevee J. Gethers,
SCDC# 343706

HORACE ABNEY AKA HERU MOSSIAH MAAT - REFLECTIONS- LETTER TO MY DAUGHTER

12 /15/13 - Dear Princess,

This letter is the toughest one I've ever had to write to you the entire 10-plus years that I've been incarcerated. It truly broke my heart to receive the news that you were pregnant. Baby girl, after the scare you had last time, and the discussion that you, your mother, and I had about this issue, you promised me that you would at least finish High School before you made me a grandfather.

Your mother, even though she was against it,' went out and got you a prescription for birth control, and you promised that you would take them religiously. Now here it is you're in your senior year and you allow yourself to become another statistic (A young unmarried African-American Teenage mother).

Before I go any further I want to apologize to you for making bad decisions in my life, which caused me to be taken out of yours. Not to say that had I been home the situation would've been any different. It may have been worse, the reason I say this is because before I was sent to prison and given time to learn and reflect on my ways and actions.

I believed that the answer to everything was money as long as I had money then everything else was irrelevant. So I chased it religiously, not thinking nor caring about the danger that I was placing you, your brother, your mother and myself in. Nor was I taking time to learn anything worth teaching to you and your brother. My only concern was balling out and keeping up with the Joneses.

Since I've been away I've learned that most young ladies seek out men that remind them of their fathers or possess similar traits as their fathers. So if I had never been arrested you would've have been seeking out a very narrow minded self-centered male that possessed no knowledge of what life is truly about except the value of a dollar. Which may have landed you in the same prison you're in now?

The thing is I'm no longer that person and since you've been of age I've been trying to raise you from a jail cell. Or at least do the best job that my current situation would allow. I know a letter or a phone call is no substitute for physical presence, but you can never say that I did not try to warn you about the decisions you are making.

I've spoken to you about the damage it causes our communities when babies have babies, and how we end up trying to be our children's friends instead of their parents, because our minds and bodies aren't fully developed enough to raise a child properly. We've also discussed the fact that a child will place responsibilities upon you, you are not ready for and wouldn't be ready for until you were a graduate from college.

Anyway I'm not going to preach, you've forced your mother and I into something that neither of us are ready for. We were just learning what it takes to be parents and already you're making us grandparents. The question is, "Where do we go from here?" You already know I got your back, and no matter what your mother may say, she has your back as well. The only thing about it is we can assist you with little man and make things easier and less stressful on you, but we cannot make decisions for two nor one.

From what your mother has told me your decision making has already gotten off to a bad start. She's informed me that you're allowing your grades to slip, that your school is constantly calling about your attendance, and you're still smoking trees. Smoking is the worse because every time you get high you're getting little man high as well. This isn't fair to him. You're killing off his brain cells before they even have the chance to develop.

Right now your mind should be focused on finishing out the school year with a bang, and taking the best care of yourself so that you can bring a healthy, intelligent, fully developed little person into this world. You must provide him with a fighting chance to make it because you already know just by being a black man child the deck is stacked against him.

So you, with our assistance, must do our best to arm him with the tools he'll need for not only survival but success as well. Starting out by getting him high isn't a good start, and if your soon to be baby daddy isn't encouraging you not to smoke then that is sign # 1 of what kind of father he will be. Even though I had my flaws I wouldn't allow your mother to smoke or drink while she was pregnant with you or your brother. What she did when she wasn't in my presence I had no control over, but when we were together I was not having none of that shit.

If he doesn't care about his son's wellbeing before he enters the world, what makes you think he's going to care once he gets here? Trust me, I know what I'm talking about on this one.

As you know I'm looking forward to coming home soon and one of my coming home presents would be a healthy grandson. Even though I'm not ready to become a grandparent, I feel I owe you, being that I missed out on assisting with your growth and development. I will do as much as I can to help you with little man.

You'll have to be patient with me at first because I'll need to get on my feet and get myself situated. I've been gone for almost 12 years and will be coming home with nothing so before I can do for you I'll have to do for myself first, but once I'm where I need to be, trust me your life will be good. I promised you that and I don't intend to break my promise like you did. All I ask is that you tighten up and make sure you graduate. If not for me or for yourself, do it for the most important reason, the person you're forcing into this world who didn't ask to be brought here. Remember a good parent is a good teacher first so what would you be teaching your son if you don't graduate from high school?

This pregnancy can be one of many mistakes that you are bound to make in your life, or it can be a blessing from the man above, but your choices you make from this point forth will determine which.

With that said I'm bringing this letter to a close.

Love always Your #1 everything Daddy!

Horace Abney aka Heru Mossiah Maat, SCDC #316024

****

Reflections - Letter to my Son

12/12/13- What's Good Little Man? There are some things about life that I want to inform you of. You are now at the age in life (13) where you have a giant bullseye on your back and every move you make will determine the outcome of your future. All of the fun and games are over with. The disrespecting of your mother and other adults, the constantly getting in trouble in school. You are only 13 and already you've been arrested multiple times. Jah, I don't know what's going on in your mind but this behavior must come to an end before you are victim to the trap that society has set for its underprivileged citizens.

You must be aware that there's a war going on around you no one is safe from. The name of this war is "Mass Incarceration." This war was waged on the American People by their own government since around the time that slavery came to an end.

To understand why this war was waged you must look back at this countries' history. The way America became the juggernaut that it is today, was because of slavery and the use of free labor or underpaying people for their labor.

After slavery was abolished, or at least chattel slavery, the extremely wealthy who had become used to the lifestyle that this free labor allotted them had to devise a way to continue not paying or underpaying people for their labor. Hence "Mass Incarceration" was born.

185

When slavery was first abolished, it was intended to be done away with completely, but after Abraham Lincoln was assassinated the 13th Amendment which outlawed slavery was amended and changed to read that slavery was illegal unless one is duly convicted of a crime, basically making slavery legal again only in a different form. Just like right after slavery, if a black man did not have money in his pocket and was stopped by the police, it was considered vagrancy and they would have to spend 7 years in prison with back-breaking labor. (Justified slavery) From that day forward penitentiaries became the new plantations.

As you know I fell victim and became a casualty of this war. For the last 10 years I've been incarcerated forced into bondage for a crime that in God's eye isn't even a crime. I say this because all crimes are biblical and nowhere in the Bible does it speak about selling drugs as being unlawful. This was a weapon formed by the government as a tool to assist them in their war. Just like many other so called laws of this land. The only crimes that are actual crimes are murder, robbery, theft, rape, and child molestation everything else was thought up by man.

I'm not telling you this to make excuses for my actions or to blame the choices I've made in life on anyone else. I'm telling you so that you'll know what you are up against and be prepared for what's to come if you continue down the road you are currently travelling.

When I was around your age, I had dreams of becoming the next Johnny Cochran (a defense attorney), but those dreams were crushed once I decided to become a product of my environment and chose to sell drugs.

From the time I was three up until I was 11, my mom had our family living in a decent neighborhood. Where there wasn't much drug activity going on at least not out in the open. So up until that age I was sheltered from the realities of ghetto life. Then because of the actions of my older brothers our apartment was raided by the police and my mom was arrested. From that day forward, my life would never be the same.

Once my mom got out of jail after staying in there for a little over a month, we started living with my aunt who was watching over me while my mom was locked up. On this side of Flushing, Queens there was a whole lot more pressure soon as I stepped outside, brothers would be in the lobby hustling selling drugs and making money. For a while I was still on track taking the bus to the school in my old neighborhood which as predominantly white.

After I graduated elementary school that next year I started Junior High and was enrolled in the school around the corner from my aunt's apartment. As I got older, the pressure of my environment became too much. By this time I had new friends that were from my aunt's neighborhood. Once I had graduated Junior High, it was all downhill from there. Seeing dudes my age 15 pulling out thick wads of money, and wearing the latest fashions. I wanted to dress and have money too, so that summer I started my life of so called criminal activity.

Then I came to find out that my brothers and my father were some of the biggest drug dealers in Queens. So once I turned 18 and they accepted that this was the life I had chosen. They started schooling me and turned me on to a whole other level of hustling.

The only thing about it is that my luck in the drug game has never been good. Just like you I was constantly getting arrested. My first arrest, they gave me probation, my second arrest they reinstated my probation. By the time I was arrested the third time, I was getting money in N.C with my brother and father. This time there was no probation. They sent me to prison for three-and-half years, which felt like eternity while I was doing time, but once I was released it seemed like it was a smack on the wrist. While serving the three-plus years I did nothing constructive with my time other than get my G.E.D. The whole time I was locked up I was making plans to get out and get back to getting money in the streets again.

Once I made it home I lasted all of about three years, which was during the time you were conceived. The next time I was arrested would be the arrest that sent me away for a very long time—30 years to be exact for getting caught with a little under a half of kilo of cocaine. They sentenced me to the type of time that even some murderers don't receive.

I gave you this brief walk back through my past just to show you how a wrong decision can change your future and how the system toys with you by first setting you free after you commit your first crime. Then they may set you free again, they might even give you a short stay which for some people usually isn't enough for them to realize the scheme. Then if you continue to live the same, they lay you down for an extended stay and for some people that is the rest of their lives, LIFE SENTENCE, which is the ultimate goal, to make a life-long slave out of as many people as possible.

Knowing this should sway anyone from living a life that could send them to prison. If this isn't enough to change your decision making, then the conditions of life back here should. You are told what to do and when you can do it, never having privacy or space that is your own. You are subjected to constant strip searches having other men look at your intimate private parts telling you to lift your nuts and turn around so they can have a look at your asshole.

You never know what tomorrow is going to bring. One minute you're sitting around watching T.V or playing chess, and the next minute the CO is yelling, "lockdown" telling everyone to report to their cells because someone got stabbed in another dorm and they placed the whole yard on lockdown.

Your whole life becomes unstable. Then on top of that the food sucks. Only about three meals that they serve are worth eating and even those are borderline disgusting. You're surrounded by men 24 hours a day except for the few women they have that work here and they only see you as another number to be counted. Your old man can't wait to hold a woman again just to breathe in her scent and to feel her soft embrace. To allow yourself to be taken away from that is madness in itself.

Then there is the strain that this place puts on your relationship with your family and loved ones. Most guys' families abandon them after a few years of the stress this place puts on them. As far as your relationships with your lady you might as well forget that because most are gone after the first couple of years, if they stay around that long.

If these things don't make you want to stay out of prison then the biggest fear all of us have back here have and that's dying in this place. Since I've been here I've lost my father who was my confidant and best friend. I've lost all of my uncles and a couple of my aunts, without being able to pay my respects to them.

The medical care you receive back here is the worse. They think all problems can be solved by an aspirin or Motrin until you're damn near dead then they want to give you the medical attention you are supposed to get. The food has no nutritional value. Everything is starch and meat. No fresh veggies or fruit all they want you to do is survive, not live, even some of the meat they feed us says, "Not fit for human consumption," on the box.

Going to sleep and not waking up in that uncomfortable thing they call a bed is my worst fear of all. Not being able to enjoy life with you, your mom, and sister or not being around to see you and your sister grow into the successful adults that I know you have the potential to become.

Every year I feel my health declining. They say prison preserves you Yeah, it may preserve the external, but it destroys the internal. You have guys younger than me that exercise on a regular basis whose organs have shut down on them. I'm no doctor but I think it's due to the lack of proper nutrition.

Just this year about two guys in their late fifties died from heart attacks after complaining about chest pains and being ignored by the medical staff. This place is a big machine that needs human bodies to run and just like when a part goes bad in a car, you remove it, discard it and replace it with a fresh part. This is what our criminal justice system is doing with us.

With the peer pressure that our neighborhood and communities apply on us along with trying to keep up with the Joneses it is difficult not to fall victim. And I know you want to be viewed as cool, but trust me Jah, the brother that's cool is the one that never comes to prison and enjoys his life to the fullest. Even though he may look lame as a teenager, once he's grown and earning a seven figure salary or owning his own business his patience and perseverance would've paid off.

Before I was given this time I possessed no knowledge worthy of passing on to you, but now I am the man I feel you deserve as a father, but if you come to prison before I can get out and show you the man I've become then my efforts to better myself would've been all for nothing.

At the end of the day I cannot live your life for you. Only you can do that. All I can do is guide you and hope to pass you a torch that's burning bright once I'm done with it, but will hopefully radiate when you are.

I'm currently working on something that can turn into something very special for all of us, and this letter is part of the foundation to the mega structure I plan to build. Your dad has his head on straight now and with the help of a special friend I'm on my way to doing big things. I just hope you are there to share them with me once I am free.

Love your old man,

Horace Abney

SCDC# 316024, aka Heru Messiah Maat

(Do you want to hear more from Heru and visit him for a month in prison via his journal? See our next book in this series: "Blindside Diaries, Life behind the Fences" coming soon in Winter 2019. See Heru's e-book which he also co-wrote. "MYA MAFIA, I'm That Girl" published by Imperial Imprint LLC currently on sale at Amazon: https://www.amazon.com/dp/B01MF8TU1K)

MICHAEL COFFIN - THE POWER OF LOVE

Dear Son,

I hope tears of regret will not cloud your eyes while reading these words. But if they do, I say this; it won't be because of the absence of love.

You see, love is the reason the unfriendly feelings come. The real person you are is your spirit, the one God gives you. You feel guilty because you know you have let someone down and are ashamed in your heart of hearts.

This is not really a bad thing though. It is actually a good thing. You see it means you care, you have goodness in you. If you would not feel guilty of wrongness, it means there is darkness set in. It will destroy all things good. It is like a disease that you may not realize you have that will rise up and make you sick. Then go away and let you believe that you have gotten better. It will come back, make you sick again and again until one day you don't get well ever.

So embrace your regret and let the goodness come in and soothe it. For every time you do this, it will become easier and easier.

The goodness of which I speak of is love. Love has no regrets, it is never sorry or ashamed. It can change any situation for the better. It will always be there for you in good times and bad, and if you let it do its magic, it can transform lives.

This world may try to make you believe that love is not always right. But I tell you that without it, we really have nothing. It is the only thing of true value, put in us for a reason; to test us, to mold us, to make us the REAL people we are intended to be.

Love,

Dad

Michael Coffin # 236693

Mr. Coffin is serving a LIFE sentence and is currently completing a college degree program to mentor and minister to others who are incarcerated.

FELIX CHEESEBORO aka STREETS - PRISON LIFE FOR FEMALES

To my young sisters,

This is your big brother Streets. Let me speaks with you for a quick minute, because I really think that I need to feed your mind with some fruitful mental food that will guide and arm you as you struggle to maintain your physical freedom.

I want to start off by advising all of you not to feed into the hyped up tale about prison. These institutions were designed to separate tight knit families and break down the power of young sisters just as much as young brothers. I know you've heard about the violence that takes place behind these fences. Instead of being filled with fear, you are overly fascinated. But it's not the violence that will affect you the most. What will affect you is being subjected to full body strip searches at any given time, being talked to and handled like a dog on a leash, being told when you can take a shower, what little clothing you are allowed to wear to the shower, and the little bit of time you have to shower. When you have your monthly period sometimes they will not even provide you with sanitary napkins. Can you imagine that? SMH... The mishandling of your property during random room searches. The CO's reading of your mail, losing your mail and even throwing away your mail. And much more psychological games to keep you depressed, confused, and contempt with the way you are being treated.

It will be the little things that will make you realize you have truly made a terrible mistake by being trapped in here. No more going to the mall with your friends, no dressing in the latest fashions, no more driving your car, no more spending the holidays with your family, no more freedom period.

Do not think for one minute that when you do time your loved ones don't do the time with you as well. The phone bill, the searches they'll be subjected to before being allowed to enter the institution to visit you, money they send to you so that you can purchase food, clothes, writing materials, and other personal needs. The worrying they go through after receiving phone calls and letters from you concerning an unjust act that was committed against you in some way.

Little sisters, they say that God does not like ugly. Well baby y'all just make my heartbeat, because He made every one of you so beautiful from inside to outside, so love yourselves just as much by doing all you can to steer away from trouble. Obtaining basic education such as reading, spelling, comprehension, and math is a must have in order to overcome road blocks that lie ahead of you. It's a shame when you're 21 years old or older and need another prisoner to read your personal letters and write responses to those letters for you. It's a shame when you're constantly getting beat out of your money because you cannot add or subtract well. Never be too lazy to do the things that will better you.

Knowledge is information and wisdom is what you receive from experience, so always supply your mind with as much information as possible, both academically and street wise. Gain wisdom and learn from others mistakes in order to dodge the quicksand; and positive pathways will open. This is my message to you baby girl, in hope that it saves you.

Love, Your Big Brother Streets, #237564 - December 28, 2013

STREETS CONTINUED – WRITING TO YOUNG MEN

December 20, 2013

To My Young Brothers,

Yo this is your Uncle Streets. Check it, I wanna holla at you for a quick minute, because I see you getting grown now, so let me put you up on this multimillion dollar business that you'll be a part of real soon at the rate some of you are going. It's called "The Prison System," and it's mainly geared towards trapping young males "of all races." The prison system knows that the younger they come, the more money they can make off of them over the years, whether they receive a long sentence, or become a repeat offender, because it doesn't matter to them....it's just business.

A lot of you do not fear coming here, because you feel that doing a bid adds to your hood cred, especially if you come in here kicking ass, or develop a mean hustle and rep as one of the heavyweights in the prisons dope game. And you're right, it does build your rep, but listen, because this is the part you do not hear about. Prisoners will fight each other over a few heated words while on the basketball court, but will not lift a hand against a correctional officer who disrespects them verbally in front of the other prisoners.

Prisoners will clique up to fight another clique of prisoners over some territorial beef, or one gang against another gang, but they will not lift a hand against the correctional officer who they see violently assaulting their fellow prisoner. The COs mistreat prisoners in lockup by making them lie down on their stomachs in the back of a cell in order for him to receive his food tray. They have two prisoners housed in a cell that's no bigger than the average bathroom, and tell the two prisoners to strip at the same time and consent to a degrading cavity body search before they are allowed to take a shower. Prisoners will clique up to go in the room of another prisoner to rob him for his food paid for by his family's hard earned money. But prisoners will not make any attempt to run up to the prison administration and try to change items that cost three times less in the stores on the streets...'hood cred'...damn shame.

Look, you want true hood cred, then the ones of you with illegal money should start a chain of business that will provide jobs for the hood, invest your money in the future of cats who have strong athletic skills, but who cannot concentrate on their school work, because of the hardships at home such as the lights, phone and water being turned off. Start a non-profit organization that's directed at bettering the hood, and build that organization until it becomes a major positive organization. There are ways you should go about getting a rep. There have been prisoners who have been released and went on to become success stories. But ask them if they wished that they would have never had to gone to prison, I bet you all of them would say "yes."

Making the right choice in life, or being mature and disciplined enough to correct wrong decisions, is what will decrease your chances of coming to this hell hole. Learn from a dummy like me who it took FOUR (4) Natural LIFE sentences before I realized that my fate was decided after I made certain choices that paved the trail straight to this hell hole. Learn, or burn. Your choice...

Nut'n but Luv 4 U,

Your Uncle Streets...

(Streets is a talented writer. See his e-book "MYA MAFIA: I'm that Girl" published by Imperial Imprint LLC currently on sale at Amazon: https://www.amazon.com/dp/B01MF8TU1K)

MARQUES DAVIS a.k.a QUEZ - A LETTER TO A FATHER'S ONLY HOPE

Son, Listen, everyone can be a sperm donor, baby maker, etc., but it takes a man and woman to be a father and mother.

Growing up I had a lovely mother and a stepfather who would teach me how to be man. I grew up in a family who raised me to be the best I could be. I always went to school and had good grades. As I got older I branched out into the streets, because that was all I knew sex, money and drugs. It started from seeing the men and the women in my family dealing with that which caused me to follow in their footsteps and do what they done for a living. My grandma always told us, "Don't do this, do this," but I always chose to do the opposite even though it wasn't right. It was just the thrill of wanting to touch fire and suffer the consequences later. Sometimes when a person gets away with doing something for a while they believe they're untouchable and this is what causes them to fall victim to prison, the cemetery or homelessness.

Listen son, I'm not telling you don't do this or that because you probably been getting that told to you already. Do what you feel, and remember that there's always consequences and repercussion to anything you do. I know you say to yourself he does it and gets away with it, so why I can't? Everybody can't hit the lottery, but some get lucky and hit it. ***There are guys behind bars that have talents that they showcase a lot back here, but for nothing.*** Some could have been music artists, basketball or football players and more but instead they are doing football numbers (30 and 40 years in prison) at a young age, with me being one of them.

I have truly learned my lesson and heard all the stories you could possibly think of since my incarceration. So, son, remember it's your life and you can only live it once, so live it to the fullest, positively not recklessly. Be all you can be, not what me or anyone else would like for you to be. I stand behind you 100% at whatever choice you make even though I might not like it! Be a go getter, and if they hate let them hate and watch the money pile up!!! So later on in the future you can look back and say "I started from the bottom...now I'm here!" I love you Son with all my heart. Stay Strong and Focus.

Love Always and Forever,
Your Father,
Marques Davis a.k.a Quez #300478

KEITH CLARK, aka KASIT - LETTER OF ADVICE TO 'SON' GOING ASTRAY

A letter to my nephew by: Keith Clark #313898 AKA "KASIT" As-Salaamu-Alaykum (Peace be upon you) My beloved nephew, my man. I pray that Allah (God) guides you so that you will have Peace and success while dealing with the everyday struggles of this life that we all have to deal with in some way or another. As you know, I have mad love for you. Everything that I tell you comes directly from a place of unconditional love.

In my life I've never had a grown man to give me the guidance that I desire to give to you. With that being said, let me tell you straight up like this man, if you don't change now you're gonna crash. Period! Before you know it you're gonna be knee deep in the mix of madness, and believe me, you don't want that!

Only you and God know what's really going on in your head. Whatever it is that keeps causing you to make bad decisions, especially when you know better, obviously means that you need help. No, I'm not saying that you're crazy. You're just another young black man that needs some sincere advice and guidance from a grown black man that has nothing but a very real and deep love for you. Me!!!

Let me start by telling you this. The first thing in every man's life whether he accepts it or not, is Allah (God) Period! And after that, his mother. Being fool or disrespectful to either one of them is the quickest way to failure in this life, and the hell fire in the afterlife. Believe it or not. That is strictly between you and our Creator, but you will eventually realize that nothing will go right for you.

Next thing, you will not find peace in a bottle of liquor or a blunt. All that does is make all your bad ideas and actions seem like it's right. There's a lot of young brothers your age in here with me that have LIFE sentences because they were high and ended up killing their girl by accident, or shot some dude because they were tripping on X or some other mind altering drug. Word!!

Every man pays for what he does, there's no getting around that fact. Every day that I wake up I have to realize that. Didn't you feel the love when I was hugging you when you came to see me? Didn't you see the tears in my eyes? This thing is real man. You're a really smart young man, but for some reason it's like you're trying to throw your opportunities for a successful life away. Who does that?

Yo, nephew, you gotta talk to me. You gotta tell me what you probably never told anyone before. You can tell me anything. Man-to-man. I'm your uncle, your main man, and your best friend. By God's will and by His guidance we can work whatever out together. Now it may sound corny to you, that's alright. I'm not trying to sound cool. I just want my nephew to get his life together. I love you man. You have to reach out to me. Come to see me as soon as you can. You have to do something that going to start bringing some positive change and progress in your life.

So until next time, wise up, be smart, be safe and be strong.

Love Always,

Your Uncle Keith

P.S. Kiss & hug your mom and stay in touch with your Grandmother.

Keith Clark, SCDC# 313898

TERRY WILMORE - LETTER TO SON WHO HE HAS NOT SEEN SINCE HE WAS A SMALL CHILD

My son,

I pray that all is well with you and the family by the time you receive this letter. This letter has been written a thousand times in my head yet I'm still confused about what to say to a young man who I call my son but know little about and vice versa.

I know you have a son. Cherish every moment you have with your son. Tell him you love him as I tried with you before being incarcerated and during this time every chance I got to reach out to you. My life flashes back to the last time I held you in my hands, a small innocent child with no cares in the world. We have come a long way since that time. We have built a lot of bridges since one of those bridges was when you gave me a chance at a relationship with you by phone. Another one was letting me know I had a grandson. But the main one was when you came to see me, a man who was supposed to protect the ones he loves, but only to hurt them. That is a burden that we as men must find a way to break through so that our family can get back the way it used to be which was caring for family.

My son if you only knew how overwhelmed I was when I looked into your eyes only to see me looking at myself at the age of 20. When I got back to my room I asked myself did I deserve a visit from you, and the answer is yes because parents make mistakes. Some are not as devastating as others but they are still mistakes. Now that you are a parent, don't try to be perfect to your child, I tell you as I told your sister many years ago. Wherever you go in life don't be ashamed of who your parents are. Keep your head up. I pray that you are guided by God and not in some group just to fit in. I said that because I need you to talk to me so that you will never have to sit behind fences writing to your child like your old man. Until we see each other again, which I am praying will be soon or drop me a letter. I won't make a promise but I will try to write more, so give me something that we can talk about. I will end this letter with the ink in my pen but not my love for you. Stay strong. Peace.

Love Always,
Daddy - Terry Wilmore - #217739

DONQUES HOOD – THE CHOICES WE MAKE

12

-10-13 -Son,

I would like to inform you of what it's like to be in prison. I do not know why I decided now, considering I've been locked up five years. I guess any time is good to inform you of the hardships of prison. First, I need to inform you about the first and most important thing: the choices we make. We have freedom to choose our friends and the choices we make. Devon the choices we make are everything. Choosing the wrong friends is definitely a way that leads to prison. Devon, don't be influenced by other people. Make the right choice in everything you do. I chose to get money the fast way and that's what led me to prison.

PRISON LIFE

Devon, currently black men make up about 14% of the United States population, but they are more than 50% of the prison population. Being in prison strips you from a lot of the freedoms you have. We are told what time to eat, sleep, and when to wake up. Officers even make us walk in between red and yellow lines on the side walk. Sometime we're locked in our cell days at a time. Devon, the food in prison is awful compared to the food you eat every day. Son, these things I'm informing you about are nothing compared to the mental strain of being in prison. Prison can destroy you mentally. Being away from your family is difficult. Some days you feel alone, although we're surrounded by 100 people daily. Thinking about family is what keeps you going. There is a lot of violence in prison, just like on the streets. So like I said before, "Choose your friends wisely." Devon to sum it all up prison is not a place for any man, black or white. Devon the choice is up to you.

THE ROAD TO PRISON

Devon, <u>greed</u> is what led me to prison. I wanted money and cars. Working at a job didn't get money fast enough. So me and some friends came up with a plan to rob a bank. Because we decided to rob the bank, I'm in prison serving a 20-year sentence for armed robbery. Devon because I made a bad choice, I hurt a lot of people when committing that crime. I hurt the victims, my family, and last but not least me. Devon *getting in to prison is easy*; staying away from trouble that leads here is hard. Once you're here this is the end of freedom. I'm going to end this part of the letter with couple of verses from *MATTHEW 7:13-14* in your Bible. "Enter ye in at the straight gate: for wide is the gate, and broad is the way, that leadeth to destruction and many there be which in there at; because straight is the gate and narrow is the way; which leadeth unto life, and few there be that find it."

REDEMPTION IN PRISON

Devon, although I'm in prison and convicted of arm robbery and kidnapping, I can change my life. I have changed. Prison is a time for making a change. There are many different religions and schools of thought in prison. I find comfort in Christianity with the Lord Jesus Christ. I fall short sometimes, but I always strive to do what is right. While you're free and on the street, seek God. God is the only preventative measure from prison. I have found redemption Devon, but I still want to come home. I believe God allowed this road for me to prison to happen for a reason. I believe it was simply to slow me down. I honestly look at life from a different perspective now. So prison has saved me to say the least. Devon seek God and you will be on the right path.

Devon, I'm sorry it has taken so long for me to inform you of my incarceration and how I came to prison. Prison is not a place for anybody. Make good decisions, Devon. Take this information and tell it to your friends, but especially to your little brother Davian. Once again, make good choices and stay out of trouble. I wrote this letter with love and sincerity, and it's all the truth.

Love,
Your father DonQues Hood
SCDC #333563

DID YOU KNOW????

DID YOU KNOW??? - *Table of Contents*

LAROLD MORRIS - LEARN YOUR HISTORY

Hey Kyla,

How things going at home? I hope that you had a very good Christmas and that you got every gift that you wanted. Well, this time it is actually harder than I thought it would be. These CO's treat us like little kids, basically tell us when to do this, when to do that, and on top of that they keep us locked in our cells a lot for the smallest things, which makes doing time a whole lot harder! I know prison wasn't designed to be fun, but how the COs treat inmates here make you think we were animals and that they should be locked up for cruelty to animals. I would say this sometimes it's good to be bored that way I can pick up a book and read something that could educate my mind when I do get out. It would be a whole lot smarter and I won't make dumb decision to end back up in prison.

I did learn something yesterday. They held Kwanzaa up in the gym yesterday morning up to 3:00 pm. I know you not of age yet to know what Kwanzaa is. Well it is a seven-day festival they hold around Christmas time every year. It's a time Black People come together and celebrate and learn about the real truth about being Black. You learn about Africa, which is our Motherland, you get the chance to learn real history. When I say real history I'm speaking about Black history. You won't learn this type of history in school, because they do not want you to know your background. What I mean by your background is I'm speaking about Africa and how Black people were taken, which means kidnapped from their homes which were villages, some were beaten to death and killed. I learn a lot from listening to those guys speak yesterday. So I feel like it's my duty to learn as much as I can so I can teach you, that way nobody can brainwash you or misguide you with false history about Africa! I want you to grow up and obtain as much knowledge and when you obtain it, use it for good. That way you don't ever have to worry about ending up in Prison!

Prison ain't good for nobody, some might deserve to be here because of their crime, but as a Black man and Black woman we gotta make a change. It's too many of us already locked up, that's why I'm reaching out to you while you are young so you don't make bad choices. You know I'm striving to do everything in my power to come home, and I love you to death, you are my only child that I have, I want you to grow up smart and beautiful like you are. Always remember being Black is Beautiful, so know you are a Black girl that rocks. Don't ever let anyone tell you different. I love you Kyla Marshal!!

Larold Morris #336461 – Q2A113

-- Stay Safe and Stay Strong for Daddy

--- Love Y'all Always!

Note from Heru, Dawn & Streets: When we went through the letters for the ones we liked the most, we originally did not want this letter. But as the book evolved, we started to add Factoids and the "Did You Know?" section. As a result, we realized how important this letter is. Mr. Morris' letter reminds us of the fact that many do not know their history (or the history of others).

Mr. Morris' "Learn Your History" letter is so important because through learning history, you gain knowledge and do not make the same mistakes or fall for the same tricks that you or others have in the past. Knowledge provides you with protection.

His-Story...is important whether it is from the past or present.

****

Two (2) excellent sources that I read from each day to STAY WOKE are The Marshall Project (www.themarshallproject.org) and The Sentencing Project (https://www.sentencingproject.org/). These two organizations keep truly care criminal justice/prison reform and people. Please check them out and support.

DID YOU KNOW ABOUT??? States Refusal of SNAP/Welfare Benefits

Did you know that when you get out of prison for felony crimes such as drugs, some states will not give you food stamps, welfare or any kind of help/housing? And in MOST cases, when you get out of prison you have to go to a Parole officer, and pay a "supervision fee"? There is a FEDERAL LAW which places a life time ban on Supplemental Nutrition Assistance Program benefits for those people who have drug related felonies; however states can choose to opt-out (not follow) this ban, and allows its state citizens to receive these benefits, the ability to buy food to eat.

How are you supposed to eat? Where are you supposed to get some clothes to wear? Where are you supposed to live? And with all that, where are you supposed to get the money to pay Parole their "supervision fees" so you can stay out of prison…otherwise you have to return. Please read Michelle Alexander's book "The New Jim Crow, Age of …" This will give you the real deal of what happens AFTER you get out of prison. Sometimes, it is even worse if you have no one to help you when you get home.[53] [54]

In 2018 they are attempting to pass the 2018 Farm Bill Act which Rep. George Holding (R-NC) added a provision to revoke/not allow food stamps to anyone with certain violent felony convictions no matter when the sentence was completed or where one resides in the United States. (See "2018 Farm Bill" - https://www.agriculture.senate.gov/2018-farm-bill)

STATES that do not ALLOW Drug Felons to Get Food Stamps

Wyoming	Georgia*
West Virginia	South Carolina
Mississippi	Arkansas

*As of July 1, 2016, Georgia lifted the ban on SNAP benefits.
(Source: http://www.redandblack.com/athensnews/new-georgia-law-lifts-food-stamp-ban-for-drug-felons/article_e047283c-1413-11e6-ad63-6767de912a3e.html)

States that DO NOT ALLOW Drug Felons to get welfare/Temporary Assistance to Needy Families (TANF)

South Dakota	West Virginia
Nebraska	Mississippi
Missouri	Georgia
Illinois	South Carolina
Delaware	Arkansas
Arizona	Texas

(Source: The Marshall Project-Nonprofit journalism about criminal justice using Source: The Pew Charitable Trust, Legal Action Center as of February 4, 2016 at 7:15am ET)

DID YOU KNOW ABOUT??? The School To Prison Pipeline

*The above infographic was created by Community Coalition http://cocosouthla.org/inforgraphics/ . The organization generously provided Imperial Imprint LLC permission to use this infographic for this book.*55

Also check out:

https://www.aclu.org/fact-sheet/locating-school-prison-pipeline

http://www.pbs.org/wnet/tavissmiley/tsr/education-under-arrest/school-to-prison-pipeline-fact-sheet/

http://www.suspensionstories.com/

Did You Know ABOUT??? Education NOT for Prisoners

Did you know that during the Clinton Administration and its being tough on crime, in 1994 Congress (both parties) agreed to STOP people in prison from receiving Pell Grants so that they could further their education while in prison? It is a known fact that the more education one has or attains; the less likely they will be to go back to prison, especially if they received their degrees while in prison. Heru's brother, Dr. Shajeem aka Bashir Muhammad-Jordan has a bachelor's degree as does Leonard "Pete" Rollock, which they received while in prison. Their reality since coming home is much more promising because they have college degrees which provided them with the ability to get better jobs or become better LEGITIMATE business owners.

Did you know that in addition, as per an article by the Marshall Project, schools are asking if children were suspended or expelled in Middle School and using that as a way to refuse entrance in to college? Most people likely to be suspended from schools are black/African-American and in addition, this is also true for Latino, American Indian and Alaska Native. Hence those of color are being given harsher punishment than whites in school even as children.[56] [57]

President Obama is in process of creating the bill so that prisoners that will be coming home within the next 5 years or so have the ability to take advantage of the PELL grant. The Pell grant is approximately $5,775 per year to be given to the school/program that provides higher education to a person to cover tuition, books and educational expenses. 'The administration can't lift the ban on Pell grants without Congressional approval, but the Education Department can use its authority to temporarily run a pilot program.'[58]

Giving prisoners education tend to be cost effective in that people have skills and can have a better chance of employment or becoming a productive tax paying citizen.

But did you know that some state senators from New York OPPOSED prisoners getting an education and felt that people who are in prison should NOT be allowed to better themselves through education while in prison and have written up a bill to STOP this? One state senator launched a petition entitles "HELL No to Attica University"

It was said that it was rewarding bad behavior and that it was "beyond belief to give criminals a competitive edge in the job market over law-abiding New Yorkers who forgo college because of the high cost." [59] (Bakeman, 2014)

The Bard Prisoner Initiative which offers bachelor degree programs while in prison have a 4% recidivism rate, versus the usual 40%.

So this is just a little information for you...If you go to prison even those who are supposed to represent the people in your government will be AGAINST you turning your life around to do better. And if you look at some of the comments on the websites regarding this issue, some people think prisoners do not DESERVE to get an education or the PELL Grant while in prison, just sit and rot in there. They feel like this, "Why should a prisoner receive a free education for committing crimes when I have to pay for my own/or my children's education?"

Luckily New York State Governor Andrew Cuomo, an Ex-State Attorney General, President Obama and others are forward thinking and support this program as well as other positive minded government officials.

***Thoughts from the author. Although my stance is to be neutral in this book, I do want to say something to those who believe that inmates should NOT receive Pell grants and college education while incarcerated. It is painful to be a victim of a crime. I have been one myself and the idea is to PUNISH the person that did the harm. Please note, most of these people did not have level playing ground for educational opportunities and were NOT guided toward college while in school as a child. Secondly, should the prisoner want to attend school once, released, they still will receive Pell grants and financial aid once, costing the tax payer even more money.

So my question to you is: WHY prolong the process? Isn't it better for the prisoner to come home prepared and ready to be a tax-paying law-abiding citizen, rather than one struggling to get by with a low level to NO level job and have to resort back to crime just to survive? Why take the chance of YOU or someone else being that next crime victim?

And for those who feel that prisoners are receiving an education for FREE while in prison, then another option could be to implement programs so that they pay back the money received via service, internships, teaching assistantships (with real prevailing federal wages ($7.25 or more/hour) not slave/prison wages (20 cents/per hour)) or paying it back once they are released and financially self-sufficient. ***

DID YOU KNOW ABOUT??? Kids for Cash

D id you know it was uncovered in 2009 that there was a judge in Luzerne County Pennsylvania who was putting kids that committed minor crimes or wayward acts into private prisons for money? See the movie KidsforCashmovie.com by director Robert May. See how Judge Mark A. Ciavarella Jr. put away around 3,000 children into for-profit prison facilities and received about $2.2 million as a finder's fee from construction costs for private prison facilities for kids; ruining the lives of these children. These kids were of ALL races.

"They were hauled into court with their parents, sometimes after being persuaded — coerced, according to at least one parent — by police to waive their right to legal counsel." (Getlen, 2014) [60]

It was not until some other leads *and a reputed underworld friend* of another judge (Judge Michael Conahan) who was putting together an investor group to build another FOR PROFIT juvenile detention center called PA Child Care, tipped off authorities about what was happening that they were able to come in and arrest both Judge Mark A. Ciavarella and Judge Michael Conahan.

The judges (Ciaverella and Conahan) asked for leniency, the same thing they did not give those children, but instead Judge Mark A. Ciavarella received a 28 year sentence for racketeering, "honest services mail fraud" and of being a tax cheat (Wikipedia)[61], he gets out of prison in 2035, at age 85. Judge Conahan received 17 ½ years for one count of racketeering conspiracy and will be released at age 74 in 2026. The families of those who were subjected to his courtroom sentences are now in court suing these judges.

Ciarvarella had approximately 2,480 of his convictions reversed and expunged.

DID YOU KNOW ABOUT??? About Marcus Dixon

Marcus Dixon was an African-American male, 17 year old a high school student with a 3.96 grade point average and a promising football career who was wrongfully convicted of molesting and having sex with a 15 year old white girl in Georgia in 2003.

He had a full football scholarship to Vanderbilt University but lost it when he was tried, convicted and sentenced to 10 years in prison.

He was found not to have raped the girl as the sex was later to be found as consensual, however due to her age he was found guilty of aggravated child molestation which carried a mandatory minimum of 10 years imprisonment.

After assistance from his lawyer David Balser who was a commercial litigator from a large firm but donated his services after hearing about the case, as well as civil rights groups and a lot of media attention, the Georgia Supreme Court overturned the conviction and he was released from prison in May 2004. Many of the jurors who found him guilty said they would not have convicted him had they known that the charge carried a 10 year sentence for consensual sex between a 15 year old and a 17 year old. However his record still shows a misdemeanor statutory rape charge.

As fate should have it, he went on to college at Hampton University, graduated in and played professional football until he retired in 2015.[62] [63] [64]

So young men, what does this story tell you???...Yep... that's right... leave 'em alone!

DID YOU KNOW ABOUT??? Which Race is Going to Prison the Most

FACT SHEET: TRENDS IN U.S. CORRECTIONS

RACIAL DISPARITIES

More than 60% of the people in prison today are people of color. Black men are six times as likely to be incarcerated as white men and Hispanic men are 2.7 times as likely. For black men in their thirties, about 1 in every 12 is in prison or jail on any given day.

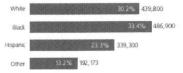

People in State and Federal Prisons, by Race and Ethnicity, 2016

Source: Carson, E.A. (2018). Prisoners in 2016. Washington, DC: Bureau of Justice Statistics.

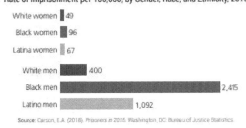

Rate of Imprisonment per 100,000, by Gender, Race, and Ethnicity, 2016

Source: Carson, E.A. (2018). Prisoners in 2016. Washington, DC: Bureau of Justice Statistics.

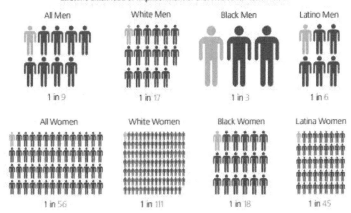

Lifetime Likelihood of Imprisonment of U.S. Residents Born in 2001

Source: Bonczar, T. (2003). Prevalence of Imprisonment in the U.S. Population, 1974-2001. Washington, DC: Bureau of Justice Statistics.

The Sentencing Project · 1705 DeSales Street NW, 8th Floor · Washington, D.C. 20036 · sentencingproject.org

Imperial Imprint LLC received permission to use the above 'Racial Disparities' infographic from the Sentencing Project. www.sentencingproject.org [65]

Also Check out: https://www.facebook.com/groups/blackmendown.missinginaction/

DID YOU KNOW ABOUT??? Black Men & the Police

We would be remiss if we did not acknowledge the issue with police brutality/killings of African American males. This has been an ongoing issue since before slavery. During reconstruction, blacks were stopped for vagrancy and put into prisons for years. There have been lynching, the burning down of cities, "Black Wall Street", the criminalizing of civil rights leaders such as Rosa Parks, Martin Luther King Jr, Malcolm X and the list goes on and on.

Due to the cellphone/mobile phone and having the ability to record videos, people being unjustly taunted by law enforcement are being seen. Many people think this is new, but we are just seeing it more because of technology.

We as a country need the police and the police need us, the people and communities. It is the 5% of rogue police officers that have tarnished the image of the other 95% of the police who are good men and women.

We must work together to get things right. As young men, especially those of color, you must be mindful that even though times are better, racism still exists. Utilize the skills and the AMERICAN privilege that you have to ensure you don't become a victim. Chances are you will be a victim, but it is important to have the tools (education, knowledge and good relationships with people who are community leaders, such as religious institution leaders, your school administration/teachers, politicians, head of your sports or community center, and the police for example) and skills to be able to combat the ignorance of racism and police brutality. Always be respectful, even if you are being disrespected at the time.

A new bill just came out in 2016 called Blue Lives Matter Hate Crime bill which basically states that assaulting a police officer is a hate crime, similar to that of a particular minority group, such as Asians, homosexuals, or a specific religious group. As per AOL.com news, Colorado Rep. Ken Buck has proposed the Blue Lives Matter Act of 2016 in the House of Representatives.[66] As per an article in the Salon.com it says, "In short, these laws make it even easier to prosecute someone for allegedly harming a police officer if there was no actual assault, and by creating a narrative that the police are the ones under attack."[67] This means that even if you hit their police car, you are desecrating/breaking the property, similarly to attacking a religious relic at a church/mosque/Jewish temple, and you will get charged with a hate crime…yes for police equipment.

Not too long after the bill passed in Louisiana on August 1, 2016, the bill was initially applied very loosely. In Louisiana in September, a drunken man cursed out the police who were arresting him for disorderly conduct of being drunk and banging on windows and overall disruptive. Aside from disorderly conduct he was being charged with a hate crime for cursing at the police officers under the Blue Lives Matter Crime act and was facing an additional 5 years in prison and a $5,000 fine. The New Orleans Police Department dropped the charges, after many groups were alarmed by the fact that he would be charged with a felony for this.[68]

So given that you are a young person of color, if you do anything, like resist arrest, you can be charged with a hate crime for putting your hands up to protect yourself as an officer grabs you. If you scratch the officer by mistake, you have assaulted the officer. And who do you think they will believe you or the officer?

This is real, and even though we have made strides in the racism and classism in this country (yes, whites discriminate against other whites) you must always be mindful.

DID YOU KNOW??? That the Police DO care about you and want to help?

At the age of 17, my youngest son decided he wanted to grow dreads [rope like strands of hair formed by matting or braiding of the hair, a popular hairstyle among professional African American athletes] I can recall telling him "Son, be careful of the attention you are about to attract". Although, I'm pro-choice, I felt compelled to warn my son about the perception, predispositions and stereotypical labels that are attached to the dread hairstyle, and how those influences sometime obscure an individual's behaviors and reactions, particularly the police.

Unfortunately, a percentage of black males who commit criminal offenses have dreads or similar type hairstyles. These same black males between the ages of 17-30 years of age are often captured by our local media outlets being apprehended by local law enforcement, resulting in the negative stigma associated with black males who have the dread hairstyle.

As a law enforcement officer and a father of 2 boys, I try my best to keep it real with my sons, I must admit, I can be a little abrasive or direct as my youngest son sometimes say, but as a father, I rather be accused of being too direct then not taking the time to explain to my boys the realities of being a young black man in America. The truth of the matter is, we have made some strides over the years, and black men have a few more opportunities than before, however, the playing field is still not level, we still have a lot of work ahead of us.

I tell my boys it's important to really get to know the individuals you associate with, that includes male and female associates. Although my boys are young adults now, I often remind them the importance of screening your friends; who you allow to ride in your car, driving in the wee hours of the morning, and more importantly the places you hang out.

Black males increase their chances of being pulled over by a police officer if you are travelling with multiple occupants in your car, more so if you are all black males, the hour in which you are travelling, the neighborhood, or any type of visible mechanical defect on your car. (i.e. inoperable or broken tail lamp etc.) Faulty mechanical equipment will give the officer legal grounds to initiate a traffic stop.

Black males who want to avoid negative interaction with the police, arrest, prosecution and incarceration, should strive to make every effort to succeed by completing high school and maintaining a GPA and test scores that will afford them more opportunities to continue their education. Additionally, participating in productive after school activities such as sports, part time employment, and/or faith based organizations would keep them busy and away from the negative influences. During my tenure as a road patrol officer, I witnessed black males driving without a valid or no drivers' license, thus resulting in the issuance of criminal citations that require court appearances and the subsequent introduction into the criminal justice system that leads to compounding issues such as bench warrant arrests for non-appearance, failure to pay traffic fines arrests, and monumental court costs and late penalties making it difficult to afford to pay, which ultimately result in reoccurring traffic arrests and the inability to seek gainful employment and a greater risk of criminal activity and arrests.

In my 20 plus years as a police officer, I can honestly say, most police officers have very good intentions to do the right thing, unfortunately, there are a small minority of officers that abuse their authority, exercise poor judgement, do not use their discretion appropriately, and aren't empathetic at all. Some argue this could be related to their individual culture, biases, ignorance, training, and supervision and leadership. I argue that it is a combination of the aforementioned, as a law enforcement executive, I hold my supervision accountable for the actions or inactions of their subordinates, the supervisors are responsible for the development of their officers and ensuring they are doing the right thing at all times.

Stop and Frisk is very effective if applied appropriately and not used as a form of harassment or intimidation. It pains me to say, there are officers who have used the stop and frisk law inappropriately. I can recall as a young supervisor scrutinizing the arrest form of a select few of officers' I suspected that may have embellished the facts in the case. My supervisory style was not the most popular with some however, I demanded everyone be treated with dignity and respect. Blacks and Latinos often feel they are targeted and believe there is a disparity in number of stop and frisks encounters with police. Data will probably suggest or confirm there is an overwhelming number of stop and frisk encounters with Blacks and Latinos. Could the disparity be related to the number of subsequent arrests and convictions? Is it related to officers patrolling in impoverished neighborhood often riddled with crime and drug related offenses? There is probably a direct correlation between stop and frisk encounters and the areas in which they occur.

Giving the tensions with police and the black community and the lack of trust with the community and police across our nation, I encourage all black men including my sons, to comply with the officers' instructions. Considering the recent edited captions of police encounters with black males, some of which the males seem to be complying with the directions from the officers, I would encourage all black men who are pulled over by a police officer to minimize the confrontation with the officer, if you have tinted windows on your car, roll all the windows down so as the officer approach, s/he will have a clear view of the interior of the vehicle, turn your radio off, shut the ignition off, place your hands on the steering wheel, the officer will approach and more than likely ask you for your drivers' license, vehicle registration and proof of insurance. If the documents are in your glove compartment, tell the officer, and wait for the officer's instructions. If you have multiple passengers, in your car, tell them to remain quiet and not escalate the situation, more than likely, you are probably being pulled over for a minor traffic infraction which usually requires an issuance of a ticket.

If you feel the officer has mistreated you, remain quiet, try and capture the officer's name from his uniform, vehicle number and the location of the traffic stop. Remember this information will be valuable if you wish to pursue a formal complaint against the officer. Refrain from words or phrases such as 'I know my rights', or 'you only stop me because I'm black'... the less confrontational you are the less likelihood things will escalate further.

Please note, due to the recent and fatal attacks on police officers around the country, officers now have a well-founded fear not just against black males, but with people in general. However, it is incumbent and more so of black men to make every effort to avoid being confrontational and follow the officers instructions. As most law enforcement begin implementing body cameras, which I think works both ways, meaning it protects the officer from frivolous complaints and it also protects the citizen regardless of race against police misconduct, we will begin to mend those severed relationship with the police and our communities.

-This message was written especially for you, young man, by a Miami-Dade County Municipal Police Executive

DID YOU KNOW??? About Convict Lease

"The Convict Lease System and Lynch Law are twin infamies which flourish hand in hand in many of the United States. They are the two great outgrowths and results of the class legislation under which our people suffer to-day."[69] This quote was written in 1893.

Convict Leasing was the outsourcing of prisoner (penal) labor to private person, companies and corporations by the prisons in exchange for money. It was used in the South during and after slavery, however it peaked in the 1880's. The prison would lease out prisoners to private companies, such as plantation owners or corporations such as US Steel and the Tennessee Coal and Iron Company. The person/corporation was responsible for food, clothes and shelter of the leased out prisoner.

Louisiana was the first state to start this practice in 1844, with North Carolina being the last to end this practice in 1933, however it continued anyway "until it was abolished by President Franklin D. Roosevelt in the Francis Biddle's "Circular 3591" of December 12, 1941."[70]

The Southern states were greatly dependent upon this prisoner labor in an attempt to increase state revenue lost because of slavery ending. In Alabama, the convict leasing revenues for the state was 10%, in 1883 it shot up to 73% by 1898.[71]

As slavery ended in 1865, the previous slave owners and the southern corporations had a financial loss since they no longer had their free labor (slaves), which of course had saved them thousands of dollars given that otherwise they would have had to pay for the labor as one paid for employees in the North.

With Convict Leasing the prison populations grew tremendously:

In Georgia the prisoner populations increased tenfold 1868–1908; in North Carolina it increased from 121 in 1870 to 1,302 in 1890; in Florida from 125 in 1881 to 1,071 in 1904; in Mississippi the population quadrupled between 1871 and 1879; in Alabama it went from 374 in 1869 to 1,878 in 1903; and to 2,453 in 1919.[72]

The underlying issue with this practice was that the convict labor was predominately black. The increases in prisoners were due to the increases in criminalizing blacks. Upon the ending of slavery came the 'Black Codes' which criminalized previously legal activities. Blacks were put into prison for vagrancy, being out of the house past newly set curfews (meant for blacks only) and standing or walking around in the "wrong"/white part of town. (Sound familiar? – Trayvon Martin?) And of course criminalizing those black who attempted to vote by imprisoning them or by lynching. The rationale for the criminalization of blacks was as per Ida B. Wells article in *The Reason*

Why The Colored American is not in the World's Columbian Exposition, states, "The Negro was first charged with attempting to rule white people, and hundreds were murdered on that pretended supposition. He is now charged with assaulting or attempting to assault white women. This charge, as false as it is foul, robs us of the sympathy of the world and is blasting the race's good name."[73] Hence justifying the need to criminalize black people in the south to put them in prison so they can make them slaves again or... just lynch them to show other blacks a lesson.

Many of the authors in this book such as Kimjaro Presley, Torrance McCray, Kevin Whitfield and Heru all mention the prison system using the 13th Amendmentas the legal justification to have prisoners work for little to no compensation. So basically what these men are saying is that they (prisoners/inmates) can be considered slaves of the state/prison. Furthermore this clause in the 13th Amendment also opened the door for mass criminalization,[74] hence mass incarceration for that time.

The 13th Amendment abolished slavery and involuntary servitude, *however* 'According to the 13th Amendment, "Neither slavery nor involuntary servitude, **except as punishment for crime whereof the party shall have been duly convicted,** shall exist within the United States, nor any place subject to their jurisdiction."'[75] Hence slavery could be used as punishment for a crime.

Okay, so one may argue, "So what? These guys are going to prison for breaking laws. They just should not have broken the laws, even if most were petty crimes that would not have given a white person in the south a prison sentence. They should have been more responsible." The response to that is "Fine, but what type of prison sentences were they receiving for their crimes, and what type of 'punishment' did they receive?"

These "criminals" received long prison sentences. In addition the brutality of the convict leasing system was more than cruel and unusual punishment, it sometimes resulted in death; for example in Alabama. "In 1873, for example, 25 percent of all black leased convicts died"[76] Some were made to work in coal mines under deplorable conditions and an example of what happened if they did not do enough work? Correspondence to the Washington D.C. Evening Star dated Sept. 27, 1892, has testimony from a prison officer at the Coal Creek prison in Tennessee who said, "Men who failed to perform their task of mining from two to four tons of coal per day were fastened to planks by the feet, then bent over a barrel and fastened by the hands on the other side, stripped and beaten with a strap. Out of the fifty convicts worked in the mines from one to eight were whipped per day in this manner."[77] In addition one woman who went to prison in Mississippi for fighting was given a 6 month sentence, which extended to 18 months because of the "costs". She gave birth twice during her time in prison but lost one due to "premature confinement, caused by being tied up by the thumbs for failure to do a full day's work."[78] (The other question would be how did she get pregnant again?)

Other cruel practices that were used during this period were Peonage/ "Peonage, also called debt slavery or debt servitude, is a system where an employer compels a worker to pay off a debt with work."[79] (Similar to Pay Day loans or getting stopped by the police and issued a ticket that you cannot afford to pay, or court fees, or when one has to pay "supervision charges" when on Probation and/or Parole) And of course the "Chain Gang" which kept prisoners chained together via leg iron shackles on both legs. And the list goes on and on.

One of the main reasons for the end of the Convict Lease practice was due to the negative press received when a Martin Tabert, a 22 year old white man from North Dakota was arrested and charged with vagrancy in Florida. His parents sent the $25 dollars for the fine and $25 to return home, however the money "got lost" in the prison system and he had to remain in prison. He was leased out to Putnam Lumber Company, where he did backbreaking work and was down to 125 pounds, when the other inmates testified that he was "strong and sturdy" upon arrival. Thomas Walter Higginbotham, the whipping boss flogged him to death with a "Black Aunty" a 7 ½ pound 5 feet by four inch leather strap used for whipping people during the time when the prisoners were in line being counted, Tabert received over 30 lashes and after the beating could not get up because he "was too weak to stand. This angered Higginbotham further and he said, 'haven't you had enough?' and began to whip him again"[80] with his foot on Tabert's neck. "Several prisoners reported that when they got Tabert in the sleeping shack and removed his clothes his "skin was all off his back in one chunk from his shoulders to his knees.""[81]

Coverage of Tabert's killing by the '*New York World*' newspaper earned the Pulitzer Prize for Public Service in 1924. Because of the publicity the incident received through the media, churches, community groups and activists, there became more awareness throughout the country about this brutal practice of Convict lease. In addition, they found Sheriff Jones, the police officer who arrested Tabert, to be '"little more than a slave catcher" who earned $20 a head picking up "unfortunate men" on trivial law violations and sending them to Putnam.'[82]

Ultimately Higginbotham was tried and convicted of murder, however he got a new trial in the Dixie County where he committed the crime but was never retried. The information for the case seemed to have disappeared.[83][84]

Through this bit of knowledge we are sharing with you, do you see the similarities of what is transpiring today? Privatized prisons (for profit), working for little to no pay and when working as a prisoner 35% goes back to "the system". Prison industries which can be helpful to the prisoner is still not being paid as their "free" counterparts with no benefits, pensions, days off, etc., hence cheap labor and a form of "outsourcing" of the job-seeking American citizen. Pay day loans, unaffordable Title loans with a balloon payment, fines, tickets and court fees that one cannot afford. Criminalizing behavior such as "San Francisco, along with eight other counties in California, is implementing gang injunctions—curfews, anti-loitering, and anti-association laws that function very similar to Black Codes for black, Latino, and Asian youth—using the pretext of gang prevention to track young men into the prison system to become prison labor, while preparing the community for redevelopment and gentrification." [85] And of course public lynchings, "I can't breathe!" Eric Garner's dying words, when he was killed by police using an illegal chokehold for selling illegal loosey cigarettes.

So know your history *and* the history of others.

Knowledge is power…Use it!

(This "Did You Know???" was written by Dawn Simmons)

To further your knowledge we at Imperial Imprint ask you to please read the below mind blowing articles to see the origins of Criminal Justice after the Emancipation Proclamation (slavery) to get a greater knowledge and understanding of how the law worked for those of color and lesser classes. (These are quick reads, but very thought provoking)

http://digital.library.upenn.edu/women/wells/exposition/exposition.html#note (THE REASON WHY The Colored American is not in the World's Columbian Exposition. This is a newsletter by Ida B. Wells, 1893, but is still relevant today.)

http://www.reimaginerpe.org/20years/browne (Rooted in Slavery: Prison Labor Exploitation)

https://en.wikipedia.org/wiki/Convict_lease (Convict lease, From Wikipedia, the free encyclopedia)

http://www.thewhitehouseboysonline.com/ARTICLE-MARTIN-TABERT-COLLIER.html (Martin Tabert, Florida's Past Vol 3 by Gene M. Burnett)
http://www.alternet.org/story/151732/21st-century_slaves%3A_how_corporations_exploit_prison_labor (21st-Century Slaves: How Corporations Exploit Prison Labor) in Alternet.org by Rania Khalek

DID YOU KNOW ABOUT??? Peonage/in the 21st Century

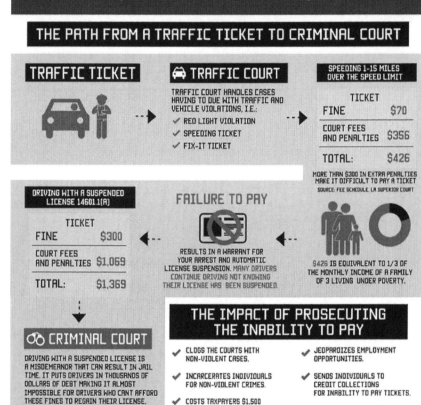

The above infographic was created by Community Coalition http://cocosouthla.org/inforgraphics/ .
The organization generously provided Imperial Imprint LLC permission to use this infographic for this
book.[86]

DID YOU KNOW ABOUT??? No Public Defenders for Louisiana in 2016 by Jayda Pickett & Dawn Simmons

Louisiana's public defender system is leaving many people incarcerated with no bail. Due to insufficient funds and decreased capacity, this is becoming a crisis. Inmates are facing violent and dangerous conditions in the overcrowded facilities, as well as being on a wait list for legal representation. The Louisiana public defender pay system "relies on court fees, collected mainly from traffic tickets, to fund the majority of local public defender budgets."[87] '"The way we're funded is unstable and unreliable and inadequate," said Jay Dixon, state public defender at the LPDB. "That will always be the problem."'[88]

With these insufficient funds, many attorneys and staff from the public defenders offices were laid off. This resulted in a waiting list across the state for many inmates. Most inmates are still waiting many months and even years to even obtain legal representation. Many attorneys also refused to do felony cases. Since those accused did not have representation, civil rights attorneys have been filing lawsuits on facilities that held inmates who had no access to an attorney. In New Orleans alone, the office's budget has declined over four years from around $9 million to $6.2 million in 2015, which is about a third of the local district attorney's budget. This results in cutting public defender jobs, investigators and administrative staff, hiring freezes and not having the resources to properly investigate the facts to support/defend the client.

The state's funds are not enough to pay the representation staff as well as rehire new ones. The waiting lists are getting larger and larger as the years go by. Poor communities and inmates are barely surviving inside jail and outside trying to make ends meet. All they can do is wait for the state to give them financial support. The inmates have to try and make it through each dangerous and depressing day behind bars fighting a hopeless battle. Innocent people could be behind bars and wouldn't be free for years due to the wait list.

In November 2015, Joseph Allen was accused of being the gunman for attempted murder where 17 people were wounded. Had he depended on the Louisiana public defenders he would still be in jail awaiting trial or would have taken a plea deal. Instead he was able to afford a paid attorney, who presented footage showing Mr. Allen at the mall with his family in Houston, Texas the day of the shooting. As a result, his charges were dismissed after spending about one week in jail.[89]

Currently lawyers throughout Louisiana are upset themselves with the way the system is working. They are being ordered to take on cases pro-bono (no fee) for criminal convictions. Most of them are not criminal lawyers and have no idea how to practice criminal law. They are real estate, corporate, divorce, tax, etc. attorneys who have NOTHING to do with the criminal justice system. They are being given a 3 hour class to tell them the do's and don'ts of being a criminal defense lawyer. These lawyers with no criminal law experience except for the one or two classes they may have had to take in Law School are being responsible for helping poor people from getting many years to LIFE in prison. How effective can these lawyers really be?

In a Times Picayune – New Orleans newspaper article Richard Lamb a tax attorney makes the analogy for unprepared lawyers to defend people convicted of criminal offenses. ""It's like asking a dentist to do heart surgery, "Lambs says""[90]

(FYI, Jayda Pickett is a 10th grade student who did the research and assisted with this essay for the book. Her dad, Lance Pickett, who completed the interview/ letter later in the book re: Coming Home, is the proud father of this Valedictorian student)

https://www.motherjones.com/crime-justice/2018/04/a-louisiana-bill-would-give-public-defenders-more-funding-public-defenders-arent-happy/

https://www.cbsnews.com/news/inside-new-orleans-public-defenders-decision-to-refuse-felony-cases/

2018 UPDATE

The situation has gotten a little better since 2016. The ACLU filed a lawsuit against New Orleans Public Defenders office and the state board however it was thrown out. Currently they are trying to appeal.

As of August 24, 2018 Judge Todd Hernandez of the 19th Judicial District from Baton Rogue granted class action status to a lawsuit where all those who were affected by the lack of public defenders in Louisiana when they were accused and arrested of a crime, with the exception of juveniles and people accused of murder. Basically the lawsuit is for the state to fix the problem, and not necessarily for those affected to get money.[91]

As noted before, the public defenders system and public defenders in Louisiana receive their pay from the from court fees from convictions and traffic tickets, unlike the district attorney's office who receives money from local and state money..

DID YOU KNOW??? Let's See Who Is Profiting Off Of Your Crime & Imprisonment(s)

(The infographics below are Courtesy of 'In the Public Interest' - https://www.inthepublicinterest.org/programs-not-profits/) [92] [93]

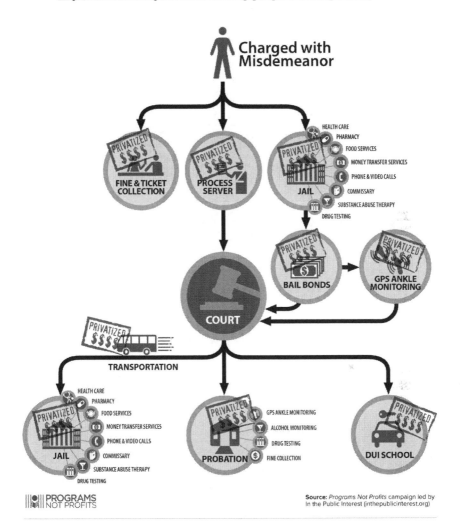

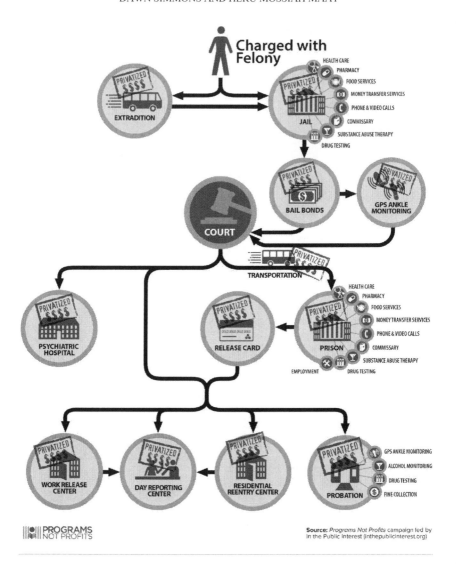

Please use the link below and see who these privatized vendors are at:

https://www.inthepublicinterest.org/wp-content/uploads/In-the-Public-Interest-Programs-Not-Profits-Felony-Path.pdf

DID YOU KNOW??? What Is Civil Asset Forfeiture?

(This information is provided Courtesy of FindLaw.com)[94]
Tim and his husband Blake were traveling to Houston in order to purchase a used car they found online. Since it was an all-cash deal, they were carrying $27,000 in twenty-dollar bills in a shopping bag. But as they got closer to the meeting place, they were stopped by the police for speeding. The officer, noticing a stack of twenties protruding from the bag, asked the men what they were up to. Not believing their story and suggesting they were actually making a drug transaction, he pressured them into handing over the cash. The officer informed the driver that they were heading to a "known drug spot" and didn't believe their story.

Neither of the men were arrested or charged with a crime, but now they're $27,000 short and not sure if they'll ever see their hard-earned money again. Can the police do this? Believe it or not, they can.

Although highly controversial, civil asset forfeiture laws allow the police to take (and keep) large sums of cash or property *suspected* of either being used to commit crimes or obtained through criminal means (e.g. goods purchased with "dirty" money). Civil asset forfeiture laws differ by jurisdiction, but generally don't require proof of the property owner's guilt (although some state laws do require a conviction).

Civil Asset Forfeiture: The Basics

Unlike criminal asset forfeiture -- a less-common action in which property used or derived from a crime is forfeited only after a conviction for that crime -- civil asset forfeiture does not require a conviction or even criminal charges. The majority of such forfeitures are related to suspected illicit drug or organized crime activities. Technically, it involves a lawsuit by the government against the property itself -- or, in legal terms, in rem. As strange as it may seem, the inanimate property (whether it's a yacht or a bag of cash) is the defendant in such a proceeding.

It depends on the jurisdiction, but typically the police (the plaintiffs in such a proceeding) are only required to show that there is a preponderance of the evidence suggesting the seized property was involved in wrongdoing. This is a much lower standard of proof than what is required for a criminal conviction (beyond a reasonable doubt), which is why property is so often seized from individuals who are not convicted of (nor charged with) a crime. Even if the owner of the property is tried for a crime related to the seized property, there's no guarantee they'll get their property back upon acquittal.

227

The seized property is usually sold at auction, with a majority of the proceeds (as well as any seized cash) going straight into the police department's coffers. State laws differ in this regard, although some states allow 100 percent of the seized property to be used for law enforcement and others earmark the proceeds for education or other purposes.

Federal Civil Asset Forfeiture Law at a Glance

The Federal Bureau of Investigation (FBI), Drug Enforcement Agency (DEA), and other federal agencies use civil asset forfeiture laws when investigating crimes. The legal authority for these actions is found in Title 18, § 981 of the U.S. Code and has been upheld by the U.S. Supreme Court.

Under federal law, the government must send written notice to "interested parties" (i.e. property owners) within 60 days of the seizure, although deadline extensions are often granted by courts. If a claimant (typically the property owner) sends a claim to the agency seizing the property, the government has 90 days in which to either file a formal civil complaint ("in rem") against the seized property or obtain a criminal indictment for a criminal forfeiture. Failing either of those actions, the government is required to release the property.

Since the action is against the property, the owner (or "interested party") generally has no right to counsel in these proceedings. One exception is if the seized property is the owner's primary residence.

Asset Forfeiture and Equitable Sharing

In July 2017, Attorney General Jeff Sessions announced plans to revive the Equitable Sharing Program, allowing greater collaboration between federal agencies and state and local police. The program allows federal agencies to take control of the assets seized through such federal/local collaborations and then return 80 percent of those funds back to the state agency (typically a state or local police department). This controversial program effectively allows local agencies to get around state laws that often limit the percentage of seized assets they're allowed to keep.

For example, Indiana state law prohibits law enforcement agencies from using any forfeiture proceeds. But under this program, Indiana police could simply enlist the help of a federal agency, have them seize the property, and then recover 80 percent of the proceeds to use within their police department.

State Civil Asset Forfeiture Laws

State laws regarding civil asset forfeiture differ quite a bit from one another and also are subject to frequent changes. Two of the defining characteristics of these laws are the burden of proof required for seizure and how the proceeds are used. For instance, Texas police must show a preponderance of the evidence for a seizure and may keep up to 70 percent of the proceeds for their department. See Civil Asset Forfeiture Laws by State to learn more.

Concerned About Civil Asset Forfeiture? Get a Free Case Review

Having something of value taken away from you by the police can be infuriating, especially if you haven't been charged with a crime. If you believe your property was unjustly taken from you, you may have some legal options for getting it back. Get informed and protect your rights with a free case evaluation by a local criminal law attorney.

(The above "Did You Know???" article was created by Thomson Reuters and is located on the FindLaw.com webpage. *https://criminal.findlaw.com/criminal-rights/what-is-civil-asset-forfeiture.html.* The organization generously provided Imperial Imprint LLC permission to use this information for this book.)

If interested in knowing what the laws are by state, please see "Asset Forfeiture Laws by State" https://criminal.findlaw.com/criminal-rights/asset-forfeiture-laws-by-state.html which is also part of the FindLaw.com website.[95]

Did You Know??? About Kalief Browder – An INNOCENT Teenager In Solitary ConfinementFor 3 Years While Awaiting Trial - By Jayda Pickett and Dawn Simmons

Kalief Browner was a 16 year old African American who was arrested at age 16 for stealing a backpack. He was imprisoned on Rikers Island jail in New York City. Because his family could not afford the bail, he had to remain in jail, which lasted for 3 years. For 400 of those days he was in solitary confinement. He had a very hard time there and attempted to commit suicide many times. He also had been beaten at times by the Correctional Officers. Off the record, some say that he may have had claustrophobia which exacerbated his condition when being in solitary, as the jail does not have an inmate's medical records and cannot initially determine if there is anything wrong, unless the inmate tells them. Nevertheless, he was only 16 years old.

In addition, he maintained his innocence because he did not want to become another statistic or go to prison for a crime he did not commit. He mentions this during his interview in Ava DuVernay's Documentary "13th"

After 3 years, and having to attend 31 court appearances where in most cases the prosecution was not prepared and asked for continuances, he was released from jail, all charges dropped as they found he was NOT guilty. He tried to resume him life and enrolled at Bronx Community College looking toward obtaining his degree, but because of the horrors of jail and solitary confinement that he endured over those three years, he could not go on and committed suicide in 2015.

His death created a reverberation throughout New York City. The New York City Council has proposed to provide bail reform for those who could not afford it for petty crimes, and President Obama weighed in with putting into motion creating laws to stop children (minors) from being placed into Solitary Confinement

On October 16, 2016 the New York Daily News provided the story, "Mom dies of 'broken heart' after son Kalief Browder killed himself last year."[96]

DID YOU KNOW ABOUT??? The Angola 3 – Decades of Solitary Confinement

Have you ever heard of the Angola 3?
Albert Woodfox, 43 years and 10 months, Herman Wallace, 41 years, Robert Wilkerson, 29 years. These are not their ages; these numbers represent the number of years they spent in solitary confinement, i.e. Lock Up.

Albert Woodfox and Herman Wallace were accused of killing a prison guard, Brent Miller age 23, during a prison riot at Louisiana State Penitentiary, in Angola, Louisiana in 1972. They were members of the Black Panther Party, but it later came to light they most likely did *not* kill him. Even the widow of the deceased, Leontine Rogers is uncertain if they killed her husband and was not pleased given the way the case was handled coupled with the racism that existed throughout the trials.[97] Albert Woodfox was in solitary confinement from 1972 to February 19, 2016, 43 years and 10 months (released on his 69th birthday) and Herman Wallace was released in 2013 due to liver cancer after being in solitary confinement for 41 years; however he died a few days after he was released.

The last of the Angola 3, Robert King Wilkerson, was in solitary conferment from 1973 to 2001, 29 years, due to a reason not related to the Miller death; however he too was a member of the Black Panther Party. He was freed in 2001 because his conviction was overturned. He has since traveled the world and performs speaking engagements telling of his experiences of prison and solitary confinement.

On October 1, 2013, Wallace was released from prison by U.S. District Chief Judge Brian A. Jackson of Baton Rouge, Louisiana. The state wanted to keep Wallace in prison (even though he was very ill and dying of liver cancer) and in turn appealed the judge's orders. As a result, "Jackson later Tuesday repeated his demand that Wallace be freed immediately, saying the state has failed to show Wallace would be a flight risk or public danger if released. He threatened them with a contempt judgment."[98]

Wallace died on October 4 a free man. One day after the state appealed to retry him again for the murder.

****

Albert Woodfox was the last one was released on February 19, 2016; the state had to issue a court order because the previous state attorney Buddy Caldwell fought to keep him in prison. Mr. Woodfox's convictions were overturned for the murder twice, however each time thereafter the state would re-indict him. Advocates, both state officials and otherwise found that he could not get a fair trial because of the racism that still existed in the Louisiana Parrish that he was being tried in and because most of the witnesses were already dead. (As the event happened 42 years ago) Finally in 2016, he made a plea of no contest (nolo contendere) to charges of manslaughter and aggravated burglary and was given his freedom.

Part of the reasons that these men were held in Solitary Confinement was because of their involvement with the Black Panther Party. As per an article in Nola.com, the then Warden Burl Cain stated: that Woodfox needed to be in a closed cellblock. He felt it in his heart. He claimed he was dangerous and posed a threat to the general population and to the public. [99] (Closed-cell restriction ("CCR")) And the Nola article also mentioned ACLU lawyers asked Cain if there was a possibility that Woodfox did not kill Miller, which was 'official' the reason that Woodfox was in Lock up—and Cain responded that Woodfox would still belong in CCR. Cain stated, "I still know that he is still trying to practice Black Pantherism, and I still would not want him walking around my prison because he would organize the young new inmates. I would have me all kind of problems, more than I could stand, and I would have the blacks chasing after them.""[100]

The fact that these men were in Solitary Confinement for decades created global recognition of this practice as cruel and unusual punishment. It took Amnesty International, the United States press and various human rights watch groups to create awareness of this situation and advocate/help these men get out of Lock Up. Even with global awareness, the state of Louisiana and the warden still tried to block their release for years.

Please note, the prison advised that they were not in 'Solitary Confinement/Lock Up', they were on a closed cell restriction (no different circumstances than Solitary) which they reviewed the circumstances of their "crime" every 90 days, and still found that they were not suitable for general population.

Unfortunately we at Imperial Imprint did not reach out to the men while they were in solitary, but we must recognize that these are men who were in Solitary Confinement/the hole/Lock Up for decades.

DID YOU KNOW ABOUT?? The Central Park 5 – Years of prison for a coerced rape confession

On April 19, 1989, five male teenagers were out in Central Park. They were being rambunctious but not in the way that they were later seen to be. At the same time, a 28 year old white woman, Trisha Meili, an investment banker was jogging and brutally raped and beaten. She was beaten so badly that she could not remember the encounter.[101] [102]

The teenagers, who were Black and Latino minors were picked up by NYPD (New York Police Department) and were questioned by police. The children did not have lawyers or their parents present. Through rigorous grilling by the police they confessed to committing the crime of brutally raping and beating this woman. In the Amsterdam News Yusef Salaam states, "I and four other teens (ages 14, 15 and 16) were innocent, but four of us gave false confessions just so that we could "go home" as police promised."[103]

Through this incident they were known as the Central Park 5; Raymond Santana, Yusef Salaam, Kevin Richardson, Kharey Wise and Antron McCray.[104] Five teenagers known for the new 1989 term: "wilding" running in "wolf packs" (insinuating they were like animals) and committing heinous crimes. They were seen as pariahs in New York and throughout the world. The current Mayor of New York City at the time said it was "the crime of the century"[105] They later maintained their innocence but no one would believe them.

These young men maintained their innocence. They even had a hard time making parole because of it. Years later, Matias Reyes confessed to the crime only to find out that he was an exact DNA match and was actually the person who did this heinous act.[106] In 2002, the boys, who were now men, were released and exonerated of this crime, but only after years of a horrible prison life (which you know is true from the letters and Factoids in this book.) The longest prison sentence served was 13 years by Kharey Wise because he was the oldest.

Once released from prison they filed a lawsuit. Certain top ranking officials of New York City did not want to compensate them for their trauma and years of their productive life lost. A movie "The Central Park 5" in April 2013 was made to show how these young men were mistreated and injustices.[107] Not to mention how it further fueled racial tensions within the city, during this crack era. In 2014, Mayor de Blasio along with other New York officials agreed to settle the lawsuit with them for $40 million, approximately one million dollars for each year that they spent in prison collectively. Even though the money was given to these men, now in their 40's, many people, former politicians and businessmen still spoke out on how they did not deserve this money. [108] [109]

DID YOU KNOW ABOUT?? Acquitted Conduct

Have you ever heard of this? This is can be more harmful than any charge that you have been convicted of.

"Acquitted Conduct" is another fact "they" do not tell you about. Brett Kavanaugh the Supreme Justice confirmed in October 2018 was directly affected by this as a juror, while as a juror in a trial for Gregory "Boy-Boy" Bell. From a federal investigation, Bell was said to be part of a criminal conspiracy with a crew called the "Congress Park Crew." Bell was acquitted of all his charges with the exception of one that should only have carried a five year sentence. However when the judge sentenced him, the judge took into consideration the charges he was acquitted of (as if he had been convicted of them) and used that as a basis to prolong his sentence to a full 16 years and 2 months.

Brett Kavanaugh was a juror on this case and was disturbed by this. In 2015, Kavanaugh wrote about Bell case saying, "Allowing judges to rely on acquitted or uncharged conduct to impose higher sentences than they otherwise would impose seems a dubious infringement of the rights to due process and a jury trial."[110]

In fact three of Bell's co-defendants had their sentences TRIPLED due to this. The sentences were tripled based on allegations only, none, of which the co-defendants were found guilty of. The accused leader, Antwuan Ball of the "Congress Park Crew" was acquitted of all of his charges (leading a drug conspiracy, selling drugs and a murder) with the exception of a $600 drug deal.[111] Because of Ball's background, prosecutors believed he should still be sent to prison for 40 years and/or given the death penalty, and by applying acquitted conduct it resulted in the judge sentencing him to 225 months[112] i.e. 18 years, a draconian sentence, even though the jury's verdict reflected that the additional charges could not be proven hence they did not convict.

So does that mean if the prosecutor and the judge does not like you, law enforcement/the prosecution can trump up charges, and even if you are acquitted of the charges, you can still get a long sentence anyway? Yes...

It is a hope that when Justice Kavanaugh is on the US Supreme Court, he will help to have "acquitted conduct" cases heard and hopefully overturned as a basis to prolong defendant's sentences. In 2014, only Justices Ruth Bader Ginsberg, Clarence Thomas and Antonin Scalia were open to hearing these types of cases.

(The full articles can be found on the Marshall Project website, https://www.themarshallproject.org/2018/07/23/punished-for-crimes-not-proven and https://www.washingtontimes.com/news/2008/jun/29/a-600-drug-deal-40-years-in-prison/)

REFLECTIONS ON WHAT YOU HAVE READ SO FAR....

What are your thoughts as you have read through this book? Do think that it is boring? Do you think that these men are just providing scare tactics and advice that make you hear "Wonk, wonk, wonk, wonk!?!" Or are visualizing the hell that these men go through on a daily basis? Some of them will be living like this for 10, 20 or 45 years and some forever and ever.

Do you think that prison is the life for you?

We just want to add one point. For those of you who saw the movie "Car Wash" and you remember Brother Abdullah (fka Duane) played by the infamous Bill Duke and the older black man Lonnie, played by a movie icon Ivan Dixon, when Brother Abdullah was going to make his last move and Lonnie challenged him. This is what this book is about. It is about "generational responsibility and guidance" as Bill Duke referred to it on the TV show 'Unsung Hollywood'. Many of you young men may not have that older person looking out for you and providing you with good legal guidance for a good life, but take it from these ex/prisoners men, who have YOUR best interest at heart...Listen, learn and see that life _outside_ of prison is not all bad. You are not living like these fellows in this book...so there is light.......

My friend Steve-O Lawyer said to me, "My worse day out here is better than my best day in there..." _Think about it!_

Please take a moment to reflect on your thoughts....

Feel free to share your thought on our Facebook page,
https://www.facebook.com/Letters2oursons/

OR

To our email address at info@imperial-imprint.com

OR with your family, friends and whomever you want to share them with.

FAMILY SHOULD HAVE ALWAYS BEEN PUT FIRST
(Part 2)

FAMILY SHOULD HAVE ALWAYS BEEN PUT FIRST (Part 2)
Table of Contents

There is a strong woman named Erica Fielder who decided that Criminal Justice reform needs to take place. After a discussion with her husband, Mr. Lewis Fielder Jr, (who is currently incarcerated for 24 years and has to do 85% in other words, 20.4 years of his sentence with NO Good time) and with guidance from prayer, she and her husband created "Hearts for Inmates".

They have mobilized many people in the state of South Carolina to get involved and attempted to get a bill passed by the state to reduce the mandatory time for 'Truth in Sentencing' from 85% to 65% for all crimes, as well as allowing prisoners to receive good time work credits. This gives the prisoner incentive to be on best behaviour, helps to provide a safer environment for both the prisoners and staff, and it especially gives HOPE to those young people who come into prison who have 60 year sentences. Imagine a 17 year old who has a 60 year sentence… Coming home at 56 years old if this bill passes, whereas they will not come home until they are 68 years old if it does not pass. When one is incarcerated for over 50 years, they will receive at least one disciplinary for something trivial or major, hence losing good time…(not able to work to receive it back) so most people do MORE THAN 85% of their sentence. And please note…not all people who have "violent" charges actually committed a "violent" act. (Such as our co-author Heru)

HEARTS FOR INMATES FOUNDERS

LEWIS FIELDER JR - FAMILY SHOULD HAVE ALWAYS BEEN PUT FIRST

My name is Lewis Fielder Jr and I am incarcerated on a 24 year sentence for man slaughter. I have been in prison for almost 10 years. When I think about the fact that I have been in prison all this time away from my wife and children it's enough to make any man wish he had done things differently. Prison saved my life and allowed me to become a man that I never thought I would become. I say that because when I was young I thought I had life all figured out. I thought the streets loved me, my homies would have my back, and that I could have any woman I wanted. It took prison for me to find my true self. The things that I ran from I now could no longer run from. It took me to come here to have the time to find Christ and to get right. I honestly, can say that I have thought about things that I never would have even had time to think about before. When was out I ran the streets nonstop, I did what I wanted to do and didn't think about no one but myself. My mom tried to tell me to slow down, pick my friends and surrounding but I let it go in one ear and out the other.

I say of all of that to say this prison is hard even the strongest and toughest men are tried and tested.

You can believe that almost every day your man hood will be tested by everyone from the other inmates to the COs. You have to learn quick to how to walk away, think, and humble yourself.

In here all you have is time to reflect on your whole life often wishing that you could relive and rewrite the wrongs you now see. Emotionally, physically, mentally, and financially prison will drain you. Every day you have to make a personal decision to not give up and not allow the time to get to you.

As a man it's natural for you to want to provide for your family and take care of your wife and children but the reality is you aren't in a position to do so. Hearing in their voice how they need you and you aren't in the position to do so make you feel even less than a man for putting yourself in the position to be away from them and then you add the constant stress of trying not to lose focus because you are being treated like an animal, treated nothing more than an inmate by staff and knowing that they don't see a man when they look at you they see an inmate is enough to break man's self-esteem. I am grateful to have a wife in my life and can remind me to stay focused and beside me as some days may feel longer than others.

I hear how they talk about the younger generation. How tough, hard headed and quick to pull the trigger and my first response is don't come to prison. I can promise you that this is not the life you want. All your freedom is stripped from you. Every second lived here you will be told when to eat, sleep shower, where to walk and you have to ask for permission to do what you should be able to do. For those who think you are ruff and never shed a tear I can promise you that this prison life will put those tears in your eyes. The same people who sat in the court room, you may never see them again. You can say goodbye to what you thought were loyal friends and family members. The few people, if a few, that will stand beside you will become prisoners too. They also begin to feel the pressures of incarceration as they spend money to help you fight your case, on food and on collect phone calls.

I know that I am one of the blessed ones because through this process I have gained a wife who stands beside me 100%, gained my GED and the opportunity to have my eyes opened to see what I could not see before. I now stand as a man and no longer play those childish games saying I am a man but actions showing differently. Young men live!! Don't give your life away for a split moment decision that could and would hunt you for the rest of your life. Forget being hood or street cause in the end it will either lead you to prison or to a grave. Every day, I am missing out on being a husband to my wife and a father to my children. I wouldn't wish prison on anyone. Prison is not the place and please don't let TV or movies persuade you that it's cool. Prison is a dark place and you are constantly reminded that you are not free. Prison life will do either one or two things. It will either make you better or bitter. I pray that these words encourage you and you think twice before coming here. You can't say that you weren't warned.

Lewis Fielder Jr.

FEEDBACK FROM THOSE INCARCERATED – VIEWS (HEARTS FOR INMATES)

I have received letters from so many people expressing that since "Hearts for Inmates" they now have hope and that their prayers have been answered. Something that I say almost daily is, "I will go even if I have to go alone." I know that we are being heard and have a constant reminder that it was something higher and greater than myself that lead us on this journey because even one year later the things in which I was told that needed to be changed is being done. I know that change will come and that families will be united.

There isn't a day of my life that I am not looking for a miracle or to get a phone call saying that this has come to an end... My desire is that somehow my words penetrate not only the legislator minds but their hearts and the family members as well. Nothing can enter a closed heart or closed mind. When the heart and mind is open, love can enter and leave freely. I am convinced that love can conquer and overpower all things even what most would say is impossible. The harsh truth that most don't want to admit is it's time for change here in South Carolina.

It's time to do what needs to be done and that is retroactive sentencing reform, re-establish the good time and work credits, increase our parole release rate, offer second look policy for those who have served at least 15 years, provide job training and skills for those incarcerated. Prison is not enough now nor has it ever been. We need policies and legislation to reflect such. Empirical data shows that people age out of crime, that crimes are situational and drug and or alcohol was involved at the time of the incident.

Here in the U.S we have a 95% plea rate indicating that people are waiving their constitutional right to go to trial not always because they are guilty but in most cases because they lack the financial support to pay for an attorney, family support or have either a public defender or attorney who advised them to take a pleas. There are ways that we can ensure public safety, save taxpayers money while creating fairer sentencing structures. South Carolina is the leader in sentencing reform however most of what the committee recommended has not been done. The Omnibus Bill of 2010 has offered some relief yet there are so many deserving and desiring of retroactive legislation that would create the opportunity to give those desiring and deserving of a second chance. States such as Oklahoma have already re-established the good time and behavior credits, Mississippi has reduced their mandatory minimums from 85% to 50% for violent offenders and 25% for nonviolent. Crime rates continue to decrease while the amount of incarceration continues to increase.

Over the years most prisons have moved away from rehabilitation and now have become the house of punishment. 95% of those incarcerated will come back into society at some point therefore we all have a duty of ensuring that they have something to come back to. Re-establishing such incentives and alternatives that

243

we are advocating for not only will encourage those incarcerated but it also can make prison safer for all involved.

In conclusion, I am optimistic that changes will take place and that disconnect between the judicial, legislative, correctional institutions, and families will no longer exist and that people who are not directly impacted by incarceration learn the harsh realities of incarceration and its effect on those incarcerated and the families.

Heart For Inmates wants to be the bridge in helping ensuring that those who are incarcerated receive every tool necessary to help them become productive during and after their incarceration.

A Note from Dawn & Heru: "Cindy Quattlebaum, whose son Barry is serving an 85-percent sentence for a DUI that resulted in death, told lawmakers, "According to Barry, the 85 percent is interpreted within the prison culture as license to misbehave. Mr. Jon Ozmint, past director of the Department of Corrections, wisely said, 'If you take away all hope from men they act like men with no hope.'"[113]

Background

Hearts For Inmates Corporation was founded on May 15, 2015

MOTTO: "WE WONT STOP, WE WON'T QUIT, WE NEED THESE LAWS TO BE FIXED"

MISSION: HEARTS FOR INMATES mission is to help, encourage, aspire, redeem, trust and provide support both short and long term for those incarcerated. By advocating for changes within South Carolina legislation and policy changes within The Department of Corrections and South Carolina Department of Pardon Probation and Parole. We will work with other agencies and organizations that support and actively offer rehabilitation services that include drug and alcohol treatment, mental health treatment, counseling, transitional housing assistance, parenting courses, educational programs, financial education, job placement and training. One of our goals is to ensure that the individual receives all the necessary help available to ensure success during and after incarceration.

Held multiple rallies at the South Carolina State Capitol

SERVICES PROVIDED: Mentor programs "Inside Out" Speaking engagements, Referrals to appropriate agencies, Community Advancement Programs& Faith based programs that all work towards being a part of the solution to counteract the effects that incarceration has on those incarcerated and the families.

ACCOMPLISHMENTS

- **Spearhead House Bill 5120 (HB5120), now H5155, Sentencing Reform**
- Host on Various Radio Stations throughout State speaking on incarceration (107.3 Big DM, Frank Knapp, Myrtle Beach)
- Featured on New Stations WIS, WACH, FOX 21
- Front Page Greenville News
- Featured twice Sentencing Project Washington DC
- Guest Speaker – DJJ and McCormick Prison, Speaking Down Barriers, Love Thy Neighbor Rally, New Deliverance Worship Center
- Community Homeless drive/ Veterans
- Member of Upstate Re-entry Coalition
- Collected more than 10,000 signatures on petition
- Met with host of legislators and Community leaders
- Met with Director of South Carolina Department of Corrections (SCDC)
- Held Advocacy Training Course 101
- Held events throughout state for family support and education
- http://www.greenvilleonline.com/story/news/2016/05/07/laurens-woman-starts-inmate-advocacy-group-seeks-reform/83866246/
- **For more information on the shocking facts of Mass incarceration, see heartsforinmates.org -> Resource Center**

ERICA FIELDER - FAMILY SHOULD ALWAYS FIGHT FOR THEIR FAMILY MEMBERS (PRISONERS)

My name is Erica Fielder and I am the proud wife of Lewis Fielder Jr. who happens to be an incarcerated man. This is the one title that I honor before all others because I am a wife who believes that all things are possible and that this prison sentence has not taken away from who we are but have allowed God to bring ashes to beauty.

I am the Founder of a non-profit organization called Hearts for Inmates. Hearts for Inmates acronym is Helping, Encouraging, Aspiring, Redeeming, Trusting and Supporting. I am often asked how Hearts for Inmates came about and I tell them that Hearts For Inmates was birthed by having a spouse incarcerated and after going to an institution year after year it's impossible to go in and not come out thinking, feeling, and willing to become better.

For years I would hear the families week after week complaining about how unjust the system was, the cost of the items, the treatment of their loved ones, and how their loved one had been convicted harshly, taken a plea or misrepresented yet so few did anything beyond complain. I would often ask why aren't they calling someone and talking to the people who make those changes? I often found myself asking questions as to what they were doing about the issues they were speaking on, who did they call, and I received the same answer every time. "I don't want to cause any problems for him." I literally would stand there in disbelief that people would be a prisoner to fear and that they would rather talk about all the issues they were having but not willing to advocate or at least go to the policy makers and legislators with their legitimate concerns.

One day I began to speak in depth on how things were and the realities that there are too many people speaking on what is wrong with the system and too few doing anything to bring a solution to any of the problems. I literally felt like I was speaking Spanish among people who clearly could speak English but for some reason they acted as if they didn't understand what was being said. That day enough had become enough.

I was sick of hearing about issues, sick of the same people saying the same thing, sick and tired of going into a place that everyone seems to conform to yet no one had brought any of those issues to those who could make changes. In my mind I couldn't understand how people would not at least bring these issues to the attention of those in position to make changes. How would they know that there were problems or other alternatives if no one raised the issue?

I can remember the day my husband and I were talking and I was telling him about everything and how it was a little upsetting to hear the same thing every week. After visiting my husband on Saturday we spoke in depth and the decision was made as to what was needed. The night after visiting I heard GOD speak to me that he could hear the cries of the people. He spoke to me that I had to go and tell them to let his people go, that he could hear the cries of those being inflicted. I know for some this may seem odd or strange but this is what I heard and I couldn't rest all night because I kept hearing these words. I asked go tell who, where do I go, how, and he then spoke to me that he would lead me and direct me on where to go. I literally felt that I was being pulled and that I had to go.

I had no clue on where to go, or who to call and despite of everything I didn't know for some reason the one thing I did know was that I had to go and I was going. (One year four months later I am still going and will continue to go)

I am often asked how do I find the strength to keep going and I tell them what I see when I look across the room when I visit my husband. I see desperation in their eyes in some, I see some are too their breaking point, some have lost hope, and I have seen some standing on a ledge prepared to jump. . .

I ask myself how it is possible that people can go visit someone and see the same look of hopelessness, desperation, despair and not extend more than a hand to help them? How is it possible to go into a prison even as a visitor and your life is not changed? I can say without thinking twice that my life (our lives) are forever changed because of incarceration. I am what I never thought I would be yet I am what I knew I had the capability of being and that someone who is unafraid of standing up and being a part of the solution to bring and reconnect families back together. This journey has not been an easy task, I have met people who have given me their word that they would be there every step of the way and to be honest I have never heard from or seen most of those people again. I sometimes often ask myself how is that people can throw "free my homie" parties and yet do absolutely nothing to help them become free. Can someone tell me what is the purpose? How much money is being sent to the homie to wife or children?

> Most of the time people only ask about those who are incarcerated because they see a family member so they at least can use the excuse that they asked about them so when they later get out they can say" I asked about you"

> My stomach turns at the thought that people can commit to getting up 4 or 5 am to attend and pay for fish fry at a prison, club all night and day, spend money or whatever or whomever but lack the same passion for standing at a rally, signing a petition, donating $5.00, calling their legislators, or even ensuring that their person is aware that someone is fighting for them.   It is mind blowing the things that people will be loyal to.

> Some days that I am hurt not because of the lack of support but I think about how it must feel for those who are enduring the pain from those families

who are not visiting, sending letters, money or standing up to help support changes that would allow them the opportunity to come home. Families need to be reconnected, men back home to be a husband, father, son, and contributing to the lives of society. Women who are incarcerated need to come home and be a wife, mother, daughter and likewise be able to contribute back to society. There isn't a day that goes by that I don't need my husband, there isn't a day that goes by that I am not reminded that his presence is missing. I don't understand how people can live their lives and not remember there is a part of them missing.

How to Contact Hearts for Inmates

Website: www.heartsforinmates.org

Email: heartsforinmates@gmail.com

Telephone Number: 864-547-0675

Address: P.O Box 1901, Laurens, South Carolina 29360

We are a recognized with state as non-profit and charity. Working on donations to become 501(c)3 with the IRS.

PLEASE SUPPORT with financial donations, no matter how small…showing up for a rally or helping Mrs. Fielder spread the word…

SHAWN HALBACK - MESSAGE TO BROTHER - DON'T FOLLOW THE CROWD

Name: Deon
Time: 7:15am
Date: 12/12/13

What it do little bro? It's me your big brother Shawn bustin' your way. Bro I know that it's been a while since I dropped a few lines on you. Well lil bro, I know that you are almost grown and that you are playing them streets heavy now. So it's my duty as a big bro to drop a few jewels on you to at least keep you from going down the same road that lead me into the slammer.

Deon, I have mad love for you and I don't want to see you taking the same road I took. All them so call friends you have is really not your friends. As soon as the law gets involved and find out about some of them crimes that y'all doing, your so called homies start snitching, signing statements, and everything else they can do to free themselves. Lil bro, I'm just giving it to you raw, look at me, I'm your real homie, real brother, and real friend, so you know that my words are true.

Don't waste your time and freedom behind a careless mistake, because once these white folks have you in their trap it's hard to get out of the system. That's when you become victim to this penitentiary crap! So keep your guard up and start doing positive things, I know that you have some of your homies who look up to you, so do what's right. And when you see some of them Black elders who need help like with their grass cut, car washed, them type of things, look out. That's how your name stays alive and ring bells by doing what's right and positive. I know what you can do to uplift and help big bro make a change! I love you no matter what, Peace lil bro....

From, big bro Shawn Halback – SCDC #283843

RICHEY L. BOYD aka SOLO – LETTER TO MY KIDS

Dear Children (Alexis, Deasia, Kemiya)-
I am writing this letter to show how much I appreciate to have y'all as my daughters. I am incarcerated at Perry Correctional Institution in Pelzer South Carolina. (Greenville County). I also want y'all to know that I miss y'all very, very much, and hope to come home soon. This is the first time that I have been away from y'all this long of a time. I know that it's hard living day to day without me being in your lives, but being my blood, and having my genes let me know that y'all will be just fine during these hard times. Life back here is no place for no one. Your freedom is one of the most important things that you can have in life. For this moment, mine has been taken away from me, but I am free in mind and spirit. The last time I talked to y'all, I promised that I will never put y'all through this type of situation again ever! I plan to keep my promise that I made to y'all. Keep up the good work in school, and always remember that Daddy's looking over your shoulder at all times.

Never give up on what you believe in. Stay focused on what matters in life and that includes Education, Health, and always think ahead for yourself. I am doing well back here in prison, but that's because I think positive at all times, y'all have to understand that sometimes in life, we make mistakes, some of the mistakes can lead you to a place like this. Some of them we can overcome because I do have a release date, and I am able to fight my case due to the fact that I went to a jury trial. Some of these guys can't say the same thing because they are _never_ coming home. So let's just say Daddy got a little bit of luck on his side.

I am very excited to be writing this letter. It brings peace to reach out to the people that you love with all your heart. Y'all are a part of me, and I am a part of y'all. We will always be as one. Alexis, Deasia, Kemiya, you are the most important women in my life, and always will be. Having you as my daughters is a blessing. Every time I show somebody a picture of y'all, they say, "Oh your girls look just like you. They have your forehead and all." I guess having a wide forehead runs in the family.

Well Daddy will be calling home soon to chit chat for a while. In the meantime, I'll be thinking about y'all, and your mother, Natasha. I love her dearly. Love is what brought y'all into this world. So that means that this family is full of love.

My time will soon be a thing of the past, and I will be free again. I really miss picking y'all up from school, and I miss y'all running up to me whenever y'all spot Daddy out of the crowd. Those are the little things that I will always remember. It's very hard to think about not being around every time when y'all are in need of me. It's very, very hard. I know that there are a lot of mothers, and fathers that are going through the same thing as us. This is what the wrong path leads us to. Thankfully, it didn't lead me to that other path of no return, as being deceased. God is within me, and God is within you all. Always believe in yourself and you will see your way through. I love you all, and I love life, keep shinning like Diamonds, and the Queens that y'all are. Daddy loves you with all his heart.

(Peace and Love)-Richey L. Boyd (Solo) #344612 -12/10/13.

CHRISTIAN COLEMAN - ADVICE TO SON

What's going on son? It's been a while since I've seen you last but got some things I want to tell you. Son, don't think for one minute that I don't love you. I just made a choice I will have to deal with. Sometimes life doesn't go as we planned and we got to accept that fact.

Son, watch who you keep as company because the company you keep sometimes determine the man you will be. Always respect those who respect you and show love to those who show it back. It's a dirty world out there and everybody is playing for keeps. Never trust a man unless he has had the opportunity to cross you because he could simply be deceiving you to get what you got.

I've matured a lot and became conscious of a lot of things pertaining to us (black men). Son, always remember that the majority of the time you will be judged because of the color of your skin. Don't be afraid of that. Embrace it because our ancestors were kings and queens. Always treat women with utmost respect, because our women have been through enough already. Also finish school and don't give up. Strive to succeed in whatever you do, so that no man alive or yet to be born can do it better. The reason why I ask you to watch the company you keep is because I don't want you to make the same mistake I made. You don't want anybody telling you when you can use the bathroom, when to eat, and tell you to stand up for count. The prison system is a lot different than the outside. It is a world of its own. Always remember don't let anyone dictate your life. Do what you feel you should do, but also be willing to accept the consequences that sometimes outweigh the rewards.

Christian Coleman # 344192   (January 7, 2014)

BRIAN POSEY - A LETTER OF REGRETS TO MY SON

May this letter find you in good health, spirits, and trusting in the Most High God. Danny, this letter will be like one that I've never written before. It is the letter that should've been written a few decades ago. Nevertheless, I've found the time, courage, and method to put together what will be a lengthy/emotional body of work for you to unpack and sort through. Please know that throughout this letter I will be experiencing feelings of guilt I've carried with me all these years. So Danny this is my letter of apology to you. Included are some things about me that you don't know that will help you understand who I am and why I've done some of the things that I've done.

When I met your mom, we both were very young. Everything that developed into our relationship was purely physical -- at least for me anyway. I could tell that as time went on she went from liking me a lot to loving me a lot. But I did not know how to give that love back to her. I was a street dude and to me street dudes did not fall in love. I'll go out on a limb, I would say that despite all, I have taken her through, she still love me today as she did 30 years ago. I share that to share this, when your mom was pregnant I was cruel, mean, and just straight vile to her. In my crazy and young mind (14 years old), I felt that if I was that way (cruel, mean and vile) towards her, she then should let me off the hook by maybe claiming that the baby was someone else's and not mine.

I didn't want a baby. I was scared out of my mind. The fear of having such a responsibility gripped me and shook me up good. It was around that time October/November 1985 that I chose a criminal path in life. Looking back on those events, I know now that I chose the criminal path in order to escape my responsibility as a father. If I am being truthful I would tell you that it wasn't until ten years ago that I learned the seriousness of fatherhood and being responsible in it. Unfortunately ten years ago I was in prison so my ability to practice what I've learned about fatherhood remains unproven. The only way to prove myself as a father and as a man to the son of mine born on July xx, 1986 is to be a friend first. Danny, I want you to know that all that I've done throughout my life that negatively impacted you and your moms life has been the behavior of a manchild/childman with a whole lot of negative adjectives in between. I can tell you that growing up without a father really cheated me out of some necessary life skills that I should have in order to pass on to you. Not that I am making excuses but an absent father leaves a young man with a void that needs to be filled.

This for me meant that I looked deeper into the streets as a way to make me whole -- to make me matter. Nonetheless, through all of the negative history of me and my life, you have stood tall against all odds. I'm glad that you are my son with my DNA but I'm glad that you didn't pick up my negative character traits.

In closing, I give that to God for blessing you and guiding you through this wicked world with the grace and moral compass of a boy-turned-man groomed by the most saintly elders. Danny, I am truly proud of how you've lived your life to this point. It's not lost on me that you have been working a job since you were twelve years old and that you have never given your mom any problems growing up. Those are qualities that have escaped most young men of your generation, and that's why I smile when I think of how much of an inspiration you are to me. So much that whenever I need to talk about an example of accomplishment and someone to look up to, in a strange but real way, I speak in the reverse of father looking up to son instead of the other way around. This is true man, and I have no problem with it because you have earned that much respect from me. Danny as you probably can tell, I cut a lot of the body of this letter out and I apologize but it is just too crazy trying to form those words. However, I look forward to sharing with you in person one day soon. Until such time, I love you, I'm proud of you, and I encourage you to continue to be the good man that you've grown to be.

Peace and Love, Your Pops, Brian Posey,
SCDC #160604 -- January 14, 2014

JOSEPH HUDGINS - TRUSTING OTHERS OVER FAMILY

Dear Sons,

My name is Joseph and I am 40 years old. My incarceration began when I was 17 years old and I have never been home since. I have been without the conveniences and blessings that you take for granted for 23 years now. I hope you will heed my words and take from me the example of what not to do!

I was arrest in 1992 for murder and given the death penalty in 1993 I was the youngest person sentenced to death in the Country (USA) at that time, but that wasn't the beginning of my mistakes. I want to tell you about the mistakes I made leading up to my incarceration.

First of all, never underestimate the importance of your family in your day-to-day life. If I would have listened to mine I wouldn't be in this predicament today. You see, I started running with a bad influence I won't give any names, I'll just call him "T." I was raised in a Christian household, was made to go to church throughout my childhood and resented it. I know now it was for my own good and I actually absorbed a lot even though I was in church against my will. When I got old enough to defy my daddy and not go to church if I didn't want to it was almost impossible to get me there. You see, I did not want the guilt that came along with listening to the preacher telling about all the things I know I was doing wrong. When me and "T" started running together I was able to get away from the strict rules imposed upon me by my father. "T"'s mom let us do whatever we wanted. She would buy us alcohol; let our girlfriends spend the night with us at her house. I was living the dream and it was intoxicating. My family told me "T" wasn't any good but I wouldn't listen. Me and "T" got in the habit of stealing things to make money and really just for the excitement of it. As my family continued to speak against him I pushed them further and further away.

We began to spend our days skipping school, going around figuring out what we were gonna steal that night or shoplifting during the day. His mom would lie to my dad for me if I needed her to cover something up for me. Things were awesome! I thought that anyway. It got to the point to where "T" Mom and her boyfriend were even telling us what to steal and her boyfriend would take us to a "fence" to sell the stolen goods. I made house payments, car payments insurance payments for them when I was only 16 & 17 years old. I felt like a big man. *The whole time I was being used.* Granted it was mutual using but as a kid I had real feelings of affection for "T" and his Mom and her boyfriend. They were to me like the family I had pushed away from and my feelings for them were genuine. I have always been a very loyal person and I would have protected them and been there for them in any possible way I could. I proved this time and time again.

One night me and "T" were in a truck we had stolen. We were using it to steal other things. Well we got pulled over by a young Sheriff's Deputy and in the process of him getting us into his police car "T" shot him with a 25 automatic that we usually kept in the dash of his truck for shooting dogs if they got in the way of our stealing. That night we ran on foot we were less than a mile from my house and that is where we ran. "T" called his mom's boyfriend to come pick him up. It was 3 days before we were caught and arrested and we spent almost every moment of those 3 days together. "T" was 18 years old and I was 17 years old. During those 3 days I came up with a plan. I was young and dumb! I did not know anything about the law and was determined to save my friend "T" that I thought of as a brother. I had genuine love and affection for him. I knew that you could get the death penalty for murder but I didn't think the state could give it to me since I was under 18. I thought I would be tried in juvenile court. That being said, I told "T" that if we got caught I would tell them I was the one who pulled the trigger. That way I could keep him safe from the death penalty and I naively thought they could only lock me up until I turned 21 years old and they would have to let me go. The plan was "T" would keep his mouth shut and I would take the rap. I figured that yeah, he would get some time as an accessory or something and we would both do a little time and we would get out and our bond would be stronger than ever.

He didn't have the same loyalty to me that I had for him. As soon as we were arrested he told the police that I was the one who shot the Police Officer, cut a deal for himself since he agreed to testify against me and got himself a deal for 30 years in prison. To make a long story short, he testified against me and helped me to get the death penalty and he got 30 years of which he served a little over 16 years and he went home to his family and I am still languishing in prison after 23 years with a natural LIFE sentence. He has never once even tried to check on me and see how I am doing. I spent over 7 years on death row and was blessed to have my conviction overturned and I was granted a new trial. In order for the State to withdraw their intent to seek the death penalty again I had to agree to plead guilty, accept a LIFE sentence, waive my right to appeal, file a post –conviction relief application, writ of Habeas Corpus of file to the Supreme Court, plus waive my right to be considered for parole or pardon, in essence turning a LIFE sentence with parole eligibility into a LIFE without parole sentence. I agreed to this to keep myself from the death penalty and spare mine and the victims' family having to go through another lengthy and painful trial process. Through all these years, the same family that I ignored and pushed away has been the ones who have been there to love and support me. Granted, I have had a couple of friends that still have love and support for me but only in the form of letters. My family has been my foundation for the last 23 years. They come and visit every week. Not a day goes by that they don't accept a collect call from me from the prison, and they always send me what money they can to my prison canteen account so I can go buy my food and supplies from the institution canteen. They are always there with a word of encouragement. Without this network of love and support I never could have made it through all this. After I was arrested my foundation in the church all came rushing back to me and I turned to God! He is always there for us in our times of need even if we haven't always served Him to the best of our ability. Even if we have turned our backs on Him, He will never turn his back on us! My family greatly encouraged my spiritual growth and I know God gave His son Jesus to die for me so that my sins could be forgiven.

I was fortunate to get off death row. Many people I knew, whom I grew to love and care about were not so fortunate. I experienced the State executing many friends that through the years I had grown to love and care about. I got to know them and their families and loved ones. One pattern always came to the fore front. The ones who were getting visits, making phone calls and that were able to go to the canteen are the ones who had awesome family support like mine. I know I am in a horrible place and often surrounded by violent, angry people but I am still a blessed individual because I have an amazing, wonderful family and an awesome, loving God that I have a personal relationship with!

Through the years I have worked hard to better myself, learn something, and become a better person to help others. I have gotten my GED taken continuing education classes, basic computer class, culinary arts class, art class, and gotten a degree as a paralegal through Blackstone Career Institute. (Which my family paid for.) I have served on the Inmate Representative Committee as a representative. As Treasurer, and as Co-Chairman. I worked in the prison law library and library from 2002-2015 with a good work history. I helped with operation behind bars for a short time trying to get my story to troubled kids to help them not make the same mistakes I made. I am now active in the Second Chance Program as a mentor at McCormick C.I. and regularly attend classes. I am blessed that the US Supreme Court made a ruling that anyone under the age of 19 years old when their crime took place cannot be given Life without Parole if that was the only sentence available so I should soon be going back to court for a re-sentencing, hopefully to receive a reduced sentence. I pray about it often!

The point I have tried to make throughout this correspondence is the importance of family and a spiritual foundation. You may think that the friends you are running with will be there for you and that they all have your best interest at heart, but I am living proof that you cannot count on that. If you are running around with someone who you know is leading you down the wrong paths, please push back from them; get closer to your family and your faith! These fair weather friends cannot be relied upon. Use your own intellect and judgment. Analyze your situation from every angle and make the best decision for yourself. Do you think I was ever considering spending 23 years of my life in prison when all I was doing was stealing? My story just illustrates for you how fast things can get out of hand and there will be no turning back. So many times in my life have I said to myself, "If only I could go back and do things differently?" Don't be asking yourself these questions years down the road. Please learn from my experience so you won't have to! I see so many of our youth coming to prison. One of the men in my Second Chance Class told me he is 21 years old. I told him "I have been locked up longer than you have been alive." For that matter I have been locked up longer than I was a free man who could make his own choices. I had 17 years of freedom with an amazing family and never appreciated the blessing I had! Now, I have had 23 years of incarceration and not one day goes by that I don't appreciate them and lament all that I have lost! What I wouldn't give just to be able to hold my little grandniece and grandnephews, to go out to eat with the family, to lay in my own bed without having to share a cell with another man, to go to a restaurant and order a meal or just spend an evening watching T.V. with the family. I have not been able to have a wife or kids. Many small things you take for granted should be cherished! Please take a long look at your life and how you are living it. Examine all the influences on your life and do away with the negative and increase the positive. Learn all you can! Your mind and wits may be all that keeps you safe and moving in a positive direction. Please, I beg you to take my letter to heart and don't make the same mistakes I have made! I will be praying for you and pulling for you.

-My Hopes and Prayers are with you always,

Joseph Hudgins

FACTOID – Destruction Of Family Bonding & Relationships With Those On The Outside

"Responsibilities as husbands and fathers are key factors that tame young men's wildness and encourage them to settle down: One longitudinal study found that marriage may reduce reoffending by 35 percent."[114] ('The Truth about Mass Incarceration', www.nationalreview.com)

Destruction of family bonding and relationships with those on the outside can be caused by being incarcerated. Unlike being on the streets when a prisoner is told something by a family member or friend like "I am sending you money" or "I am writing you a letter" or "I am coming to visit" or any other promise, he looks forward to that family member or friend to do what they promised. But a lot of times the person in society does not realize this, nor do they realize that the prisoner does not have anything else to look forward to. So when the promise is not kept or broken, it causes friction, and the repeated broken promises leads to separation and ultimately destruction of the relationship.

Imagine standing in line day after day waiting for your name to be called during mail time, but it never is. Or getting dressed waiting for a visit and that person never shows up? It is embarrassing and creates heated emotions. I hear it all the time when I go to the phone room. "You just say fuck me hunh?"…or "I don't understand why you shittin' on me." Or "Just tell me you don't give a damn about me!"

A lot of times the person used to procrastinate when the prisoner was on the street, but it did not matter then. Family members and friends think that the prisoner will be all right if they put off tomorrow to write, not be there to take the prisoners call or late to send him whatever else. They feel like "Where is he going? Nowhere…" or "It doesn't matter of he gets it now or later." And that is the problem…it does matter. Now the son is arguing with their mother or father, husband arguing with his wife, brother with siblings or friend.

On the reverse side, the prisoner forgets that their friend or family member is still living in the busy world doing things that tire them out and cause them to forget. But the prisoner does not care because to him, that family member or friend is free, while he is restrained. That letter, visit, money or whatever is all they have and how they cope with doing time. I have witnessed prisoners cursing their loved one and friends telling them to go to hell, killing any further communication. I have witnessed prisoners getting letters or talking over the phone having the person tell them that they are not having anything more to do with the prisoner anymore because he does not appreciate them.

Then you have relationships that were on shaky ground when the prisoner came to prison because when the prisoner was on the street they did not treat the person (on the outside) well. Now the person one the outside is shitting on the prisoner now.

Prison, it destroys families and friendships like a wife or a girlfriend being caught in your bed having sex. And sometimes letters are lost by officers, visitors are turned away for bullshit reasons but the prisoner can go off so badly before it is discovered that it was not their family's or friend's fault, that the damage is done to the point where it cannot be repaired. Some of the closest knit families and tightest friendships have been destroyed due to the separation of incarceration...sometimes the prisoner's main man or brother and the prisoner's wife are together so much helping the prisoner that they wind up getting into a relationship because of the stress and working together taking care of the prisoners needs.

For the most part if you have a woman who loves you and you receive an extended bid (sentence) over five years, you may as well prepare yourself for the Jody moment. I know you are asking "what is a Jody moment?" That is when you call home and another dude answers the phone or when you say I love you to your lady and she does not return the favor or calls you by another dude's name. Or when you are calling and she does not pick up the phone as much as she used to. The most hurtful case is when she straight up puts a block on the phone.

Prison places a strain on all relationships from family to friends. The reason being is that you become a burden to most. Having to ask for money or wanting them to take time to write you or come and visit you. Then when they come they have to leave you there which is hurtful for everyone. In some prisons they want to search your loves ones before they come in. In some cases the visitors are subjected to demeaning strip searches and they have not even committed a crime. This gets old to most people. All calls from the penitentiary are collect and this too places a financial strain on your loved ones; especially those living on a fixed income.

And now some prisons/jails are using video call through Securus[115] that cost as much as $15 for 15 minutes. You can no longer visit your loved one through the glass (which is free) and have a contact visit. This in itself is a way of keeping loved ones apart not to mention bilking families out of money to visit their loved one. In addition, sometimes the videocam is not properly working or it is not focusing on your loved one, but once your time is up, that is it!

I know dudes who call their people back to back to back when they first arrive in prison. Then when they call and hear the automated voice saying

"Sorry the number you have reached is blocked." They walk around looking sad in the face.

I have also seen dudes get on the phone have the audacity to curse their loved one out whether it be their mother, sister, woman or child. This is the craziest thing I have ever seen. Then when those same people stop coming to see them or they put a block on their phone, the dude gets mad and slams the phone down, while the rest of the prisoners around think "You are a straight idiot!"

My advice to you is if you are in the streets committing crime, NEVER burn your bridges with your loved ones. Break bread with them every chance you get and always tell them how much you love them and appreciate them. If you don't, when you get back here, those will be the same people you have to lean on for moral and financial support.

There are cases when you trust your "girl" or "homies" who were in the streets with you that had questionable character and when you leave the money with them and you find that all of your money is gone, especially if you have a long bid/sentence. And let's not forget, the people that you should have been looking out for that truly love you such as the people who have shown true sacrifice for you, such as family members, long-time friends, your lady/partner and your children are the ones that will stick by you. Be good to them, cause your "good time friends" ain't going to be around if your sentence is long.

From Blindside Diaries: October 5
1:38pm.

I was called for a visit. My mother, brother and one of my sisters came. It is so good to be able to see your family and hold them. Before I was incarcerated, I had a pretty good relationship with my family. We are very close knit. But now it's even more intense with everything we've been through in the past 20 years. I'm so thankful for them, they have kept me sane. No girlfriend has stuck by me since I've been incarcerated which has kind of worked in my favor because I've been able to easily shut my emotions down and focus on rebuilding myself. Not saying I don't want a woman, because I do. But in this situation you want or need less stress as possible. You don't have time to be worried about whether she's cheating or not. Look, she is a woman in the flesh with fleshly needs. What do you think she is doing? Why haven't she wrote? Why haven't she sent that money? And why won't she answer the phone? These are questions that will drive you absolutely insane. Snapping at everyone for nothing, have you chasing a high, any high trying to suppress the pain.

A CULMINATION OF LETTERS FROM FAMILY - LIVING ON THE OUTSIDE WHILE YOU ARE ON THE INSIDE

It is really hard to have a loved one in prison. You may think that just because you are the one in prison that you are having a hard time, but the one(s) that love you, like me, are going through it with you.

So you may be hungry because the food is horrible and in portions that would only feed a child. They have stopped commissary so you cannot get extra food to supplement your meager diet, for some B.S. reason, or because they said you did something wrong and gave you a ticket. How do you think I feel on the outside being helpless not to be able to give you something to eat when I know that you are ravenous and having terrible hunger pangs?

Or what about when some dudes are trying to exhort you or just giving you beef because they don't like you, you are from a different gang or different part of the state/country? How do you think I feel knowing that your life is in danger and there is nothing I can do about it? I feel powerless scared and can't even concentrate.

How do you think I feel when I know that you are locked down for days because the prison is short of staff or some idiot in your cell block wants to stab up people every time you all are allowed out of your cells? You are doing the right thing but the other prisoners are not, because after all you are in prison with criminals who just don't care? I suffer waiting for your call or your letters that do not come because the prison staff denies you to make calls or even go to the mailroom to send letters since there is a lock down. I am anxiously waiting on pins and needles for a call or a letter that does not come.

How do you think I feel when you want me to be there emotionally for you, send you letters, visit you, and send money, when you did not give me the time of day or was stingy with your time when you had your freedom? Or what about when you treated me badly and still treat me badly by talking to other women, maybe not because you want them, but because you are lonely and need any kind of attention? Why should I be faithful to you as a friend, lover or loved one when you were not totally there for me?

What about when I come to visit you and deal with the demeaning way SOME of the correction officers treat me. Strip searches because I have my period and want to see my bloody sanitary napkin, or just because they are plain evil, sadistic and know they have the power to treat and talk to me and you ANYWAY they please and there is nothing we can do about it?

What about those female officers that may be attracted to you and make it a point to stop me from being with you. Are disrespectful to me and I know for a fact you are having some type of emotional and possibly physical relationship with them maybe because you WANT to or out of survival?

Another thing I have learned is the phrase "jail talk" which is when you promised that you would do the right things the last time you were in jail/prison and got a slap on the wrist or a short bid. But then you come home to do the same criminal activity or don't try to go to school or work against the odds the legal way, like you never even went to prison, and now… you are back in prison AGAIN with an even longer bid…or never coming home!

How about the fact that you are in prison and now the money has run out? I have to take care of the kids by myself; I am struggling with money and still have to send you some. Then you want to talk to the kids about doing the right thing when you are sitting up in prison for doing the wrong thing? How do you think it makes me and the kids feel? Why should we respect you, even though we try to show you respect? And then what's worse is that you may even accuse me of being unfaithful when the million dollar question is would you have been faithful to me if I were in prison?

And lastly, how do you think I feel having to ride out this prison sentence with you? Dealing with the ups and downs of the pain and trauma you go though and yet I am powerless to do anything. Yes, I can write letters to the warden and the administration, but who is to say that they will not retaliate against me or you now or at a later date?

In the end, yes we can blame it on the prison and the correctional officers for making OUR life miserable, but in the end, we must tell ourselves the truth and it is YOU the prisoner, who has messed up and put yourself in this nightmare of prison. The reality is that YOU have taken me and a piece of my soul in there with you.

****

Visiting loved ones in prison

Having a loved one in prison is one the hardest things to deal with next to them being dead. I can only see you after being screened by the prison system. Sometimes visitors are approved sometimes they are not. I know some cases where wives are not approved to see their husband and the husband has a 30+ year sentence. How can you maintain a relationship that way? Traveling short or far distances to see your loved one is sooo mentally and emotionally draining. I have seen visitors get turned away from a visit because they had the wrong clothes on, or the prisoners dorm is on lock down so they are not having visiting hours for them that day, and that may be after you have driven 2 hours to see them. The worst thing I saw was when a grandmother, a white lady in her late 70's with difficulty walking, drove 2 hours to see her grandson. She had forgotten her id in her car and went back to retrieve it. There were no signs saying you cannot go back to your car. When she did finally get to the front to be processed they told her she could not visit that day because she had gone back to the car. It was so painful seeing that elderly woman crying as she had to drive back 2 hours without seeing her grandson.

Aside from being turned away, even though many of the correctional officers try to make it a pleasant experience for the family visiting, it is still hard. You see some of them talk to your loved one any kind of way and there is nothing that you or he can do. If you say something you risk being kicked out and taken off their visiting list. And if they say something about the disrespectful treatment, they can get a ticket and go to the hole AND lose privileges such as visits or even the ability to have commissary/food.

I went to visit once and my loved one wanted to give me an extra hug. The female CO on duty was so mean and nasty she yelled at him and told him to stay away from me or she will take away his visits...over a hug (I was in line to be processed out with 8 people ahead of me) After the visitors were processed out, she thought we had left and started screaming, yelling and cursing at him. He talked back to defend himself, but then stopped. She then started threatening him and telling him just wait until she sees him on the yard. It was not until the Lieutenant came in and asked what was she yelling for? She told him and the lieutenant asked, "Well what's the big deal if he wanted to give her another hug? His loved one travelled far to see him and she comes every few months." This is the kind of demeaning and petty treatment that you and your loved one can be subjected to.

But at the end of the day, having visits is *NOT* a right it is a *PRIVILEGE*. So it is so very hard to go on visits not 100% sure you will see your loved one. However as mentioned, most of the Correctional Officers and Administration do try to make the visit pleasant for the family during the visit. So that time you spend does make up for all of the despair you feel outside of those few hours.

ONE APPLE CAN SPOIL THE BUNCH

Sons, daughters and those who read this letter, I would be remiss if I did not mention one topic. There are people in prison who prey upon those who are sympathetic to the incarcerated. They meet men/women on chat lines or pen-pals and PRETEND to love you. They use their terrible plight of being in prison to get the woman (in this case) to send money, do favors for them (both legal and illegal). They have you visit them, buy expensive vendor food while on visit and sometimes have you do or buy things for their friends and family. All the while you are giving up your time, worrying about their circumstances, waiting for their calls, doing the time with them emotionally, and living in the prison of your home because you feel as if you are a prisoner yourself since you have decided to be faithful to this person. However, the prisoner may have two or more other women feeling and doing the same thing you are doing.

These people, who prey upon the goodness of your heart, are confidence tricksters aka con artists. They do not love you. They use you and will toss you to the side once you have nothing more to give them, such as your time, money, visits, doing favors, etc. They have a masterful way with words that make you believe you are the only one and they make you feel so good about yourself. They will talk to you for hours on end if possible, run up your phone bill or have you pay for their contraband cellphone and maybe even tattoo your name on their body and have you do the same. They may even PRAY with you, tell you that they will marry you, send you cards and letters and tell your kids that they love them and will be a good dad to them.

Why?

- Because they are lonely
- They do not have anyone to support them emotionally and especially financially.
- They have learned how to use and manipulate people as their only way of survival. (See Letter by LA Bernsten)
- Most of all because of Selfishness and GREED for money, support, companionship, ego, etc.

Part of reason is also due to learned behavior from the inhumane conditions in which they live inside the prison walls, but mostly it is because it is *their character.*

Most prisoners DO NOT do this. They cherish their loved one, make their love public and their queen known, but for those who don't there is always *one apple that can spoil the bunch.*

Written by: A Woman ~~Scorned~~ Enlightened

266

MAN 2 MAN

KOBE CARTER aka ½ - HELL ON EARTH

D ear Son,
I'm writing you this letter because I love you so much and I don't want you to make the same mistakes I did growing up. Son, I want you to know that I love you and I will always be here for you to lean on. I've been gone away from you since you were four years old and now you're 16. I've missed 12 years of your life by being locked up behind bars because of some bad choices I've made in my life. Son, I don't want you to think that you have to grow up all perfect and be trouble free, I just want you to make better choices in life and try to strive to do the right things in life.

I realize that there are two heavens and two hells. You have the real heaven, where God and the angels live, and you have hell where the devil lives. On earth you have heaven and hell also. Heaven on earth is freedom, living life in the real world, with your family and friends who love you and care about you. You have hell on earth, and that's where I am at, in prison, and being in prison is not the place you want to be. Son, there is so much I can tell you about the bad things that go on in prison, but it will take a whole book to tell you. There is one word that can describe this place and that is "HELL."

I don't want you back here in hell or in hell with the devil. That's why I'm asking you to please think about the choices and actions you make in life. I know you are going to have your ups and downs, just pray and keep moving forward in a positive way and everything will fall in place for you. I'm doing O.K. back here behind the walls. You are my motivation to strive to do better and stay focused.

I'm helping and teaching young brothers that are in jail with me how to make better decisions in life and letting them know that it's more to life besides drugs, robbing, stealing and other bad things that can land them in jail. My goal is to become a better man and father so I can make it out this place to enjoy heaven on earth with you.

I thank God every day for blessing me with a loving and caring son like you who understands that your daddy loves you.

Your father,
Kobe Carter "1/2", SCDC# 296132

(Mr. Carter is an extremely talented artist with Imperial Imprint. Please see his art at www.imperial-imprint.com or www.fineartsamerica.com) He is one of our star artists. He is absolutely talented. See his work on the following page.

WAYNE "AKBAR" PRAY - WAS IT WORTH IT?

Today June 21st, 2015, marks a milestone of a sort and on some levels a celebration, it is Father's Day. A day I am assured to from my small cadre of sons and daughters; a day of family visits and laughter. However, for me in many regards it will be a day of laughter tempered with a tinge of sadness, for it was on Father's Day, June 21st 1999, that my son Sultan Pender Pray was killed, the innocent victim, at 19 years old, of a drive by shooting gone horribly awry. It was also on June 21, 1988, 27 years ago now, that I was arrested in Boca Raton Florida and began the service of a No Parole LIFE sentence. Hence, today for me carries a mixed message, the joy of fatherhood and the unceasing pain of incarceration.

Time in many regards is a human construct. Our one-minute is an ant's afternoon. Twenty-seven years in many regards seems to have gone fast and in other regards it seems to have stretched on ad-infinitum. Over these 27 years I have watched men come and go then come back and perhaps go again. I have watched strong young, sane men become in some cases, decrepit old men or men trying desperately to hold on to some semblance of sanity, as they watch their youth disappear, family members die and friends fade like vapor. At times in the grip of it all, you ask yourself "was it all worth it?" Were the honeys, the money, and the trips abroad: Vegas, Atlantic City, Europe and South America...all worth this moment now?

You have then to ask yourself, "If I had the chance to do it all over again, would I make the same choices?" Fortunately for those of you reading this book, the question is a hypothetical one. However for many of us locked behind these brick walls or razor wire fences doing unconscionably long sentences, the answer, sometimes whispered in the still of the night, in a cold or far too hot cell is an emphatic NO, not if I had it to do all over again.

Again, if you are reading this book homie all of this is hypothetical to you. You understand it intellectually, but not viscerally, not in your gut and I pray that you never will never be asked to go to the chapel to hear that a loved one or a family member has died or been killed. I hope you never have to look at solemn faces in a visiting room, to hear that your son or daughter is missing and there is virtually nothing that you can do about it.

It is at these moments and others that will tell you that you should have chosen differently, taken other options, made other choices. I understand the temptations, we all do. I know better than most that the game is addictive, habit forming. That the same chemicals that a person's body is flooded with, dopamine, endorphins and adrenalin, good feel chemicals when a person takes a hit of coke or whatever their drug of choice, these same chemicals flood your body, give you a rush as you engage in the trap we have euphemistically referred to as the "game."

All addiction homie aren't drug related in the common sense of the word. There is addiction to gambling, addiction to sex, addiction, even food addictions or cravings (sugar being a case in point) and of course as Jay Z rapped in the song of that name "Addicted to the Game." All of these addictions are costly and have a downside, but the addiction to the game can cost and has cost many their freedom and many others their lives.

Again, I understand the temptations. I know the job market is horrible for minorities of all colors. However, in closing homie bear this in mind: 9-5 even at $ 10.00 an hour beats 20 to life at $ 0.14 cent an hour, the average pay in a federal penitentiary. Smart is the new rich, smarten up.

One love.

Akbar Pray

About Mr. Pray... Akbar Pray (born Wayne B. Pray on March 22, 1948) is an American former and once "untouchable" reputed drug kingpin in Newark, NJ who headed one of Essex County's largest narcotics operations bringing millions of dollars worth of cocaine and marijuana into the county since the early 1970s. He operated in New Jersey during the early 1970s to the late 1980s. The Essex County, NJ based African-American organized crime network headed by Pray is believed to be one of the largest in New Jersey at the time. The Akbar organization called itself The Family, and consisted of more than 300 active members.

Currently in his 28th year of a life sentence, Pray has shed the shell of his past; emerging as a wise, educated leader. While continuing to fight for his own freedom, Pray takes the time to be an example and an inspiration to those around him. He has become an accomplished author, penning the myth-shattering cautionary tale "The Death of the Game", warning youth of the detrimental realities associated with the street life. He is also a columnist and regular contributor to Don Diva magazine, a contributing writer to Nikki Turner's "Tales From Da Hood" and co-author of "The Street Chronicles" with Nikki Turner. Respected and revered as a street legend and talented writer, Pray also serves as Editor in Chief of Gangster Chronicles. Pray's CD "Akbar Speaks" invaded the mix tape circuit and allowed Pray's voice to be heard via a medium relevant to today's youth. (Source: http://www.akbarpray.com/the-author.html)

TIMOTHY K. STROMAN - ALWAYS STAND FIRM

Dear Son,

First let me apologize. For it's my fault in bringing you one step closer to your demise. There's going to be things in this letter you won't understand. Listen and take notice becoming a man. No doubt you are wondering why I wrote this? Simple, son. I want you to take notice. If I didn't care for you I wouldn't even bother. Yet I know the meaning of not having a father. Things will get harder for you as time goes by. Remember, son, it's not always wise to cry. For tears are for the mourning and the weak at her heart. Me and strength are what you'll have from the start. Why? No questions needed, place her above any other! Life is a game of chance. The players are money, sex, greed and romance. The path you're on has many twist and turns!

Just remember water is wet and fire burns! Lessons can be taught in many ways. It's on you to seek the real, scratch the fake, and find what pays. A female will be the destruction of a man, or the money that touch his hands. Love your mother for what she is and your grandmother you do the same. Meaning the word bitch will never be their name! The words they speak shall be nothing but the truth. Things that will mold and make your youth! For my eyes can only see you as a man. To teach you and make you a true souljah is my plan. It's not hard.

Damn, son. Listen because I can only say these things to you one time. You take this letter and do with it what you may! I don't care just as long as you feel what I say! Your old man learned the game of life by making mistakes. I almost mastered it, but no man will ever really have what it takes, for life is tricky, people are picky. But I know enough now not to let these people get me! You, your mother and sister, brothers know I love them and my family more than life itself. I know behind y'all I'll catch my death. So you should have no problems when you get older. Real recognizes real, no matter what you do! Remain righteous and real at all times and you will shine. It took me jail time to learn about mines. Just be wise about life. You may live by the gun but you can die by the knife! Hold your head and you'll make it long. Always stand firm and you will forever be strong!

Sincerely Yours

Timothy K Stroman,

SCDC #265993- Q2A-208 December 17, 2013

CORNELL SIMPSON - A LETTER TO THE YOUTH OF POSITIVE ENCOURAGEMENT

Think about this? You can find yourself coming from anywhere nowadays and get shot. Not realizing that your life could end any time. By someone who's thinking criminal minded just like you, the fear of violent crime-murder, rape, robbery, and assault-that grips so many people today. Thousands of abused children grow up being deprived, unloved, showing deep hatred, unhappiness, and depression. Many become juvenile delinquents, alcoholics, and drug addicts who assault, rob, murder, and commit suicide. Most of all these children desert their homes and/or refuse to obey their parents or guardians. They drop out of school without a good reason. There are many problems related to their personal problems making them commit criminal acts. Most of these cases are children who come from a broken home, poor supervision by parents, lack of affection, slum conditions and lack of self-discipline. All this has to do with the family and relationship between parents and children. Some are disciplined by their fathers who are overly strict in their discipline, or fail to apply any discipline, or are strict one time and do nothing the next (inconsistent with discipline).

Many boys have mothers who fail to apply good supervision over them, or do not check on them, especially where they're going or have been. The close physical union of the family is very important. A home that is only a place to eat and sleep, with no feeling of being together, or doing things as a family is a poor home environment for a child and a close connection to problems. Society is conditioning the young people to fail, and conditioning them to become alcoholics, drug addicts, and violent. Society is giving them no other means with which to cope.

The response to the children's problems is to educate them effectively—making sure they get a good education. There are a lot of people who see the rage and frustrations, but simply will not be realistic about what is happening in the ghetto and address it. No one is filming it. No one is writing about it. No one is doing stories about it. It just seems invisible. If you go out into the streets you will see a lot of young men and women with no place to go, nothing to do, no jobs, no point in living. They seek any form of escaping that they can find, whether that form is drugs or alcohol or whatever.

We need more organizations to assign a big brother or sister to the youth who need male and female role models. Parents can join with other partners to find better ways how to raise children. Youth groups should be organized spending time discussing the individual problems of their members while others seek remedies to change the common issues that the youth are going through in society. Go out and meet people who need help working out their difficulties. They might be in your family, a friend or maybe in your neighborhood. Give your information to those you want who are interested in starting new groups in other communities.

Some youth hang around a friend that is so important to them that they are rarely totally free of the influence over them. Our peers may tell us a C is a perfectly acceptable grade, and our parents may find only A's acceptable. One's self image and behavior are greatly influenced by peer pressure. Within every group, whether a class in school or friendships and gangs, there are people who influence the behavior of others. Many young people belong to violent gangs that sometimes terrorize their schools and neighborhoods. Gangs commit roughly 60% of all juvenile crime. With many of them you can hear their stories about how they got shot and are not afraid to show you their scars left by a bullet. They may be proud of the scar. You probably know someone like that, a leader of a street gang who is always getting into trouble and getting out of it.

One day the Kxxxx a street gang of about two hundred members had a rivalry between their hated enemies, the Hxxxx gang, which is the most vicious and largest street gang in the area. It all started with fist fights two years earlier in a school hallway. Then someone brought a gun to school, and the killing started. The estimate was seven members of the Hxxxx and ten members of the Kxxxx. People get high and just don't care sometimes. Don't let anyone influence you to the point that they push you to join gangs because of peer pressure or whatever the case maybe.

When someone says, "Let's go do something wrong." Don't be game for it like everybody else, because they don't want to look like they are scared. But after a while, you will be. Because when you go to prison they break you down and the personality you had on the street is no more.

In prison you become helpless and confused. They (the Department of Corrections) have total control over you. Making you feel completely dependent on them. **You cannot eat, sleep, go to the toilet, or leave your cell without permission. You are constantly harassed by the guards**. You become a prisoner, completely cut off from the outside world. The letter that you receive from your families is received when the guards see fit to give them to you. Without the support of relatives and friends, each person's self-image begins to break down.

Prison makes you physically weak. The allowance of food is limited so you are rapidly losing weight and strength. Inadequate diet, lack of sleep, and torture weaken you to such an extent that you are no longer capable of having the mental effort in making the right decisions. When you come to prison you lose all your freedom and personal privacy.

Prison doesn't reform inmates. Prisons are schools of crime. First time offenders learn the tricks and attitudes of hardened criminals. Many young men who come to prison join gangs. Some get killed or raped. Being in prison for a lot of time under these conditions cause many inmates to crack or become embittered.

276

This letter is to the young generation. I hear your cry. **While many sit back saying they are praying for you but ignoring you.**

Time is passing and most of you are running out like the tide, deeper and deeper grows the ocean of lost humanity. You stroll along the quicksand of everyday living. You are sinking and I think you know. Still you are holding hands of love and hope to each other. I give you a strong word to pull you up. "Hold on!" I see some of you sinking, holding on to each other—forming longer lines every day. The older generation say you are the future, you are to follow us. Ha! Come, to see the older generations are following you and not wisely. You are taking them with you into the quicksand but them fools are heavier, burdened with time and experience. Following you they sink faster.

Don't let doubt obstruct the progress that you're trying to achieve. Bring out that inner life to fulfil that lifelong goal. You may be feeling like you're nobody right now, but have faith because one day you can be the best around. Just take pride in yourself and think positive. If you like to act, take part in talent shows as that will help you feel at ease on stage when you get that big role. If you had dream of becoming a singer or rapper, you still can make them dreams come true by practicing. Look beyond any doubt of failure of becoming what you want to be, because one day you can record that hot mix CD to make your dreams a reality. Whatever you want to do in life always make a difference. Keep that firm belief in yourself that you can be a star and help change the direction of others who think that they can't make it. The one thing about life is it's important to stay well balanced. Make sure your education is still number one no matter what happens. Whether you succeed or not, you've got to stay focused. Look at all your options. Don't be in no hurry, just keep things balanced.

Whatever it is that you love to do, work hard while pursuing your career goals. Never try to be something that you're not. Just try to be who you are, but better than before. In order for you to get to the place that you want to be years from now, you will have to choose the right roles you want to play. Sometimes it might mean that you can choose to work on smaller, low budget projects if you don't have the money to work bigger ones. There are a lot of things that can help you to be successful if you put a lot of effort into or preparing for yourself a dream role.

There are so many obstacles that we all have to face in our life. Many are when people don't like you or laugh at you because of your disability. But remember this; don't let hindrance become a mental block. Stopping you from progressing from achieving your goals in life. Let your faith be in the Most High God and let Him direct your path. You are gifted and you have the power. Don't be shy about who you are, and let it result into doubt, thinking that you can't make it. The sky is not the limit; it is much more out there waiting for you. That's if you're willing to search for it.

Just because many of you come from the low income housing you have a natural born talent. Life is dangerous in the housing project and you have got to be aware of that. The danger of everyday life of violence and drugs should make you want to focus on doing something besides selling drugs and being a criminal all your life.

What about your family? Finding the right path, making the right choices because you must not lose sight of what's ahead of you. Where there is no vision, you will perish from a lack of knowledge. There are so many people who have no positive vision or dreams. Some people say that they know who they are and where they come from, but in all reality do they really know who they are or where they're going? Let your imagination work hard for you so it will stop you from going crazy from the pressure of the world.

Work hard to make a name for yourselves. Self-expression is the goal. Just be real about how you feel. Whether it's singing or dancing, performing comes from the heart. We all build up make-believe descriptions of our lives. Those descriptions need to be challenged. That's because when all is said and done, we have to take the responsibility for ourselves. We are the ones who have to answer for where we have been and where we are going. It's nice to have lots of money, but it's even nicer to help fund programs that support families in need, giving children the opportunity for a caring education. The whole point to your life is to demonstrate that there is a joy and peace to be found in God. There is no need to go out searching for drugs, sex, and alcohol. Don't give up! Sometimes it will take a while to find fulfilment in your current way of life.

Just because you are different and feel like a weakling, don't let that change your concept of who you are, to be friends with people who are in gangs or getting in trouble, going to jail, or getting gunned down in the street. Sometimes when you feel as if nothing is going right, and you might have no money, feeling absolutely at the lowest point of your life, depressed and ready to quit, have faith, and keep on doing what you love best because one day you're finally going to get your big break.

Whatever you do, make sure you keep hope alive and become a winner by being a good role model for younger kids. Keep on moving forward in a positive light. The past is done with. Get on with the future! Because it's sure looking bright for you. Life is full of choices and challenges. Make sure you understand the difference between right or wrong. If you have a vision, remember it takes determination to make your dream come to reality. And don't give up until it's complete. I know some of you live in bad neighborhoods and have to deal with the reality where you live, because I have also been there too, but don't let that be an excuse and interfere with your progress. You have the power to create anything you set your mind to by using your imagination. Keep on going, work at building up your strength and try to better your life. Whatever you love to do, fall in love with it, as long as it is legal and not lawlessness. Continue to work hard at it constantly to show it to be true that you get what it takes to be a star. Whether it is football, baseball, track and field, soccer, tennis, an artist or whatever it may be, preparing yourselves for life, you can't miss out on opportunity that's waiting for you. Think large. There are plenty of schools where you can go for business courses. Have faith and believe in yourself and take that advantage when you can. So you can get everything that's due to you. Then you will see that all your hard work paid off.

By Cornell Simpson
Released from Prison

KEVIN D. COX - A VALUABLE LESSON LEARNT

D ear Son,

With so much to say I question where to begin, for I wish to be as stern as a father yet as compassionate as a friend.

I'll never forget the promise that I made to myself. "That I would never leave you, that I will protect and teach you to be a better man than my father taught me." I wanted to be there to teach you how to play sports, about the birds and the bees, about culture and religion, freedom, justice and equality.

I wanted to shape and mold you into a man of knowledge, wisdom, and understanding. I wanted to be there with you to teach you how to drive your first car! Yes my expectations for you went so far.

Instead I failed you, wasn't there to do all of those things, that's what a prison cell will do. I would condemn myself every day for wronging you in that way. Then I realized the opposite of negative is positive, and though I was not there to teach you everything that I wanted you to be, I taught you what not to be, and that's like me. A valuable lesson learnt.

Kevin D. Cox
#232745 – December 9, 2013

RAS BAMON aka CURTIS PRICE - FROM RAS BA TO THE STRONG MEN

May these words find you well in body, mind and soul. I am known to many as Ras Bamon (Bah-mon-ee) (formerly known as Mr. Curtis L. Price). As a 39 year old father of two sons and a grandfather of two beautiful grandchildren I write this letter from a prison cell here in McCormick S.C. It is my desire to relate to each of you how I came to be a prisoner and enlighten you to the realities I know of prison.

On June 29, 2003 I was racially profiled, harassed, chased, run off the road, crashed into, beaten, tazed, stripped naked and hospitalized then falsely arrested for an armed robbery I had nothing to do with. It all started after my ex-girlfriend (who happened to be white) had attacked me after accusing me of being unfaithful, she had poked me in my eye as I attempted to dodge her swing. There I was hundreds of miles away from my home in South Florida, in the hills of South Carolina, at 11pm on a Sunday night. Thankfully she had stopped at a red light before she spazzed out, which allowed me to exit the vehicle quickly and able to avoid further in query and retaliation for some perceived offense. I happened to have a huge bag of kind bud stuffed in the cargo pocket of my jean and carrying a nickel Colt 45. I learned a few lessons that night. A) To not interact with white females for dating and as well as mating purposes. B) To leave white females for their God given mates – white males. C) That it is not good for our well-being to be caught up in a situation that position us to interact with cops, while with a white female; and D) to drive in the driver's seat.

On July 23, 2004 I was wrongfully convicted of armed robbery. Not only was I convicted of a crime I did not commit, to add insult to injury I discovered years later that I was convicted illegally in violation of the US and South Carolina Constitution – my rights to due process, assistance of counsel and a fair trial were violated. I was convicted of an offense for which I was not indicted for by a legal Grand Jury in Greenville, SC I had been sentenced to 35 years in prison at the age of 28. All while the State appointed lawyer (Mr. Ernest Hamilton) failed to object to violation of my "rights." No one prepared me, I had found out why the South is called the "dirty" South. I now know without doubt after I was cuffed and abducted in the court of the so-called Honorable C. Victor Pyle Jr. In 2009 my appeal for relief was denied.

That was on a Friday that I was convicted then Monday morning I was transported to Columbia S.C. where I would be "processed" upon reaching Kirkland R&E. I was shocked to see so many black faces both as prisoners and prison employees. After leaving the mostly white run jail; having over a foot worth of dreadlocks hanging from my crown seemed to cause State Employees to target me to be first in the barber's chair. Of which I refused stating that as a Rasta I choose to be ital. (natural) it is lnl way of life (what most call a "religion") our native culture. I was attacked by several Guards who had spayed a chemical that took my breath away and burned my eyes, nose and mouth before being robbed of my dreadlocks. I was then placed in isolation until August 19, 2004 when I was transported to McCormick Correctional, where I've been ever since.

I was not prepared; no one warned me of the difficulties I'd face growing into my manhood as a black male. I was never told how we as a people (Black males & females) were targeted by our historical enemies who kidnapped, tortured, whipped maimed, raped and murdered us with impunity in order to enslave our people for hundreds of years. I was miseducated into believing all was well since freed we won the civil rights battle and were "integrated" into mainstream American society. I was told and believed that as long as I worked hard I'd be given opportunities to prove myself able to succeed. Little did I know that the author of the integration idea had such lowly roles reserved for me and those who look like me.

I was allowed to believe that our country men were our neighbors and friends. It wasn't until I had graduated that I learnt of the real deal of the so called European "Explorers" and "Settlers who invaded and attacked every land and people they came in contact with. And how the black male is viewed, that our very existence is viewed as a threat to their literal survival and continued domination. I was never told that the so called "Founding Fathers" and successor have been attempting to solve the problem that the enslavement of our ancestors created, long before the Declaration of Independence back in 1776. In history class the "Black Problem" was glossed over. What to do with the millions of souls held in bondage who provided the labor power that produced the Capital that feeds Capitalism?

The criminalization of the black male image is key to the plans our enemies have derived against us. Mass incarceration – slavery has been big business. It's the "Golden Goose" of Capitalism, which has handicapped our efforts to live life and love to the fullest possible extent. We must learn the truth and know who is who and what is what, if we are to overcome the system which has destroyed countless lives. No one would dare fight to protect "criminals just as no one fought to protect the "savages."

Not everyone in prison is a criminal. Many are brothers who had a bad day, who made bad choices born of desperation and ignorance. Yet the fact is that upon entering prison you don't know Abel from Cain and that could very well be the last mistake you make. The predator/prey dynamic at all levels of American society – even the lowest levels. Everything in the wilderness is aiming to survive, just as everybody held captive in this concrete jungle is driving to keep from "going under". Most have been indoctrinated into the dog-eat-dog ideology that puts man against man, which is producing much of the problems we experience. Most have been ill-prepared to handle the ups and down, ins and outs and especially the "gray" areas. Most of us are or were lost, after having our identities stolen, and need only remember.

We would expect that being in such a crisis we would figure that unity would be our greatest tool in fixing our collective problem. Yet that is not what happens. No, we are kept from uniting and organizing ourselves by the power that be (the State) and of our own hands. We are warned by the correctional staff to "mind your business" and told that "this does not concern you" when a prisoner challenges the status quo and dares to resist conforming to "policy." It is really a simple solution, unite and fight against our common enemy. Race, color, black or white is not the issue, power is. The fact the wealthy European have wed the poor exploited and non-European is oblivious to any who have eyes and see how things have played out throughout the past 500 years. Yet it is the weakness of our unity and not the strength of our enemies which enable them to dominate our lives.

Prison reveals to you your mettle. Inside we have time to think and ask questions people not in such a position have no time to ponder. So caught up in the "rat race" the struggle to survive, most fail to take time to stop and ask questions to think! Many have experienced depression from isolation or maybe they were abandon or some other condition. And as a man one must ask himself questions in order to discover for oneself why?

Everybody needs somebody, some help at times. And as prisoners, we sure could use a helping hand in fixing the problems – the conditions we suffer. The prison system and the judicial system are dysfunctional and cause more problems than they solve. We need our best and brightest minds employed in the occupation of problem solving and troubleshooting, if we are to reverse the mass incarceration of a generation.

In prison we are warehoused, stuffed into cramped overcrowded unhealthy cells and forced to survive in conditions which in a civil society would be viewed as criminally cruel. We are expected to rehabilitate ourselves with little to no means, and very little support from society, which most of the prison workers and guards ignore the fact that the system they work for is degrading and inhumane; seeking to explain such treachery on the basis of needing a job. Many of once decent individuals continue to profit that system.

The most challenging aspect of being eaten alive by "The Beast" is the isolation, being separated from my family and friends. Being the youngest of my family I'd gotten used to having someone I could call in time of need. While I was recuperating and held incommunicado, my Dad had passed away. I had found out almost two months after being kidnapped by police that my family was shaken by the loss of my father. I was angry and hurt at the same time. Uncertain of what to do on how to do it I prayed, asking the Creator to bless me and allow my father to continue to aid and assist me somehow.

From time to time I'd have dreams where my dad would come talk with me and help me feel not so alone.

Not being allowed to maintain the relationship we had prior to incarceration has been most effective in dividing our communities and families. It's hard to repair a broken relationships from afar and just about impossible without regular interactive communication that comes with a 15 minute, $2.50 call. Not being able to "comfort" my woman, I lost her. After we discovered the limits of what "affection" the State would allow us to have, slowly we drifted apart. As a heterosexual brother I was shocked to know that I am denied one of the most basic human rights, love and physical affection. We feel disconnected from our nature in a major way. It's almost seems as if the State is promoting unnatural relations in prison.

The food here is terrible. It is of the lowest quality possible, not only does it look nasty, it tastes like it looks. The chicken they serve used to come in boxes which read "Not for Human Consumption." I'm glad I stopped eating meat long before being imprisoned. The food served here could not be sold anywhere. DHEC would rush to shut down such and establishment if the people didn't burn it down first. The canteen/store sells nothing but junk foods. We are denied fresh healthy food in the kitchen nor can we purchase such foods from the canteen store. I'd enjoy snacking on an apple or a banana, an orange would a dream come true. Something must be done to address the lack of nutritious and good tasting food we are subjected to have. (They do this because they say people will make wine with the fruit)

Most have to choose between going to the store or going to medical – which costs five dollars each time and usually we would have to see the nurse three times before seeing the doctor, costing $15.00 and that's not counting prescriptions given costing another five bucks. I present owe the State $481.10 for medical, mail and legal copies. So if I receive any monies the bulk of it sees to pay the bill and am allowed to keep $6.40. Staying in good health is not easy here since we are prevented from having access to a well-balanced diet complemented with regular exercise and a well-rounded social life.

After 11 ½ years of incarceration I still have to resist being institutionalized. Resistance is my weapon. I will do the opposite of what is called for like food. I regularly skip meals throughout the week. Not allowing myself to fall into the habit of eating when I'm told to. I've found other ways to keep from conforming and accepting the status quo. Apathy is the most insidious aspect of being broken. Most succumb eventually and become fatalities and give in. But not me, I know I will be victorious and succeed in returning to my family, friends and community long before my max out date in March 2034.

Even though many of great persons were held prison in their lifetime, Malcolm X, Martin Luther King, Jr., Mandela, Marcus M Garvey, I am looking forward to when this chapter of my life has passed and I awake from this nightmare of mass incarceration. Yes I've learned much since I've been held captive and am hopeful that I am able to share lessons that will enlighten others so that they can learn through my experience instead of the misfortune of finding out the hard way for oneself.

I encourage you to read of the experiences of often starting with those who look like you. And see how they handled situations and circumstance they faced in life. Doing so will prepare you for what life may bring your way. Also pick up your pen and write, share you experiences. For in doing so you may somehow aid and assist someone survive and thrive through their experiences.

As black males we must grow into our manhood accepting all that comes with it. As a people we must embrace our peoplehood and address issues which have be left undealt with for too long.

The genocidal policies of those in positions which impact our people must be challenged, just as the attacks of our hearts and minds must be resisted. Know that prison is an advanced form of genocide being carried out right here in the United States, is a form of warfare that is scientifically used to down press our people.

Awareness of a problem is necessary in order to solve it. Now that you know how things are, how there are persons in prison whose only crime was ignorance, let us work to raise each other awareness. Together we can win! So let us begin by uniting to fight our common enemy, ignorance of who we are. Then we will be able to organize ourselves and develop idea and strategies to overcome the tactics used to keep us divided and conquered. The old saying "each one teach one" is a step in the right direction. Yet before one can be taught one must be reached.

In closing, I hope this letter serves to open your eyes to the truth, to some degree of the challenges we as black males must face in actualizing and exercising our full potential and power to be, do have and give our best as Blackman. Feel free to write me a few lines anytime.

Mr. Ras Bamon (Curtis L. Price) #303786

Ridgeland CI, SA-0017-B

5 Correctional Rd,

Ridgeland, SC 29936

May the Creator-Father- Mother Keep blessing in all.

One Love, Ras Ba

PHILIP COPELAND - PRISON IS NOT A RITE OF PASSAGE

Peace be unto you:

My name is Phillip S. Copeland, my artist or creative name is also my stage name Money $ Montana. I am a song writer, artist & motivator. I am originally from Baltimore, MD. I was in South Carolina for 11 months before I caught a murder charge. I was 17 years old, had already lived a scarred and tormented life. I fell victim to my own ego. I did something stupid because of it something seemingly unatonable.

That was 1992, now 2015. I am about 60 days to max out this 30 years that had been weighing me down for years. I have 2 years consecutive for some assaults on officers. And 30 days, simple assault on another officer. I was never a "model inmate" anyway. But the pivotal moment was in 1995 when they locked up over 30 five percenters (5%- Nation of Gods and Earths), in the guise of STG "Security Threat Group." Before then, I was reading books and manifesting that day's degree but when they locked us down for no reason. I blinked out! I said, "They don't want me to learn and teach? I'll show them what I am without culture!" I jumped completely off the hook.

My father died in 1999 and it turned me up loud. First, I was tired of losing family members while in this beast's belly. One brother died of AIDS. Grandfather drank himself to death. My father died of emphysema and my oldest brother was killed in an armed robbery. Some kid wanted what my brother had worked so hard for.

Well I'm in this cage, with only months left after all the time I've done. I've been in solitary confinement 15 years together almost 12 years in super max, for hostage taking and assault. While at SuperMax, I strove to study business, marketing and finance, etc. I was determined to turn that little cage into my Gymnasium/sound booth/temple. On my own dime, no help from SCDC. In fact, they wanted me to stop!

Everyone asks, "you been locked up x-amount of years. How do you do it?" and I tell 'em, "You have no choice, unless you commit suicide." With that said, you have one life. If you decide to be all miserable and depressed, so be it. But if you look at it like, "Just cuz I'm locked down doesn't mean I can't find solace within myself." See it's hard to explain to someone what it's like to be in prison, with a lot of time, solitary confinement and Super Max – Heavy if one hasn't lived it. It's hard to explain.

They'll ask, "What is it like?" See, society has drawn up their fearmongering and have unleashed it many times before as the roughest "hood" in America. So, people have a misconstrued position on the goings on in prison. Like, it's a 'Right of passage' for niggaz to be flirting with you cause you new, or "fresh meat." Trust me; they know their distance to keep. But because our so-called leaders keep up the whole "Don't drop the soap" myth the followers that respect them will take what was said literally. Predetermined face value as if it was Gospel. People know the food is nasty. And truthfully you are NOT given visitation and other privileges like being able to use the phone or move as you wish. But, I'm here to tell ya, that's all trivial shit compared to what it slowly does to the psyche. You never expect your mind to make your heart so hard. Refusing to relinquish obsolete thoughts that will hinder you and destroy you from the inside out.

There is nothing good that comes out of prison experiences. Some may say that it saved them or whatever but the fact remains…prison only takes, she does not give. They try to break you down subtly and then leave you in pieces. Then they say "Ok, you can go home now." Yet, my mind is twisted up like a pretzel. They try to condition you into code of policies. Where there is always take and never give and when you rebel, they ejected me with a cocktail of liquid Prolixin and Haldol (antipsychotic drugs). The dosage last 2 weeks, then they add another higher dose. I was a psychotic zombie, until, some 'Gods' (fellow 5 percenters) built with me and brought me back. I refused all medication and they would force cell extract me, beat me and put me in the restraint chair. Some kinda medieval contraption (which straps down all of your extremities – arms and legs and body) that is legal torture and it is for 4 hours at a time! You are sore and everything. Then, they throw you back into your cage, physically bruised, emotionally torn. I had to extract as much feeling and emotion from my person as possible because the idea of loved ones is soothing, but at the same time, it is also heavily weighed on your heart and mind, and that's not a good feeling.

I choose to speak mostly on psychological issues in prison, rather than the usual us versus them sequence although right and exact, the psychological part become a flaw that not too many take seriously because it is an unseen illness. But **mental illness** is very real. Just ask any one coming home from the wars in the Middle East, and they've gotten PTSD. Well, long stints in prison, especially doing it in the way I did it, cause the same reactions. It is hard to return from hard long time. Institutionalization is real! Very real!

In fact, when I left Super-Max in April 2015, I felt new. New like another person. But, I had gravely misjudged and underestimated the affects that coming from there to here. Essentially, from one prison cell to another, only within a new prison solitary confinement (the hole) at that! Then coming back to this "RHU" building was a super hard readjustment of its own. I can only imagine what it will be like after 24 years in prison and going home. A quarter century of life, given to the devil, free of will. Crazy part is that I've heard "reputable" figures such as Judge Greg Mathis. I love his show but he is a provocateur. He leads people to think that he did all this long heavy time; when in fact, he only did 90 days in Juvenile Hall. He has created ways for prisoners, to re-enter in ways but he still promotes this "Tough Love" bullshit.

Your kid is a shoplifter. So, you put him through 'Scared Straight' and do what Judge Mathis says, "'Tough Luv" let 'em go to jail and he'll learn his lesson." That should be the reality of it, but check it, first you gonna give *your* child to the corrupt ass system to be indoctrinated?! Thinking you are doing the best for him but all it takes is a matter of days and your little shoplifter will be gangbanging, whipping white and stealing cars by the time he gets out. You won't know him, he'll have a disdain for the establishment. Prison is a Gladiator school. If five prisoners are in for the different things, drugs, stealing cars, guns, murder and fraud, by the time he leaves everyone who had an "M.O." (modus operandi), now knows their own, also everyone in that group.

Don't think that these CO's "got it down" on us because they are mostly cupcakes. (Although they have the right to tell you what to do, treat/talk to you any kind of way, without respect, and take away any little privileges or cherished items away from us, like sneakers, a watch or a picture) SCDC doesn't pay one enough to have shit and piss slung in their face. Beaten down or stabbed. So they let us live all that TV/Scared Straight shit – Nah! These pigs are not stupid.

So to my son and to my sons, prison is **_not_** a rite of passage. You don't need to prove you are real or tough. It is **_not_** a badge of honor. But, if you happen to find yourself there, make it worth your while. Study, exercise (Mind, Soul, Spirit, Emotions) and plan intricately. Don't ever be scared to learn something new and don't fall in love with the bottom.

Love Peace & Harmony

Money $ Montana aka Philip Copeland

(Released: to a neighborhood *near* you)

GERALD BROWN - FOR ALL THE OTHER CHILDREN INCLUDING MINE

I once read somewhere that the pen would be mightier than the sword—
I have also read that it takes a village to raise a child.

Over the years I have come to realize that both of these statements are indeed divine words of wisdom. These are a couple of the reasons why I sit here with pen and paper, attempting to be on the Village elders, doing my duty by enlightening our children to the various struggles and inhumane treatment of prison life. American Culture (especially rap and hip-hop culture) glorifies and celebrates certain aspects of prison life. We must change our way of thinking; it is imperative that we eradicate the acceptance of prison life and culture out of our psyches. With the diabolical scheme of mass incarceration in many of us have accepted and even embrace the possibility of going to prison.

Although with the promotion of mass incarceration with in the United States, the possibility of getting locked up is an everyday fact of life, Nevertheless, we cannot except this as a <u>normal</u> part of our lives, Unfortunately those of us whom have found themselves in prison, have become so psychologically victimized and traumatized that wear the years that we spend being tortured and dehumanized like badges of honor, or an testament to our strength, our ability to survive under such brutal and inhumane treatment, we must stop treating prison as if it is a rite of passage that we must go thorough to prove that we have transitioned from boys to men, or that we are somehow "real" because of a prison bid. I know from personal experience that brothers whom have been incarcerated for decades (10, 20, 30, 40 years) When asked how much time they've done, say those astronomical numbers with pride, as if all of those years that they've been locked up are a testament to their undying manhood. I am ashamed to admit that I have been a victim of such psychological trauma myself.

Dear Future – I say dear future, because the children (you) are the future, and I am writing this to you, for you, out of love in hopes that you will listen and learn, because you're very life may depend upon it. I know that you are fearless, you ain't (you're not) afraid of anything. Future, that's okay, there's nothing wrong with being fearless, it's okay to be brave, not being unaware, uniformed, or unconvinced about the dangers of Mass incarceration and what really happens after one is locked-up, is not being fearless, it's not being smart – it's being unintelligent and in fact stupid. And though I am a black man, this message is not only for black children, because the system sees all of you in one color – green. Prisoners are new cash crop. One can be assured that most people in prison never thought that they'd be in prison. As Tupac Shakur so poetically states "who'd think in elementary, hey! I'd see the penitentiary one day."

Prison is not something that people plan for—this is not a damn vacation! Only those who've been systematically and psychologically conditioned ever even consider the possibility of prison; Even then, coming to prison often times stems from something that is a simple mistake, or lapse in judgment on our behalf. Yes! Believe that! You can end up in prison for a simple mistake. The system of mass incarceration is more concerned with putting you behind bars than it is with furthering your education, and in fact, it is not concerned with furthering your education at all, because it (the system) knows that with the proper education, you will by-pass all its traps and snares that may lead one to prison. The choice is simple, and there's really no comparison – education or incarceration. Please consider your choice

Gerald Brown --July 2015

LIL BRUH by LUMUMBA K. INCUMAA

Peace Lil Bruh,

Let me drop a few words of wisdom on you, it won't take but a few moments of your time, and then I will be through. I need to build with ya on some serious facts of truth. What is the image of Black people you see projected on the news, television and radio? Are we all lazy and criminals or is there more of us to show? Lil Bruh, as Black people in America we have endured much and still do. Just look at how we are being treated as a people and you will know this to be true. They say we are US Citizens and we have an equal share in the American Dream, but in truth we don't have the same equality as others—it seems. And the justice whom we receive is most definitely not equal; we are treated as second class citizens and an enslaved people. Why do you think in the US prison system black people are the majority, but in US citizenry we are counted as a minority? We are racially profiled and treated like animals to kill, stalked in stores and on streets and then gunned down at will. By white neighborhood watch vigilantes and the police. Trayvon Martin, Sean Bell, Ramarley Graham, Jordan Davis, Eric Garner, Kalief Browder (who was innocent) Philando Castile and all the others to and added to this reality of hell, is Blackman killing Blackman right in the very communities in which we dwell. Gangs fighting gangs and brother killing brother which in turn makes the people in our communities are petrified of each other. Our families are broke and our communities have become political and economic gold mines for politicians and businessmen to become powerful and rich while our communities steadily decline.

These are the realities which we daily face. But Lil Bruh they are not by accident, they are designed to emasculate and destroy the Black race. Lil Bruh just look around and see all the traps which have been set, gain as much knowledge as you can gain and elevate above them. Those lies and illusions designed to bring the Black youth down, into a broken existence, incarceration or 6 to 12 feet into the ground. Lil Bruh, *the intelligence of the divine, is within your mind.* To help you see what you need to stay away from, by showing you that if you go in that direction what you will become. Your knowledge will help you predict any and all potential conflict. Your wisdom will help you perceive, and endeavors which you can achieve. Your understanding will help you anticipate, any and all changes which you must make with in your life before it is too late.

See Lil Bruh, by using knowledge, wisdom and understanding which you gain to navigate your life in the right direction, you increase you potential to create a life within the conditions, of Love, Peace, Happiness and Success, because when you properly educate yourself and open your mind, you will see that your opportunities in life are limitless. Let nothing or no one cloud your decision making or pressure your will. Always control your own mind and be master of the emotions which you feel. Lil Bruh the present existence of your life is yours to make, just always remember that what ya make now will determine the future you will create. So move on Lil Bruh knowing these serious facts of truth, and don't be afraid to share them with other need to know youth.

Peace!
Lumumba K. Incumaa

(Currently in prison with a LIFE sentence. Released into general population after 20 years in Solitary Confinement (2016))

WAKE UP CALL

WAKE UP CALL - Table of Contents

KEVIN WHITFIELD - SHOCK TREATMENT

Just like the feeling we receive before death takes out life. We also feel before coming to Hell. (Prison) My "Shock Treatment"

My legs began to buckle, my body went numb, and everything before me seemed like a blur. My throat was dry and my bowels felt weak. My ears were popping and I don't think I heard him correctly. All I could hear were the cries of loved ones in the background as he passed down my sentence.

I could see his lips moving as he held a wicked grin on his face, I swear, Lucifer himself was staring at me. I thought I was having an out of body experience as I watched myself at the defendants table, shackled like a slave.

The room was cold as ice, and I could not stop my body from shivering.

"TWENTY SIX YEARS!" were the words that came out of his moth that brought me back to reality. And for the very first time, I felt vulnerability because I had allowed another man to hold my fate in the palm of his hands. I could see my life flash before me. All the things I had planned on doing would now be put on hold.

Then I started to evaluate things, on how I could have done things differently, but it was TOO LATE, because my Poor decisions have caused my ultimate down fall.

"Baby I hope I will be here when you get back," was the words of my grandmother which brought me to tears. Knowing I would never see my loved ones in the flesh ever again.

"Damn Kevin!" I wanted to question myself.

"Let's go!" said the officer trying to escort me out of the courtroom. But my legs would not allow me to move, still shocked from the 26 year sentence I had just received. I tried my best not to look back because I did not want to see the hurt and disappointment on my family's face. So I kept my face forward and focused on that big black door. Walking like a duck as the leg irons limited my movement. I made it to the door, not knowing what to expect beyond that corridor, but I knew one thing fo' sure. That my life would be changed, forever......

Kevin Whitfield

TORRANCE MCCRAY a.k.a. RA SAFARI M. KAMAU - AN ANIMAL IN A CAGE

As I sit here thinking about my past life, I was once a made man, making nothing less than $50,000 a day. The streets knew me as (T.D. The Don) A Don to the game which is really not a game at all, but a fantasy, a dream of becoming a rich man selling poison to our people. This was my everyday thing, hustling. Not for fame or a name, but because I believe I needed to for my family. A young kid I was at the age of 16 in those streets, from state to state moving and hustling dope and ganja and cocaine. But now I sit in this cell feeling like an animal in a cage, with stained white walls, steel bed, steel toilet, steel window, steel bars, an animal! Damn, how things can change at the drop of a dime. Now I am a Black man doing 30 years straight and all I hear is cries and screams of brothers going insane. Cow Chains and handcuffs with leg iron is now my new bling-bling. This is what they put on us every time they move us. No more big boy watch, no more jewelry, no more beautiful women, but the young sister in uniforms. Sex has become two minutes of hand play, fantasizing of women from back then.

Tears have become our new rain, pain our new friend, terror our new happiness, and murder our new passion. My life has become a curse. It hurts to see this when you have been exposed to what we thought was the good life. A life which you fantasize a child in the hood, slum or ghetto. A fantasy of being a baller or rich nigga in the hood, but behind these walls there is no hood or safe place to hide. Every day I must walk with a crew or group of brothers for which have my back as I have theirs. See in order to be a man for which you think you are you going to have to show it to the next man, may it be whipping a man ass or murder if it comes to that. Whichever one comes first. This is the lifestyle we are forced to live, because of our environment of the street life. Every man must man up or become someone's bitch, girlfriend, or wife back here. Don't think that you won't be put to the test because you will only be lying to yourself.

See the sun don't shine anymore, the wind don't blow anymore, the rain don't fall anymore, there is only the dark, to some of these men, nothing matters, for the coldness of the soul is the only way to survive. And the food is a mystery "not made for human consumption." Yet this is the only thing they feed us, a mystery for food. Even the cats that run around on the yard won't even eat the food here for which we are forced to eat. You are told when to sleep, shit, eat, and when you can or cannot talk. Men are now looking at other men for sex, love, passion and even marriage when they have fully been broke. Some of these men feel or think this form of action is the only way for them. They are selling their bodies for food and drugs. Out of 1,400 men 40% is doing or having sex with other men because they desire to be with a man. The other 10% may have been raped. A lot of these young kids that enter into this place have been raped on the streets by a family member or friend, so they just continue what they have been already expose to.

The Officers are younger than me, women and men are getting jobs here starting at the age of 18, and they are ordering us around like we are animals. Screaming is all you hear in your ears like we are in the Army. The water smells like boiled eggs or someone's ass. It is so hard that it does not soften your skin, it just roll right off your skin.

Yet here I sit, being counted nine times a day like we use to count the animals on the farm to make sure that they all was accounted for each day. Men sleeping on top of men and men sleeping on the floors, like they were on those slave ships. Men running to these prison kitchens cause they haven't eaten in 3 to 4 days. Men killing men over food, watches, shoes, drugs, raped by friends, homeboys and family members because they look good to the next man. Why? Why should any man be exposed to this life? This is not living. This is not even surviving. This is wickedness at its fullest: Wicked people who have wicked thoughts or ways of thinking. Why should anyone force a man to live under these conditions? This is not a prison; this is an institution designed for the mentally insane. The game for which we call it is not a game at all, it is the keys to the promise land which is the grave yard or it is the keys to anyone of these institutions that have been built for you and me.

I am one of the many voiceless people affected by the systematic imprisonment of poor men, women and children, and the dehumanization process in which they go through. We as a Community must realize that crime is directly related to the social conditions of a people. Understanding that fact makes it easier to see that the criminals mentality is being allowed (knowingly or unknowingly) to be nurtured in the poorer communities. This amounts to an attack (direct or indirect) on poor people. Those who have a voice must speak out. To give a child who is 15 or 16 years old a sentence of 30 years at 85% in one of these institutions "shows" change further proves the opinion concerning rehabilitation that this system takes is biased and that the methods for inmates release eligibility need to be revisited. The statistics only solidifies the fact that rehabilitation is not this country's objective at all. The present prison system is not even a Band-Aid that can stop the bleeding of our communities.

Torrance McCray #293580
a.k.a. Ra Safari M. Kamau

MATTHEW RADFORD - PRISON LIFE - What You Are Missing – The Real Deal

Young man, this letter may fall on deaf ears, but if you know what's good for you, you'll listen. I am currently serving 45 years for a variety of charges, including 1st Degree Murder, Armed Robbery, 2nd Degree Arson, 1st Degree Burglary, and a host of other charges. I started right where you're at now. I was young and stupid, feeling like I was untouchable with something to prove. Let me let you in on a little secret. You ain't invisible. Not even close. Everything you do will come back tenfold. Even if you're not caught doing a certain crime, it will come back to bite you in your fucking ass.

I've been locked up for 12 years, since the young age of 17. Can you imagine coming to prison and can't even buy a pack of cigarettes? I'm in prison for committing an adult crime and I can't even buy myself some fucking cigarettes! What kind of shit is that? That's the kinda shit I get for trying to act like I ruled the fucking world. Now I wake up every morning and eat grits for breakfast, then turn around and eat rice for dinner every night. For 4,380 days I have had the same thing to eat every fucking day. I don't even remember what a pizza looks like. The only way to get a break from "state food" is if you're lucky enough to have someone that loves you enough to send you some money. Believe me though; they'll get tired of sending you money real fast! Especially when you are asking for money every week, cause the canteen is so fucking high. Do you play video games? Well forget that. The only time you'll see a video game is if you're lucky enough to see it on TV.

The point I am trying to make is that this shit is not a game. It may seem fun now when you are out there running the streets, but when it catches up to you, then all the fun stops there. Some people are lucky enough to catch an eye opener. Meaning that they get arrested for something petty, and realize that they need to fly straight. But for someone like me, my second chance will come when I am 60 years old. Forty-two and a half years' worth of lessons! Don't be a hard head. Let this letter affect you in a good way. Let it open your closed eyes. I ain't your momma, daddy, brother, or sister. I am just a regular ole stranger that has been in the exact same shoes that you're in right now. And do you know where them shoes will take you? Straight to a 6x9 cell with a metal sink and toilet built into one. You don't want to piss where you wash your face at.

Peace, Your Future. Matthew Radford, SCDC# 298022

(Do you want to hear more from Matthew and visit him for a month in prison via his journal? See our next book in this series: Blindside Diaries, Life behind the Fences, coming soon in Winter 2019)

BRANDON CHRISTIAN - A PRISONER WHO'S MISUNDERSTOOD

June 15, 2015

Dear Youth,

My life isn't my life anymore. Day in and Day out you have to become trained like animals and that is not good. Yes, I've made some not so wise choices in my life but no human being should be treated like an animal. Not knowing what something mean could be misjudged by another person and turned into something bad. I am a Black Leader of an organization known to others as Bloods and stereotyped by Governments and outsiders looking in as a "Gang Member."

I am for the up lifting of my community as a communist. I specialize in unity and not individually. United we stand divided we fall. Sure you have certain individuals who say they are Bloods but they use and go off of colors, signal, etc. those are the ones who give my brotherhood a bad name. So being Blood is "not" what's bad, its saying your Blood and not knowing what you stand for nor your purpose. Prison is no place I wish my worst enemy because no matter the fight we as Black people are still in the same struggle S.T.G (Security. Threat Group) is a terminology used by the system to pin point who's Blood, Crip, Folk, 5% etc. and it should not be like that. One thing to always keep in mind is no matter how much good one does people will always remember the bad even if it was not meant to happen how it happened. Looking down on my Brotherhood because one not knowing what we are judging me by it is a form of oppression and I stand against oppression, any and every where...

Sincerely yours,

A Prisoner Who's Misunderstood

Brandon Christian #350508

301

EDMOND GOODMAN - MY CHOICES & VIEWS WERE SO WRONG

Dear Sista and Brother

I never ever thought I would submit to a life so distant in chains. From a steady progression of ignorance to following the lead of so many different men. Fueling my own desires, to do what I felt was right in my life, when in the end. "My choices and views were so wrong..." I can write to you and blame the misfortunes in my life on so many different opinions, but would this logic be right and exact? I get the fact that I grew up poor uneducated, and Black but I also understand you make your own choices in life. You see family my mistakes should be your escape because my escape is to work in the cafeteria seven (7) days a week. The personal property that's taken form me is how the Correctional facility insults my dignity, and here I stand firmly rooted in prison sanctioned with thirty (30) years feel me?

If I could say one thing that could touch your sanity it would be this: "I would give anything just to see my lil' girl, Just to watch her grow into her own, I would also give anything to take a shower when I wanna and that when I choose." Since I'm fed scraps in a big prison scheme how I wish I could eat a huge helping of my mother's favorite dish. But that's just wishful thinking to you, but to me it's the world... Then again if only my fine could end and I wouldn't be stick with dis 30.

P.S. I remember the first night I had my room shook down or searched by contraband (Correctional Staff) now understand to have your personal property invaded is insulting to man but it is "prison" who know what one may have in his cell by the way my name is Edmond Goodman #271444 Cell Block Q-four Aside room at Perry Correctional Institution.

(Do you want to hear more from Mr. Goodman and visit him for a month in prison via his journal? See our next book in this series: "Blindside Diaries, Life behind the Fences" coming soon in Winter 2019)

EUGENE GLOVER - CREATE YOUR OWN TITLE

E. Glover
500 Get Rich St
Urban, SC 29999

I'm what you call a 'surviva' doing this time! But looking at these fences (prison), I become uneasy. I don't like looking at them. Me and a white friend of mine had this real solid plan of getting away from this certain institution...I'm not going to say which one, but now I am glad I didn't do it. It was so well thought out I just know it would have turned out real good. As I walk through the paths of this journey, you would feel and know what it is to be behind these different fences. I don't want to talk about the "was escape" plan; we'll talk about that later on. But I want you to know this...doing this time will take a toll on you if you are weak. Don't get it twisted, ya feel me?

But oooo when those cellphones, flips first then touchscreens etc., then tobacco and trees (weed). Anyway to make money it was all sorts of ways. You got some crazy cats that wash niggas clothes...Naaah homie don't play that shit. I wash my own gear, ya feel me? Yo, yo, yo I got it, you had some real soft ass guys here who get work to put in work and if they soft...like in won't do shit to nobody, a nigg would just take his shit like phones, chargers, tobacco, food, weed, etc. They call him "soft" and he still won't do anything about it. Oh I forgot, TV's also. I know if a S.O.B. take my shit oh Imma get back in a worse kind of way. Yeah a shame how some of these broke ass guys try to spoil it for getting $$$ guys because they don't have the mentality of hustling to get their grind on. I gets my hustle on to try to keep food and soap in my locker because nobody isn't going to give you nothing and the way I see it, you're a grown assed man, no one is going to keep on giving you shit! These damn people here calls theyself coming up off the inmates by giving everyone their canteen back so yo' people can send you their hard earned money and overcharge you with these high priced canteen food knowing you can only spend but so much. That's why it's good to have some kind of hustle.

Okay, let me take you back to when I was at the county jail that used to be on Calhoun Street in 1990. I was in the county security cell because I was fighting too much. Yes, I decided to cool off, plus I had gotten this dude ass, so his close friends were after me. But while I was in my holding cell for numerous reasons because I got into another fight with this dude call "RC".

He said some smart ass shit so I told him I'll see you when we goes to the shower. So they had him on the bench when I came out so I jumped completely on his ass, but he was holding his own until I scooped his ass up, that's when the CO broke us up. So this other guy named J thought I said I was going to get him next, they put RC up but they let me and J go to the shower so old J sucka punched me and nearly broke my left jaw. Before I

303

could get to his ass the CO's got in between us but I told him that whenever I see him it's on and popping.

About three weeks later it was time to shine, old boy RC started a fire there and it was so smoky there until they had to let a lot of us out of our cells. So I sees this bitch ass nigg J, the half white in fucker man the dude actually done thought I forgot his soft ass; so I made pretend that I don't see him. So right as I got ready to pass him I turns around and really fast and hauled off and slapped the shit out of him. I done it so fast that this clown rushed me so somehow I grabs this dudes head and caught him in a headlock, backwards! That means I can lift his whole body up if I felt like it. So I started doing it to let him know don't do nothing stupid because you are in no position, so it started going down with this clown. Then someone out of the blue said "Stack, let him go before you choke him to death!" So I got up first and he started rising, so as soon as he got on his hands and knees I uppercut his ass, then m-f's started holding me. And the whole time, I didn't know that I was punishing "a killa!" Let me get into that then I'm going to go up some years on this OK? So check it. Breeze through this. This when I found out he was lying me too and that he was a killa the whole time. Boom! Check it! I was looking at the news and he was there! Real talk, true story! The news stating that he kidnapped this old white lady, raped her and was riding around with her dead body in the trunk of her car.

But prior to that, he raped his own grandmother....Daaaamn! Some crazy shit hunh? But prior to that he was telling me before we got into all that shit, that his partner snitched on him that he had some stolen goods in the car, that's why he was in jail...lying S.O.B.!

Oh yeah, his mom was white and his daddy was black because you know me, on visit I was sweating the hell out of his fiiine ass sister, yeah put this wood all the way on her, because the sexy bitch kept giving me panty shots every time we be on visit, she be smiling at a nigg the whole time. True story!

Check it, I don't likes to lie on what I got into while I was bidding, for one, I'm not going to lie on myself and for 2) I am a realist and for 3) I've become a very intelligent man, there is no need to play stupid or silly games. This is what went down.

Editor's Note: 20 years later: Mr. Glover is a man who does not get into trouble in prison anymore and tries to do the right thing. His charge is NOT murder. This letter reflects the effects of prison life/stress over the years coupled with a little to no support from outside/family.

MICKEY JOHNSON - FROM THE STREET TO THE PEN

August 2015

First off, I want to say peace, love and respect. I'm not going to waste much time on introduction so I'm just going to get straight to it.

I'm 31 years old. I have been locked up since 2011. I was given a LIFE sentence in 2013 for "Conspiracy and Accessory before the fact to a murder" and sent to the Department of Correction. I am currently classified as "S.T.G (Security Threat Group)" because of my affiliation with a street organization known as 135 Piru." Let me give you a brief history on how I got here.

THE STREETS: I had what one would call "A Solid Rep" when I was on the streets. In 2009, I had begun doing shows at different clubs, music videos, and stayed in the studio recording Rap music at least 4 days a week, and on my off times I was with my homies or either getting my hustle on (or both). I was "putting on for my city" In September 2010, I decided to move from Sumter, South Carolina to Virginia Beach with my wife (at the time) in pursuit of a better life. 4 months later, I made one of the dumbest decisions in my life and moved back to Sumter... (For various reasons). I wasn't even back 3 months before I got cased up with the charges that I am now serving a LIFE sentence for.

Some guys who I was associated with (at the time) ended up committing a robbery that went sour. Their way of taking the fault off of them for what they done, one of them devised a plan to use me as their scapegoat. So one of them ended up telling law enforcement (after they was charged with the crimes) that I have a high rank in the 135 Piru street gang and I "ordered" him and his co-defendants to go kill someone (supposedly a retaliation hit from an event which happened earlier that day.) *__Of course this was not true at all__*!

But nevertheless, it satisfied law enforcement and I was eventually indicted and convicted after a three day trial. These guys used my affiliation and reputation to paint a picture for law enforcement as means to why a crime (which they committed themselves) happened for.

As I sat there at the defense table at my trial, facing a bias jury, a non-understanding judge, a crooked prosecutor, and some lying co-defendants. The main thing that I kept hearing in my head was "Look at all the bullshit I'm going through all because of my affiliation." My family sat behind me the whole time looking scared as ever, not knowing my fate in the hands of this "supposedly" fair justice system. I didn't even shed a tear when the judge sentenced me to LIFE in prison. I did not shed a tear when my parents stood in front of the judge pleading my cause. But the scared look my parents had on their faces and me knowing that it was nothing I could say or do to erase that look hurt me more than the sentence I had heard the judge give me.

THE PEN: Coming to prison was not a new experience for me at all. Actually, this is my third prison bid (not including all the time I served in Juvenile Prison and the numerous times back and forth to the county jail in the past). But this particular prison bid really opened my eyes to a lot of overstanding that I wished I had on the street.

Coming into the prison system, you first have to go through R&E (Re-Evaluation Center). You will stay here anywhere from 30-180 days before you are transferred to a particular prison (according to the crime/crimes you was convicted for). Here, you are basically locked down in a tiny cell with two other people 24 hours a day (unless they let you out for a shower, phone call, or to walk to the mess hall to eat).

In prison a lot of dudes tend to align themselves with a particular organization or group (mostly for protection and other times just so they feel like they are a part of something). I done been stabbed, seen dudes get stabbed and killed back here, and let me tell you "ain't nothing fun about it." Who the hell want to be here when you could be at your house, eating whatever you want to eat, washing yourself whenever you want to, watching whatever you want to watch on TV, and most of all "Being able to spend quality time with a female" and also your family?

On the streets you never even plan to come to prison. Dudes tend to have that "It is what it is mentality" until they are in an interrogation room or standing in front of a jury (who already presume you guilty). A lot of us miseducated brothers will sacrifice even our own lives for certain people who would "never" do the same for us. And the people that's always in our corners and love us unconditionally, these are the people we tend not to listen to. Why are so many of us like that?

We never listen because we always think that what they are saying is just the same "Legendary Speech" that one of our family members would always give (tell us). And while they are giving us that same old "Legendary Speech," our response usually be "Yeah, I know that already" or "Yep, you right." But in reality the only thing we be trying to do is bring that "Legendary Speech" to an end.

The only advice we would rather listen to is 1) Our own advice or 2) The advice we get from our homeboys/homegirls. We have become a generation that does not want guidance. We have become a generation who would rather follow the people who we know deep within don't love us unconditionally. Why are so many of us like this?????

This is not just a letter I'm writing! This is my life! I just wanted to briefly share a small segment of my life with y'all hoping that my words open your eyes in some way... Prison is NOT where you want to be! Trust me on that! I guarantee you that if you ever come here, the main people that are going to be in your corner is your family. And if you were to catch a long prison bid, please don't expect your homeboys or your girlfriend to stand by you every step of the way!

Take advantage of every opportunity/opportunities you have while you are out there in the world to make whatever dreams you may have become reality. Please don't wait until you get where I'm at (or worse before you realize exactly what you should have been doing in life. Either you take heed to this letter or end up where I'm at or worse). I did not write this letter to try and scare you either. I wrote this letter to help you and keep you from going through what I'm going through now (fighting for my freedom against an unjust justice system).

I had a lot of good things going on in my life before I came to prison. Only if I could rewind the hands of time…Only if I could go back and correct all the faults I now see… Now that I think back, I should have took heed to the "Legendary Speech" my parents used to give me over the years. But now it's too late…

Had I listened and followed all the wisdom that was given to me by the people who really cared for me the most. I wouldn't be here in this tiny prison cell writing this letter right now. Now I finally realize that a lot of times in life, "it's a blessing to learn by "Example" rather than by "Experience."

Bles Freedome Ru

I give Imperial Imprint permission to use this letter in their "Letters to Our Sons Project." I understand that I will not be compensated for my participation. But I will receive a copy of my letter and a copy of the complete work once it is done. I agree to turn over all rights/copyrights of this letter to Imperial Imprint.

Mickey Johnson #298814, Q4B-0213-B
P.C.I.
430 Oaklawn Road
Pelzer, SC 29669
8/30/15

Please feel free to contact me anytime at the address above

DEATH ROW

JOSEPH HUDGINS - COMING TO DEATH ROW AT 17 YEARS OLD

Dear Sons,

Hey, it's me again, Joseph. The last letter I wrote explained to you a lot about what went on that lead up to me being arrested and convicted of Capital Murder at the age of 17. I'm told you need to hear more about my experiences on Death Row and how I felt while there.

Of course when the Judge said, "I sentence you to death in 30 days and may God have mercy on your soul." I was rightly scared, hurt, lonely... So many emotions go through you in a flash and it is completely overwhelming. I can remember a feeling of aftershock, and then my lawyers asked the Judge if my dad could have a few minutes before they took me away. All I remember is shock, despondency and then daddy was giving me a hug, holding me and we are both crying like babies! I couldn't help myself. Everything had to come out. If not for dad right then and there I'm not sure I would have made it further with my mom intact. I know I came close to the breaking point for my sanity. Giving my life to God also helped tremendously because knowing where I would go when I died was a comfort. I felt like my life here was over!

I was driven from the Courthouse at a very rapid pace and we set out for Broad River Correctional Institution where they had Death Row at that time (Dec. 1992 Arrested-1993 Convicted and placed on death row.) S.L.E.D agents had to take me everywhere I went because the Court didn't believe I would be safe with any County Officers. They always kept me segregated so as to keep me safe. I never really understood that because these were the same people who helped get me sentenced to death but that is just the way it is! For the most part the S.L.E.D agents always treated me okay they even bought me a drive thru McDonald's meal on the way. (I guess they knew I may never get Micky D's again.)

When I got to the row the first officer I came into contact with was Officer Langston. He hated me on sight. The first thing he said to me was. "You know you are lucky that you got here." Of course I asked him why that was, and he said, "Because I used to work in law enforcement and we would have killed you before you got this far." I knew exactly how he felt about me and that made me not to be able to stand him as well. I was also always very leery around him because I knew if I gave him reason he would try to do me harm. I just avoided him as much as I could. Not all of the Correctional Officers were like that though. Most of the officers back then were hand-picked to work on the row and to keep things calm. The first place they put me on the row was in a suicide watch cell. I remember asking them why and they said. 'Because I was so young they wanted to watch me and see how I adjust.' They kept me in that cell (4) days before they put me in my regular cell. I was very worried about the kind of people I was locked-up with but I really shouldn't have been. The guys on the row went out of their way to help me cope with life the way it was for me then. As I got to know the guys on the row with me, my anxiety about them began to fade away. Don't get me wrong, there were some scary guys there and you were stupid if you weren't leery of them. Only an idiot swims with sharks and thinks they aren't in any danger, but for the most part I got pretty close to a lot of the guys on the row with me and their families which I was able to meet during visitation. I was so depressed and messed up mentally that I pushed almost everyone-away (mostly friends because the family wouldn't allow me to push them away.) I felt like my life was over. Some of the guys did explain the appellate process to me so I no longer felt like they were gonna kill me in (30 days), but I still felt dead already and I pretty much gave up for a while.

I gained weight because I didn't do anything but lie in bed and watch T.V. while eating junk food and drinking sodas all day. Most weeks I drank at least a case and a half of soda. My weight got up to 289 lbs. and I am only 5'10". I was a fat cow! I didn't like myself and just wanted it over. Slowly I built some awesome and amazing friendships. When you are around the same group of people day in and day out for years you become close and familiar with them. Some you even build long strong friendships with. This is a form of mental and emotional torture though because while you are building these great friendships you know in the back of your mind that one day the State is going to kill the person you are bonding with. The whole thing is really sick and perverse. Any relationship I forged could only end in their death or mine. Not exactly how you want to begin a friendship but I did form many strong friendships nonetheless!

A group of guys invited me to play Dungeons and Dragon, a role-playing game, with them and I really enjoyed it. Role-playing games proved to be very therapeutic for me since I could use the game as an avenue to exercise my imagination and escape reality if only for the time the game is going on. (Kinda like an emotional re-charge.) So, I became very close to this group of guys, even more so than all the other guys was I was getting to know. Going through something like death-row together forges some very strong bonds. One of the guys was even an ordained minister and even though we didn't have access to a baptismal he still baptized me right there on the spot.

These guys introduced me to reading Epic Fantasy novels so I developed a deep love of reading. I read everything, but Fantasy and Sci Fi were my favorites and still are up to this day. We played handball together and lifted weights to stay healthy. We even played tackle football on concrete but only once a year because after the game everyone would be injured. I did the best I could to make the best out of a bad situation of course I was scared of dying but the thing that hurt me the most was how it affected my family. When I was sentenced to death my Dad's health got worse and I would of sworn that he aged ten years in no time flat! I have always felt horrible for the way this whole situation has affected my family. It has been so hard on them. When bad things happen to you they happen to the people who love and care about you as well. Which brings me to another of the more cruel things that comes along with the death penalty. Those same guys I developed such strong friendships with were subject to be executed at any time.

Getting so close to people and then have their deaths approach is one of the most helpless feelings you will ever feel. You try to prepare yourself - emotionally for the time to come but you never truly can be prepared for the scheduled death of friends and brothers because some of them were as close to me as brothers. We would always write some of the guy we were closest to the night before the scheduled execution day. I still have several letters written to me before the executions of my friends and I take them out from time to time and remember my friends fondly! I have lost so many and each of them hurt to my core. When they killed the man who baptized me it hurt like losing a beloved family member and I still miss him to this day. I think of him often and will never let his memory die or even fade. (My tribute to him.)

Since I was so young when I got to death row all the guys really tried to look out for me. Even though I started out scared I never had anything to worry about from them. Unless you done something bad to them. Then all bets were off. I learned a lot from some of the guys who had been doing time for a while. They had a lot of wisdom to offer and I listened to all they had to teach and learned how to do time and stay true to myself. The lessons I learned early on the row have been invaluable in helping me make it this far. I am now starting my 24th year being locked-up and have had the opportunity to pass along a lot of lessons I was taught so in that way I am passing along the legacy of those who showed me the ropes. Each time the State would kill one of my friends it would tear me up inside but we all supported each other in times like those.

A lot of the guys I was on death row with have also gotten of the row and I see them on the yard with me. When I meet anyone on the yard that was on the row with me, I automatically feel a connection to them on so many levels because we went through hell together and came out on the other side. I can explain until I run out to breath and still not be able to explain the bond formed when you go through that particular situation together. Even though I'm not on the row anymore it still hurts every time the State has an execution. Even if it is someone I don't even know; I just know how many people are hurting with him.

They even moved death row to Lieber because the death house is at Broad River and they didn't want S.C.D.C Officers to get to know us and then have to be the ones to kill us, so they moved us to another prison and only took us to the death house when your time runs out. Thank the Good Lord I never had to experience that and that my family hasn't had to go through that emotional Hell! There were some very talented people on the row too: Singers, Artist, Writers, even Builders. I saw tons of original creations. So much wasted talent! I even tried my hand at Art. Turns out I was pretty good and never knew it. My family even sold some of my paintings to help me with some extra money. I got a good feeling of satisfaction when I created something unique and that had value enough to others that they would spend their money on it. One of the few good experiences that came from being incarcerated. I got me a job as a run-around while on the row so I could at least come out of my cell each day to work. The work included cleaning up, passing out the kitchen trays and drinks, and heating up people's food in the microwave. Once again another good way to get closer even to most of the people there.

I went through a lot of depression and had pretty much given up at one time. I was unhealthy and weighted 289 lbs. My friends were encouraging and eventually I pulled out of it and decided to continue to struggle. I lost over 100 lbs. and got healthier. I put in to try and get my G.E.D. which they wouldn't let me try for while still on the row. Guess they felt like I wouldn't need it! I spent over 7 years on the row before I got a new trial granted. I had a lot of mixed emotions when I found out I was granted a new trial. I was happy, thrilled, hopeful, blessed, and relieved but at the same time I was sad to leave people I cared about that I would never see again! So you see, even the good things can damage you emotionally and stay with you for the rest of your life. I was however, thrilled my family wouldn't have to experience the loss that would have come with my execution! I know just me being locked-up is hard on them but nothing like it would have affected them had I been executed. I left a lot of friends behind but they are happy for me as I would be for them. Some of the ones I left behind got off the row as well and when I see them on the yard my heart soars for another brother that will live another day.

Yours Truly,
Joseph Hudgins

315

KEVIN MERCER - THE BLACK HOLE–From Death Row To Living A Lingering Death

BUT YOU GOT THE WRONG MAN!!... Despite the serious doubts that surrounded my case, on April 26, 2006, I was sentence to Death by Lethal Injection for a crime I did not do. Now, I was living in **THE BLACK HOLE**.

The title fit the description about death row because I actually lived there for eight long, hard, devastating, miserable years. I truly believe that when you're sentenced to Death Row it is like living in "Hell" without living in its flames.

I remember hearing my mother's voice saying to me when I was a little boy, "Kevin you'd better get your act together with your way of life because there's always a place worse then what you can imagine". But, like any rebellious son, I had to do it my way.

The Creator of all beings has been protecting me from many encounters with death because of His love and mercy upon me. But I still ignored the warning signs because I thought that I was living the life, I thought I was invincible.

Being sentenced to death at age 24, truly, there are no words that are created to express what I felt. It's a feeling that you cannot imagine unless walking a mile in my shoes. But, being sentenced to death for a crime you did not commit brought its own additional set of pain and raging anger. For me, it is someone telling you step right up and put your head on the chopping board knowing you were going to be beheaded.

Because I was a man and taught from the streets to be tough and invincible, I thought although wrongly accused, I would take it like a man. The moment I heard the words "sentenced to death by lethal injection", those were the worse words I've ever heard in my life and the worse feeling I've ever felt in my life! I couldn't believe it...Me, Kevin Mercer, sentenced to death and living on Death Row! My mind went numb and everything I thought about, knew or didn't know prior to being sentence didn't mean a thing to me because now I had to prepare and face Death. For the first time in my life, I was being faced with death, faced with the unknown

For months and years, I lived without any meaningful human contact and that produced great mental anguish. My life became a vicious cycle, every night having nightmares seeing myself being injected with a lethal injection and dying a painful horrific death. Wondering what death would be like, wondering if I would suffer. Wondering if I would fight for my life until the last breath left me even though I know it was the end for me, but still I fought. Receiving a letter asking me which way I wanted to be killed by either Lethal Injection or the Electric Chair and them wanting me to sign on the dotted line. Wondering if I would or could condition my mind in a way until I could face the lethal injection or the electric chair. Nightmares after nightmares, worry, worry, worry, thinking, thinking, and more thinking is all I did for those eight years wondering when they were going to call my name. It's a horrible way to live no human should live like that.

The First Day on Death Row

That first day was surreal. One can't even imagine what it was like to walk into The Black Hole unless you were one who lived it. No amount of reading about it or seeing a movie could prepare me for this, it was a trillion times worse because all of this was happening to me.

When it was time to take me to my cell, they took me down this long dark hallway with broken light fixtures. There were blood stains on the walls along with big rats running down the hall. There was writing on the wall that said "One Way In and NO Way Out".

The officers that took me into the death row lock up section that looked like Satan's demons. They wore their clothes dirty and they had evil smiles on their faces. One officer said to me, "Well, well, well, we have another lost soul entering the death trap... I hope you are ready after you pass these doors because what happens on 'Death Row' stays on death row."

One of the officers, who I did not like because of how he treated me, gave me a push into the "terror dome" and when I looked back at him he said. "Good luck because you're going to need it". Once inside the cell, the heavy metal sliding doors slammed in my face, I turned around only to see the worse place on earth, Lieber Correctional Institution's Death Row House.

As I walked further into what was to be the last place I would live on this earth, I suddenly turned around to look out of my cell, a metal door with a window only big enough to receive a food tray and the receiver of a phone.

I started out with a bed made out of concrete material then I was moved out of that cell to another cell with a bed made out of steel both had paper thin mattresses. My cell was moldy and I was placed in a cell where an inmate committed suicide. Although, you could see where they tried to clean the cell from the previous evidence of human blood, there were blood stains and spots where it was evident someone had lost a lot of blood. I often felt like my head would explode with pain and at time I would have welcomed the explosion for relief of this hellish nightmare. The mental pain grew worse than the torture I felt in my body from sleeping on the concrete and steel bed for many years. I spent every waking and sleeping hours locked alone in my small, windowless cell, sealed solid steel door. I was fed in my cell. My food was passed to me on trays through a slot in my door. Although I was told when entering on death row that I would get daily showers, there would be days even weeks before I received one.

Once in my cell, I saw a few officers in a corner in front of an inmate's cell. When I tried to get a better view, I saw six officer's escort an inmate's body out of his cell. Then about five minutes after that, on the third tier of death row, I heard an inmate jump, and then I heard a big crack! When the sound of the loud crack was heard, there was a loud scream that turned in a ferocious roar like a thousand lions. I joined in and continued to yell for help with the others trying to alert the officers that a man may be dead or badly injured. The officers appeared to take their time. Later, I found out that the inmate had died from a broken neck. When the officers came to his aid, although appearing to be dead, as they took him out, they had handcuffs on him and his hands where cuffed behind his back.

Although I was told that I would be locked up for 23 hours with one-hour recreation, there were weeks and even months I would be locked up for 24 hours a day every day of the week. The anxiety and fear of being locked up 24/7 took a toll on my body and mind. I had no physical contact. No one could or would touch me. The only time I was touched is when I was placed in shackles and chains and escorted to the doctor to be seen. The food I ate was horrible and sickening; I became sick to my stomach as I saw rat droppings in my food on several occasions. The food looked, tasted and even smelled like garbage. The food was not even fit for a dog to eat. I was being treated like I was not even human.

My Eight Years on Death Row

I want to write more because believe me there is so much more, however, there is a lot that seems to escape me, it appears that I can't remember as I use to. I developed diabetes, high blood pressure, heighten anxiety and PTSD. Most of the time I am angry and then I get depressed and the cycle is repeated.

What kept me sane and what continues to keep my sanity to this day is that I believe that one day someone is going to help me and look at my case and I will be free. I don't believe that my higher power would leave me here to die for something that I did not do. I have my mother, wife and children to continue to believe with me and for me that one-day justice would serve on my behalf.

I realize that death row is not meant for a walk in the park, however, no matter what, I should've still been treated like a human. My Eighth Amendment rights were violated, my punishments on death row was very, very painful mentally, physically debilitative and cruel.

I am still living through hell as I am now in general population which now I have to always be on guard not to be killed. To this day, I'm being approached by my lawyer trying to coerce me into signing papers stating that I did the crime after 15 years in prison to include eight years on death row but I refuse. To this day, I am still being threatened to be sent back to death row. But I'm going to keep holding off signing those papers as long as I possibly can, hoping that help will come soon. There are a lot of inmates that have been killed or have killed themselves there are no exceptions.

Although, I should be bitter and angry, rightfully so, I have learned how to forgive, understand and appreciate people more, especially my mother. My perception of life and the way I saw people has changed greatly. Case in point, I thought that all white people were against black people and really believed it until in 2008 when I was escorted to court for new evidence. A white man an inmate by the name of Kevin Fuller, tried to save my life by insisting that the killer was living in the cell with him and another inmate and insisted to speak with the prosecutor on my case or threaten to go to the media. I never ever laid eyes on this Kevin Fuller because he was in prison some 200 miles from where I was.

That day, as he was escorted to the witness stand cuffed, almost immediately before his rear hit the seat, he froze in midair and said aloud, "Where is Kevin Mercer?! Where is Kevin Mercer?!" The Judge ordered him to sit down. Then he made another outburst, "Where is Kevin Mercer?! I just want to see him! The Judge then said, "if you don't sit down, you will be in contempt of court!"

He then sat down, and said "I am just doing what my grandmother told me to do; I am trying to save an innocent man's life." He said "the killer is living in the cell with me. The killer told me and my roommate every detail of how he killed the victim." Well, I watched them shut him down almost immediately discrediting everything he said.

The prosecutor said that Kevin Fuller was speaking on my behalf to lessen his current charges of a domestic violence charge. Nonetheless, that one event changed my mind about how I looked at white people. I realize that there are some good people out there in the world no matter what color/race.

I was always embarrassed for being labeled mildly mentally retarded when I was a little boy and got picked on a lot because of it. However, I believe now it was a blessing in disguise. I realize that being labeled Mildly Mentally Retarded was the best thing that could have happened to me, that diagnoses saved my life. Although, my mental information, other pertinent documents and evidence were held back at my initial trial, in 2011 they overturned only the sentencing phase because in South Carolina a mental retarded person cannot be executed. The mental evaluation my mother had me go through at the age of eight years old is what got me off of death row and I am eternally grateful to her for that.

Thank you Mom.

I remain.......

Kevin Mercer (former death row inmate)

(Kevin is currently off of Death Row and serving a LIFE sentence without parole. He has maintained his innocence and has asked that if there are any lawyers that can help him with his case to please contact us. He has faith that one day his innocence will be proven and that he will be a free man again. He knows that one day this nightmare will be over.)

DRUGS ABUSE AND ITS EFFECTS

DRUGS ABUSE AND ITS EFFECTS

Table of Contents

****

D rug Abuse is a huge problem in the United States. Drug sellers and drug users are caught up in the web. Those who are drug users are usually self-medicating themselves for an underlying psychological issue. Those issues can be due to mental illness, self-esteem issues, feeling of hurt and in some cases an individual may have used a prescription drug and became physically addicted to it. Either way, this section will show how people became to abuse drugs and the effects it has had on their lives as well as those who love them and or have been victimized by them, because of the drugs.

Also currently there is an opioid addiction that is affecting mostly people who live in the suburbs and are white Americans. The government has turned it into a state of emergency advising that drug addiction is a disease. Unfortunately, when people of color, and particularly black Americans were addicted to crack and heroin, people of color were called "junkies, crackheads, and many other degrading terms"

Given that addiction is a HUMAN issue, we need to find a way to help ALL of those who are dealing with this "DISEASE of ADDICTION", regardless of the drug of choice.

On the next page, The Sentencing Project provides an infographic Fact Sheet on the effect of drugs and the penal system.

Number of People in Prisons and Jails for Drug Offenses, 1980 and 2016

1980: 40,900 individuals
2016: 450,345 individuals

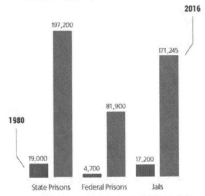

Sources: Carson, E.A. (2018). *Prisoners in 2016.* Washington, DC: Bureau of Justice Statistics; James, D.J. (2004). *Profile of Jail Inmates, 2002.* Washington, DC: Bureau of Justice Statistics; Mauer, M. and King, R. (2007). *A 25-Year Quagmire: The War on Drugs and its Impact on American Society.* Washington, DC: The Sentencing Project; Minton, T.D. and Zeng, Z. (2016). *Jail Inmates in 2015.* Washington, DC: Bureau of Justice Statistics.

DRUG POLICY

Sentencing policies of the War on Drugs era resulted in dramatic growth in incarceration for drug offenses. Since its official beginning in the 1980s, the number of Americans incarcerated for drug offenses has skyrocketed from 40,900 in 1980 to 450,345 in 2016. Furthermore, harsh sentencing laws such as mandatory minimums keep many people convicted of drug offenses in prison for longer periods of time: in 1986, people released after serving time for a federal drug offense had spent an average of 22 months in prison. By 2004, people convicted on federal drug offenses were expected to serve almost three times that length: 62 months in prison.

At the federal level, people incarcerated on a drug conviction make up just under half the prison population. At the state level, the number of people in prison for drug offenses has increased nine-fold since 1980, although it has begun declining in recent years. Most of these people are not high-level actors in the drug trade, and most have no prior criminal record for a violent offense.

Imperial Imprint LLC received permission to use the above Drug Policy infographic from the Sentencing Project. www.sentencingproject.org [116]

***Note: In 2015, the United States kicked out many prisoners out of prison who had non-violent drug offenses and gave them a second chance. This did not include people who had an excessive amount of drugs and were considered "trafficking". They continue to remain in prison with draconic/extremely long prison sentences, such as Heru aka Horace Abney and Kobe Carter (two of the authors in this book), who is still burdened with a 30/25 year "Violent-Trafficking" offense…he had no weapons nor did he assault anyone or commit any violent act as the cause of arrest.

BRIAN SCOTT STAPLETON - THE PURE PASSION & DELIGHT OF DRUGS LED ME STRAIGHT DOWN THE ROAD TO HELL

I'm writing this letter to the youth in hopes of changing the course of life for those who are headed in the wrong direction. 1 want you to know that the choices you make early in life will determine what becomes of your future. Some of the choices you make will have consequences and some reward, but if you don't learn to make choices that will bring you positive results you could end up spending the rest of your life in prison or even worse-you could end up dead.

I have been suffering from the consequences of my actions since I was a young teenager. At the age of 13 I began to smoke pot because at the time that's what all the cool kids were doing or so I thought. Little did I know those were not the cool kids. It wasn't long before I began descending into a cloud of darkness on a road that I will call Black Hollow Highway. Little by little I began to experience with other drugs that made me feel like at times I was lost in a chamber of fun-house mirrors where everything including conversation was distorted and nothing quite made sense. The drugs were like a nostalgic power that grabbed a hold of me and wouldn't let go. Everything around me was intensified and the way it made me feel was exhilarating. Everywhere 1 looked Dangerous temptation spun and leaped at me like a tormented spirit. I submerged myself in these temptations and never even cared about the consequences or who would suffer from my actions. Getting high took me to a whole other level of pure, passionate delight. Whiskey fumes and marijuana smoke smelled as sweet as salvation to the point where 1 was blinded. It's all that I lived for and nothing else in my life made sense. It was a mystical feeling as if I was in a new dimension.

Little did I know the road I was on led mile straight to Hell. At the age of 16 1 dropped out of school and because of that my driving permit was suspended. By the age of 17 I was arrested for failure to stop for a blue light, simple possession, and driving under suspension. I was a little bit worried because of all the stories that I had heard about jail, but as soon as I made bond all my fears vanished. Once I was released I continued to indulge in drugs as if I had never been arrested. In my own mind I didn't have a problem, but I couldn't have been more wrong. I began taking and stealing from people in order to support my drug habit and didn't care who I hurt as long as I got what I wanted.

In 2002 I was put on probation for trafficking more than 28 grams of liquid opium, possession of controlled substance, and conspiracy provisions of drug law. Seems that would have been enough for me to learn my lesson, but It wasn't. In 2004 I went to prison for possession of cocaine and violation of probation. After being sent to prison for the first time I didn't know what to expect. I had heard all kinds of terrible stories, but now I was about to find out for myself. I appeared to be tough and to some extent maybe I was. But deep down I was terrified because I didn't know if I would have to kill or be killed in some black moment of the storm. I always told myself if I made it out alive that I would never come back, but I always seemed to find my way back as if prison was meant for me. I kept committing the same crimes and doing the same drugs expecting different results, but little did I know that's called 'insanity'. I had an addiction but was not willing to get help. I was court ordered to attend a 30 day inpatient drug treatment program, but didn't receive the help that was offered because I wasn't there because I wanted to be, I was there because I had to be.

I never took the time to look within myself to see why I felt the need to escape reality. I felt like I was blinded by the darkness of a troubled heart and was not willing to talk to anyone about it. I thought I had it all figured out. I would just continue to numb the pain with drugs and alcohol then everything would be alright. But it only made things worse.

My father was never there for me and he passed away in 2002. My only brother died at 37 years old in 2003 from an accident. My mother, who was closer than any of them, went to rest in 2004 due to bad health along with my grandmother in 2005, not to mention my grandmother on my dad's side of the family in 2002— two weeks after my dad passed. I used all these reasons to get drunk or high when in all reality they should have been reasons for me to sober up and start a family of my own.

It is now 2018 and I have a 9 year old son whose name is Brian Edward Stapleton. And son if you are reading this I hope that you can forgive me for not being there for you as a father should be. I want you to know that I would give anything in the world to change that. There are so many things that is special to a father and son like hunting, fishing, playing ball and just enjoying all of the accomplishments that you will achieve in life. It is these moments that I will miss out on and these moments that will hurt me the most because I know that there is nothing I can do to get the moments back. All I can do is pray that you don't grow up with hate in your heart because of my absence. I want you to know that I do love you and I really hope that it's not too late to be a part of your life.

I currently have 13½ years left to serve on this 25 year sentence, but I hope and pray that God will one day soon open the door for me so that I can get out and raise my son like a father should. I hope and pray that this letter will convince whoever is reading it to make better decisions in life because prison is not a place you want to be. And unless you make some changes, you just may end up spending the rest of your LIFE here in prison.

Brian Scott Stapleton - SCDC #308556

JAMES SENN - DON'T DO DRUGS

My prayer is that this letter helps to change the direction of a young person's life. My name is James Senn. Due to some poor decisions, I have been incarcerated for nine years and I have 12 remaining. When I was young, I made the mistake of experimenting with weed. Before long that led to experimenting with LSD and Cocaine. The next bad decision that I made was to sell weed for a living. Well that did not work out so good. The next thing I knew, I was spending my money and my connection's money to support a crack cocaine habit. Seventeen years old and hooked on crack—not exactly the place I saw myself being at that age.

For the next 10 years I stayed in and out of trouble. Staying high had become a way of life for me. Time flew by until I was 27. In between, I did lots of things that I am NOT proud of. The worst part of it all is the problems and pains I caused my family especially my mother and father. Even my younger brother and sisters had problems due to who I was and the decisions I made. People wouldn't give them a fair shake because of who I was. Glory be to God, I'm not the same person.

Shortly after I turned 27, I was arrested twice for trafficking meth. Drugs and so called "good times" cost me 25 years of my life. Please kids, don't make any of the decisions that I made. Stay away from drugs and people who are a one-way street to prison.

So the next time that you are fixing to fire one up or about to chop a line, remember where I ended up because of the same decision. My prayer is that this letter will make at least one of you stop and think and decide not to use drugs.

God Bless,
James Senn
SCDC #313954

DONALD HILL, - I'm In Control Of My Drug (Ab)Use!

Dear Lost Ones,

What can I say that you have not already heard? What can I say to get you to change your ways? I can only start by saying that long ago, I was in your shoes. I can say **now** that I wish I would have listened to the ones telling me what their bad choices got them. I used all kinds of excuses about why I used drugs. I always believed that I was the one in control. I always said I just liked to get high. I always thought that I hung out with the "cool" people. I don't need to say to you about how many times that I was wrong. You already know, don't you? This knowing is what it will take for you to get control of your life. You must begin now to change your ways.

First lesson is, it isn't on anyone else but you. It isn't about where you are from, how much you have or don't have, it isn't even about who you know or don't know. I'm here to tell you that when you fall, and you will if you continue on the path you are on, you will see quickly who your friends really are. You will be forgotten by ALL of your "friends." The only ones left, if you are lucky, will be your family for which you are now a burden to. Each mistake I made was like an atomic bomb going off. Imagine a rock being thrown into a pond and you will see the waves as they ripple out...you get my drift...one action effects many others. It has taken me many years to finally see the light. Drugs have only **taken** from me and my family, not to mention any victims I piled up.

I reflect on the money and time that drugs have taken from me and all the people I've hurt. That is now water under the bridge. The only thing I'm left with now is what can I do or say that will perhaps get you to Stop and Think and Change the path you are on. What can I say or do? You **must** be the smart one here; you must make the right choice. You have so much potential and you are wasting it on getting high. Some of you will say, "Yeah right," but my hope is that at least one of you will change. For those that say, "Yeah right. It can't happen to me," well, I can only tell you that I said, "Yeah right, it can't happen to me." You will be thinking about what I just said when you are in your 50's looking at all the time, money, and family you have pissed away because you thought it couldn't happen to you.

Well my friends, you on drugs, you, an addict, only have four choices:

(1) If you are lucky, jail,
(2) Not so lucky, the crazy house because you blew your mind up;
(3) Death; or
(4) I'm hoping you will choose this one, Change!!

My hope and prayer is that you leave drugs behind and take control of your life as only you can. Involve yourself in school sports and your community. There is help out there, seek it out and don't be like me in your 50's, wishing I would have got it many years ago.

PROVERBS 7:24-27 *Now therefore, listen to me, my children, pay attention to the words of my mouth: do not let your heart turn aside to her ways, do not stray into her paths: for she has cast down many wounded, and all who were slain by her were strong men. Her house is the way to hell, descending to the chambers of death.*

By Donald Hill, SCDC #341279

MICHAEL MOORE - BASIC ADVICE

Hello Fellow traveller,

Do you have plans for your future? Dreams? Are there things that you want to accomplish? I did too. That was 20 years ago, before my bad judgment caused another human being to lose their life. Prison is a graveyard for dreams. Every single day is a repetition of the day before. I didn't have to be here, but I didn't choose my priorities well. Instead of thinking about my future, I only concerned myself with the "NOW" I found myself in. I can admit now that my parents were right and that they only wanted what was best for me even though it seemed as if they were trying to stop me from becoming who I was meant to be. Even though their advice and admonishment seemed to contradict everything I believed in, they were right. Hindsight truly is 20/20. Discovering yourself can be extremely confusing and painful. There are people in your life that you should and can reach out to whom can help you. We all like to think that we can lean on our friends, our peers. They can't help you anymore than you can help yourself, as they are going through the same transformation that you are.

Believe it or not, alcohol and drugs don't make life easier. All these things do is mask the pain and blur the issues, not help you deal with them. When you sober up, guess what? All the BS is still there are you still have to deal with them except now you probably have a nasty hangover to add to it all. Running from your problems only makes them hang around longer. And even though you don't believe it now, it really does not get any better. It is not all bout the "NOW" because in ten years the BS that you think matters today won't. Do you hear me? It will NOT matter! One bad choice can ruin your entire life and end all of your possibilities, so focus on where you want to be and not where you are. That's what matters—our success in this life, not our failures. All that being said, take some advice from someone who wishes they had listened long ago.

Stay in school and learn everything you possibly can. Knowledge is power, popularity is not. Be yourself, not a clone of those around you. Don't drink and do drugs excessively, your brain is still developing its maximum potential. Choose friends who want success in life and don't associate with those with no direction. Quit looking for the love of your life, you have many years of living ahead of you and believe me, you will find love when you least expect it. Most of all, listen to your parents. You don't appreciate just how little time you have with them in your life. Even if they live into their 90's, it is never enough.

When you read this, before you completely dismiss my words, please remember, I have been where you are, and I did none of the things that I talked about and look where I am now. Had I listened to a small amount of my own advice, my life would have taken a different path. All I ask is that you simply consider what I have said, perhaps it can help you. It certainly can't make your life any worse. NAMASTE!

(Michael Moore (#219515) is an extraordinary artist, not only can he draw from memory or from a picture, you can tell him your vision, he will envision it and draw if off the top of his head, this man is so talented...yet has been incarcerated for over 20 years. See his art work at www.imperial-imprint.com or www.fineartsamerica.com.)

COLIN J. BROUGHTON - THE EFFECT OF DRUGS

DRUGS -- Colin J. Broughton #337151--- January 6, 2014
I really don't believe that my name is important. For the last seven years, I've been incarcerated physically, but for a very long time my bondage was always in my mind. I am 29 years of age, and I am serving a LIFE sentence without the possibility of parole.

I can't really complain about my upbringing, but at the same token my childhood wasn't perfect. I made good grades in school, and my dream as a boy was to play for the NFL. At first, I wanted to be a running back just like Emmitt Smith, but then I changed my mind. I wanted to be a wide receiver, like Michael Irvin and Alvin Harper.

My parents took good care of me and my sisters, and we lived in a small country town, I can remember when I was five years old, I stole a piece of candy from the store that sold fruits and vegetables. I was with my aunt, and when we got back in the car, I showed it to her like it was a prized possession. Well, she yelled at me and quickly went inside to pay the clerk. When we got home, I ran under the table, and pulled the chairs in as close as I could. I had my arms hanging through the legs, so if my aunt and mother tried to get me, I would just hold on to the chairs as a shield. As I look back, I put myself in a "jail cell" underneath that table. My mother waxed me good, and so did my aunt, then they ate the candy together.

As I got older I stole bigger things, I learned that if I tucked action figures, candy bars, or whatever I wanted into the waist band of my pants, they wouldn't fall. By age 11, I tasted my first cigarette and yes, I was dumb enough to think that it was cool. I didn't know how to smoke, but I had seen my father smoke for years, so I thought that's what men did. Me and some neighborhood kids started stealing cigarettes, cigars and chewing tobacco from a local store. One of us would go in and ask for a pickled egg or sausage, which were in the back of the store. While the clerk went to the back for the food, the other kids or myself would snatch what we could grab. One time we slipped up and swallowed the juice of the chewing tobacco, which made us really sick. A few months later, a cousin of mine taught me how to inhale, and the Black & Mild cigars made me very dizzy

The Christmas of 1997 is one that I'll never forget. I was 12 years old, hanging out with the big boys. We had bottles of malt liquor, Old E to be exact, and I joined my first cypher. I smoked marijuana for the first time, and that led to a life of addiction, I started to smoke just about every day, and my tolerance for alcohol grew. I ran with a gang of young people who would break into cars, and eventually houses. When I turned 17, I tried ecstasy, and to be honest it was a high that I didn't like. On occasion I popped prescription pills, but ecstasy was different. Then, I tried cocaine. My first hit of coke didn't really do anything, so it left me curious, I graduated from high school in 2002, and that summer, the forecast required "snow." Coke made me a zombie. I had a job. I would spend my whole paycheck on it. I was still breaking into houses, and got involved in other crimes. I couldn't sell drugs, I would use them. When I turned 21, I smoked crack cocaine for the first time. Excuse my language, but my life went to hell in a hand bag. I started robbing folks, including my own family, just to smoke. I had sex with all types of women, married women especially. My family wouldn't see me for days or weeks at a time. I share all that with you because my mother always told me this "The choices that you make today will determine your tomorrow!" She was very correct on that. The choices that we make can seem so small but can have a major impact on our lives, and the people that love us.

You may think "so what if I smoke a little herb" or "having sex isn't a crime." Those choices can cause destruction. If my mind wasn't so foggy, maybe I would have listened to my parents, my teachers, and my family. When we are young, we tend to think that our parents are mean that they don't love us, or they don't know what they are talking about. We think we have all the answers when we haven't even lived life yet. (My job was to go to school and be a child). I chose otherwise. Like I stated earlier, my childhood wasn't bad, but I chose to do drugs over a future. I come from a family of athletes, so the talent is there. I just gave up on family dreams and gave into peer pressure.

No matter what, you don't have to do anything that you're not comfortable with just to fit in or be "cool"

A real friend would never hand you a gun, a beer, or a crack rock. While you have the chance, think about your goals and dreams, and start making plans to accomplish them. Never allow anyone to discourage you from your dreams. You can do anything, but it won't come easy. You have to work hard in life, because nothing will be handed to you. Whoever reads this, please be informed that you are the future. You will vote, make laws, and one day have children. You are our future government, scientist, teachers, and blue collar workers. The prison system is packed, and it's not getting any better.

Enjoy your freedom. Live life, and never for a moment overlook the small things in life. Appreciate the opportunities to take a bath, to walk in the mall, or eat a home cooked meal. Enjoy sleeping in your own bed, and using the toilet in the comfort of your home. In prison, you don't have a room by yourself. You live in a small bathroom, with another person. Just imagine living in your bathroom at home better yet, maybe you should try it. Go to the smallest bathroom in the house, and stay in there a day or two. Sleep in there. Have someone bring you a meal or two. If you chose, do it on a day like your birthday, Christmas or anytime you think is important. Cause in here you experience birthdays, holidays, deaths, and so on. It's always easy to get in trouble, but it's too hard to get out of. Things can happen really fast and next thing you know, you have on handcuffs.

Life is good, too good. It's not about money, fame, or popularity. It's about being you. You were created to be unique. There's only one you, and you're here in this world to serve a purpose. A part of my purpose is to make sure that you wonderful children don't make the same mistake that I did. I can blame the world for my incarceration and throw myself a pity party, but that will get me nowhere. If these words can get one child, male or female, to stop and think, then I did what I set out to do. This is a place that I pray you never see. I'm 29, and there are men in here that have been incarcerated longer than I've been living. DMX made a song called "Slipping." If you've ever heard that song, it has a powerful message.

For years, I've been "slipping" and now it's time for me to stand up and walk as a man, despite of my past. No matter how bad you feel, no matter how bad you think you may have messed up your life, get back up and stand tall! No matter if people told you you're stupid, ugly, you're not good enough, please put all that behind you. Personally I had to, because the power of words can really hurt. You're smart, you are worthy of a chance, you are pretty, and you can do anything. Your father may have left the home, your mother might be on welfare, you might not have the name brand clothes, but you are special, you are somebody. I hope that you grab a hold of your own destiny and please, never let go. Nobody can stop your shine but you!

Take these words to heart, and think about how you want to live your life. It's never too late to start over. When you finish reading this go hug your mom or dad, and tell them how much you love and appreciate them. Start sitting at the front of your classes. Ask questions, take notes, study! Look in the mirror. What do you see?

ONE LOVE
Colin J. Broughton, SCDC# 337151, January 6, 2014

JAMES HAYS - BACK AND FORTH TO PRISON... THANKS TO DRUGS

To My Dear Nephew Chris,

Being away from you is so hard. I sit day in and day out living with regret. I have to watch you grow up through pictures no man should ever have to watch a love one grow up through pictures. I want so bad to see you grow up and be the man I wasn't. You have a very loving father and you are surrounded by people that love you and care for you. I want you to see me as your Uncle. Not a criminal. As you grow up and begin to understand things about how life is and works, you will understand better of me.

Growing up for me was simple. I grew up in a nice and loving home. Our family did what most would say was normal we went to church like most families did. Vacation every year like most normal families would. I remember long ago when I was about your age; my mom would always say a prayer every time we got into the car to go anywhere. This would be her prayer that always keeps us safe. "Lord I ask that you take us to point A and to point B safely. I ask that you watch over us and bring us back home safely. Amen." I also remember that my mom would always make sure that my sister, brother and me said Amen too. Always at the end of the prayer. I felt safe. I felt loved. I just knew everything was going to be okay. This was normal right? It was my normal.

Growing up I was very adventurous. I loved to explore the woods. Walk miles of Green. I remember your daddy "My brother" and I after school almost every hot summer day ran down to the swimming hole, it's what we called it, and go swimming. I can remember as we got home from school and we just came from throwing all our school work in the house, we would race to the swimming hole. Your dad always beat me. Those are days I'll never get back. Days I'll never forget.

There was this little bitty pond near our house and I was going to build what I thought was going to be a livable log cabin. I was only 9 or 10 years old at the time. The mind I had. So I begin to cut all these little pine trees bunches of them. I then gathered them all on the ponds dam. That's where I began to build my log cabin. Or so I thought as I got going I quickly realized I was so out of my mind. So the log cabin was forgotten about as fast as it had started. And I moved on to another grand adventure of mine. I did that quite a lot through the years start something but never finish it. Today though, I have learned that if you start something then you must finish it.

By the time I was fourteen years old, things in what I thought was a normal family began to become un-normal. I was heartbroken. No not by a girl silly by your grandma and grandpa. They grew to the point to where they just could not live with each other. They broke up the normal family. My normal family. I asked myself what did I do. It wasn't my fault was it? Of course not. I can vividly remember that being the pivotal moment that began to rock my life.

I want you to get out of this an understanding of what it's like to grow up in a home where you live mostly with one parent and see the other every so often. Just like the situation you are living now. I hope this helps you to make wiser decisions. Remember that it is not your fault. You have to still make the right decisions. I don't want you to grow up and be like me buddy. Life is precious.

So, time had passed since that first day when I came home and my Mom was not there. The day I said my heart was broke. I remember seeing hurt in my Father's eyes. Pain...Defeat...So much hurt, I hurt. It was so hard to be normal. To go on as it had before. At 14 I was confused. I didn't understand any of it, I soon adapted and it became easier. The next few years were chaotic. Somewhere along all the confusing I ended up with my Mom in Texas. Yeah, Texas. She felt it was best we go there. I didn't know why I just went; I was snatched out of school then thrown into another school there in Texas. We stayed with her Aunt and Uncle. So I had to make new friends. New adventures. In Texas I was a thousand miles away from the normal life I use to know. That was taken from me. I was still hurting and asking the same questions over and over. Why? Every day I would think of my dad. I wondered if he thought of me too. We were there only 5 weeks.

We returned back to South Carolina. It was difficult on me from what I can remember. All the hurt and the constant demand of having to move from place to place have been etched in me the memories will never go away. My life was not normal anymore.

My mom got a little three bedroom house in downtown Edgefield, SC which is rural farmland. From there it's where it all began to go downhill. Soon thereafter I was introduced to pot, drinking, and smoking cigs. Being there with only me and my mom I had not felt so free in my life. After all I've been through already, I just felt settled. I began to roam the streets at night. No harm. No foul, right. Curiosity began to scream inside of me. I started to go inside abandoned ware houses. Sit atop them and drink and smoke pot. By then I had met a friend. Travis we did everything together. I remember we would go to the town pond at 1:00 a.m. in the morning and jump off the dock and swim out in the lake. It was awesome until the cops showed up and shut us down one night. The next day a sign was posted up in front of the dock. "No Swimming" Dang it.

Travis and I finally broke the law. We broke into a liquor store late one night. We stole beer, liquor and smokes. We got away for the moment. A few weeks later Travis was picked up by the cops and he spilled the beans. This was my first encounter with the law. At the end of the day, I went to Juvenile for a couple of months and then was sent to a boys group home for a couple of months and then was sent to a boy's group home for 6 months. I did that and coming home was supposed to have been a new beginning for me. Before I went to that Group home my mom met a man. At first my Mom thought he was an okay man. He wasn't, come to find out he was a drug addict. She didn't know this at first. It was painful to see her living that kind of life.

When I came home I went to live with the two of them. They had moved and were living in a trailer park that was infested with drug addict neighbors all around them. Really?!? The first day home from the group home, it was the best day ever. My granddad picked me up and we went to eat. After leaving there we drove to his house. There at his house I was given a truck. I had no idea. Oh, it was awesome. He also helped me get a job. It was at a BP station changing tires and oil on vehicles. I loved it. Time began to tick away the past was moving away as I worked, made money and met new friends. I was living life. I was just doing it all wrong. At the time I didn't know it. I was putting the cart before the horse. That was what my Granddad would say to me. I was given everything I needed but not showed how to use it. Life doesn't come with a user manual. It's why you have family and friends. As you grow up please listen and take all advice given to you. If there is anything that bothers you, talk to someone. If there is something you do not know ask someone that does.

All was going well. So I thought. I had already started back smoking pot, drinking, partying and screwing girls. Whatever I could. There in that trailer was where I smoked crack for the first time. It changed me forever. I remember it being a low time for me. I remember seeing my mom at her lowest. We lived together. We did drugs together. By then I was burning bridges. Rebuilding them and re-burning them. It was like that for some time. Somewhere along the way we ended up going back to Edgefield, because the trailer park was not in Edgefield. It was in Aiken. Anyways, by then the truck I had, done died on me. The transmission went out. It was said to have been my fault. I ended up buying 1994 Honda Civic. The next year was my lowest. I became homeless. I had done made an enemy of my Stepdad. My Mom and Stepdad had moved back to Edgefield and were living on his Moms property in a Clubhouse. I lived out of that car with no Insurance. Riding around as a zombie. Had no care but to get high. I felt that no one cared. Everyone did. For instance, during this time I went to live with you Aunt Amanda she welcomed me in to her house. I worked and tried to maintain sobriety clean. I just didn't have the strength to do it. I relapsed. But not after leaving your aunt's house to return back to my comfort which at the time was drugs. That high you just can't describe with words.

I lived around the town of Edgefield again for some time. (Now work with me, a lot of this is a blur. So much has happen and events took place that it's hard to put it all in order.) I started to live with a friend of my Mom. I also was several hundred yards from my Mom. Every day I yearn to live a normal life. Every day I searched for meaning, yet everyday turned out the same. What I was chasing was normal. But every day started and ended the same. You have to want to change. You must change your thoughts – ways.

This woman I lived with didn't have to do what she did. She knew my situation. She knew I was or had been on drugs. I had ruined the relationship with my Mom and Dad. She knew I was lost and confused. Yet she still helped me. Let me do yard work. Paid me for it. Fed me. Took me on like a Son. But I wasn't her Son. I was the Son of the woman down the street who was shooting dope, smoking crack. The Son that lost his way. No one really grabbed a hold of me to get me back in line. The pain I felt every day for how my life was going was pain I refused to feel. I channeled it through drugs – lies- cheating – stealing – manipulation I became a mad man.

I got on drugs at this time pretty hard. I began to deal with a pretty old fellow in the next town. He urged me to steal more. "Come on bro. We need to get more dope for tonight." I was exhausted. I was getting to my limit. Yet that's what I thought. I sold my car one day. Got 100 dollars for it. Bought crack. Smoked it all up within a few hours. I did all this at this old man house. Down the road from his house was this little bar. So, one Friday night I was there and lost. Lost as in what I was doing in my life. I remember sitting on a picnic table out front thinking all this when a van pulls up 2 old woman were in it. They got out to stretch and walk around. I'm sitting there thinking. I need a ride back to town. "Excuse me." I said.

"Yes" one of the ladies replied.

"Which way y'all going?" One of the ladies points towards the wrong way. 'Damn, went through my mind'. "I'm trying to get to Edgefield. My car broke down and I need a ride to Edgefield." This came natural. Lies. Manipulation.

"Well," one of the lady answers me "We going to Aiken and I've gonna make it back to Edgefield in a couple of days. We gonna see a few friends of ours. You more than welcome to come with us and we will get you there soon."

I thought for a second. I needed a break. I hadn't slept in a few days. Oh, what the hell I thought. What could go wrong with two old ladies? "Yeah sure. I'll go along."

That was that. I told you this to show you how careless I was. I needed to show you that you can find yourself in a situation that seems fine but can turn out to be devastating. Although nothing happen with me and the old ladies. I made it back to where I wanted to go in a few days unharmed, but it could have turned out a lot worst for me.

I got dropped off on my stepdad and mom's property in Edgefield. I walked around a little while to clear my thoughts. I really wanted some crack. It had been a few days. I also wanted some food. I ate very little with them ladies we ate once at a friend of theirs. I walked to where my mom was staying at, in the clubhouse I referred to. I noticed my Stepdad was gone. I go up to the door of this building and knock. No answer, more knocks. No answer. I walk to my Mom's window. Knock-Knock. No answer. I sit down after a few attempts. I begin to think of my next move. What was I gonna do to get high? My thoughts were interrupted when the door opened. I looked up and there was this woman I could hardly recognize. Oh, it was my Mom. See, I knew two sides to her. I was the only one, early on, that knew that side of her. My sister and brother never saw her do drugs. They never actually witnessed low moments with her. I did though... her long, bushy, curly hair was a wreck. It looked like a bush that was in desperate need of a trim. Her clothes clung to her; begging to be washed.

"What you want son?" She started with that. Her tone was 'Damn you'. With her, I would not come around for a while and then just pop up. I had to keep my distance because of John, my stepdad. She wanted to help me. But she knew she couldn't. She was so dependent on John. He was her bread and butter and her way to keep getting high. Nothing is accomplished here. I told her I 'needed somewhere to sleep that night. She told me that at dark she would put a blanket and a pillow in her truck so I could sleep in it. She told me to be quiet when I came there. I also had to leave at daybreak.

The temperature that night was in the 30s.

Not long after, maybe a week, I broke into a house down the block from where I slept in my mom's truck. It didn't take long for the cops to pinpoint the crime to me. I was arrested early one morning. My mom knew about what I did. I told her about it so the cops knew where to find me because my mom told them that her son was the perpetrator. I sat in the County Jail for about 3 months. I pleaded to 2nd degree burglary. I was sentenced to 90 days shock probation. From the time I was arrested I was gone for about a year.

When I got out I went to live with your father (my brother). He was doing good. Had a good job. Good girl. Nice house. It was a good fit for me to go live with him. Not long after living with your dad he lost his job. He lost the girl he was with. Lost everything. Things begin to go downhill fast from there. My situation was doing fine. I had gotten a job doing roofing. The boss would pick me up and drop me off every day. So when my brother lost his job, the bills still came. That was when the house went into foreclosure. By then he met another girl. Your momma. He began to live with your grandma (your mother's mom). Then they would live with friends and then finally get their own little place.

But I was there staying at the foreclosure house. I was having faith that I could figure out something that would get me my own place. I remember feeling helpless at times. It had only been months since I had gotten out of Prison. So there I was in a foreclosure house with no job. Because by now I had given up on working. Things just wasn't right. Nothing felt normal. I can say now though I didn't try hard enough. But soon though I had no money. No car. Nothing. I knew the house I was staying in was not permanent but I had to do something. So I started roaming the streets again repeating all over again the one thing I felt I knew best and what could get me quick cash. Then I began to feel the urge to smoke crack again. So I started to rob houses again. Stealing whatever. Everything I stole I took to the dope man's house. I began to smoke again. I just couldn't let it go. After that first blast I knew I was going back to jail. I had been clean for over a year now. I mean, come on. I had nothing. I was staying in a house that was going into foreclosure. Lights had already been turned off. I was hardly eating anything. My family wasn't buying into anything I had to say. Even if I wanted help I was better off getting it from a stranger than my family... I had nowhere to go with stability. I was losing focus. I had slowly evolved into a maniac, a criminal thinker all over again... So at some point during all this I decided I would go hard on stealing until I was dead or in jail. I finally gave up. So late one night after I just robbed a house I was picked up by the cops and arrested for a shoe print that matched the print left on the trash can I stood on to climb into a window. Also I left my fingerprints.

Months later I was sentenced to 15 years suspended to 90 months. I was on my way back to prison. I served my time and was released not to my family. They didn't believe in me. I was gone a little over four years I had plenty of time to think over what I needed to do. I believed in myself. I just didn't have my family there to back me. It was hard.

I went into a halfway house called Soteria. It was in Greensville S.C. Church oriented. Nice environment. You could almost come and go as you wanted here. You just had to sign a login book and be in by 11:00 p.m. The place was in an all-black neighborhood in West Greensville, a three bedroom house. If you were to drive by, you would never have guessed it was a halfway house.

After a little while there I had figured out that if I had the money I could get my own place. I could just leave. I went to the halfway house in March of 2010. I got a job working at the Chick farm in Greenville not long after being at this place. Everything was going very well. A good job. I was making close to six hundred dollars after taxes a week there. That was a lot of money for me. I just got out of prison. I was on cloud 9. I was finally doing the right thing. I was saving all my money. Paying my probation every week. By July 1st 2010. I had enough money saved to get my own apartment. I was stacked on my days off I would go and check out apartments in the area. All I had at the time was a bicycle. I would also use the city bus when needed. So I had finally found a nice apartment close to my job. I needed to be close because I had to ride my bike to work. I filled out the application to this apartment. Everything came back clear. Oh my, was I excited! I was finally doing the right thing. With my life and I was doing it all by myself.

I needed the first month rent up front and the security deposit. The total amount needed to get this place was like $1,300 dollars. I had that. Easy I paid my light bill up front. Renter's fee. All that. I did all this a week or so before July 1ˢᵗ 2010 because I couldn't move in till then.

Well July 1ˢᵗ rolls around and I moved in. I had moved into a 1 bedroom apartment. I was excited. I needed a mattress. At first I was sleeping on the floor I had nothing. I did end up buying a bunch of things from the dollar store.

Back near the halfway house was a woman that had a bunch of things out in her front yard for sale. All kinds of stuff. Among all this was a king size bed set. Mattress and all for $100. I bought it and she delivered it to me. So I had a bed now. Things went on well for a while. I was still working hard. Saving my money. Thinking ahead in life in to what I wanted to do. I had bought me a laptop and was doing a lot of online schooling. I chose "Westwood" online. I was going to do "Art & Animation." I was stoked.

I met a girl named Crystal a couple of months after moving in to my apartment. I believed to this day had I not meet her I would not be in prison now. I have to back up before I met Crystal. I let your dad and mom come stay with me. Not long after I moved in. I thought it was a good idea which it was. At the time you were just born when they came to stay. Miranda was like 5 or 6 years old. I was going to get gas and groceries one day by myself. Your Mom and Dad were back at my apartment lounging at the pool. At that Gas Station is where I met Crystal. From there it was up and down. I remember in November of that year I got hurt at my job and was out of work for a month. Crystal was staying with me and her two daughters. Your mom had some kind of court date she had to make.

Anyway that November I learned that Crystal used Meth. So of course I began to use. That whole month out of work I smoked Meth and blew through all my money I had saved. When it was time to go back to work me and Crystal had ended our relationship. It ended because I had enough of Meth. I couldn't take it. Now with no money and the bills still came. I got behind in bills and the rent. I stopped using Meth. But since that month of November I went downhill. I kick myself in the rear end every day. Things just kinda slumber by from then. All I had dreamed of, hope for was just not happening. I had screwed it up. Around April 2011 I lost my job. I was already behind on bills. Rent. I was fast falling into my old ways. I lost my

341

job due to an accident, I drove a 5 wheel tractor trailer. I moved full trailers of chicken around on the camp and I was backing up a trailer one morning and hit a building. The damage wasn't really bad but I didn't report it and was seen on camera. I lied when I was asked about it. In May I was being told I had to move from my apartment because I was being evicted because I hadn't paid my rent in almost two months. I began to panic. I had gotten a truck around January of 2011. I was paying $300 a month. I figured I would live in it if I had too, but I even had stopped paying for that. So I was thinking that it would be repossessed so before I knew it I was buying crack and breaking in houses and then sitting in jail with 10 charges. Looking back at the last 15 years is so hard. *I've given up so much for so little.*

If I was honest with you, I have to say that I didn't learn anything when I got locked up the 2 times before now. It seemed I only learned how to get better at doing wrong. Of course I didn't get too good at what I was doing (doing wrong) because I still got in trouble.

Please look at my life and try to understand what it was I did that caused me to do wrong. So you don't have to go through what I have. I know it is hard living with only your dad. I know. But you must not let that get in the way of being a man. You must let that motivate you to push harder for Success. Think ahead.

Drugs are not an answer to anything. I always thought that it was. It is not. Buddy I know you miss me and I miss you bunches also. Take care and always know that your Uncle James loves you. I can't be there right now but the time is coming sooner than you think and feel.

Love, Uncle James

(James Hays is a talented artist. Some of his work can been seen on www.imperial-imprint.com)

STANFORD TUCKER aka SADDIQ HASAN SHAKUR - ARMY+PTSD+DRUGS=PRISON

To THE YOUTH OF AMERICA,

Please let me introduce myself. My name is Stanford Byron Tucker, aka Saddiq Hasan Shakur. I was born in the state of New York, but my father moved his family to South Carolina for a better life. Let me tell you a little something about my life. I am the oldest of four siblings. My father is middle class, so growing up half in the south wasn't hard. I played football and was very good at it. I earned an athletic scholarship for the sport after a couple of semesters in "*the* Big College." I said to myself this is not what I what want to do, sure I was playing the sport I love the most but I was missing something. So on my next holiday break we had I talked to my family, about a life and career in the military. So I spoke with a recruiter, took the necessary tests, and the next thing I knew I was doing my basic training at Fort Campbell in Kentucky.

I became a staff Sergeant in four years, but wasn't satisfied with the rank. So a navy seal I knew said that I would be a good DS, (Drill Sergeant). So I packed up and went to Fort Benning in Georgia. I became a Ranger, and the name of my unit was called "Bravo." I was a sniper, and the best at what I did, which meant killing people, that were a threat to the US and the world. After my post graduate advanced infantry skills, I was placed into a division called, LiF (light infantry fighter). I travelled all over the world doing my duty for this nation. Ten years passed, and in 1990, I was ordered to ship out to Kuwait for 18 months, nine months into my mission, I got injured in a four hour fire fight with the enemy. So I was given an Honorable medical discharge. I was ready to leave the army because I was tired of killing "The Bad Guys," I have 17 confirmed kills on my record. The most in my unit because when I was given my orders and target it was 'lights out'.

Well, I was shipped stateside, and started a very long journey to recovery; my family gave me 100%, love and support, and helped me deal with my situation at hand. But I started using painkillers like M&Ms due to the sleepless nights, and the images of the dead people I killed in my head. I still saw them at times. I started using stronger drugs, such as cocaine, marijuana and alcohol and they do not mix well. That got me into my first fight, I went to prison for six months, got out and started all over again.

For three years I didn't do anything but stay in and out of prison. My mother would beg me by saying things to me like "Son, I didn't raise you this way" or, "You're making our family look bad." I was really out of control, really! I went downhill from there. I was married, with a baby on the way. No one could tell or show me anything until I was charged with first degree murder, now I am here with 40 years to be served. *Taken away from the ones I love, like a slave, and looked upon as a social outcast.*

This place they call prison is pure hell really. If you think that you're big and bad, think again. There is someone bigger and badder—that's the C.O. (correctional officer) that watches and is in charge over you. He will tell you when to eat, sleep, shower, talk, see your family etc. You can lose your life behind these walls. If you don't listen to anyone out there who loves you, then please listen to me. Stay in school for one thing, listen to your parents they really do know what's best for you. Choose your friends wisely. They may say, "We love and care for you." I'm speaking about the gang life. *(It's the beautiful lie, if you really listen to it.)*

This is no place for anyone, do you hear me? The things you will see in here will humble you, and make you appreciate the life you had, because when you pass these "Gates of Hell" I will be waiting for your ass, and you won't like me!

Peace, Stanford Tucker,
SCDC#194427

(Mr. Tucker is also a talented writer. See his erotica e-book "Taboo" published by Imperial Imprint LLC on Amazon: https://www.amazon.com/dp/B01MCV3P0H)

ALLAN L. HAWKINS – MY LIFE & DRUGS

There are times that I find myself silently screaming from my heart at my television where I see children having children and children killing children and it seems that no one is asking the question, why? What causes innocence, in its purest form, to be so distorted in their thinking? What persuades a young female to sleep with multiple partners, only to end up pregnant with no way of providing for herself, let alone her child? What causes so much anger inside of a teenage boy that he would want to shoot out of a car window, hoping to hurt someone for street cred or intentionally walk into a school building and shoot multiple classmates to get his point across? For me to assume that I could tell you why an individual acts the way that they do would be foolish, however, I can tell you how my innocence became distorted and the reasons why I did the things that I did. No one ever asked me why I was behaving the way that I was behaving either or at least I never heard them. Even if they would have, I don't believe that I would have been able to answer at the time. I was 31 before I received a clear revelation about my life and if you'll allow me to, I'll share it with you.

I believe that in order for you to fully understand the end, or should I say where I am now, you'll first have to understand the beginning and the middle. My story is a little different from most common prison stories. I didn't grow up without a father, in fact, I lived in a two parent home most of my life. What I didn't realize at the time would be the impact of not having my birth mother actively present in my life.

At a very young age, my mother left my father. Of course, I was too young to remember any of it but at some point she met another man and one day, she, my older brother and the new man left for Georgia and since I was so small, she left me with my Granny Kay, her mother, and said that she would return for me when she was settled. I guess that day didn't come for a while because my grandmother called my father and told him that she couldn't raise any more children so he needed to come and get me. That day I went to live with my father at my other grandparent's house. The Hawkins side of my family is very old fashioned so it wasn't just me and my father; it was also my Aunt Carla, my cousin John, and my uncle Mark, along with my grandparents. Looking back, I believe if my Uncle David, Uncle Wayne, and Aunt Lynn hadn't married and moved out with their own families, it would have been all of us in the house. That's just the kind of family I had.

When I was 4 years old, my father met a woman who would later become my stepmother. She loved me and treated me like I was her own child. She and my dad married rather quickly, my dad was granted custody of me, and it wasn't long before the three of us were living together in our own house. At the age of 6, my sister was born and you would almost think that I would be pushed to the side, especially from a woman that didn't give birth to me but that was definitely not the case. Of course, my sister was the focal point because she was a baby but their love for me remained the same. We were all, in much regards, a happy family. We were always together, either at my Aunt Lynn's or my Aunt Carla's house on the weekends. Again, my family, at that time, was very close knit. Everyone worked all week and the weekends were spent at the house of one or the other. You may be wondering what all this has to do with the book that you are holding in your hands. It has a purpose. Just because something appears a certain way doesn't necessarily mean that it is, indeed, that way.

In the custody arrangements, my mother was granted visitation every other weekend and holidays. I can't remember exactly how I felt during the early points of my life but I can remember how I felt when I reached a certain age. I can remember going to my mother's house for the weekend and crying when I had to go back home. As time passed, I remember the weekend trips getting further and further apart. I can still recall the pain I felt sitting on the front porch waiting on a car to pull up in the driveway but never showing up. I guess that is what made coming back so hard, knowing that I never knew when the next time would be. It's seems a little contradictory doesn't it? I had everything that I could possibly want in a home but I didn't want to come back to it. It took me many years to fully understand why that was. The one thing that I needed the most at that time of my life was the one thing that I could never find. Acceptance! I just wanted my mother to accept me. Yes, I had a mom at home and she was awesome but she wasn't my mother. No matter how much she loved me and how well she treated me, it would never fill the vacancy in my heart. The same went for my father. I could not have asked for a better dad but even in his strengths, he wasn't strong enough to fill the vacancy either. All those years spent incomplete set the tone for my life.

Being accepted is what each of us desire, whether we choose to admit it or not. More than that, being accepted by our parents can determine how we view the world's system of acceptance. If there is a void within our being, stemming from the absence of a parent or the neglect of a parent, more often than not, we tend to seek acceptance in people or things that can be detrimental in our personal development. Trust me, I write from experience. I spent the majority of my life seeking a replacement acceptance that I was missing from my mother.

I chose to start smoking weed at a young age, partly because the ones I thought were the "cool kids" got high and of course, I thought if I got high, I would be accepted by them and partly because it took my mind away from all the pain and anger. It worked. I was accepted and I was running with the people everyone talked about. I went out of my way to make sure I was accepted by other people. I had to fill that vacancy, a vacancy, mind you, that I didn't even know existed at that point in my life. Before long, I was stealing xanax and tylox from my father's medicine drawer to take and to sell to "my friends" and this behavior pattern had begun before I reached high school. I became the kid in school that people would come to when they wanted to score some weed or some pills. I wasn't the only person but everyone that was in my circle came to me and it made me feel important. I felt accepted. It was difficult for me though. I became two different people.

My father and step-mother would never approve of the way I was living so I had to master living in both worlds. Education was very important in my house so I had to maintain my grades and at the same time, I had to maintain my "coolness". High school came and the partying intensified. I was holding down a part-time job at Arby's, selling small amounts of drugs, and trying to stay above water at school. I managed to stay afloat my freshman and sophomore year but eventually, I couldn't outrun myself. During my junior year, I was partying more than ever; I was getting high almost every day, even bringing vodka to school in my orange juice bottles. Mixed with xanax, it was nothing but a recipe for ignorance. With only a couple of months left of school, I made one of the worst decisions of my life. I could have graduated a year early but a few too many Xanax on a particular day ended my school career. I walked out of Wren High and never looked back. That was the decision that took my life to a whole new level, and not in a good way.

Remember that I had to learn how to master two different lives, one of which was with my parents at home. Well, there was no mastering this. I knew that the moment I told my dad that I had quit school would be the moment that I would have to find a new place to live. At the age of 17, I left home. I didn't know where to go at first so I asked my mother if I could stay with her for a while. I guess part of my thinking at the time, if I was actually thinking at all, was maybe I could catch up on all the lost time between me and my mother. I had been dating Melissa for a few months, not nearly long enough to discuss living together, so I went to my mother's house. Not long after moving in with her, I met Scott, a guy who would soon become "my right hand man". He was into the party lifestyle, a lifestyle that had become all too familiar to me so he and I spent a great deal of time together. Scott had his own ceramic tile business and soon after we met, he offered me a job. Obviously I was going to need money so I started working with him and when we weren't working, we were partying. It was that simple. I was a grown man now, doing my own thing, not accountable to anyone, so I thought. I was a complete idiot and had no idea of the reality that was unfolding in my life.

My mother was more like a friend so she really didn't seem to mind what I was doing. We even partied together. I continued to buy and sell a variety of drugs, mostly to be able to party at the expense of others. I thought I had the world figured out. Scott and I had become inseparable, to the point where you didn't see one without the other and more often than not, when you saw us, we were high on something. The more I was high, the less I had to feel anything else and looking back, I believe that is all I wanted, to just be numb to everything.

Melissa and I had gotten very serious in our relationship along the way. We had been dating for a couple of years and finally moved in with each other and it didn't take long before the way I was living became an issue with us. She didn't like me drinking or getting high so I had to do what I did when I lived with my parents. I had to learn how to be two different people once again. For the record, no matter how good you think you are, no one, and I mean no one is capable of wearing a mask for very long without someone seeing you with it off. I thought I had mastered the technique but in all actuality, I only mastered fooling myself. I may have fooled some people but I didn't fool everyone. I'm sure some even tried to tell me about myself but I was so far gone that I couldn't hear any of it.

I had graduated from hustling small amounts of drugs to larger quantities. I went from just enough to get high for free to getting high and living how I wanted to live. I had started breaking the law on a whole different level. Check fraud, stealing heists, rolling people, nothing was off limits. My thinking became very distorted and to be honest, I was completely out of control. It wasn't long before I started using and selling ice, cocaine, weed, and pills. And guess what? I was accepted by the streets. Every time my pager went off or my phone rang, I felt like somebody. It gave me a sense of power and when you have that kind of sense of power, you don't even look to be accepted. That is what I mean by distorted thinking. Things that are not real appear to be real and things that are real don't appear at all. It's called being lost but you couldn't tell me that at the time. You couldn't tell me that everything that I was doing was in an effort to fill a vacancy left from a very young age. All I knew was I felt accepted and that was all that mattered.

In the Spring of 2000, I came home to find a positive pregnancy test waiting on me. I was going to be a father. I was both excited and afraid. I was, by no means, living an intelligent life at that point but even I was smart enough to know that I had to change some things and I needed to change them fast. The problem was that I had reached a point some would refer to as "the Rubicon" that point where turning around is easy to talk about but difficult to do, so not much changed and instead of Melissa and I getting closer through this experience, we seemed to grow further apart. Because of my selfish living and my immaturity, I missed the most special moment of my life, the birth of my daughter. BreAnna was almost two weeks old before I held her for the first time.

At that time of my life, I had been high on many different substances, but I have never felt a high so intoxicating as I did when I held an angel in the palms of my hands. I remember looking at her in that moment and telling her that I would never leave her or cause her to feel the way that I felt. No matter how much I wanted that to be true, it's obvious that I didn't hold up to my end of the deal. Melissa and I finally split up and I tried moving to Tennessee to get a fresh start. It worked for a brief moment but one thing I have learned in life is that you can never outrun your demons. I ended up meeting some people there that would play a big role in the downfall of my life, as I knew it. I stayed there for a while, getting my daughter on the weekends and sometimes during the week. I was always an active part of Bre's life, but I couldn't be the father that I needed to be.

Again, I was very ignorant and immature. I thought that as long as my daughter didn't see me selling drugs or getting high, I was being a good parent. I was around her so I thought that was all that mattered, but just because you are around someone all of the time doesn't necessarily mean that you are impacting their life effectively. When your thinking is distorted, it's almost like sailing across the ocean in a dense fog trying to find the lighthouse. You know it's out there somewhere but you just can't seem to find it and before long, you hit something that you never knew was there and your boat sinks. Well, I hit something!

I moved back to South Carolina and like a dog returning to his own vomit, I foolishly returned to the same streets that I tried to get away from. I was moving more Oxycontin than before and because of the "new friends" I met in Tennessee, I was trafficking across state lines. The value was almost double up there, and I was the "new guy", in the "new group", in the "new state". I was accepted and more than that, I was needed so the sense of power that I referred to previously grew more intense. My brother and I was dealing and using more cocaine than we ever had, and I starting messing around with guns. I moved in with a woman named Kim, got married, got custody of BreAnna, I had everything, so I thought. I was an idiot! This was the beginning of the end of the life that I knew, if it wasn't already. I thought I was untouchable, a superman of some sorts. I had got to the point where I walked around with a 45 on my side most of the time, like it was supposed to be there. I wasn't afraid of the law, I wasn't even afraid of God. Then the inevitable happened.

On November 22, 2005, during the course of, yet another drug deal, everything went wrong. I got into an altercation with a guy that I had known for years, guns came out and I fired a shot. Ultimately, that shot proved to be fatal and that shot changed everything about my life and the lives attached to me. Being the immature kid that I was (may I remind you that I believed that I was a nan), I panicked and fled the scene. It was almost a week later when I turned myself in to the authorities. The damage was done. No matter what I said, it wouldn't change the fact that I fled the scene with a man bleeding. No matter how justified I felt, I shot another man and was charged with murder.

I would like for my next sentence to be that the moment I was handcuffed it changed my life for the better, but I can't do that. Two weeks later I went up for my bond hearing, I was given a bond and went home that night. Remember when I referenced "the Rubicon"? Well; I had reached that point with no return in sight. I continued down that dark and lonely road. I stayed high on oxycontin every day, more than likely it was because the reality of what happened didn't exist in a drug induced fog, either way, I chose to stay there. I ruined my marriage and most of the meaningful relationships (there weren't many of them) along the way. In the state of ignorance, where I lived most of the time, I believed that the court would view the shooting in the way that I viewed it, justifiable homicide, and I would never see a day of prison time. Obviously, that was not the case. After four days of trial and thirteen hours of deliberation, the jury found me guilty of murder and I was sentenced to thirty years in prison.

At 27 years old, I was sentenced to more time than I had been alive. All those years of wanting to be accepted by other people. For what? Now I was going to have to learn how to accept thirty years behind bars.

Again, I would like for the next sentence to be that those bars closing behind me woke me up, but unfortunately I cannot write those words. After a couple months in R&E, I was transferred to McCormick Correctional in March of 2008 and was sent to Unit F1A, a medium custody wing at an Upstate level three institution. I was told that the worst of the worst is housed in this wing, and when I walked in the front door, I was scared to death. I had never been in a place like that, and I no longer felt the sense of power that I once felt. I was completely powerless but I knew enough about prison stories to know that I could never let my fears be realized by others. I stayed to myself and it didn't take long before I was around the people that I wanted to be around. I was accepted once again. I was taught the ropes and even got high from time to time. It didn't take long before the street life that I had been so accustomed to come out behind the fences.

I started hustling cigarettes and eventually scoring pills. I was such an idiot. My life and many other lives ruined by the very thing that I continued to do after I got to prison but you couldn't tell me that at the time. I was making the best of a bad situation, so I thought. This behavior went on for a couple of years and in 2010, the light finally came on. I had just scored 90 oxy 80s and it was wide open. Everyone that I ran with was high, just like the streets and I had regained that false sense of power. I was needed and I felt accepted.

Leaning on the upstairs rail in F3, I was watching the guys that I ran with and noticed that they were chasing a needle. One of the guys in our group was a full blown hepatitis C patient and he had the needle. Everyone knew he had Hepatitis C but no one seemed to care. Turn after turn, they passed the needle around and it was that moment when deep inside, I heard a voice saying,

"Allan, what are you doing?" These guys were risking their lives just to get high on the pills that they were getting from me. I was playing a vital role in their downfall and they didn't have a clue. I stood there, slouched over the rail, thinking about how many people I had harmed because of drugs.

I couldn't help but to think about how many kids went to bed hungry because their mom or dad wanted to get high more than they wanted to feed their family and I ended up with the money or how many families, not including mine, had been torn apart because of my selfishness. What was I doing? It was definitely a good question and I didn't have an answer for it. I was still doing the exact same thing behind the fences that I was doing in the free world. Thirty years! Was that not enough to say enough is enough? It was that moment that those words I said to my daughter as she lay in my arms came creeping back into my mind, "I will never leave you and I will never cause you to feel the way that I felt as a child". I did the very thing that I promised I wouldn't do. How could I have allowed this to happen? I spent the next few days thinking about the lies and deceit that I had lived by for so long, all the pain that I had caused my family, all the affairs, all for what? A brief moment of satisfaction to be accepted?

It didn't happen overnight but I made a decision that I had to make some changes in my life. I couldn't continue living the way I was living. I had hurt enough people, especially my family. I didn't sell another pill after that day and shortly after, I stopped doing drugs myself. In January 2011, I took my last drink of alcohol and smoked my last cigarette.

I had always known God, or should I say known of Him, but I had never allowed Him control over my life. On my knees, I cried out and asked Him to help me. I needed to change and I couldn't do it on my own. I didn't get an earthshaking answer and a bush didn't catch on fire, but I felt His spirit rest over me. I had always heard of the "jailhouse religions" that goes on behind the fences and I promised God that I would never play games with Him. I needed Him and if He would fix my brokenness, I would give myself to Him. I didn't understand how a relationship with Him worked at the time but I asked him to help get my life on track and to help me to see my daughter again. I hadn't seen her since coming to prison because my name wasn't on her birth certificate. To this day, I still don't understand how it was so easy to be awarded custody but so difficult to have her added to my visitation list. I promised God that if He would help me to be able to see my daughter; I would never go back to the drugs, phones, alcohol, and the lifestyle that came with those things. He didn't answer me immediately or even in the next several months but I knew that He heard me and I trusted that He would answer me in His time.

A little over a year later, I sat across the table from my mother and told her that I forgave her for leaving me as a child. Through tears, we talked about

351

the pain it caused and I learned more about my mother that day than I had ever known before. It wasn't the things that were said that settled inside of me, it was an enlightenment that could have only come from God. I wasn't the only one walking around with a vacancy. She had been carrying that same pain around also. Before I was born, she watched my oldest brother get run over in front of her and helplessly had to watch him die from the injuries. She never recovered from that. I would never be able to associate with that kind of pain. My mother didn't leave me because she didn't want me; she left me because she didn't know what else to do. She didn't know how to deal with the pain that she was carrying and I'm sure that played a huge role in her decisions.

After that visit, our relationship began a healing process that continues to this day. We no longer just have the friend type relationship we once had; we have a healthy mother and son relationship as well.

In 2013, I saw my daughter for the first time in five years. There was a lot of red tape with my name having to be added to the birth certificate but God was faithful. Because His timing is perfect, not only did the judge instruct DHEC to add my name to BreAnna's birth certificate, she also instructed them to change her last name without me asking. Not only was I going to be able to see her again, she would now have my last name, a desire that I had since she was born.

I was so nervous the first weekend she was coming to see me, partly because I hadn't saw her in all those years and partly because I didn't know how she would feel seeing me in prison. All of those feelings vanished the moment I put my arms around her. In a moment of time, it was as if we had never been apart. Five years later, I have a relationship with my daughter that I never dreamed possible, especially being in a place like this. She has become my best friend and more often than not, my drive and my strength. In a life where I once thought that I would be her rock and her strength, she has shown me that life isn't always what you think it is and it don't always play out the way you expect. At almost eighteen years old, she has become the strongest person I know. I would not want to imagine my life without her in it!

Do you remember when I wrote at the beginning that in order to understand where I am now, you would first have to understand the beginning and the middle? I am who I am today because of everything that I have experienced in my life. I spent much of my life on a journey to find acceptance, having no idea of the journey I was on or what I was even looking for and it caused a lot of unnecessary pain along the way. I went through the things I went through in order for you to be reading these words today. Everything that happens in life is for a reason, one way or the other and I know, beyond doubt that my life is meant to help change someone else's. If there is one thing I have learned about being accepted, it is the moment that I realized that I am accepted by God, my entire life changed. I no longer needed affirmation from someone else. I no longer needed to feel accepted by someone else.

Don't get me wrong, it's nice to hear "you're doing a good job" or "I need you to do such and such" but it is no longer what drives my life. I have found my purpose in life and when you find your purpose; that alone, is all you will need to be effective and live prosperously.

It took me coming to prison to learn these things but it doesn't have to be the same for you. If you are reading this book, you still have a chance to set the course for your life, a course that doesn't have separation from loved ones, three hots and a cot, community showers, others dictating when you can and can't do something, a course that you can determine the outcome. It's all up to you.

Thank you for taking the time to read this and I can only pray that at the very least, it causes you to stop and think.

--Allan L. Hawkins

BRIAN SCOTT STAPLETON - COPING WITH ABUSE

A buse is more widely spread than most of you realize. Every hour 5 infants in this country receive injuries from their parents to the extent of broken bones or skin. For most of us who have suffered physical or verbal abuse find ways to bury the pain that we have endured because we don't know how else to deal with the situation. Some of us cover up the pain by staying busy all the time and some of us by using drugs or alcohol. I chose drugs and alcohol, but I wasn't aware that I was just finding ways to cope with my situation. I thought that I just enjoyed the way the drugs made me feel and to a certain extent that may be true, but I later came to the understanding that this type of behavior usually stems from something dramatic that has happened in someone's life at an earlier age whether it be physical abuse, verbal abuse, or just the fact that their father or mother wasn't there for them, but for the most part we are not aware of that because we refuse to look inward.

This is true for most people in life. We tend to run from our problems or should I say we bury them with what is called coping methods instead of looking inward to see where the pain originates from. When we run out of or stop our coping methods those layers are slowly peeled away until the pain we have buried resurfaces again, and we are back where we started. We have not even begun to solve the problem. In fact we have tricked ourselves into thinking that these problems are gone, but in reality we just continue to cover up the pain that has been inflicted by someone else at an earlier age in our life.

Brian Scott Stapleton

MENTAL HEALTH

MENTAL HEALTH - *Table of Contents*

This is a Section of Great Importance. Most prisoners have some type of mental disability however due to the closing of hospitals more and more are finding themselves in prison. Non-compliance with medication, an inability to afford medication as well as issues of poverty, contributes to those finding themselves in trouble with the law.

Furthermore, the conditions in prison can be so stressful, frustrating and dehumanizing that many are given psychotropic drugs just in order to cope from hour to hour. It does not matter how weak or strong you are mentally…mind games by staff, other prisoners and loved ones on the outside, actual fear for your life (whether it be sexual and/or physical violence), claustrophobia as well as good ole "indifference" can drive someone to insanity.

Many of the men wrote letters that touched upon mental illness but did not fully go into it. As a result we will address the issue in a few Factoids.

Congressman Timothy F. Murphy (Republican) from Pennsylvania who worked tirelessly to get H.R.2646 - Helping Families in Mental Illness Crisis Act of 2015 (114th Congress 2015-2016) in Congress passed on July 6, 2016 with a (422-2) vote. *(The bill was passed on December 7, 2016)* This bill will increase beds in psychiatric hospitals, increase treatment for young mental health patients, and establish a new assistant for substance abuse/mental health in the Department of Health and Human Services (HHS), expanding Medicaid & Medicare spending expansion and as well as other provisions. [117] [118]

Again, we do not have a lot of information on Mental Health issues in prison for this book. Please read this article on the internet in the Free-Times, which gives you some idea of what people with Mental Health issues deal with THROUGHOUT the United States. It is not just confined to this particular prison or state.

(http://www.free-times.com/cover/horrors-behind-these-walls-012214)

FACTOID – Mental Health - Manufacturing Madness in the Prison System of America

It is well established that isolation and sensory deprivation can aggravate or even cause a variety of psychiatric symptoms. Inmates subjected to prolonged isolation may experience depression, despair, anxiety, rage, claustrophobia, hallucinations, problems with impulse control, and impaired ability to think, concentrate or remember. I know inmates that have reported on the devastating effect of extended isolation, including a progressive inability to tolerate even ordinary simulation. Some cut themselves, just so they could feel something. The courts have recognized that solitary confinement itself can cause a very specific kind of psychiatric syndrome. For instant I was placed in what they call ""the box" for 13 months for something that was a right, but I was told to shut up by the Captain and I wouldn't. So he lied on the charge paper. But they didn't know that I was trained by the army for those kinds of conditions.

See the decision to isolate an inmate may be made without any formal proceeding, and the period of isolation most often has no defined end point especially when isolation is imposed for "administrative" rather than disciplinary reasons. Note: Lock up time is determined by prison authorities rather than the courts. Inmates constitutional rights to due process of law are not recognized at all. The worst stages of lock up can lead to agitated, hallucinatory, confused psychotic state often involving random violence and self-mutilation, suicidal-behavior (and other) agitated fearful kinds of symptoms. How would you like to be woken up every hour throughout the night by a flashlight shining in your face? Listen inmates are so ill, that they all tended to be ill in very similar kinds of way, and were so frightened of what was happening to them that they weren't exaggerating their illness. They were tending to minimize it, deny it. They were scared of it really. This constitutes a very large percentage of the prison population.

Whether the origins of their problems are neurological, socioeconomic, or both, these populations often experience the greatest difficulties in following prison rules, controlling their own anger, or handling the prison social environment his own anger, or handling the prison social environment. This will result in being placed back in isolation.

There is a legal case, Austin V. Wilkinson, which sets an important precedent because the court certified that incarceration lockdowns is a "significant hardship." The legal standard for a claim under the due process clause of the Bill of Rights future litigation defending prisoner's rights will be able to draw on this precedent to argue that lock up undermines basic constitutional rights. In closing, this culture of violence is profoundly destructive to those who suffer its effects, brutalizing not only inmates, but also Prison Guards and Officials who become the daily agents of inhumanity. The larger community is also gravely harmed, not only by the practical difficulties of reintegrating human beings who have been so deeply traumatized, but also by the profound erosion of our simple humanity. Here, as in every arena of life, violence only breeds more violence. Institutionalizing the use of violence has created, in our communities or in our world. All have little or nothing to do with the safety and orderly operation of correctional institutions and everything to do with the spread of a culture of violence, retribution, dehumanization, and sadism.

Peace,

The Mind of Saddiq

Stanford B. Tucker

Dated: November 4, 1437 A.H./2015 C.E.

Read this from the Quran please Ins Sha Allah Quran: 26:79-81

Dawn,

Use this as a "Factoids" for the book Inshallah. If you need more just say the word, I'm at your call. This needs to be addressed, because it's one of the main reason(s) why so many Black men are being locked-up. And this would better help the people on the outside to help with the problem(s) of stopping that mass incarceration of our Brother, Fathers, Uncles, Children etc.... and by the way thanks for the updated newsletter of the company. Listen I can't say this enough thank you for all that you have done really, I'm grateful for you and the things you have done for the company. And "DON'T EVER GIVE UP! NEVER!" Keep the faith. I have it in you. Trust me. The Quran says: That we will be tested by Allah ta ala. Always keep that in mind.

I remain.

(May you be blessed & protected)

"POSITIVE PEOPLE DOING POSITIVE THINGS"

I like that...

Peace,

Stanford B. Tucker, #194427, U8-104
Tyger River Correctional Institution
200 Prison Road
Enoree, SC 29335

ROBERT TODD – PATHWAY TO DRUGS & CUTTING

When I was 7yrs old my dad started beating my mother and when I would try to make him stop he would beat me also. There was a few times when it was so bad that he would knock her out. About a year or two later he started hitting me for the smallest reasons and sometimes for no reason at all. He would hit me with anything he could get his hands on such as drop cords, chains, wood, his fist, and when he did beat me with the belt he would hit me with the belt buckle that was big as hell and had a hook in it.

Both of my parents were strung out on meth so I wasn't allowed to have friends over from school and we lived way out in the country so there was no one for me to play with so instead I played with our dogs. When I would come home from school I would either lock myself in my room or play in the woods all day with my dog, that was until I found my dog limping one day and as I got a closer look I saw a hole in her stomach from a gunshot wound that my dad had inflicted and when I mentioned it to him he told me to stop being a little bitch and put her out of her misery, so I did. Two months later at the age of 9yrs old I ran away from home and went to live with my grandma like my big sister had done already, but my grandma said since I was my father's son she didn't want anything to do with me.

DSS (Department of Social Services) got involved and they immediately made me move in with my old babysitter for 90 days while they looked into things. After the 90 days was over they placed me back with my parents. Everything went well for about 2 or 3 months then things slowly began to get worse. I started hearing voices, starting fires, and thinking of ways to torture people. After starting a few fires my mom took me to see a mental health counselor, but there was no point because I didn't trust anybody enough to talk about what was wrong with me.

At the age of ten or eleven my parents separated and I began smoking weed, popping pills and drinking. I would steal my mom's Xanax and my little sister's Adderall to get high because when I was high all my worries would cease to exist. I got in trouble with the law for the first time when I was 12yrs old for petty larceny, malicious damage, and trespassing. I was sent to a camp and did good while I was there and looking back on it I always did good when I was in a structured environment. After being there for seven months I returned home and it wasn't even two weeks before my mom caught me huffing gas.

She sent me back to the camp and I stayed for 12 months this time. When I went back home this time, my uncle gave me my first shot of meth and within a few months I got locked up for 3rd degree assault and battery. I was sent to DJJ (Department of Juvenile Justice) for 35 days and was released. Within four months I was locked up again for 3rd degree assault and battery. I was sentenced to 3 months in DJJ and when I was released I went to a mental hospital for 5 months.

During this time my dad and I was working on building a relationship so when I got out I moved in with him instead of living with my mom. He always kept the refrigerator filled with beer, and there was always weed, meth, and pills in the nightstand and he gave me full access to both. After moving in with him two weeks goes by and he calls my probation officer and tells him that I'm on drugs and running the streets. I felt betrayed and pissed because of what my dad had done. I was placed in the hospital on suicide and homicide watch because I made a statement that I was going to kill myself. I was only there a week before they let me out and this time I moved back in with my mom. I met this dude on the street and within a month and a half I started going over to his house to smoke weed and sell pills.

One day he came on to me and tried to molest me. In self-defense I stabbed him 27 times. I was only 15 years old when this happened and was sentenced to 30 years in prison for what I did.

After coming to prison my victim's sister contacted some people back here and made a deal with them to come after me. It wasn't long before I was robbed. After being robbed I tried to check into protective custody, but the CO claimed that there wasn't any available rooms in lockup. So in order to force the CO's to place me in lockup I went to somebody who I got drugs from and told them I needed a knife. He wanted to know why so I told him what I was planning to do and that's when he said that if I cut myself they would send me straight to lockup, so that's what I did.

I liked how it felt because I got a rush from it and it was the only thing that made all my worries, stress, and anger just go away. At one point I had 46 staples and 11 stitches in my arms. It doesn't really hurt when I cut, I feel a little stinging but that's all. I started off just scratching, but after a while scratching didn't satisfy the urge so I started cutting. I would make 4-5in long cuts that would go all the way through the muscle into the tendons, but after a few months of that it wasn't enough to take the urge away so I started cutting veins and arteries. I wasn't trying to kill myself but if that happened I didn't care.

It wasn't long before they placed me in CSU (Crisis Supervision Unit) and in there I wasn't able to get a razor so instead one day I saw a spider and I let it bite me 2 times. I refused the medicine for it because I liked the pain. Not only that, I liked going to the hospital because the few hours that I was there I got treated like a real person. I've even swallowed razor blades and told the SCDC prison nurse and all they say is "it'll pass." But when I'm at the hospital and tell the nurses they raise hell about getting me help.

The last time I cut, I cut a main artery and filled up two Styrofoam trays with blood. I couldn't even beat on the door to tell the CO that I had cut because I felt like I was going to pass out, so I threw the trays under the door so that the CO's would see the blood. I was rushed to the hospital and pumped full of IV's. I was very close to dying that day but I didn't care. The next day they sent me back to CSU and they were able to help me stop by keeping me close to home. The only thing that helps is seeing my family.

If you're going through something like this find someone to talk to about it. Don't just keep it bottled up because that can just cause more problems. Find a counselor that you feel comfortable talking to. I went through multiple counselors before I found one I could be honest with and it really helps. Take the medicine that you are supposed to take even though they may not fix what's wrong, don't stop taking them.

Don't self-medicate, smoke, drink, or pop pills that don't belong to you. They may help you for the time being but the outcome is worse. Don't sell drugs because they will put you at risk for prison or death. You may end up hurting someone or someone may hurt you.

At the end of the day it ain't worth your freedom or your life.

---Robert Todd

ANONYMOUS - SOME OF THE TWISTED MENTAL EFFECTS ON LOCK UP

Dear Dawn,

Just a little note, some of these brothers who have been here after 20 to 30 years in lock up are institutionalized nuts and sexually sick crazy men. The kind that believe in choking women while having sex. A man may feel that he's GOD's gift to women and they should adhere to his sexual needs. Some are very talented music wise on the raps and R & B tip or with art and drawing skills. But he may be sick and a walking contradiction. He can be school or self-educated as well, but he can be like a wild animal caged up in a cell. A pill junky who takes a cup of different pills to keep him high so that he does not have to cope with boredom and loneliness of being in prison.

He may be on medication to help him stop masturbating so much (But of course he does not take it) I mean he is sick with it, and gets highly upset if someone gets in his line of view for jacking off a female that may be in the area. And he may fall dangerously in love with certain women. He grabbed one female at this same prison when she stuck her arm through the window to gas him, and tried to break her arm. He has mental illness. He needs to be complimented, he needs people to talk to him, and he cannot function or perform without getting high. He is going to be like the white dude who played the new "Joker" to bring his career back, but overdosed before the movie came out, or either he gonna kill someone because he gets overexcited and overreacts. He may be soooo talented but so fucked up. He cannot be a part general population, trust me; he is destined to crash and burn. Look in his eyes.

So many on lock up for indefinite sentences are like this and they say that Lock up is not "cruel and unusual punishment." However look at the monster it has created...with mental illness and sexual/criminal deviancy. Be careful young men, because this can become you, if you are on lock up long enough, have no contact with family/friends or the outside world and you are treated worse than a caged wild animal. In some lock-ups they will not even allow you to have pictures of your family or loved ones for YEARS. The only recourse you may have is psychotropic drugs to melt away reality and jacking (masturbation) to make you feel that you are still a person with primal needs. The drugs and the ejaculation are the only way to express or satisfy your needs to provide you with a short lived pleasure, making you feel human, no matter how twisted it may seem.

Sick isn't it?
Realities of prison....Anonymous

FACTOID: Suicide – Ending It All

"I CAN'T DO THIS SHIT NO MORE! IMMA KILL MYSELF!!"

A common occurrence in prison. It doesn't matter what race, how physically big, or the baddest reputation. Yeah, I have witnessed a straight hardcore badass OD on pills to end his life, because one day he realized he could not do the remaining thirty years of his sentence. He was only 34 years old. He had been in prison since he was 17.

"That shit will never happen to me." A prisoner told another prisoner. But three years later, he was on lockup in the security watch cell with no clothes on and nothing else in his cell because he tried to hang himself when his baby momma sent him a 'Dear John' letter and refused to accept any more of his calls. Prisoners attempt suicide because of loneliness, depression, death of a loved one, a female has ended the relationship, or because they just can't do the time any longer. The majority of suicide attempts occur on lock up, correctional officers can also put so much pressure, such as mind games on a prisoner that they kill themselves to end the abuse.

The pressure of not being in society any longer can cause a prisoner to call it quits, especially during Thanksgiving and the Christmas holidays. Childhood memories of those days can lead to depression. Seeing and hearing about certain events that are taking place in society is a hurting feeling when you know that you will not be able to participate for years and for some of us NEVER. Too many young cats are killing themselves knowingly, and unknowingly. Even sadder is that some of them have seven years or less to go before they are released.

When I say that they are unknowingly killing themselves, I am referring to those who have decided to get put on psych medication so they can get high in order to deal with the stress, not realizing that those medications are tearing at their body and mental bit by bit. We have young brothas receiving grown men sentences. I mean 50 years, 80 years, LIFE, Double LIFE or FOUR (4) LIFE sentences like I have.

After years of filing appeals that are not granted, hanging with their homeboys, or homies, drinking, smoking and fighting other prisoners and guards, the realization of their situation starts to kick in. No more hanging out with your family and friends, no more home-cooked meals, or eating at your favorite restaurants, no more pushing whips, no more clubbing, no more sexual relationships with females, no more sports parties at the crib, no more bike week, no more clothes, only the same state issued clothes you wear every day until you get out of prison, and basically no more freedom. That is when the depression creeps in and grows like Stage 3 cancer; then ultimately death. It is our attempt as prisoners who care about the youth and the mass incarceration of our children and fellow countrymen, to get you to end all the negative things you have or think about getting involved in and begin a more productive lifestyle. There isn't anything *"real"* about coming to prison and ending it all. Real talk from yo' Uncle Streets.

Also Remember: Suicide does not necessarily mean that you have mental illness.

Excerpt from "BLINDSIDE Diaries": 8:50am.

One of my co-workers is having a very bad morning. He is crying about why the world hates him so much. Everybody thinks he is soft and he is not. They are going to find out soon. Everyone is always trying to get something from him because he is Mr. Nice Guy. His girl has left him. He changed religion, tired of working, got a LIFE sentence and tired of doing time. This guy is really depressing me but I'm trying to talk him out of cutting himself or any other suicide attempt he might do.

Damn how the hell I get myself into this when all I said was, "Good Morning. How are you?" I bet I won't ask him that tomorrow. Fucking up my day right along with his.

GETTING HELP

Many of the prisons are doing a poor job with Mental Health services. Most staff has not been properly trained for mental health/psychological issues. Inmates need more assistance and lines to the outside world with those who can provide mental health counseling or just someone to talk to.

SUICIDE HOTLINE: 800-273-8255

Unfortunately prisoners do not have access to this number, unless they are using a contraband cell phone. If they tell the CO that they feel suicidal, instead of compassion, a prisoner will be stripped naked and thrown into solitary confinement. Or strapped into the chair where they are immobile for 4+ hours and if they need to use the restroom, they have to go on themselves.

Correctional Staff and prison administration, please properly assist the prisoners with REAL MENTAL HEALTH services, empathetic listening/counseling, fresh air and professional help...*at the end of the day, we are all human beings and it is not your place to judge.*

Whether you are in prison or NOT...

If you need someone to talk to, PLEASE, PLEASE, PLEASE pick up the phone and call to talk to someone *you trust* or the Suicide Hotline. Someone will be there to hear you speak your thoughts. Suicide is up 30% in the United States right now (2018). People feel sad, isolated, hopelessness, overwhelmed, stressed, scared....

If you feel suicidal, it does not mean that you are mentally ill. You may just be going through something...but you are NOT alone. At some point in our lives we all feel that way. It is not always mental illness; it can be a situational experience that makes you feel as if you have no other options except death, *but* you DO have options. You may also need professional help. It is okay to ask for help.

TALK IT OUT!

Pick up the phone and talk it out. Don't act on it. Call a dear friend, trusted family member, a stranger...or the suicide hotline.

You can ALWAYS also pray for guidance, strength and protection from God/Allah/Creator.

Sometimes when you talk things out, you can find solutions and sometimes you find that the situation may not be as horrible as you think it is...

LETTERS TO PARENTS
(THOSE BOTH INSIDE OR OUTSIDE)

LETTERS TO PARENTS (THOSE BOTH INSIDE OR OUTSIDE)
Table of Contents

CREATING A CRIMINAL PSYCHOPATH

When children are raised up by parents who beat them the abuse they receive will have an effect on that child for the rest of their life. In some cases the child will grow up thinking that it is ok to be cruel to others because he has learned so from his parents. This child has not only experienced brutality but has also experienced survival. In most cases he will become violent because in his own mind this is what it takes to survive. He is full of hate even though he may learn to hide it by being polite to others. These people are interspecies predators who use charm, manipulation, intimidation, sex, and violence to control others and to satisfy their own selfish needs. Lacking in conscience and empathy, they take what they want and do as they please, violating social norms and expectations without guilt or remorse and the prison system is full of these people.

-- Brian Scott Stapleton

DUPREE EVANS - HOW TO SPEAK WITH YOUR PARENTS

Greetings Readers and Young Minds.

My name is Dupree, and I am locked up serving a natural life sentence without the possibility of parole for murder. I often ask myself how did I get here and the answer that I have come up with is that I have been hard headed and refused to listen to those who had my best interest at heart. Most specifically, my mother told me numerous wise words of wisdom that I refused to take heed to. It sounded like riddles then, but now I know that she had been 100% correct in all that she told me in her riddles. "A hard head makes a soft ass" which had been her favorite, because I got beatings for the same thing twice. This has been applicable to a lot of things when I take time to think deeply on the subject as you should.

"Never be a follower, always be a leader" had been one of her favorites. So and so doing this that and the third, so I will go and do this that and the third. So and so, getting away with it, and I get caught basically being a follower imitating the actions of others.

"You think you know it all" and "there is nothing out there in them streets but trouble that will leave you in the hospital, dead, or in prison."

Readers and Young Minds, what I am presently experiencing is something that I would not wish on my worst enemies, not on someone's child, niece, nephew, daughter or son. I am writing to humbly ask you all not to disregard your parents or uncles, or older siblings so easily when they tell you things or be quick to go off on a journey thinking that you so slick or tough that nothing can harm you.

I wish I had stayed a nerd in school, and avoided the crowd I chose to hang out with because all of us found ourselves just like moms said: in the hospital, dead or in prison. It is a lot of truth in that.

I've been told that "Conversation rules the nation." And its truth in that too! So talk to your family. It takes courage and may seem doubtful but try *and if they always yelling and screaming ask them could they please stop yelling and that you don't like to be yelled at, and ask them how did they feel when their parents yelled at them, did they like it or dislike it? I am sure you will have their undivided attention if you are not yelling yourself and tell them whatever is on your mind.* Tell them your hopes and your dreams and ask them for help with achieving your hopes and dreams and to lay out your alternatives.

Be proactive with your life and not reactive. I am quite sure it's a lot of you who lack the courage. I suggest you write a letter and ask questions, speak your mind and be 100% respectful. Letting them know that you do not seek confrontation, merely a better understanding because I assure you, that if you take the necessary time and make the effort to understand, it will go a long ways towards being understood. Trust me, you are on the same team, and are misunderstanding one another due to a lack of communication. Tell them respectfully what you don't like and listen to what they have to say. Truly listen and ask them how can we both get what we want, and honor your agreement. The first step to being treated like an adult is acting like one.

Dupree Evans
SCDC# 322078

*(Like what Dupree has to say? Come visit with Dupree in prison for a month via his journal of day to day life in prison in our next book-"*Blindside Diaries, Life behind the Fences*" coming in Winter 2019)*

HOW TO SPEAK WITH YOUR CHILDREN

Mr. Dupree's letter is important because this speaks not only to the youth but to parents also.

Parents, YOU are responsible for your children.
I am going to be blunt and frank.

DO NOT have children with someone that you do not love or who does not love you. Especially when you do not plan on spending the rest of your lives together. Divorce and Death do happen, but why bring your children into a situation where there is no love and a broken home?

Also stay away from someone else's husband/wife. Chances are they will not leave their spouse for you and why have all that drama, jealousy and possible criminal actions that will leave someone scarred, maimed, dead…or in prison? What will happen to the children left behind?

You are responsible for your children. If you cannot afford to have them *or* do **not** want to do your best to take care of them the best you can *without* money, then just don't have them. Even if you do not have money, children need your love and attention. That goes a LONG way and they will cherish that more than anything.

Don't curse and use profanity in front of your children or to your children. I have heard people calling little 3 years olds "cocksucker" "mutha-fuckers", "bitches" and the list goes on and on. What kind of language is that to use with a child? That is truly despicable behavior, and then you wonder why the child has no respect for you when they get older.

Some parents love their children but do not listen to them. They impose what they want the child to do or be. Some do not get involved in their children's activities or schools. It is VERY IMPORTANT to know what your child is doing. You will never know what they are up to 100% of the time, but it is important that your child knows they can talk to you and you will support them (after you scream and yell)… but whatever you do, do not curse them and berate them. In the end, the question should always be "Where do we go from here?" They need to know that you have their back.

Attached is something found on the Internet. It is United Kingdom based and it is not foolproof, but it should assist in helping with keeping your child on the straight and narrow. https://www.nidirect.gov.uk/articles/preventing-involvement-crime

Some of the highlights of this website are: providing reasons why children commit crime, such as poor grades, truancy, drugs and/or mental health issue, difficult family relationships.

It suggests that parents have good communication with love, have clear rules and boundaries as well as knowing where and who your children are with

Lastly it suggests that a parent should be very involved with your child's school and with extra-curricular activities or within the community.

We can try our best to teach our children right from wrong, be there for them and try to give them a better life than we have had, but at the end of the day, it is up to your child to do the right things, and you will have that sense of comfort if you have instilled good values in your child. It is not foolproof, as nothing is; however, at least you have done your best.

The next letter is one by a father who realizes that the way he spoke to and encouraged his child may not have been the "right" way.

GERALD BROWN - WORDS HAVE LASTING EFFECTS ON CHILDREN

Dear Salam,

Son, it seems like many years have passed since I last heard from you; although it's only been a couple of months. Everyone (including your mother) says that you are the big man now. Although I can't quite understand how you could be the "big man" at only 14 years old. I still look at you as my little boy. In a good way I can see how you could be "the big man," but not in the way that I'm hearing about. Yo', hold up and let me start over by saying this: It is mostly, No! -- It's all my fault that you are in the streets and have the outlook on life that you do.

When you were just a little boy, I taught you how to fight and win; even taught you some real dirty fighting tactics. My father always said that there is no such thing as a fair fight. If a nigga (someone) is tryin' to hurt you, you hurt him first – in any way that you can. It is my fault that they call you 'Killa' now. That's what I started calling you after you beat up your first little bully. I was so proud of my little man steppin' up, taking care of himself and not letting no one bully him. Although, over the years it seems that that name (Killa) has been a curse, because you feel as though you have to keep proving that you are indeed "a Killa." Son, I apologize for misleading and misguiding you in the way that I have. Don't get me wrong, because there is absolutely nothing wrong with defending yourself. Though at this point I believe that you may be becoming your own worst enemy; and thus, you're going to have to start defending yourself from yourself. What I'm trying to say is that as I sit here in this 10/6 foot cell, I can visualize you sitting here with me – ALLAH (GOD) FORBID son, there are young men all around me that remind me of you; some just a few years older than you – 17, 18, years old.

Salam, I hear that you are knockin' niggas (people) out, taking nigga's (people) packages (drugs), and all other kinds of shit. My dear son – I love you more than anything in this world. I'd give my life for yours in an instant. I'd do anything to protect you, but I can't protect you from you – that is something that you'll have to learn yourself. As a child, I wanted you to be tough to be prepared for what this ol' cruel world has in store for you as a black male child. Therefore, I thought that I had to teach you "the ways of the world"—I was wrong—not in my intention, *but in the way that I went about teaching you.* Son, I humbly ask that you give me a chance to start your teaching from scratch. See, I was attempting to teach you something that I didn't quite understand myself – how to be a man. It's like reading a book that has every other page torn out to it. It's impossible to understand, so you just try and fill in the gaps. What your mother and I were doing when we started raising you. "Constantly trying to fill in the gaps." My father wasn't really there to teach me how to become a man and so I vowed to be a better father, a real daddy to my son—ironically it seems I may have been even a worse father than my own.

Son, I named you Salam and even before you were barely able to walk I started calling you Killa, one of the many contradictions that I've placed into both of our lives. Titles, names, and /or whom or what we are known by hold much more then what most people realize. I named you Salam before I truly knew the significance and understood what it meant. Salam means Peace. How in the hell could I ever start calling you Killa?

Son, I am forever sorry for being a contradiction in your life. Though from this point forward, I promise, that I will never misguide you again. Though, the fact still remains that I am the reason why you are who you are and why you do some of the things that you do, my dear son, I pray that you can live through my prison experiences and won't have to have these inhumane experiences for yourself.

As you know, I am Muslim and at this present time, the entire Muslim world is going through the Holy Month of Ramadan. During Ramadan Muslims fast from sun-up until sun down (4:45 a.m. until 8:40 p.m. for 29 or 30 days. In free society you fast all day and eat once the sun has set. But here in prison, locked behind steel doors, you have to wait until the Correction Office (C.O.) brings you your food. You ain't got no refrigerator to open up, much less reachin' in and getting something to eat. There have been nights wherein I haven't gotten any food until 10 or 11 o'clock at night. Some nights the C.O.'s brought me nothing. This is prison life – a life that I wouldn't wish upon the devil himself. In prison, the guards don't care if your name is Killa, Salam or Dr. Martin Luther King Jr., because all are treated the same – like dogs. Your fellow suffers (other Prisoners) might be afraid of Killa and may perhaps even respect Salam, but the guard and other prison staff don't give a damn about Killa's street rep, because they are part of a legal organized gang that can beat you down and even kill you with impunity and immunity, these are people whom are numb to your feelings. They deal with mass murderers, serial killers, and baby rapist on a daily basis. They don't give a fuck about Killa or Salam.

Please son, I am not trying to frighten or scar you straight, I am not trying to beat you down with verbal gymnastic, or trick you into walking down the straight path. Son you were raised in the streets, and thus you can peep game and also recognized bull-shit when you see it. And that's why I'm appealing to your intellect—yes I am telling you the truth about prison life knowing that you are intelligent enough, smart enough to know and understand that this is not the life for you. I taught you how to defend yourself. I taught you street game. I taught you how to read and write, I even taught you how to respect little girls and woman—Please son, let me teach you NOT to end up in prison like me, your father.

The first step that will lead you away from these prison walls is to realize that you don't have to prove your toughness, your "manhood" to anyone. Son, you ain't no Killa, you are a peace loving man who's trying to transition from boyhood into manhood at much too fast a pace; and on top of that, you don't have me (your father) there to help in your transition. Please know this son – though I am not there physically to take you by the hand and guide you, I pray that these words written in ink will soak though this paper into the bright consciences of your brain and into your psyche of the intelligent human being that you are and guide you *away* from these prison walls.

Peace, Love Respect
Your father, Gerald Brown #174505
Abul Wahiid Batiin

JAMES SIGLER – FATHER LOST CONTACT DUE TO INCARCERATION & SON PLACED IN FOSTER CARE

Decmeber 28, 2013 -- Dear Jaiheam,

First I want to start this letter off by saying I love you. And everything I put in this letter is because I love you and want nothing but the best for you. For years I know you've been hearing stories of what got me in prison and you in state custody. Imma give you my story and let you decide who or what to believe. Follow your heart. Growing up, I think the biggest mistake I made was not being me for a long time. I was being what everyone else wanted or expected me to be. Even though at a young age I knew right from wrong and knew that most of the choices I was making were wrong, I still did them because I knew they were what everyone expected. At the age of eleven I knew of stealing cars to selling dope, shooting people trying to hurt them. Some were way afraid of me. It seemed like every day, week, and month I graduated to a bigger wrong.

Even though through it all, I kept the tough guy personality, deep down I knew I was wrong and something was missing. But still I chose to ignore that. My biggest thing was I wanted to make it! Be somebody! Everybody around me that has "something" was guys on the streets. Those were the ones I saw in the flyest cars, baddest females, toughest gangs and lots of money. So I felt to gain what they had I had to do whatever was necessary, and I did. I couldn't wait to grow up and get big overnight! My whole youth went down the drain when I made the decision that whatever it took to get wealth I was gone do it.

Even though I grew up in a two-parent home I never had anyone actually sit me down and take the time to understand me and guide me. So I had to teach myself. By the age of fourteen nobody could tell me what to do and what not to do because I felt I knew it all. I was seeing people gang banging, robbing, and selling crack like it was going out of style! But the whole time I was killing myself inside because I knew what they were doing was wrong I was trying to have sex with any and every female I came into contact. That was what my days consisted of. That's what all the rappers were talking about in their songs and that's what was on the TV's too. It looked like the cool thing to do. The whole time I was suffering from a mistaken identity not knowing who I was or what I wanted out of life.

At the age of seventeen I got your mother pregnant and everything went haywire from there. It seemed like everything I was doing had to be turned up times ten. And the only thing I learned from my father was that if you ever plant a seed you start to accept your responsibility and help that seed grow. So my plans was to get everything ready so my unborn (you) wouldn't have to worry about hardships in life. In the process of me running around reckless telling myself I had to do this or I had to do that I got locked up and sentenced 16 years with the Department of Corrections. One of the things I realized is that the whole time I was telling myself everything I was doing was because of you, I had to realize it was really just because I was being myself. Even though I knew you would be a major part of my life, the fact was, I loved the lifestyle. The streets were providing me with (another thing I know now is that nothing good comes out of evil gain).

The biggest shocker came to me when I found out that the whole time while on the street I was thinking I was a man, I wasn't. Because I was paying bills, had money to blow and was living with your mother, I had to be a man. A boy couldn't do these things could he? Even a few years after being locked up I still hadn't grown up (reached manhood) I was still lost and trying to find myself. You may not remember the times you came to visit me while I was locked up, because you being so young then. But nothing made me feel better, made me want to do better, then the time I spent with you. Back then I knew I had to grow up. Since I was locked up and missed your birth and years until you turned three, the times we shared on visits meant more to me than anything.

Every time I looked at you I would think, *"Wow that's a little me!"* That's not me to be a better person, but to actually grow up and become a man so that I could raise my son to be a man. And that I knew how to do this, but that could be one who spoke words but didn't practice what he preached. So I started studying and became the man I wanted to become for you that know nothing about. Every time I got a chance we would communicate. Everything was going well (under the circumstances) until your mother made the decision to move to another state from where you were born and my family was located. My family was devastated because you all had a relationship with exchange other and it was now being torn apart. All that I could do was trust that your mother was making the best move for you all and do whatever that could so we (you and me) could continue to communicate. Because although y'all was moving to another state that wasn't losing complete contact that just wouldn't be able to have our visit that I enjoyed so much. This hurt me more than anything because my whole part was for my son! And now you were getting stripped from me when I decided to change my life for the one thing that believe.

After that it seem like everything that went down from that felt like I had lost because even though I was promised constant contact with you, it seemed like we only got to communicate once a week. That was undisputedly my best day of every week. I thought that my lack of constant communication with you would make you forget who your father was, however it seemed like the opposite happened every time I talked to you. You would remind me of the times we shared together. So then I continued my studies in prison but I was half in, half out. I felt like now I had to gain funds to get my son and make sure he was alright. Then they came. That hurt me more than I have ever been hurt. This is (Department of Social Services) DSS contacted me saying you were in their custody and had been for a while. First thing they did was contact my family so they could get in contact with whoever they had to get my purpose back in my life. There was but only so much I could do, I had already started working and sending money to your mother for your care but it hurt me every day thinking about what you may have been going through. I got in contact with one of the case workers and she took a liking to me because she saw that my goal was the betterment of my son. For a while that helped because she would send pictures of you and send brief letters about what you like and didn't like. But nothing could replace the bond that we shared. For the first time in a long time I prayed and asked God to help my son and protect him from evil. Also for as long as I could remember I was scared that if I lost you, I would never get the chance to raise you, teach you about the mistakes I made and how important education is.

A couple months later my worst fears came true. DSS refused to give you (my only son) to my mother due to the fact they wanted all your brothers and sisters to stay together. I was devastated but I kept pushing because I was determined to get my child back.

Today I feel as everything that ever happened is my fault. I have told myself the 'if onlys' so many times that I can recite them by heart. Due to the fact you are African American and have 'my' blood running through your veins, I know your struggle is the same as mine was at your age. So trust me when I tell you I understand your pain. There are some things I want to say to you from the heart.

Enjoy your youth! Be yourself and never let anybody persuade you to do something you don't want to do and know is not right. And education is the key to success. Knowing is the first step to being successful and as long as you know, no one can delude you with mistrust. Learn your history! Before you can get something you gotta know where you came from. No matter how hard the road may get never turn around! Always keep pushing forward (and most times the short cuts that present themselves are no shortcuts but dead ends). I am a living witness to that myself. Trust in God and let your mind and heart be your guide. This is a law to me that I wish had lived before I got where I am today. Stop and think! As long as you live by that you'll never go wrong.

Know this above all, if I could take back everything I ever did, I would in a heartbeat, just to be in your life. But I can't. I have to make the best of the future. One thing for certain though, I love you! Even though I'm not able to reach you and touch you or communicate with you, have NO doubt that you have a place in my heart. You are my heart! The life I decided to live when I was on the streets wasn't worth losing all the years I've lost with you. I could never make that up. Trust me, all the things the guys in the streets are doing, joining gangs, selling drugs, and partying isn't worth your life wasting behind these walls. Never think because it is hard, you have to do this or you have to do that, nothing worth keeping/having comes easy! And it's the hard times that make you a man. As long as you endure and don't let the evil doers of the streets seduce you, you'll always be the victor. No matter what you have or who you with. A man's worth isn't judged on what he has or doesn't have but his integrity! Tell yourself you can make it and you will. Remember this discipline as the training that makes punishment unnecessary! You don't need anyone to tell you what's right or wrong. It's already within you, just follow your heart! You don't need anyone to punish you to make you do better, punish yourself!

To my 10-year-old child who I haven't spoken to since you were three. Know this, the love I have for you is indescribable! And if you ever feel as if no one loves you or even feel as if your biological parents don't love you. Read this and know that you are my heart and I love you more than life itself.

Don't make the mistakes I've made. Take your father's mistakes and learn from them, grow from them. Believe me there's a better way. Fortunately in a few short years I'll be by your side because I won't rest until I find you! When these gates open for me, you're the first thing on my to-do-list. I feel if I can get into your life I could help so you'll never see the inside of these fences. Because all it takes is one mistake and they could take your life away. Again fortunately I am one of the lucky ones that are coming home. Most guys here with me will never see the streets again. They will die behind these walls. Don't be one of the one's that say, "Only if I had listened" or "Only if I didn't follow behind this person." Like they said, all that it takes is that one night of so-called "fun" to ruin your life forever! To the child that I haven't spoken to in five long years, hear my cries and listen. To my son that I love more than anything, Aim high! Dream big! Then reach out and grab it. Nothing is impossible! Whatever you want to become you can be. All you have to do is believe.

To my child that fills my dreams every night, I love you, I wish you the best. Remember: For God so love the world he gave his only begotten son so that who so ever shall be believe will have Everlasting life and not perish: John 3:16.

---Sincerely Your loving father, James Sigler

(Released in 2018)

(James and his son finally made contact and saw each other recently. His son has been adopted by a wonderful couple who allows him to have a relationship with Jaiheam, who is now 14 and a fine young man)

(Would you like to hear more from James "Yuk" Sigler and his former life in prison? Come and visit him for a month in prison via his journal, see our next book in this series: "Blindside Diaries, Life behind the Fences" In addition, Mr. Sigler is also a talented writer. See his e-book "Twisted Loyalty" published by Imperial Imprint LLC currently for sale on Amazon: https://www.amazon.com/dp/B01M9BYL6O and "Susie Q" (A gangster deeply in love and would do anything for his an HIV+ female childhood friend) coming out Winter 2019.)

COLLATERAL DAMAGE: GOING TO PRISON WHEN HAVING KIDS

"...it opened my eyes to the fact that there is a whole new generation that is getting ready to be raised by their fathers in prison if we don't do something to stop it out here." [119]

Darryl/Bruce Goodman ("Generations of Philly families are Incarcerated together" by Samantha Melamed)

In the United States 2.7 million children (1 in 28, basically one child in every classroom) currently have a parent who is incarcerated. [120] [121]

Children of incarcerated parents are six times more likely to go to prison themselves. [122]

Children of an incarcerated parent also tend to wind up with twice the chance of having learning disabilities and ADHD tripled, with basic behaviorial problems. Boys are more physically aggressive and tend to get into fights and girls looking for attention as well as promiscuity. [123] [124] [125]

Some laws that affect you and your child when you go to prison [126]

- The Adoption and Safe Families Act of 1997 (AFSA) This means that parental rights can be terminated if your child has been in foster care for 15 of the past 22 months.
- The Welfare Reform Act of 1996 - If you have a felony drug charge some states have created a law that you are no longer eligible for food stamps or welfare benefits. (So how do you eat and take care of yourself when you get home?)
- Housing Opportunity Program Extention Act (1996) - If you are looking for housing they can do criminal background checks and deny you housing if you have a violent/non-violent felony. Where are you and your kids going to live when you come home?
- Violent Crime Control and Law Enforcement Act of 1994 - If you are currently incarcerated, you cannot receive Pell Grants and various financial aid. So basically when you could have been getting your college degree while in prison to give you better opportunities to take care of yourself and family when you get home, the laws changed and cut it.

PRISON IN GENERAL

PRISON IN GENERAL - *Table of Contents*

389

ANDRE CANNON - PRISON...IT CAN BECOME AN EXTENDED VISIT

Dear Youth,

My name is Andre Cannon. I'm 40 years old serving a 22 year prison sentence. I've been incarcerated for eleven years now, and I hope that I can encourage you not to take the same route me and many other inmates did. Every inmate at some point in time before their incarceration has thought, *Never me...I won't get caught...I'll never catch all that time like they did.* The truth is, eventually you get caught. Could be sooner, could be later, but you will be caught.

The overcrowding of prisons is evident. As an inmate, every day is a possibility of unpredictable events you may face. The everyday life of a prisoner can be full of negative surprises. Things happen when you are locked in with people who have lost all hope in life, and have nothing to look forward to but how to survive in prison for years and years, and some for LIFE. The environment is dangerous. You could lose your life, or be badly hurt over the smallest things, such as a simple disagreement over a football game to not giving someone a pack of cookies. Everyday your life is at risk in prison. My worst fear is being put in a position where I may have to defend myself, and making the worst mistake of hurting someone or even mistakenly killing someone. Now you are facing more time than what were given or maybe even Life. It happens a lot. You have inmates here that had less than three months left to do after being locked up for years, and in one stupid incident, they ended up losing their life, or they took someone else's life, and now will never see freedom again.

Young generation, I hope this letter opens your eyes to the realities of crime. Imagine having to wake up every day in a place that you hate the most. No longer are you treated like a man. You are now the equivalent of an animal. You are told when you can eat, when you can sleep, what you can wear, when you can shower, when your family can see you, etc. Your daily movements are decided by people who think you don't amount to nothing. No matter how much you try to better yourself, in their eyes, YOU ARE NOTHING.

Young people, imagine being forced to share a room with someone you cannot trust. How about an individual who will rob and steal from you in a minute or even a roommate who is known for raping some of his past roommates? These are some of the situations, young people that could cause you to lose your life or even your manhood. You are literally put in a world in itself where there is always fighting, stabbings, rapes, diseases, disrespecting, awful food, nasty living conditions. Officers who come into work looking forward to making your life a living hell.

So young people, if you chose to live a life of ANY CRIME—you are guaranteed to live this prison life eventually—this I promise you. It's true that crime doesn't pay, and living this type of life isn't worth the crime. Every day I wish I could go back in time and do it all over again. What I'm telling you was also told to me when I was younger. I hope you don't make the same mistake I made by not listening to the person who is living a prison life.

Stay focused young people. Take advantage of having good education, and work hard to achieve the life you want and deserve to live. Why choose to live my life? It's the life everyone hates.

Yours Truly,
"Inmate"
Andre Cannon #257968

Mr. Cannon is an extremely talented artist with Imperial Imprint. Please see his art at www.imperial-imprint.com or www.fineartsamerica.com) He is one of our star artists. He is absolutely talented. See the beautiful work he does on the following page.

BRIAN ATTAWAY - THE PREDATORS & THE PREY (I)

Prey in the Pen, Predator in the Pen. Niggas make shit go down behind these walls every day because it's always somebody that looks to get involved in shit every day. You got your "doers" and your "watchers". Niggas that make shit happens and Niggas that watch shit happen.

I seen people get hit up in the kitchen and in the unit on the yard plus in the gym. You can't hide from drama you just got to know how to handle it when it comes your way. It's a saying, you must heard before when New Niggas come into the Pen "Fresh Meat." To become fresh meat is like being hunted and you are the deer standing in bright headlights; Niggas will take advantage of the weak all kinds of ways and you can never be respected as a man because of vulnerability. You can be the hardest Niggas off the hands but still run into a Nigga who will set you up just because you is a threat, because it's something to do...you know? Like entertainment.

You must always remember where you're at and who you surrounded by. It's killers, thieves, robbers, dealers and cons so it's how you bid and what you allow is who you become. I prefer to stab your ass up until my arms get tired so the next don't want to fuck with me. If I fistfight with you I'll still want to stab you because sometime that's the only thing people respect back here. It's called gun play and it's a lot of gun toters and you got to be ready at all cost. If these doors get popped you got to have your banger or bangers because you don't want to be the one slipping without yours or you're done.

These prisons got real convicts especially where I'm at. The same shit you see on TV and movies does happen and this shit is real serious because if you was to come and get me out my comfort zone I'll have to send you just so I won't have to watch out for you in the long run unless you got connect with people on another yard, because then I got trouble with people on another yard, then I got trouble back here because you deal with gangs too. I'm a man who knows how to bid and I had to learn fast because I've been in situations that couldn't be avoided. If you got your freedom, keep it because this is a grave yard in many ways and a place of suffering because you can see all the mental patients running to the pill line trying to escape this reality. *Don't come here if you don't want to risk changing your life forever.*

The food is garbage and these Niggas are stank because a lot of them don't wash their ass.

This is No Life
This is the hunting field don't become a deer
Real Talk

JAMES SIGLER -THE PREDATORS AND THE PREY (II)

There are two types of people here and they are the predators and the prey. And in prison those two are multiplied by ten. On the walk in here, right then and there you will decide which one you are. From the Officers to the Inmates you will be challenged...big fish eat little fish.

When you first walk into the prison walls the Officers will see if you are a pushover or somebody who's not to be taken lightly... Then when you are finally placed with other inmates you will be tested again. Everybody wants to make a name for themselves by proving that they are bigger and badder than somebody! Robbery, Extortion, Rape are just a few examples... Either you are strong or you are weak, protect yourself or become somebody's girlfriend, laundry man, do-boy, or simply there yes man. Once it is established who/what you are, this will follow you throughout your stay on ANY yard.

The one thing that's misunderstood is that every day, every minute, every second, you have to be on guard... because even if you are not weak and can protect yourself, there is always somebody bigger, badder, stronger, then you somewhere! The only question is when y'all will meet and how you will meet... It's a big training camp everywhere so you'll see prey pumping up getting ready for the next attack plotting, scheming, on who the next victim is someone norm. So you either train or become prey. Become somebody do boy, laundry boy, girlfriend...

Everybody around you, it has been said, is not fit for society; they are a menace to society and therefore that is why they are in prison! So being aware is essential to your well-being. Rape is constant, extortion is every day, being preyed upon is an everyday thing for some people. And for them there is no peace ever! Most people are forced to join gangs, or religious groups to have some sort of protection... But that's not even fool proof. If a group knows your purpose is for protection, they will accept you but not protect you. Sometimes you won't even be accepted. Sometimes it doesn't matter who you are with or who's behind you. If you're weak, you're weak! You will be preyed upon! They do not care! If you got it and they want it, they are coming to get it! Regardless of what it is!

And even leaving one prison to go to another won't work because your "prison status" will follow you throughout your stay. It will be whispered that you are the weak guy! And soon the wolves will come a sniffing and this will not be lived down until you become one of the same people you despise... You will have to do something very dramatic to earn your "good name" back... Most times it is a stabbing of an Inmate/Officer just let it be known that you are not to be taken lightly! Survival is an everyday battle for everyone back here. Prey watching out for the predator and predator looking for prey to make their way of living more comfortable... The man/boy who comes to prison for driving drunk, parking tickets or any little small thing will still have to live around rapists and people in for murder, robbery, etc....

Come in for a speeding ticket and get raped!

Come in for driving drunk and pay extortion!

Come in for a school, bar, street/brawl and never leave because you had something somebody wanted and they killed you for it! Multiple stab wounds!

It is said that prison is like a Jungle... lions, and tigers and bears oh my!!

Now I will be fair and say that you have 'in between' but that person is someone who has predator tendencies, most likely had been a predator, but have advanced so far in his studying that he is humble... Only attack when threatened... Allowed to study so he can advance because he's made it known he is not prey! Forcefully made it known!

I've seen prey kill themselves not to go through the torment! I've seen in order for prey to survive is that their family on the outside pays handsomely to someone back here to protect them...weekly...consistently.

Once you are classified as prey.

You have nothing!

Your life isn't your life anymore... It belongs to someone else!

(Would you like to hear more from James "Yuk" Sigler and his former life in prison? Come and visit him for a month in prison via his October 2013 journal, see our next book in this series: "Blindside Diaries, Life behind the Fences" In addition, Mr. Sigler is also a talented writer. See his e-book "Twisted Loyalty" published by Imperial Imprint LLC on Amazon: https://www.amazon.com/dp/B01M9BYL6O and "Susie Q" coming out Winter 2019.)

FACTOID - Homemade Weapons (Shanks)

A nything can be made into a weapon also known as a "shank" in prison or any detention center. The long handle of a cooking spoon off the scooping part, the silver part of a clipboard, the thick iron bar on the top of a swinging door, even the iron drain in the shower can be made into a deadly throat cutter once it's sharpened right. There are two types of knives in prison. A flat blade and an ice pick.

Flat blades will cut a victim open and cause a lot of bleeding quickly, whereas an ice pick will poke the insides of a victim and cause internal bleeding which is why it is the preferred weapon of most attackers who have intentions of killing the victim, but in truth, both weapons will kill a person if the attacker strikes the right places.

Some prisoners become so obsessed with stabbing their foes that they make their homemade knife a special way so that if it is stolen everyone will know it is his. With the flat blades prisoners will cut the blade to make teeth ridges or put a curve at the point. And some prisoners make holders to tote their blade in because it has dried up feces so that when the victim gets stabbed, the feces will be in their victim's system and possibly kill him eventually. The biggest weapons are wooden stakes made from broomsticks, long steel pieces broken off the beds, and any type of heavy pipe which are made into machetes.

Homemade knives/shanks will always exist in prisons and be used to intimidate, seriously hurt and kill their victims. So stay away from prison, it is not a playhouse.

PHILIP COPELAND - FEAR AND ITS EFFECT ON THE CRIMINAL MIND

Fear is bigger than emotion alone. Fear is circumstance. Fear is the object of the Devils affection. Fear is a tool, tool used against the slave, devised to slow their conscious perceptions, aims & directions ... conceptions.

In retrospection – Fear is the Devils greatest weapon. Fear has been known to silence the bombastic. So eloquent over talking the filibuster, wolfing him down, encapsulate in his words inside of a silky smooth garment of shame, pain and fright , w/out ever even raising a finger, for fear, is embedded into the conscious minds & psyches of the fearful captive.

Fear is control in its most pure form. Cowards, weak germs, thin skin yellow bellies & spineless slithering worm of no great concern. Oh Lord to Hell They Burn!!! Proclaimed wishful thinking. As they reflected on the pain of fears oppressive whiplash. The one that left the gash along the valley of wishful thinking shoulder blades, wishfully thinking that the pain that fear constantly implemented would soon end.

Fear had effectively changed the conscious thought, into the wishful thought. Wishful – according to wishes, rather than fact. Fear is a state of being. An unacceptable state of being. To fight back is as much of nature natural selection. The emotion of fear is to adapt and conquer is man's natural charge. Therefore, when this Prison Industrial Complex, fear is used interchangeably.

Prison Rape: Prison rape is no myth, it exists but it is Highly Exaggerated. The heads of the Prison Industrial Complex has for years promoted the aspect of "Don't Drop the Soap." Prison rape as an instrument of fear, under the guise of "deterring children from going to Prison." Although, I do not want nor advocate children going to Prison, I also do not want society to think that you either being forcefully fucked in the ass or forcefully fucking another man in the ass as a rite of passage for Prison adjustment. Actually, homosexuality is highly frowned upon, especially rape because most convicts are "affiliated" w/something: Islam, 5%, Noge, Crip, Blood Etc. And neither advocates faggotism and usually a severe penalty of death follows. Then, it's just plain wrong.

But, it does happen, in my 24 years of incarceration, I've witnessed w/my own eyes maybe 6. Probably countless others that are too ashamed to report it or check in on PCC Protective Custody or "cheap check –in" (Catching a stupid disciplinary to go to lock up (Administrative Segregation), MSU (Maximum Security Unit or Super –Max). Fear is multiplied exponentially instituted in multiple ways, by administration & prisoner, alike. They have their solitary confinement, where I spent 15+ straight years' 12 of which in Super Max (MSU). Just being in a cage for 16 years can be fearful, until you learn to understand the tactic of divide and conquer. They merely want to have free control of you and what better way than to extract you from your affiliates', and limit your access to the outside world, make nasty innuendo about the poison they may have or may not have put in your food. Knowing that if you do not eat, you'll become weak, thus, not able to fight back, if necessary.

You also can be what is called "dry celled" or "Stripped out", depending on the reason for drycell, no food, no drink, functionally, usually, when you are suspected of having contraband hidden inside the cavities of your person. You may be subject to a "Cavity search" where they physical restrain you and go inside of your asshole w/gloved hands extracting the contraband from inside of you. Or the less evasive, X-raying your pelvic area. I'd recommend the latter, in a regular cell (your toilet is about 2-3 ft. from the head of your bunk) Dry cell has no toilet at all. No eating, drinking for days, cleansing you. Defecate and you will not be able to dispose of the contraband. Just you, four empty walls and piles of shit on the floor.

Me, myself I used to make the Pigs "suit up" every morning and form an "Extraction Team" for force cell extract me. Why? Because I am a Prisoner: I am here against my will. I am in the struggle because I was forced into resistance, just to resist indoctrination; I gave my Physical and Mental Health, not all of it, but just the worst of it. I decided to paint their walls w/ the pigs' blood, rather than relent to his forced fear. I hadn't feared that devil since I was a little baby. I never loved him because he gave me nothing.

I cannot and will not comment on the Good and or Bad of a Pig D.O.J's, Administrative employee or the like 1) because I have brothers who have to spend the rest of their days behind the walls or at least until they're physically liberated and I will not violate the G-Code. 2) Because, it still takes a certain psychological gene for someone, especially the majority Black Pigs, to decide to put chains on his own kind for a living and sleep good at night. Fuck what ya heard.

Although there are always those that come to work to do their lil job and go home. Then there are those who were bullied as little kids, or house niggaz/peckerwoods and are trying to boost their ego. If you a pig, you roll in pig shit. If you cool, you cool, you just can't dress worth a fuck, in their training, they are told that; musically, politically and culturally, they have absolutely "nothing in common" with you the prisoner. You don't like the same sports team, style of clothes, food, anything. They are told to put their foot in your ass for the Warden's sake. You are merely an insignificant "inmate" to them & their patent leather steel toed boots. The male pig can only receive my malice and venomous rebuke. The female pig can only watch me masturbate until I skeet cum onto the nasty prison floors. One shot, one kill on that uniform. Still again, in some instances, the pig (administration workers) can be your closest fear as a powerful entity. All else I'll say I'll say about the pig (Admin.) is know your enemy, as if knowing yourself. Friend and foe are counterparts, when left in perspective.

I do want to touch on the D.O.J's Dark Secret: The Psycho fuck shit they mentally put your mind thru before them trying to place you into some kind of "Step Down Program" to ease you either back into population, or in my case, society. After 16 straight years of solitary confinement, is what I need not "release" out of prison? I've been to the Psychiatric Hospital 4 times, and I am prescribed a plethora of Psychotropic medications. Even held down and forcefully medicated. I have never been a model inmate. Not even with 8 months left???? I'm to just push some imaginary button and change when I will be released? But I digress…

"Liberation, Mental Health is so rampant, and yet still so confusing. I have seen a brother I'd know years before Super Max…Now "Rico" had plenty swag, hustle, and good sense. After meeting back up years later at Super-Max he was so completely out of his mind, that when he was released, his family repeatedly called MSU and Headquarters like, "What the fuck did y'all do to him ?!?!" He was out of his fucking mind. Ain't it some shit how four walls and just you alone can fuck up some sensory shit? Yes, it is. I've seen and felt it. And it ain't pretty looking in that mirror.

The best thing I found to do in those solitary cages, for me was to stay productively busy: Drawing, reading, writing, composing music and other intellectual properties. *Something tangible to look back at if only to remind me that I am still alive; because many times I had to find a way to feel alive because I didn't feel it.* I don't know what the hell it was, but it was "NOT" life. Build positive builds w/positive people, not militant minded individuals whom are into rebellion because if you get it in your head that you can't beat 'em, you join 'em…Out of fear.

Fear is a powerful muthafucka!

~FEAR~

Money $ Montana AKA Phillip S. Copeland

(He was released from prison in 2017 and now living in a neighborhood with you)

398

FACTOID - Always Being On Point/Aware Of Your Surroundings

I magine This" You are in a large warehouse packed with the worst of the worst criminals in the world.

There are over 500 dangerous murderers, serial killers, rapists, thieves, con artists, child molesters, armed robbers, mentally challenged and violent drug dealers all around you with very few security to watch over the criminals and the warehouse., Also some of the security officers are in cahoots with some of the criminals so sometimes…Anything goes.

You are locked in this warehouse 24/7. This is where you eat, sleep, watch TV, talk on monitored phone, take your shower, use the restroom and have your recreational time. Everything is done here. Remember, the worst of the worst is here so your guard has to stay up because people will steal, rob, rape you…do unimaginable things to you. Getting hit in the head with a lock on the end of a drop cord is common…hearing someone get raped in the middle of the night always happens…even when you are taking a shower, one of your friends has to stand guard to ensure nothing foul happens to you…because rape, murder, robbery is common. The security even turns a blind eye to it.

You are always looking, watching, and expecting something to happen. One would say that you are paranoid, but no…this is not paranoia, it is real and needed at all times, for you to survive and stay alive.

Imagine this…before you go anywhere you have to scan the area or get raped…when you eat you sit with your back against the wall for fear of getting stabbed in the back. When you are taking a dump, one leg has to be out of your pants and something or someone has to be present or anything is liable to happen. Anything…pick your poison, it is only any crime to choose from.

Remember this… you know no one in this warehouse. There is no one to trust…So if a murderer wants something from you, what do you do? Give it to him in hopes of "that's it?" Take a chance on getting everything taken by force? Or are you bad enough to go up against X amount of guys with everything they could find sharpened to a fine point? Who do you trust? Who can you talk to? Even the people you knew before you went into the warehouse, how can you trust them now? Thrown into a situation like this? Who's to trust?

Security…Don't even think about it! Most of them look at you like you are the scum of the earth. Like you are worse than the dog poop that may have gotten on their shoe. Most of them are trying to get a promotion. So harassment, provoking you to act out is their high…That what they live in the warehouse for. The other…are on the same side as a lot of the criminals! Where do you run? Where do you hide?

Resisting the security officer is the "wrong" thing to do. The same people whose place it is to maintain your security also have the power to throw you in the "hole" (solitary confinement). A room all by yourself with no windows where you come out every other day (if you are lucky) to take a shower. Some security will even wrong "you" and swear on their mother that YOU started it! You are nobody/nothing but a criminal....Who would believe you?

How does this sound so far? Somewhere you would want to be? Can you make it here? Do you enjoy taking showers with no privacy with killers and rapists all around you?

And remember this; telling on anybody about anything that has been done to you will only cause further retaliation towards you. So will you take the chance of telling now, rape later? Is it worth it?

Nowhere is safe. The Guy at the microwave warning up his food isn't really a guy warming his food up...Yeah, it's more confusing than that...The guy at the microwave is really the guy who doesn't like the fact that you have more than them, so that food is actually urine and baby oil that has been warming for a while now. So he dashes it in your face, causing your skin to melt away from your face oozing like goo...looking like Freddy Kruger.

What about talking to family members and friends because the security guards said you acted up so your privileges were taken away? How do you deal with all of this? Drugs? Mental psychotropic medication? Something to ease the pain?

Now what if you could not cope so you cry for help...Your cries go unanswered...Unheard...Even the ones of committing suicide...But instead of receiving help when you mention suicide, three or four guards tackle you, strip you naked, and throw you into a room with nothing. You bang on the door, even your head. And then they come and put you in a chair. They strap you in there for hours. No matter how much you yell, scream, and even tell them you have to use the restroom to get away from that chair, they won't take you out for nothing! How does that make you feel? Can you take it?

Oh, did I mention that everyone around you is the same sex? So everywhere someone is horny...Who do they desire? Who is lusting after you? The only women around you have power over you to dictate your remaining stay in this warehouse. These women will walk past your living quarters, or shower. And if she sees you masturbating can charge you with all kinds of lewd acts. So imagine men around you that haven't seen women in years! Dogs! Animals! Dogs I tell you! No respect! Even women who they would not look at twice in the street catch their eye...gets their nature to rise...Anything starts attracting them. SO the key is "Don't be handsome!"

Imagine this, bums...dirty, smelly and stank! All of this around you. Beggars begging for anything. Con artists trying to con you out of anything.

Bums will rob and kill their mothers for food! What will happen to you? Think you are badder than these bums? Tougher? How about three or four of them together jumping you? Taking your things? What then? A Gladiator Challenge is what it is!!

Would you spend a week here? A month? How about a few years? Where the security can come into your rooms and make you strip off your clothes, lift up your penis, turn around and bunk over while spreading your butt cheeks? Some people do HIDE things in their anus you know...Throwing your things all over the place, searching and stepping on all of your personal valuables, and sometimes even stealing them from you. Is this a place where you want to be? Anywhere else this would be considered sexual assault and vandalism, but not here in this warehouse, because anything goes, remember?

Imagine this...you and your friends are up to no good. Things go bad and you all are caught. Everybody turns on you! Says it was your idea and YOU made them do it. So they send you to this warehouse for 5, 10, 20, 55 years. Maybe even for the rest of your life? When you will NEVER leave this warehouse! Could you do it? You could show your gladiator skills right? Sound cool? You could get raped by three or four strong guys then go home and maybe tell your "same" friends who put you there. Sounds cool?

Well this is prison. This is the life you live in prison. Away from society, away from everything. You don't know what is going on outside of prison. Everyone forgets you because you are no longer there or will be there for??? Would you tell mommy and daddy that you have been raped by 3 or 4 guys on the monitored prison phone? (You can NOT tell them about how someone raped you or a bunch of dudes are trying to stab and/or kill you on the phone, because the prison administration will find out and put YOU in that hole "protective custody" indefinitely).

Well don't come to prison!

Because in prison, you are on your own. Think about this the next time you are doing something illegal with your friends...think about this.

FACTOID - Shake Downs & The Shake Down Team

Shake Downs are another reality of prison life. They even have special teams that are specially trained and hired by the prison to go from prison to prison to conduct shake downs. At the institution where I am currently located, they call it the burgundy team, due to the colors of their uniforms. They come to the institution approximately twice a month, sometimes more if the warden calls for them.

When the shake down team (aka burgundy team) comes, most of the time they choose one dorm. Whichever dorm they select is in for a long day, because they are placed on lock down from that morning until mid-afternoon. When a dorm has been chosen to be shook down, they lock all the Prisoners down (lock down) on both A and B sides of the dorm, and you will be locked in your room from 9:00 a.m. till 4 or 5:00 p.m., with your toilet and water turned off. Your will be served food in a bag for lunch and dinner which is one bun with two ham sandwiches, and one cake...

There are approximately 14 burgundy team members. When they arrive to the dorm they conduct a check of the recreation field. Then they divide up in to teams of two and start searching cells. At times they turn off the water so no one can flush anything. Can you imagine going from 8a to 4p without any running water? If you did not wake up early enough, then you are unable to brush your teeth or wash your face or take a poop.

Once they arrive to your cell one of the prisoners have to step outside while the other is strip searched. After both occupants of the room are searched and handcuffed behind their backs they are required to sit on the cold concrete floor. It normally takes about 20 minutes to conduct a search. The whole time you are required to stay seated on the cold hard floor while officers step over you. At times they have the drug dog with them that is walking over you as well. Sometime the dog handler stops right in front of you and the dog can flip out and attack you and there is nothing you can do to protect yourself because your hands are cuffed behind your back.

While they are in your cell they have the dog jumping on your bed, sniffing around while the officer's rumble through all of your belongings, reading your mail, take all food out of your locker and toss it on your bed or floor. Then when they do not find anything, you are allowed to step back in your cell having to straighten up the mess they made feeling both violated and degraded.

SO AGAIN VISUALIZE THIS, you have a neat clean cell. Then burgundy team comes, make you strip off all of your clothes, search your genitals and anus, (*basically being sexually violated*) make you sit on the floor naked outside of your cell handcuffed behind your back. During that time, about 20 minutes, they are in your once clean room, pulling everything out of your locker, on your desk, walls, boxes where you have your personal or legal papers and throwing it on the floor, including your food. Going through your personal things, pictures, letters reading them and throwing them down on the ground, including your clean clothes. Touching over everything, pulling off your sheets off your bed, while the men on the shakedown team and the drug dog and it's nasty paws are walking on your personal belongings sniffing for drugs. Once completed if they find something, they take you off to lock up/solitary confinement with your roommate responsible to put your things up in ONE bag.

The rest of your stuff that doesn't fit in the duffle bag gets confiscated. Which is usually your food because your other property such as your clothes, electronics, and legal material comes first and your food is the last thing they pack so if it doesn't fit the C.O keeps it and gives it to their snitches when they come to them with information.

If the Shake Down team does not find anything once completed their shake down, they uncuff you to let you back into your cell that has been ransacked; leaving you and your roommate naked to put back on your clothes and clean up your room. How degrading, humiliating, sexually violated and angry does that make you feel? Too bad…that is just prison life.

BLINDSIDE DIARIES: October 14, Monday, 1:30 A.M. (When people are usually sleeping)

There are about eight COs in the 6 by 9 cell trying to shakedown, all of them hoping that they are the ones that find some major contraband. So that they can say they were the one that was sharp enough to take me down. (To Lock up and mess up my good behavior reputation) I'm just a simple dude that don't have two of anything, so what can they take down? I'm not indulging in anything and if I was it definitely wouldn't be in this room. I've never had a drug charge. I've never even failed a piss test. If there is one thing I've learnt in my life, is that, you should never lay your head on a pillow of dirt. My dad taught me at a very young age that when you are in the mouth of a beast the worst thing you can do is make his mouth water. So instead of cussing them out like I would like to, I just simply complied talked real gentle and told them have a nice night. But one of the guys is so racist and pissed off that they didn't find anything, so he took the radio that belongs to the Chaplin that all the coordinators use and said that it was contraband. The Chaplin, Major and the Warden will talk with me soon. They'll apologize for the inconvenience and give the radio back. It's approved for it to be in my possession. This guy is just trying to make a scene.

7.15pm.

On my way to pill line I saw the officer that took the Chaplin's radio. He is very upset. They must have had a sit down with him because he is a burgundy and he is threatening me a hundred different ways. It's really quite comical if y'all could just see him right now. He keeps saying over and over that he is going to stop me. What are going to stop me from doing? Tutoring, laying bricks, drawing, what?

FACTOID - Dry Cell

Dry Cell is a procedure used by the prison system on prisoners who they suspect has swallowed illegal drugs in order to hide the drugs in their bodies. This is one of the most degrading security procedures that a prisoner is forced to go through. What happens is that the guards will take you to a vacant room somewhere in what is called "Operations" like the Administration area of a school. Or they will take you to a vacant cell in lock up. They will give you something to drink that will make you have a bowel movement, then give you a 2 ½ foot bucket to sit on and shit in, with the hopes that whatever they suspect you are hiding inside of you will come out in the bucket.

I don't know what is more degrading, making the prisoner sit butt bone naked on a big plastic bucket to shit in or the guard who puts on the latex gloves and a mask, then he searches through another man's feces. Can you imagine someone standing across the room watching you sitting butt naked on a bucket waiting to see your shit fall in a bucket? What kind of state of mind would a man have to put himself in to stand there and watch a butt naked man take a shit?

This type of treatment a prisoner can face four times a week if prison officials want to do it to him. All they have to say is "we have received information that you have illegal contraband in your system." Or that "while searching your cell, or tussling with you to search you, they witnessed you swallowing contraband, or something that they believed to be contraband."

What is really bad about them using security to dry cell you is that a sour prisoner could send Investigations an anonymous note saying that he knows another prisoner be swallowing drugs while on his visit. But is actually lying on the other prisoner with the visit because he hates or is jealous of him. That prisoner with the visit will be put through dry cell without an investigation into the allegation.

When your freedom is taken away from you, this is a part of the new life that you will be a part of...degrading as hell!

405

TYRONE D. TISDALE - RAW & UNCUT

Dear Young Brothers of the Struggle:

You don't know me by name or even by reputation, but if you look closely I am known everywhere by statistics. The ratio of 1 out of every 3 "BLACK" males born in Amerikkka is pre-destined to experience prison or some form of the penal system is me. I know exactly who you are because you are me and I once was you, but together we can break this cycle of ignorance by sharing and passing information. This letter to a lot will appear like some tell all type of thing, but I assure you that it is everything but that. This my brother is raw and uncut until your nose bleeds type facts from one who has lived this life for the past 12 years.

Kill or be killed is the most sufficient way to illustrate everyday life in Maximum Security Prison. Just like the "real world" you have the predator and of course the prey, I think I speak for a great percentage of prisoners when I say that as soon as the gate slams and those bars lock behind you, you have a decision to make and that decision becomes a matter of life or death. Will you become the predator, the prey, or one who's strong enough both mentally and physically to remain neutral? Believe this or not, but many guys in prison weren't even the predator on the outside regardless of how the media portrayed their accused crimes. They were actually the ones being preyed upon by crooked cops, sell out lawyers, and ass backwards court officials because they are so easily accessible. Their low self-esteem combined with their lack of education made them targets for the growth of statistical pulls. They place no value on the very life that they live which makes it virtually impossible to value the life, liberty and well-being of another person. Not to mention those that are mentally ill from disorders ranging from Post-Traumatic Stress Disorder (PTSD) to mental retardation and made to stand trial and sentenced even though it is crystal clear that the man is not competent.

Given 20, 30 or even LIFE sentences to serve at institutions that don't have adequate mental health departments; 1,500 mentally ill with one psychiatrist and 4 counselors to fill the caseload day to day. Many are assaulted by staff because the staff is not qualified to deal with people of that caliber. Who do you think looks out for those guys? Not the brother who has just as much time if not more to serve and damn sure not the officers. Those guys are exploited in the worst ways imaginable. They are normally those victimized by sexual assault and rapes. On top of being fucked up in the head and not being able to decipher right from wrong, his manhood is violated by a predator all because he wanted a pack of cookies or a candy bar. It's sickening! You got idiots in here who truly believe that because he's never getting out alive he can rightfully rape another who doesn't openly consent. What is a homosexual? Is it not a person that knowingly engages in intercourse with the same sex? Well try telling one of those predators that he's gay and watch him try to kill you. In their twisted and distorted mind the man being raped is the homosexual. Now where the hell they do that at?

Or how about the youth that come here already scared to death not knowing what to expect and instead of guiding him to the law library, so he can find loopholes in his case to free himself they take turns turning him out? By the time they're done he won't even feel that he deserves to return to society in that state of condition. Are you sick to your stomach yet? How about AIDS and hepatitis diseases passed from intercourse. You should be about ready to throw up now and I'm just getting started. This is all raw & uncut! Young brothers we must really learn the difference between fault and responsibility as a people. If you murder someone and you are sentenced to LIFE in prison it is not my fault, but "Guess what?!" I am responsible because had I wrote letters years ago I could've saved two lives.

Let's look at masturbation as opposed to homosexuality. In many prisons masturbation, commonly referred to as "jacking" is a norm. It is normal and natural remedy to achieve sexual gratification, but here's where it becomes a problem for the one engaging and those around him. It's an issue when you jack outside the privacy of your cell or in a shower alone. When you reach the point where it's satisfying to expose yourself to female officers, case workers, etc. you are half way there to being gone. When you expose yourself openly, regardless who's around and watching, you have officially lost your mind and became part of the "system". Would you believe that the average "jacker" actually thinks that because a female did not move out of his view or write him up that she enjoyed the act? Truth be told the lady was afraid for her well-being and didn't want to provoke him to become violent again, this is a Maximum Security Prison. When your masturbation is not controlled it becomes a disease that no medication can cure. Some say I rather jack than fall victim to homosexuality and I agree, but nonetheless, one must control one self. It is just that simple. If you smoke and the institution you're at doesn't allow smoking what do you do? Do you roll up grass or leaves just to blow some? Hell no! You just don't smoke. Not only are you destroying yourself mentally, but you are destroying yourself physically. The seed of the "man" is to be preserved for the womb of the woman period.

If you have never experience being lonely take my advice and don't experience it from a prison perspective. Imagine being confined to one cell 24 hours a day by yourself; no one to talk to, no books to read, or no incoming mail. I lived just like that for 4 years in Super Max Custody and I tell you, I'm strong minded but even I was on the brink of falling apart. Loneliness really settles in at the realization that it will be very long time before you will be free again.

Friendships and bonds are strained during long bids and often times broken before release. In the beginning your girlfriend came to visit every weekend. Then that turned to every other weekend gradually descending to once a year to ultimately not at all. You feel hurt and deserted never once giving much thought to what she goes through just to spend a few hours with you eating from a vending machine that is expensive as hell. Or the gas and mileage put on her car the average prisoner can't contribute to. How about the friends and family that talk shit to her telling her she's an idiot running up and down the road to see you with that LIFE sentence. What if she had the LIFE sentence and your mom continuously ask you what the hell can that girl do for you with all that time? Go ahead give me your best answer... I guarantee it will fall along the lines of some of the dumbest shit you've ever said. You see her dilemma? How about when she has to get damn near naked and some cases nude just to gain entry to the prison? Or she has traveled 5 hours only to be told that she can't come in, because she has an extra set of earrings? Regardless what you say, that's enough to discourage anybody. Then you get mad and now she's all kind of stinking, no good, dirty bitches and you still have the audacity to call her phone collect. Really?! Once again this is raw & uncut. When she has finally had enough and decides to move on you actually have the nerve to hate her. Question? Who put you in prison again! Oh yeah, you did! You resent her so much that when you are blessed enough to receive another companion your first objective becomes to manipulate the relationship with false love and hopes only to protect your selfish heart. Young brothers don't become one of those types of statistics.

Another issue is having no moral or financial support from the outside. A lot of guys come in with a support system, but lose it because caring for a grown man in prison, who want this, that and the world is like caring for a child from birth to 18. If you don't know how much that cost then ask your mother. Simply put...Nobody's got time for that! You then have to depend on the state to adequately care for your adult needs which isn't going to happen. Let's look at the prison I live in and what I'm given to survive. Every 30 days I receive 3 bars of generic soap smaller than your average bar, two 4.7 oz. bottles of shampoo, one 2.75 oz. tube of generic toothpaste which contains a lot of the same ingredients used to make explosives, 15 sheets of typing paper, 2 envelopes, a flex pen, and a flimsy toothbrush that the bristles fall out of while brushing. Now if I shower every day for 30 days my hygiene pack won't last but 2 weeks. Once that is gone it gone until the following month. Some guys have to resort to doing things they never imagined having to do like washing another man clothes by hand just to get by. Can you live like that without committing suicide? Many can't and trust me I know this.

Try swallowing this... I lived next door to a young black guy of age 19 serving 15 years. His support system was actually in place and strong. In fact, his older brother had recently signed a professional football contract for seven figures. Sounds like he would be okay right? Well he hung himself from the top tier railing with a bed sheet and he was one of countless others that cry themselves to sleep after taking handfuls of psychotropic drug just to numb their realities. Who in their right mind would look at prison as a badge of honor being subjected to those sort of conditions? Violence is at an all-time high. You have no choice but live and try to get along with various groups of people. Crips, Blood, Gangster Disciples, Vice Lords, Latin Kings, Neta, Aryan Nation, KKK, just to name a few. Everybody in prison belongs to something and if you are not, you are normally the prey. You will meet guys who profess not to be affiliated with no organization which very well may be true, but 9 times out of 10 he is paying for their protection. Extortion in its purest form and it ain't cheap either.

What's sad is blacks are the majority in prisons but kill more of one another than all gangs, sets and organizations combined. We always got something to prove. Whatever we have not killed or harmed is considered gay and you wonder why I say pull your pants up. From a psychological perspective your pants get lower every year. Pretty soon you will be stepping out of your pants and into a dress. As you can see, I would not wish this life on my worst enemy. But when you are in prison, some people who have LIFE sentences themselves will taunt and mess with you so that you add time to your sentence and sometimes a person with a 3 year bid can wind up with an additional 15 or 20 years or LIFE, and be stuck in prison forever just like them.

Being in prison is likely the closest to death you will ever come to in a lifetime. What you feel and experience at any point in life is totally up to you. It is all governed by your state of mind. If you believe that you are nothing more than a statistic, then prison or death is your destination, but if you believe that you are somebody with a will to succeed, you can own Wall Street one day. Having knowledge ain't shit, but INFORMATION is POWER. When you are informed, you are empowered. Once you're empowered you're on point.

I'm gone but hopefully not forgotten!

Peace, Love & Respect Young Brothers!
Tyrone D. Tisdale (August 2015)

FACTOID - The Infamous Chair

The punishment chair, as we prisoners call it, was designed to protect prisoners from harming themselves such as cutting or stabbing themselves, banging their head and hands against the door or walls, and anything else to hurt themselves. The chair is a black and hard plastic chair that hugs the sides of your body and your back and shoulders. It sits in two 4 ½ foot long flat heavy slabs in the front and back that lay on the floor. There are a few rods connected to the two slabs that support the chair a foot high off of the floor.

The prisoner use to be placed in the chair with his feet chained on either side of the chair, 5 inches from the front with their hands handcuffed around the back of the chair and a seatbelt like strap that is wrapped around their waist, but that has changed since over three years ago when a prisoners back was broken while he tried to break out of the chair...so they allege.

Now, the prisoners are forced to bend over with their hands cuffed with their feet. They are left in this position for four (4) hours straight before they are taken out to use the restroom and to be examined by a nurse. (Sometimes they cannot wait and have to use them restroom on themselves, not by choice) If the nurse clears them, the prisoner is sent back to sit in the chair for another 4 hours. Some prisoners were place in the old position for eight (8) hours in order to break them. To say that this experience was humiliating would be an understatement even though we are only allowed to wear a pair of boxer shorts. This was torture and misuse of disciplinary treatment.

If you spit at, or on the guard, you were put in the chair, if you threw liquids or food at the guard you were put in the chair, or if you kicked on the door repeatedly, after being told to stop, you were placed in the chair.

After an hour the joint in your shoulders, knees and ankles would start aching, and then the sharp pain would form down your back. Hours later your entire body will start experiencing great pain, numbness, tingling and stiffness.

I have heard prisoners shouting in pain while in the chair, begging the COs to let them out of the chair. A lot of prisoners such as me are suffering from major back problems from the effects of this chair. It felt like the stories you read about the way captured soldiers were treated. And when they put the motorcycle like helmet on your head to stop you from banging your brains out, you feel like a patient in a mental hospital. It is an experience that will leave you traumatized for life and cause you physical pain for years...and yes it is legal and there is NOTHING you can do about it you are in prison. And what is worse, if you feel, say or are suicidal, instead of giving you someone to talk to and give you counseling for more than 15 minutes, they sometimes will just put you in the chair...Yes, really helpful when you are feeling suicidal already. I do not see how this chair can make you feel as if life is worth living.

And please note that this can happen in ALL jails and prisons throughout the United States. In some cases, they put juveniles/minors in the chair.

(To see some examples see http://www.mentalhealth4inmates.org/videos) Just be aware that it is graphic & gruesome stuff)

TERRANCE D. MCCALL - DESCRIPTIVE OF PRISON LIFE

T o Whom it May Concern,
It doesn't matter if you're man, woman, black, white, yellow, or brown. It doesn't matter because prison takes all. All law breakers allowed.

Before we start, I would like to invite you in to my home. This is an imaginative invite. Seeing that you're out there living in the free world and I am living in prison for the next twenty years of my life. And yes I did say my home. Because once you break the law and be sentenced to do time in prison, then prison becomes your home. You will eat here, sleep here, get your mail here, and work here. That makes prison your home. No more nice apartment. No more living off mom and dad. No more spending the night with your girlfriend or boyfriend. All that's over with until you max out your prison sentence. That's if you were lucky to avoid a LIFE sentence. Just to make sure that you know what a LIFE sentence is. It means that you will die in a prison cell most likely all alone.

I've seen young men as young as eighteen years old with a LIFE sentence. I've seen men, young and old get gang raped. I've seen them hang themselves because they couldn't handle the long sentence. At least twice a week you will witness a stabbing. You will witness stuff in prison that you think would never happen to another human being. The worse thing I ever saw was a young gang member get hot boiling water thrown in his face. The way human skin melted when hit with boiling water. It was horrifying.

I'm sorry; I got a little ahead of myself. Let's get back to the imaginative invite. Now let me give you a tour of my home. First, if you have a car. Drive to a place where there's dirt on the ground. If you don't have a car, ask your mom or dad, or a friend to help. Anyone with a car is invited. Once you have the car on a dirt road, get out of the car. Find a stick, or something to draw with in the dirt. Once you have something to draw with. Draw a box around the car. Make sure that you get as close to the car as possible. Now that you have done that, pull the car up about ten feet. Now walk back to the drawing on the ground. Welcome to my home, I have to ask you to be very quiet because I have a roommate that I really don't know.

In prison, you don't get to pick who you want to live with. Whoever they place in that cell with you, then that's who you will be living with. This person could be a killer, a rapist of little kids. He could have AIDS, but it doesn't matter. The state don't care who is in the cell with you. As long as you are off the streets and no longer breaking the law they don't care. Now back to the box on the ground.

As God is my witness, this is truly the size of the cell. Now walk to the spot where the car motor would be. This is where a chair and small table would be. Now walk to where the trunk of the car would be. This is the only door to the cell. While standing there, lift up your left arm. This is where the toilet is. Now walk to the middle of the box, go to the line on your left, this is where the bunk beds are. Now step outside the box. Take a good look. This is how we live in prison; men living in this small space for twenty years or more.

You have no more privacy to yourself. Whatever you do in this cell, your roommate will see. You have to use the bathroom while your roommate is three feet away from you. There will be times when you will be eating dinner and your roommate will be using the toilet. There are no doors in the cells. Everything is out in the open. Just in case you don't see how small these cells are, I want you to close your eyes. Picture a 1990 Crown Victoria car in your head. Cut the roof off. Take out all the seats. Now put a chair and table at one end then put a toilet at the other end. Then put a pair of bunk beds in the middle. Welcome to my home in the South Carolina prison system!

Now let me tell you about your roommate. First, there is no such thing as a good roommate in prison. You know nothing about this person. It would be like your mom was driving down the road and saw a homeless person sleeping on the side then she pick him up, and bring him home and said that he will be sleeping in the room with you. How would you feel about that? You don't know if this person is a killer or if they have HIV/AIDS. How would you feel if you had to live in a box with a person with AIDS? In prison, you don't have a choice.

Now let me tell you a little about the guards. First of all, they don't care nothing about you. If you are getting raped, robbed, stabbed or just getting a three man beat down. They will not help. They are not going to help you because they don't want to get blood on them from someone with AIDS. Then there are the 3:00AM shake downs. They come to your room, ransack your room and your belongings, and make you take off all your clothes. Then you have to bend over and let them look inside you. They be looking for drugs and cell phones and yes men would be hiding stuff inside their body.

Now let's get to the food. You have to eat to live, that's life. But once you get behind these bars, you will have a new outlook on food. I have seen dog food that I'd rather eat than this prison food. On the box that the meat comes in it says 'not made for humans' to eat but they feed it to us anyway. There will be no more K.F.C., no more Burger King, no more going out to eat with your family. No more cooking for your girl, boyfriends. Now you will be eating slop. Slop that may be cooked by someone with AIDS. You don't know if they put blood in your food or not.

I know you may have read many different stories today about prison. Some may be true. Some may not be true. But what I have written is 100% true. I have no reason to lie to you. I don't know you. You're not my kid or my friend. I don't know your mom or dad. I just don't want to see another human being living like a wild animal in a cage.

413

I have not told you not one time to, "Stay out of trouble." Nor have I said, "Don't do this," or "Don't do that." I haven't told you to, "Stay in school." I am sure that you have heard that all before. I remember when I started getting into trouble. My grandmother use to say that if I don't stop acting up, I was going to end up in prison. I had heard it all before and it went in one ear and out the other.

Telling our kids to stay out of trouble has been going on that way for thousands of years. And it didn't help. So I am not going to waste your time by telling you something that you have heard over and over. What I am telling you is what's waiting for you when you come to prison. So the next time you go out there and sell drugs, or rob a store, or kill someone, you better think of what's waiting on you. I am in this box for the next twenty years. What I have told you is for real. So from this day on, you can't say you didn't know. I have told you the truth about prison. There are more bad things, but I am not allowed to write about them.

YOU HAVE BEEN TOLD. THE CHOICE IS YOURS. LIVE FREE OR LIKE AN ANIMAL.

BY: Terrance D. McCall, SCDC #339911

CORRECTION OFFICERS

CORRECTION OFFICERS: WHAT ARE THEY LIKE? AN INMATES POINT OF VIEW

Coming from South Carolina, Level 3 Prisons (Maximum Security), you have a mixture of CO's that work back here. And each and everyone have their own story to tell. However this is true for most, if not ALL, Correctional facilities throughout the United States – both private and public.

I'm going to use three stories John, Dave, and Alexis. None of these are true names. All are true stories.

John was a 25 year old white male CO I use to know, while on lock up (a jail within the jail) I spoke with him at depth about what it's like to work here. We would talk at long intervals of time about his life, his fears and how working in prison really changed his daily lifestyle activities. John was a normal working class man who didn't want any trouble. He only wanted to clock in do his job and go home. John was fired after only 8 months of working in the SC D.O.C.

Now the behind-the-scenes story. The administration likes to see monthly paperwork. If an Officer does paperwork, that is deemed as doing a good job. Writing an inmate up is their way of keeping a disciplined yard. But what are the reasons for writing inmates up? You have Officers who talk trash, do sneaky things and overall harass inmates. That way they get a negative responsive reaction from the inmates which give them a reason to write them up. Now before I go any further, I will state the fact, not all Officers are like this. You do have good and even very helpful Officers back here, as I stated with John. I spoke to him a month ago and John has a new job. He stated "I'm glad to be free of the tension. You're harassed to write people up on one side, but when you look around you see grown men trying to make life a little easier for themselves. I couldn't do it.

****

Dave was a 32 year old white, racist male. I met him early on in my bid. His favorite activity was to shake down rooms at night. And his favorite rooms to go to were the Black males. Dave was a lieutenant and also a Mason. So it was easy to throw his weight around. Daily life on his shift was simple. Stay out his path and off his radar. During a shake down, Dave would casually throw out the "N" word. And if the inmate reacted, he would then mace him and writes him up for assault. This had been going on for months, until he set his eyes on a new inmate. After two shakedowns in a row, he used the "N" word. Dave was sent to Greenville Memorial Hospital for multiple stab wounds and a broken jaw and cheek bone. He now is retired after a career of 17 years. These are the types of things that become daily life to us. Each yard has its own Dave; usually there are two or three of them.

They stay together for safety. And will always back each up on paperwork. Makes for the perfect team right?

We deal with these kinds of Correctional Officers as best as we can; coming together as a community to try and give support to those who are affected. But sometimes drastic action occurs. What can you do to a man with 19 LIFE sentences and just disrespected in the worst way? The state had judged him to die back here, giving him no hope for the future, so all that builds up. Then the pressure is released on the next person to disrespect him.

****

Alexis was a 23 year old beautiful Latino woman. Anytime she walked on the wing the atmosphere would immediately brighten. She could take a tense situation and say a few words and calm everything down. All the inmates adored her and knew not to disrespect her. For her first 3 months, I talked daily with her. Trying to see just what kind of mind frame she had to want to work in a Prison. Her favorite saying? "Why not bring a little joy to a place such as this? You have been denied everything else but I will never deny you a smile." We had so much fun at that desk. She would take the younger inmates and try and encourage them to get their education and become something in life. Alexis was moved to a Level One camp a year after she started working, why? Lack of paperwork.

No matter the officer, the results are always going to be the same. Administration holds the door shut on uplifting our Prison community. Put in more trade skills, education and job opportunities. Quit price gouging canteen. Quit controlled movement and let inmates experience a little more freedom behind these fences and Prison will change for the better.

Joseph Aljoe #340500

(...and by the way, Joseph is white)

Real Talk about Correction Officers - from Uncle Streets Point of View

Listen, this is yo' Uncle Streets again to come at you with straight talk. After reading a lot of the letters in this book I feel the need to cut it straight with you again. As you know, most of these letters are from prisoners who are doing time in South Carolina. Cats don't get raped like you would imagine although it does happen. Rape is looked on as some sick shit. As far as gang activity is not as bad as in others states.

Don't get me wrong, when shit get real heated, a mutha will get his ass wet up (stabbed up) and even killed, and if it is gang related you will see at least four or five cats bleeding like a busted water pipe. And because they don't want any problems with administration, they will not let medical know, so victims of stab wounds, or part of an ear torn off, have to pray that they don't get infection or need stitches for their wounds.

There is a lot of violence in prison however the shit the CO's put you through along with the shit with the system in general will be the thing that messes with you mentally. No matter where you are in the world if you are in prison. You can be 200 pounds, muscles popping with nice fighting skills, but when you are on lock up and stuck behind an eight foot tall five inch thick steel door, the body weight, muscles and fighting skills will not help you after being sprayed with two cans of mace, all because you wanted another tray of food instead of the one that they gave you with mouse turds in it. Or because you want your letter that the guard gave another inmate by mistake. It will frustrate you to tears knowing that you would punish the guard if you could just get your hands on him. You bang on the door, kick the door, shout threats at him until you are out of breath, but there is no way you are getting past that steel door. It's the things that are done to you or towards you that you can't do anything about that will take a psychological and emotional toll on you.

Like them turning your visits away, finding you guilty of prison charges that should have been dismissed (note you cannot have an outside lawyer help you with prison charges, one of the STAFF helps you…yeah right!) Then after finding you guilty of a charge and throw you in lock up, then take all of the little rights that you have such as going to the prison store, visitation, telephone calls and sometimes take away your work credits or your good time that are supposed to help you get out of prison sooner than your set max-out date (Charges such as disrespect, AFTER they have baited and disrespected you or striking an officer, AFTER they have struck you or pushed you first. Or even put you under investigation for extended periods of time with NO CHARGE, just because they can) Or the room searches where they throw your personal belongings all over the room, stepping on your loved ones pictures, just for the hell of it knowing that you can't do anything about it because your hands are cuffed behind your back and if you do go off about it, they will beat you down, pepper spray you, and take you to lock up and throw you in one of the dog cages outside on the recreation field with nothing on but a pair of boxers and your hands cuffed behind your back. They will not bother taking the handcuffs off, they'll just cut your prison clothes off and leave you lying there---like a helpless slave or roadkill. (Note, this happens to you whether you are a mass murderer or stole food from a grocery store because you were hungry...when you are prison for the most part everyone is treated the same...treated like nothing)

That's why we are trying to get through to y'all hard ass heads out there, 'cause I know you love your music, concerts, cars, cell phones and computers, females, family and freedom to do whatever the hell you want to do. All that stops back here, even for the ones hustling hard in here. Ask them would they trade it in just to live a simple free life and watch how fast they say yes.

If you gotta do dirt make sure it is worth the chance you are taking because this prison life is designed to control you and treat you like a bitch--- think about it young brother. This is no place for a real man. Do you wanna be treated like a soft ass pussy boy?

A prisoner violates you, you serve him instantly, but if one of these out of shape guards violate you, you bark at him but walk away before you catch a serious prison charge that will get you thrown on lock up for a year or two, or a fresh street charge that will get you MORE prison time. The guards know you don't want more time so they have no fear of your threats unless you carry them out. And then you will have to be a beast for weeks to make them respect you because you will receive retaliation for your actions. And what gets me is that prisoners will go through all this harsh treatment for months or years then get out of prison and see these guards, who personally made their life hell, on the streets somewhere but do nothing, not even confront the guard about his actions when he was helpless.

I am willing to bet that the CO's heart stopped not knowing what to expect from the prisoner he mistreated. Then instead of the ex-prisoner staying away from trouble, them cats come right back in there where the guard can treat him even more like a soft ass because he was out and didn't do anything.

Why would a prisoner use the strength to avoid the guard on the street so he won't come back, but not be strong enough to avoid the shit that lands him back in prison, in the hands of the same abusive COs? This is no place for a real man, so start being a man and do what's real to avoid this plantation---- and that's REAL TALK!

(Streets is a talented writer. See his e-book "MYA MAFIA: I'M THAT GIRL" published by Imperial Imprint LLC on sale on Amazon: https://www.amazon.com/dp/B01MF8TU1K)

CORRECTION OFFICERS - From Another Prisoner's Point Of View

It's really kind of hard to find a starting point to describe the staggering number of Officers who come behind the shiny walls of confinement. I'll start first of all by telling you get a glimpse of my Correctional Institution. Two vehicles ride around the institution 24 hours a day in opposite directions to prevent escapes or to prevent inmates from getting contraband thrown over the fence when a window is taken out of the dorm. The contraband packages are generally weed, tobacco and any other item of desire. Control movement wasn't always a practice but now is and it is a real pain in the ass to have to wait to move every hour on the hour, walking inside a yellow line to and from your destination.

At this moment, I'm sitting on one of the two tables that hold a microwave. I'm on the third tier. Each side has four tiers, four showers upstairs and four showers downstairs, Four 25 inch flat screen TV, Five dinettes in front of the TVs.

The rock area is always gang infested and trouble starts in this area 99% of the time. Whatever you do in the streets will follow you to the joint and that beef has to be dealt with. Oh I forgot about the stairway. There are two sets of long stairs that has fourteen steps each, one on both sides of the Rock area, Two sets of stairs that with 6 steps each that leads to the fourth Tier, the bottom Tier stairs that comes up from the bottom Tier called the flood zone has 6 steps also.

All day, every day, you can hear the grinding of steel on stone, it's a crazy world, and most of the male correction officers are gay and have absolutely no qualms about letting it be known. *(Opinion of the writer)* They prey on young playas that have drug ties and love to smoke weed or snort coke. We can own a 13 inch flat screen colored TV for your room viewing pleasure, but the price is close to $200. (On the street $200 will buy a 32 inch color flat screen…)

It is really shocking to see a male who actually believe that his back is as good as any females. The female correctional officers are just as bad, they pick and choose inmates to have sex with as readily as the males, they to participate in the drug and cell phone trade.

Ninety percent (90%) of the female staff will watch an inmate masturbate publicly in the cafeteria, the mailroom window, canteen or commissary lines and pretty much anywhere else they choose to stroke themselves. Of course, they still keep their erections concealed or least some of them do. There are those who actually whip out and slay in public. They call it gun slangin'. Truthfully the women are as perverted as the inmates but to hear them tell it they can't stand that kind of action, even though they walk around with their panties soaking wet all day. As crazy as it may sound masturbation in public areas of the institution has become a widespread disease, it is spreading for the same reason, and sex seems to dominate the minds of the inmates as well as the staff.

As a straight male, I have to admit that some of my sistas come through the gate looking absolutely delicious and very pleasing to the eye. I'm a stone cold freak for the ladies with 20/20 vision, but I have absolutely no appetite for the male. I've been married to my right and left hand for almost twenty years and rolling. Back in the day when I was slingin' crack I've dealt with female officers both White and Black. My personal preference is petite females like my baby mama, the sex is better. The snatch is tight and I get to pick them up and drop them around here and there.

I was vibing with one (CO) sista from XXXX. She and I made plans of getting money. The agreement was that I would kick out seven hundred and fifty dollars for each pound of weed. She opened up to a point that we would sit for hours and talk about everything from giving each other oral sex and to whom she had sex with first. She would come to work asking where I was because she like the way I rapped. But I told her, "Baby, you've got to talk to other people or they'll lie and say that we're having inmate/officer relations just to keep us from talking." As much as I hate to admit it I've experienced quite a few very rewarding healthy relationships with a few of them, but some were so rotten that the stench rose all the way to heaven.

Case and point there was one sista who made it known that she felt like I belonged to her and she acted like it. She came to my assigned room one day in anticipation of having sex, but I asked her to go pick up a pound of sticky green from one of my partners, that heifer ran from the room screaming that I want her to be a drug dealer.

Back then I was kind of green and scared as hell to touch anything that wasn't mines, let alone pull her pants down and penetrate her. She was bad; Boom-Ba-Bang with a pretty smile and cute face, she even had pretty white teeth and eyes.

LETTERS FROM LAW ENFORCEMENT
(Corrections/Police Officers/Prison Staff)

To ensure that this book is telling the WHOLE story, an unbiased view and not only showing sympathy to prisoners, we reached out to some people who work in the prison system and police officers to get their point of view. We want you to know that they also care about you and do NOT want you getting into trouble or to prison. Furthermore, the comments provided are honest and sincere. These comments are from COs/POs that care about saving YOU, even if some do not care for the inmates in general.

We are providing you with their responses because not all law enforcement is bad. Most are just doing their job.

Questions asked by Imperial Imprint LLC:

- How many years as a CO/PO? Male or Female? Current or Retired?
- What would you tell your male loved one about getting into trouble and to avoid going to prison?
- What are the realities of what it is like to be a Black/Latino/person of color versus a white male and the criminal justice system?
- What are CO's/PO's really like and what do they think of the "inmates"?
- Do you think that the inmates are exaggerating about the trauma they have to deal with while incarcerated? Do you think that they deserve the treatment that they are given? Do your colleagues feel that they deserve it?
- Do CO/PO's see "convicted prisoners" as people? Animals? Nothing?
- Give an example of one bad and one good experience/situation (from the perspective of a CO/PO)
- Should there be criminal justice reform and if so, how so?
- Any other thoughts, comments or concerns?

Participant #1

How many years as a CO/PO? Male or Female? Current or Retired?

I'm a retired New York City Correction Officer.

What would you tell your male loved one about getting into trouble and to avoid going to prison?

Prison/jail is not where you want to be short term and definitely not long term. No matter how hard life gets, it get even harder behind bars. You would want to work to survive in the world than trying to survive behind bars.

What are the realities of what it is like to be a Black/Latino/person of color versus a white male and the criminal justice system?

What's the difference between minorities versus the white male in justice system? This question needs no answer from me, because you already know...if you don't pick up a newspaper, watch the news. In my opinion the white is treated different from the arrest to the sentencing, they are treated in a humane way.

Do you think that the inmates are exaggerating about the trauma they have to deal with while incarcerated? Do you think that they deserve the treatment that they are given? Do your colleagues feel that they deserve it?

1. Being a Correction Officer is a job that I'm paid to do. It does not get personal for me.
2. Unless the inmate makes it personal. I'm there for care, custody and control.

Do I think inmates exaggerate while incarcerated? Yes some do, they use it as badge of honor when they get home to impress their friends. (Stupid mentality).

The treatment is fair when you abide by the Institutional rules...I can't tell you how my colleagues think and feel.

Do CO/PO's see "convicted prisoners" as people? Animals? Nothing?

Do I see convicted prisoners as people? Animals? Nothing? I see all prisoners as people who made mistakes in life, but honestly some prisoners and crimes/murders they commit it's hard to see them as God's children...leave it at that...

Give an example of one bad and one good experience/situation (from the perspective of a CO/PO).

The bad experience I seen was a Latin gang member was going to be released the next day. The gang wanted him to smuggle contraband back to them when he's free...He told them no, he wanted out...The only way out of this gang was a gang jump which consists a beating and stabbing ...sad to say he survived but lost a lung from being punctured in the stabbing.

A good experience hearing an inmate realized that this life is not for him.

Should there be criminal justice reform and if so, how so?

Any other thoughts, comments or concerns?

The reform is starting an organization to help prisoners find good paying jobs when released. This will help them to stay away from committing crimes to support themselves and family.

Participant #2

How many years as a CO/PO? Male or Female? Current or Retired?

I am a male working in this field for currently 28 years

What would you tell your male loved one about getting into trouble and to avoid going to prison?

It is not a good place to be in or a part of. It is unclean and dirty both mentally and physically.

Do you think that the inmates are exaggerating about the trauma they have to deal with while incarcerated? Do you think that they deserve the treatment that they are given? Do your colleagues feel that they deserve it?

- I feel that because of our system in the country as Black/Latino person you are treated differently in every which way. (the percentages show it clearly)
- People are different and come from all walks of life. There are officers who make judgment on others

Do CO/PO's see "convicted prisoners" as people? Animals? Nothing?

I don't think officers see prisoners as animals. For the most, inmates are treated according to their behavior. There are times when officers treat inmates unfairly by taking things out on them (the inmates)

Give an example of one bad and one good experience/situation (from the perspective of a CO/PO)

No Response – Did not answer

Should there be criminal justice reform and if so, how so? Any other thoughts, comments or concerns?

Yes, the criminal justice system should be reformed.

Participant #3 – Derrick (Cousin of Heru Mossiah Maat

How many years as a CO/PO? Male or Female? Current or Retired?

I have been employed in juvenile corrections for 21 years plus 5 more in a non-secured detention which is the same population placed in a group home setting. I am currently actively employed.

What would you tell your male loved one about getting into trouble and to avoid going to prison?

I have continuously stressed to my two sons the dangers of getting into trouble and facing the hazard of being in detention including the gang violence as well as the dangerous kids we house.

What are the realities of what it is like to be a Black/Latino/person of color versus a white male and the criminal justice system?

- The reality is that without question, the penalties (sentences) are much harsher for minorities. Without a doubt, white kids are given favoritism as compared to black and Latino children.
- COs/POs (Police Officers) definitely vary. There are many that are truly here for the kids and many who could care less about them. There is also many staff that operate on the level of the kids and are also gang members or clearly afraid of the kids so they allow mayhem.

Do you think that the inmates are exaggerating about the trauma they have to deal with while incarcerated? Do you think that they deserve the treatment that they are given? Do your colleagues feel that they deserve it?

I think that for the most part, the trauma is definitely exaggerated. While there are some kids that clearly do NOT belong in this situation. Most of the people incarcerated are where they belong and are operating in their comfort zones. As far as their treatment, it is increasingly becoming more and more a joke as the days past. Inmate rights are quickly becoming all that matters and the staff is the ones in danger.

Do CO/PO's see "convicted prisoners" as people? Animals? Nothing?

I believe that it's clear that CO/PO's see prisoners/inmates as people with some exceptions but, the animosity is growing due to the changes in the laws which are tilting severely in the direction of the inmates.

Give an example of one bad and one good experience/situation (from the perspective of a CO/PO)

- My personal bad experience occurred about 5 years ago when I used my authority to simply handcuff an inmate to prevent him from attacking another inmate which was effective and resulted in NO injury to either inmate, but resulted in myself receiving a 15 day suspension.

- My favorite experience occurred in my 2nd year on the job when a young man with clear anger issues challenged me physically which resulted in a physical confrontation which he clearly got the worst part of and eventually caused him to swear that he would kill me if he ever saw me in the "world". I came across this young man the following year on the subway at which point he shook my hand and thanked me for instilling discipline in him. He also let me know that he was working 3 jobs.

Should there be criminal justice reform and if so, how so?

I think that reform is definitely in need as there clearly are different rules. While I don't believe that Blacks and Latinos who are repeatedly breaking laws should be released, I do feel that white people should be held to the same standards. I also believe that there definitely needs to be increased consequences for inmates housed in detention centers as this would provide incentive not to return to these jails.

Any other thoughts, comments or concerns?

In closing, I have friends and my family member, (Heru) the inspiration for this book, whom are in prison and facing ridiculously long sentences, so this book definitely touches me personally. However I do not feel that jails should be shut down or prisoners should be released. I merely feel that the punishment should fit the crime.

Participant #4 – Detective Samuel Amoh Antwi of Ghana, West Africa

How many years as a CO/PO? Male or Female? Current or Retired?
Previously a Police Officer (PO)/Detective in Ghana, West Africa for 12 years but now live in the United States.

What would you tell your loved one about getting into trouble to avoid going to prison?
Don't get yourself involved with a criminal gang, avoid doing drugs or trading in it, keep yourself busy with some positive activities, be law abiding and live uprightly, respect the rights of others.

What are the realities of what it is like to be a Black/Latino/person of color versus a white male and the criminal justice system?
There is growing frustration with America's criminal justice system because there exists racist arrests and sentencing disparities between black/ Latino offenders and white offenders. On the average, blacks are made up of a total of 13% of US population. Out of this number as much as 37% are prisoners due to mass incarcerations. There are more black men in prisons today than they were enslaved in 1850 according to Michelle Alexander, a law professor from Ohio State University.
Read Michelle's book "The New Jim Crow: Mass incarceration in the age of colorblindness"

What are PO's really like and what do they think of the inmates?
- PO's really like law abiding citizens and inmates who are respectful and ready to reform so they don't come out to still join bad gangs
- PO's think some of the inmates were not given fair trial and some of them were wrongly incarcerated. Notwithstanding this PO's think inmates will learn some kind of jobs during their time of incarceration.

Do you think that the inmates are exaggerating about the trauma they have to deal with while incarcerated? Do you think that they deserve the treatment that they are given? Do your colleagues feel that they deserve it?
No I don't think so but sometimes they over exaggerate. No, not all of them deserve the treatment but the hardened inmates who also break the rules whilst incarcerated are forced to go through such treatment in order for them to reform. Yah some feels they deserve it base on their respective ideas.

Do PO's see convicted prisoners as people? Animals? Nothing?
They see them as people.

Give an example of one bad and one good experience/situation from the perspective of a PO.
One bad experience was when an inmate lost his life when he was manhandled after he attempted to escape from lawful custody. One good experience was when an inmate was reform and he is now working as a fashion designer.

The differences between the US and Ghana?
Again, in Ghana the prisons are choked to the extent that a room which was to accommodate about 40 inmates is now accommodating about 200 inmates whilst it is not like that in the U.S. The prisoners in Ghana sleep in the prison yards; eat there as well but their condition is not up to standard since they need to expand the inmates place of abode and the food given to them are not sufficient at all. In conclusion they need better conditions there.

Should there be criminal justice reforms? If so, how?
Yes

Any differences between the male and the female inmates in Ghana?
- Difference between female inmates and male inmates is that they are separated from each other. They don't sleep at the same premises and they don't mingle with each other. Female inmates can easily be reform comparing to male inmates.
- I prefer to work with both of them but more especially with the male inmates since the female inmates can easily be catered for by female police officers.

431

Participant #5

How many years as a CO/PO? Male or Female? Current or Retired?

I worked at the Department of Juvenile Justice for 25 years.

What would you tell your male loved one about getting into trouble and to avoid going to prison?

I would tell him it's easy to get into trouble and hard to get out.

What are the realities of what it is like to be a Black/Latino/person of color versus a white male and the criminal justice system?

If you are poor white trash you get treated as a minority.

What are CO's/PO's really like and what do they think of the "inmates"?

Don't think much of them (the inmates). If they follow the rules and respect, they will get much respect.

Do you think that the inmates are exaggerating about the trauma they have to deal with while incarcerated? Do you think that they deserve the treatment that they are given? Do your colleagues feel that they deserve it?

If they do a horrible crime, then yes, they deserve what they get and my co-workers feel the same way.

Do CO/PO's see "convicted prisoners" as people? Animals? Nothing?

No, I don't think of them as animals however their behavior... (crossed out and did not complete the thought)

Should there be criminal justice reform and if so, how so?
Any other thoughts, comments or concerns?

Criminal reform, YES. The residents should be doing hard time, cleaning the highways, painting buildings, etc.

Give an example of one bad and one good experience/situation (from the perspective of a CO/PO)

Good experience for me?? Is getting my paycheck.

Participant #6

How many years have you worked as correctional staff in a correctional facility? 20 years Male or Female?
I have worked with both men and women in maximum security prisons. This job is not for everybody because you can get caught up easily in the drama. You cannot walk with fear. Your enemy is not always the inmates. You must be careful at all times. Because you are dealing with people who will never come home in some cases. Some of the CO females will get down (sexual relations) with the officers for protection.

Have you worked with Men and/or Women? What are the differences?

- Prefer male inmates although they have a propensity of violence between themselves and the CO's. Men are less troublesome and less aggravation. When men have problems it is usually for owing money, stabbings or slashing (NOTE: Slashing is different...snitches get stitches – across their throat, down their face, which is used a sign and tag...jail code for "Snitch")

- Females are crazy and they will do whatever or say whatever to destroy you. Very emotional and operate on feelings. For example, a male inmate will say, 'Yes I can do this time in prison'... a woman does not know how they are going to do something. They are wired differently. They leave different things/people behind that they nurture to. Man will do a buck fifty standing on his head. Whereas women flip out. Stark raving mad!

- One woman, she used to take sharp object and stick them in her stomach around her navel. She would not be in pain because she did it so often that she would do it without feeling anything. Why did she do it? Because she had nothing better to do with her time and would hopefully be able to get out of prison to go to the hospital...she wanted a change of scenery. Another would swallow sporks. Why? "Because my wife and or/friends would not speak to me today."

- When men are trying to get to the hospital, they are under some type of threat such owing someone money or being stabbed or killed and they don't want to go to protective custody ("PC") because of the stigma associated with PC. They also go usually because they are actually sick. Men usually do not pretend to be sick for attention.

- And women tend to be cutters. (Cut themselves) Why? Because they feel it is a release. Some men do, but not like women. (Men instead tend to jerk off in front of others) And women are liars, (plotters and schemer &

433

knivers). But the men are more about getting their personal stuff/contraband and will fight over that. Men are 150% more respectful.

What would you tell your male loved one about getting into trouble and to avoid going to prison?

- I will tell my male loved one, 'I am not coming to visit and I am not sending a package to you. Prison is a very violent place. It is not a place you want to go to, you can get killed at any time.'
- If you see a woman who is not doing the right things and doing illegal things, regardless of where they are...*RUN!* Run far, far away from her.
- You need to get God to help you if you cannot get your life together yourself. Get your life together with some help if needed, because you do not want to go to prison to get it together.

Prison does not help you to rehabilitate NOTHING!

- You can't save anyone. In some cases, prison does save lives for some people because otherwise they would be dead in the street.

- If you are going to prison, you need to be going to get paid (i.e. you are an employee and receive a paycheck). That's it!

What is the main reason women go to prison?
The main reason women go to prison is for drugs. Supporting their drug habits. Some are boosters (thief), because when they were younger they got into trouble and they cannot get a decent job, but they want to maintain a high class lifestyle. Because they are narcissistic and only want to wear designer clothes, get their hair and nails done by the best, drive expensive cars and live in expensive homes, they will live a life of crime because they do not want to work hard and make money the legal way.
However most women are coming in for drugs.

Do women go to prison because of helping or covering for a man?

- Back in the day, women were going to jail for a man...Nowadays they are doing it because of themselves. They are going to prison for their OWN crimes.
- Women are rapists, pedophiles, set fires, murderers, bank robbers; the list goes on and on.
- It is a mix of women that come into prison. White/black trash, educated with college degrees, no matter what, they can still be murderers.
- Some women are very pretty but just as deadly; or deadlier than men. They will sleep with anyone. Correctional officers and other inmates to get what they want.
- They will sleep with the CO's and then save the sperm to get the CO's in trouble if the CO does not follow what they want from them at a later date. Women are very smart and can be ruthless.

What are the hardest obstacles that women have to deal with when they go to prison?

Aside from being separated from their families? They do get sanitary napkins. If they have heavy bleeding they can go to medical and get the expensive pads that hold more blood on order for them. They do get expensive medications if needed. Some commit petty crimes so that they can continue to receive the treatment. Especially with regard to the people who are dealing with sex change. The medication is very expensive. In some states, inmates have to pay each time they go to medical, however in other states they pay nothing.

Do their mates/loved ones/partner come to visit them while incarcerated? Are their boyfriends/husbands supportive of them when incarcerated?

Women will come see their man, put money on their books, but men will get another woman and move on after a while.

What are the realities of what it is like to be a Black/Latino/person of color versus a white female and the criminal justice system?

Big difference! You have Latino and Black that are very pretty they will have it easier because they will get favors from the CO. The women alter their prison clothing to make it tight fitting to show their shape/figure. They want to feel pretty (normal female behavior). With the Latinos they are either extremely religious or at the other end of the spectrum and using a CO.

When you are white, you are right, doesn't matter if you are trash or a snitch, but the people of color have to dance a different dance.

What are CO's/prison staff really like and what do they think of the "inmates"?

In certain regions 'niggas' is 'niggas'.

An inmate better walk inside of that yellow line and the inmate better have their head down without a damn thing to say. Stop at each yellow line and keep your head down and do not appear to be a threat.

Some of the white COs in certain areas (rural areas in particular) call the black inmates monkeys, niggas, etc. And even if you are an employee of color and see the COs doing this, you have to walk by and act like you did not hear what they said to the inmates and YOU the employee of color ALSO better act like you are not a threat either!

In the rural areas and the South, they are more racists with the inmates.

Department of Corruption

Honestly however, there are some good Correctional Officers that play by the book but the system itself can be corrupt.

Do you think that the inmates are exaggerating about the trauma they have to deal with while incarcerated? Do you think that they deserve the treatment that they are given? Do your colleagues feel that they deserve it?

Some of the inmates deserve the treatment and others don't. How do you kill your wife in front of your children? A CO will not care about how that person is treated. Some inmates are treated better than they deserve. But people of color are usually treated unnecessarily cruel. "Cruel and unusual punishment"

You must realize that not everybody is going to heaven because there are some EVIL people to the core (male and female). They are just sheer evil and you can look in their eyes and see how evil they are. Evil has a look. I don't care how they are dressed, their hair is done, the way they speak and how they preach religion...

EVIL has a distinctive look

This is why you must stay from getting involved with people doing the wrong thing. There are some pure evil people out there that will let you get caught up with their evil ways. (Remember "if you want to know me, see my friends?" Or "Birds of a feather flock together?") You may not be evil and just going along with the crowd who are PURE EVIL but it is YOU who will get caught up in their evil deeds. You can get the same criminal charges and the same prison sentences even if you did not actually do it. You were there with them so you are just as guilty. (Re-read Letter by Charvus Nesbitt. Did he really deserve that 40 year sentence?)

Furthermore when you are in prison you are locked up with them and treated the same way they are treated. You have to live with them every day maybe even for the rest of your life. If you are a decent person, how will you truly be able live with the devil himself? These type of people don't care about anyone or anything! Most people in prison are not pure evil but there are A LOT of people who are. In some cases they will be your roommate. Will you be able to sleep at night much??

Does CO/prison staff see "convicted prisoners" as people? Animals? Nothing?

It depends on the individual some staff treat them as people, others treat them as animals. Some inmates will try to play a staff member and because of the inmate's actions, the prison staff may not treat them well after that. Also again, it does depend on how heinous the inmate's crime is.

Most people say they will take back their crimes when asked. When asked, 'Do you wish you could take the crime back and never have come here?' They will say "You ain't never lied!" They wish they could have never have gone to prison, and as a result will try to make the difference while in prison.

Those that are pure evil get no attention…in my opinion the best revenge is to move on and have a better life for you…not to slit their throat, which is the case for some people who have killed their lover/spouse in front of their children.

You have some EVIL people. Evil has a face and you can look in their eyes and see it.

****

Most officers will call you all kinds of horrible names if your crime was heinous even if you are white.

Some crimes are so heinous that even if an inmate does start doing the "right thing" and through good behavior gets assigned to the Honor dorm/unit, because of the heinous crime they committed, some CO's still will treat them the way the "deserve" (badly).

Some crimes are just not a "One time mistake…some the crimes last for a lifetime"

If the woman is white with a heinous crime the white women are treated differently (not so bad), EVEN if they have done the heinous crime. But with white men it depends, however for the most part the COs will still treat them bad. But a black male or female, NO WAY, you are going to be treated like dirt no matter what!

****

Some CO's try to be tough guys but that is not always wise.

Give an example of one bad and one good experience/situation (from the perspective of a person of a who works in a prison)

- One of the best experiences I have had is when released inmates see me on the streets and they tell me how I helped and inspired them to do the right thing, which was to get and stay out of jail. They also say I always told them the truth, which they appreciated.
- Bad experience, an inmate wrote letter saying that I was doing her favors (giving her contraband), but that was quickly rectified given she had psych issues and we were able to prove that she was lying.

Should there be criminal justice reform and if so, how so?
Yes. Starting at the top of the food chain. Got to get new people in with new vision and new insight. Cut spending, spending too much money to incarcerate people with petty crimes (25 years) and the tax payer has to pay for them, whereas you have real murderers that go free; such as Trayvon Martin's killer who walked, even though he had a history of violent behavior.

Start from the top and trickle down because people (employees) follow of their leader. They get the spirit of the leader. If the leader is corrupt, they get corrupt. If the leader is just, then the people are just.

Any other thoughts, comments or concerns?

God help us all!

Participant #7

In 1988, as a rookie police officer in one of America's largest police forces, I found myself racing 30 city blocks north to respond to the scene of a police officer shot while effecting the arrest of a drug dealer. Later that evening, as we helped secure the crime location, we learned that the police officer died of his wounds. A short time later, we were horrified to learn that yet another officer, on the other side of the city, was also murdered under nearly identical circumstances.

Yet the deaths of those men, and sadly far too many more like them, began a movement in my city to take back the streets from the lawless, based on a simple premise- that it could be done. It only took the courage, then lacking in the politicians and opinion-makers of all ideologies, to see it through. It required the election of men unafraid to say that out of control crime did not have to be an unalterable fact of life; that the government did not have to wave the white flag and forsake, out of political correctness and fear, its primary duty to it's citizens - to keep them safe.

By 2016, I am 4 years retired and observing the current administration of the city I worked for trying its hardest to undo the safe streets gifted to it by its predecessors. Even sadder, not to mention destructive, are the conscious attempts by the current federal government to change the direction of the national dialogue on crime in such a way that stands common sense on its head. Politics and ideology have been brutal cudgels used against populations throughout history. Here in the United States however, free citizens allow themselves to be deluded, in spite of our history, into thinking that the police are a savage occupying army that the release of convicted criminals, some for truly heinous crimes, will solve injustice, and, yes, that it is understandable, even desirable, and that our ethnicity should divide us. Worse, national discourse is made more savage, cruder, and combative by destructive internet "culture". The current crisis level attacks on police officers and the skyrocketing crime rate are the very tip of this frightening trend.

So, to the authors of the accounts in this book and their families, you may have already made your minds up as to my opinions, and to what sort of person I am. I suspect that should we ever meet, in official or personal circumstances, you would be quite surprised, perhaps pleasantly so.

There is no man or woman among you that is irredeemable, for we are all sinners. I do hope that your experiences, for those of you that will walk outside the walls of prison one day, will not allow you to pick up the same path again. Having said that, however, there are few innocent men and women in our prisons today, and I say to the readers and the authors herein that you are all fully aware of that. There is, in my opinion guided by experience and information, no crisis of mass incarceration.

The real crisis in our society is between citizens on either side of the civic, cultural, economic, educational or racial divide who have been coarsened and hoodwinked into forgetting our bonds as humans and citizens.

Mass incarceration has occurred in many societies in the lifetime of living men, but not here. Across the globe, at varying times, men women and even children learned to fear the late night knock on the door, endless interrogation, and the cattle car to the camp. We do not have that here...not now.

But it can come, though if it does, no one will be safe, for the enemies of the state can change on a dime. Appreciate the adaptivity of our society, don't exploit it. Continue to educate yourselves, your families, and embrace your God. Finally, remember that safe streets and stable society begins at home, before it ends in a prison.

COMING HOME
&
HEALING

"After being incarcerated you can find that your life still matters and you can still make a difference."

Pastor Jack Royster, formerly incarcerated
Co-chair of the Harlem Republican Club &
a Sponsor at Narcotics Anonymous

COMING HOME AND HEALING- Table of Contents

As a formerly incarcerated person who has survived the abuses and horrors of incarceration I am here to say that the collateral damages of incarceration is manifested on multiple fronts long after a person has completed their sentence/parole/probation on the Individual, Family, Community and Societal levels. The stigma and discrimination is continuously being played out through the various systemic barriers in place to further oppress and discourage those who have had previous Criminal Justice involvement by locking them out of full participation and reintegration within society. Most affected by these racist discriminatory policies are people of color.

Until we change the policies/laws that affect this classification of Human Beings we will not experience the real changes that are needed to include people who have had previous Criminal Justice involvement and create a more fairer and just system for all people regardless of previous history.

Victor Pate
Chairman, Second Chance Program
National Action Network (NAN)

CONVERSATION WITH STEVE-O LAWYER - PERSPECTIVE OF EX-FELON

Mr. Lawyer is a Black man in his late 40's who is a family friend of both Dawn Simmons and Heru Mossiah Maat. He has been incarcerated multiple times throughout his life – Dawn interviewed him for this book project

•What do you want young men to know about getting into a life of crime?

What I want them to know is that nothing is what it seems. Even though it seems like it is an easy route it is the hardest route to a life of success. Because what people see and don't understand is that they only see the bling, the fast and immediate gains but it is really a fast route to nowhere.

Sometimes out of desperation when you are someone who comes from nothing or no where you look for immediate gains for success but there is so much of a down side that comes with that.

I don't know anyone…and I know thousands of people, who are happy that they took that route (life of crime). Because if you look deep inside. Everyone who has taken that route is desperate to legalize their life and grow in a desperate life and struggle, so much pain misery and loss that come with it. You sign your life to the devil. You don't know what you are prepared to give up and the things that you will have to give up. Prison, murder, giving up people that you love, giving up being with your loved ones, and people getting put away for the rest of their lives.

I know people with millions of dollars, but still sit in prison. They say if they can get my life back I would. Everybody says the same thing. "I was a smart person but I made the wrong choices."

•In hindsight what were the worst things about prison, what was helpful and the interactions with staff/other prisoners

The worst thing about prison you literally sign your life over to someone else. You are no longer able to be 100% of a person, a man. Because like a child you are told what to do, how to do it and when to do it. So you have enslaved yourself to someone else.

•I have known you since high school, so over 30 years. So I am going to ask you, why were you going in and out of prison?

Because the process of life is that we don't ever learn how to change our thinking. So when we go to prison at a young age, we learn the wrong lessons. So when we get out, we think we can do the same things (crime) better. And that is considered insanity: To do the same thing over and over and expecting different results.

We tell ourselves we are still going to do the wrong thing…but better now.

…And that is the biggest lie you sell to yourself.

•Upon coming home, what were your biggest fears and what were the biggest challenges/road blocks that you have had to face?

The biggest fear is being able to not regain your life back. Meaning you left with a certain status and habits and you want to regain that back and want to fit right back into society but that is a misconception. But your support system has become weakened since you have been away from society and you have changed, times have changed. People have their own lives while in the meantime you are trying to catch up.

It becomes so much harder and people will do less things for you as you get older.

If you take an athlete out of the sport for many years he is not the same athlete, even though you have those same desires even though you think you still have the same skills, you're not who you were before AND with less support, and more responsibilities but less readiness

•How was/is it like to be on Parole/probation?

Parole is very different from probation. Parole is like being on a long leash. Because you are free from the walls of prison but you are still being controlled, you have a curfew (sometimes like 7:30p), and the places where you have to be. People are still controlling your life while on the outside. You still have to answer to someone just like you are a child. And they can snatch your freedom away from you any day of your life. And can make you leave your job because of curfew hours, like if it is goes until after 8p, you can't keep your job because you have to be in by 7:30p.

You are a free man with no freedom- PAROLE

So you have to ask yourself are you really free?

Dawn: So that's not good.

Steve-O: …Not at all

•Who was helpful to you when you got out? Were they the same people who held you down when you were inside?

Through the Grace of God I have a loving family. My sisters were my sole support. No body that you think will support you will be there because they have their own lives. And it gets worse and more and more lonely as you get older.

When I saw you the last time you were in prison you told me that you had less stress this (last & final) time because you were not in a relationship.

Not having a girlfriend when in prison was more peaceful but more lonelier because people go crazy over their girls if they do not receive mail, their girl does not answer their phone calls, they wonder if their girls are cheating, and that creates even more stress. So this last time with no woman, it was more peaceful.

Most dudes when they go to prison worry about their girlfriends/wives and if they will cheat, be loyal, will they visit, send photos, will the girl wait on their phone calls?...they want their girlfriend to do the (prison) sentence with them.

•What steps have you taken to "heal" from the traumatic experience that is prison? Or have you?

To a degree you never really heal and that is a scar on you that you will have for the rest of your life. Even at 49 years old I seek therapy for that. I have PTSD for things that I have seen, encountered and endured while in prison.

Things such as being locked away in a box for 23-24 hours a day, with MAYBE one hour of "Rec" (recreation time) away from others. It is inhumane and dehumanizing. Locked away and rec in a cage with you in chains and 2 showers per week.

Your shower can be 8 to 10 minutes. They will just cut the water off on you. Don't care how soaped up you are. Time is Time. So you learn how to do things really fast. (Like take a shower)

•Why do people go back to crime after coming home and what can they do to protect themselves so that they can lead a positive and successful life?

We go back because it is a comfort zone. But what we fail to do to stop going back to prison is to change our way of thinking.

So the first time you went to prison as an adult, like 30 years ago, you told me about "jail talk" (people who talk as if they will do the right thing while they are in prison, but go right back to the same things when they come back home)...So why does it occur?

When you are in a vice, with it clamping on you, squeezing you in pain, then they will say something different. But once people are out of the vice, they forget the pain they endured.

You want to remember how painful it was (in that vice) so that you do not go back to that (prison).

That (prison) is the next step to death.

•So you don't know if you will go back to your old ways when you change in prison?

No, not unless you change your way of thinking...

Some of the smartest, strongest people are in prison, then why did we have to go to prison to find that about yourself? What a waste.

•In a later conversation we discussed how people are wanna be thugs/gangster.

Dawn: You said somethings that were funny but true

Steve-O: These guys are wanna be thugs and gangsters but real gangsters don't publicize their crimes. You see these guys rob, steal and then post it up on Facebook or some kind of social media. You see them with all the money they stole posing with it in their hand, in front of the building where they live with their address showing.

Dawn: (Laughs)...that's crazy...

Steve-O: Yeah and then they wonder how the police found them. Real gangsters are about _not_ publicizing their crimes. They don't want no parts of that kind of conversation.

•You have known Heru and me for over 30 years. You and I went to high school together and have some of the same friends. Heru was only 8 years old or so. Why did you not follow the road I was taking with regards to going to school, doing the "right" things and getting a good job?

Ummm. Because even though we came from the same place, we went different routes. When you see other people take a different route, in your eyes you think that they are working harder than they need to be. 'Dang, she is going to school working hard every day. But I make over $20K in a day.' (As a drug dealer)

I see those guys that looked up to us and they were working hard back then on their (legal) jobs, they would borrow from us. Now, they have lots of money or are successful. Some are (retired) Police/Correction Officers now. They have and are successful in their kid's eyes. Do I look successful? Not at all. These are people that can sleep well at night. They are established. Doing the right things, building slow, while I was living fast. Where are all of our goods now? (The cars, bling, jewelry, money, women, etc.) We had it all, but we could not keep it.

I now respect those who got it slowly and looked up to me.

They have the bank accounts and good jobs.

The ones who I laughed at are the successful ones driving nice cars, have nice homes they paid for, and can sleep well at night.

All I have are memories...

•Why did you not try to mentor Heru and advise him that drug dealing was not the way to go because even though he was not violent, he still wound up in prison, with a longer sentence than anyone we know for a non-violent crime?

This is the exact thing that we try to make people see in this book. When you look up to people for the wrong reasons, you buy into the dream and the façade and can get into trouble.

We make whatever excuse we tell ourselves. Not realizing that quickly, overnight when you least expect it, you can go to prison. This is what you don't realize. You don't know what the law term, "conspiracy" is. You can go to prison because you are around someone or know someone, not 'cause you necessarily did something. It is about the decisions you make.

With Woo, we were so caught up in our own lives (20's and early 30's) that we did not take the time to really set him straight because we were still in that life. We saw him as a younger dude, 'he wants to touch this money, wants to see what it's like.' But even if you say something to them (these young guys who are looking up to us and want to be like us...drug dealers) they don't want to hear what you are saying. You have some people who say they live the life that they have never lived (like some rappers). Some people create an image in these young dude's heads, when they were really not gangster like in the video.

•Any other comments?

For young people that is in the struggle of wanting to be successful. Don't worry about getting nowhere fast. Take the time to look deep in yourself and realize the talent and the great things within yourself because most of the time we don't see the greatness in ourselves until it is too late.

It you have taken the time and utilize it in the right direction and right path, you can have a successful life rather than turn yourself over to slavery.

449

CONVERSATION WITH L.A. BERNSTEN - PERSPECTIVE OF EX-FELON

Mr. Bernsten was in prison in 1976, out for 6 months then back in from 1978 until his release in 2014. He is a White man who has seen it all in prison. He also participated in our first project 'Blindside Diaries, Life Behind the Fences', so you can live with him while he was in prison back in October 2013 in our next book in this series.

•What do you want young men to know about getting into a life of crime?

It is not a life of crime, it is lifestyle choices. It may be quick easy money but the time you spend trying to get someone from getting your money, you are better off working a minimum wage job. Selling dope, robbing and stealing is a lot, a lot of work. People think it is easy.

•In hindsight what were the worst things about prison, what was helpful and the interactions with staff/other prisoners

The worst thing is the loneliness even though you are surrounded by people. You burn a lot of bridges. You think you are doing the time by yourself, but everyone is doing time with you. Even your victim's family.

•Upon coming home, what were your biggest fears and what were the biggest challenges/road blocks that you have had to face?

My biggest fear was believing the propaganda. That you could not make it and how hard it was for a con to get a job. If you are a sex offender no one will hire you and judge you. The fear of not being given an opportunity or change even if you know that if you were given the chance you could do the job, you are not your past circumstances. Judged on behavior back then.

It took me 2 days to get out of the big house. It was Spartanburg, SC a fairly large city and for so long I had lived a structured lifestyle in prison. Day in day out it is the same thing. I go from making 15 choices a day to 3,000 choices a day. So it was overwhelming.

For someone with no support system and the network it would have been a place to stay, a job, transportation to and from work. Clothes to wear. In SC, they give you the worst pair of blue jeans you can image. They are thin and terrible. They give you a thin blue shirt and in the winter a thin jacket. All you will have are the clothes you have on. No money in your pocket. They will give you a bus ticket to anywhere in the state in SC. If you are from out of state they will give you a ticket to the state line. And you figure it out from there.

•How was /is it like to be on Parole/probation?

In a small county called Gathee, SC it is sweet. When I first made parole, I told, Mr. Thomason my Parole officer, I wanted to do this, that, the other...he looked at me and told me what you are going to do is sit down, take a deep breath, and told me 'You have been locked up longer than I have had this job. There are lots of things you want but I will allow you to go to AA and your curfew is at 7:30p. But you can leave the house at 6:30a.' In hindsight that is about all of the freedom that I could have handled at that time. After 7:30p I had nowhere to be anyway.

Being in Spartanburg was arduous, because the toll took so much time. Initially, You had to go one per weeks for 2 hours a day and after about 90 days, then once per month. When you go for the job, the PO is open from 8-5 M-F, so if you get a job, you have to ask your employer for time off. You have to have an understanding employer. Knowing that you will be off from 10 to noon. What I found, if I had to work an extra 15 minutes after closing time, I don't tell him that he owes me extra money. He knows I worked, and I am not going to bring it up. It you're willing to go the extra mile. The employer will meet you more than half way.

Supervision fees are $50 month. They cannot violate if you do not pay the $50/month, as long as you are making the effort. If I become indigent they will waive the fee. The parole officer has the authority to ask them to waive the fee. But most judges will waive the fee.

If you have a new car, and not paying, if you can afford the car, you can afford the fee. In my opinion, some of the parole services are trying to balance the budget on the back of those who are least able to afford it. And they will attach a garnish to your state income tax and report it to the credit agencies.

The difference is from Maryland to Florida to Texas, is a different mentality, like a southern revenge mentality. You broke the law and we are going to punish you. Like a slavery mentality, given the history, versus the North, which is shown by the way the South incarcerates people. Some states may handle it better, but it is that divide and conquer mentality. We are going to have Tier Monitors (a guy in charge of the tier- he could beat you up and rob you and the CO would take a blind eye to it) Ward keeper is the same thing. Theoretically it has been outlawed by the Supreme Court but still goes on in a lot of prisons.

•Who was helpful to you when you got out? Were they the same people who held you down when you were inside?

No. The people who helped me when I got out were Celebrate Recovery and AA. They were about 10 people at the gate waiting for me to get out it. They took me to a restaurant. And they don't sell pork in the prison system.

So the first thing I got was bacon. At Cracker Barrel restaurant and the lady waitress asked "what kind of bread do you want?"

I said, "Well what kind do you have?"

She said "Wheat, white, multigrain, pumpernickel, etc...."

So I said, "Well give me one of each!" ☺

I was with people who went out of their way to make sure that I would be alright and do the right thing.

****

I will tell you...I have a friend named Bill, Federal prosecutor. Kairos prison based Christ centered program. He made it a point to look me up when I got out. I met him. Went to court with him and prosecutor, judges have their own door to get in. And everyone that saw me was acting like they were happy to me. When I came back by myself, it was a totally different experience. They were like who are you? What do you want? Etc.? I said I was on electronic monitoring. What's your name, who do you want to see? Adversarial situation. A voice comes out asking who I was looking for. They told me go down the hall to take a left.

My friend Bill took me to Walmart, bought me blue jeans, socks underclothes, all the kinds of things you have to have. Because I did not have anything. He did not have to do this. Bill went out of his way a couple of times to make sure I had clothes and food, if you fall behind on your payments, there are people who want to see you do well.

Nobody was there for me when I was in jail. I was involved in a lot bad stuff for survival when incarcerated cause I was in for 35 years.

•What steps have you taken to "heal" from the traumatic experience that is prison?

Oh my Goodness. Stay in my bible, stay in AA. And my home group (the group that you go to once a week, and everyone in that group knows that I was in prison and everything about me) They were welcoming...and that is an understatement. They just opened their homes and hearts to me. Gave me clothes, iPad, when I bought my home and had a housewarming, they brought furniture, gift cards. And one of the ladies in my group son is a federal parole officer. It is amazing. I tell these guys.

The groups, healing, support, God, Washington Baptist Church in SC. My first Sunday there, Pastor Stan, he called me out in front of the whole church. He said I was just out of prison and said all these wonderful things about me. The people in the church were wonderful towards me. No bad reactions. Ironically enough, the church is in the same city as the prison was in.

•**Why do people go back to crime after coming home and what can they do to protect themselves so that they can lead a positive and successful life?**

I think it is because we don't develop the right mental relationships that we need. Most of our mentoring comes from guys like Frank Lucas. He would be held as an icon. He could have been ingenious at a Fortune 500 company. Nicky Barnes, John Gotti. They could have used those skills in a POSITIVE way.

We should be mentored by people like Warren Buffet. (LeBron and Warren, he will not be one of those NBA players who is broke after he gets out the league)

All the guys that I admired were "stand up" convicts…Someone you could respect. Handles his business does not rat, but in reality 96% of them were NOT stand up convicts. Everything you were told not to do, they were doing on the down low. – Doing it on the sneak.

The hardest thing for me is the technology, the phone and the computer. Not learning at the speed I would like to learn at. There is such an abundance of stuff, food. I was walking and I went by a store that sold nothing but olive oil/ How do you that?

I used watch PBS when inside. I would watch Ru Steve Europe and he would travel in Europe traveling, immersing himself in the culture.

How did I mess myself so bad that I could not even do anything? I did not know what a bagel was until I was 40 years old.

I would see people in restaurants and imagine myself. About 60 days after my release, my friend Bill took me to an Asian restaurant called Monsoon. I used to watch people on TV do this. Now I am in this restaurant like a regular person just enjoying life. It was a surreal experience.

•**Anything else?**

What I have really seen is there is a lot more friendliness between the races in the US, than it was before. 1976, 1978…

Prison is a segregated society. There is some mixing (of the races), but generally speaking, you roll with what you are, in some places it is mandatory.

Also what I have noticed since I have been out is all the white men that are dating and marrying black women. I am like "Man, I have been gone a long time"

A younger white guy told me that said that my generation did not have the same problems that your generation had.

I have been so blessed. I have people hold me accountable, I have so much abundance. Need to have someone to tell me I am thinking crazy. The bible speaks of a regeneration of your mind. If you don't do it before, you will go back to what is easiest and what is most comfortable, it has to happen before you get out.

•**But some of those guys in prison, they are acting like they are hanging with their homies all day or something. No change in mindset or seriousness about coming home.**

It is like old homeboy week for some. Had I been going to church, doing what I was supposed to be doing, I would not be here, with Life without parole.

If I could tell anyone who is incarcerated this.... if you don't start preparing yourself to get out when you first get in, you are way behind the curve. I don't care if you have 5 years or 10 LIFE sentences you have to start preparing yourself for that release.

(Do you want to hear more from LA and visit him for a month in prison via his journal? See our next book in this series: "Blindside Diaries, Life Behind the Fences" coming soon in Winter 2019)

CONVERSATION WITH LANCE "BUTTER" PICKETT - PERSPECTIVE OF EX-FELON

Young men need to know that getting into a life of crime is a temporary means to a negative end. It seems glamorous and fun in the beginning but the lifelong price that you will ultimately pay isn't worth it. That felony will be with you for the rest of your life and will forbid you from being allowed to do many things.

The worst thing about prison for me was being away from my family and friends. Being that I was incarcerated out of state, I feared every day that if something happened to my mother that I would not have been able to attend. Somethings that were helpful in doing my time was to finally come to grips with the fact that it was nobody's fault but my own for my incarceration. Next was to begin programming (working, doing recommended programs i.e. AA, NA, Anger Management). Do your time, not anyone else's. Last but not least, leave the guards alone, they're there to do a job and you're there to do your time.

Upon coming home one of my biggest fears was what was I going to do to support myself, could I adapt to the changes of the world during my incarceration or was I going to resort back to a life of crime? For all being released from incarceration the biggest obstacle is always finding and securing gainful employment. I don't care what type of degree or skills you may have, once the average employer sees the "yes" box checked off where it asked have you ever been convicted of a felony, they automatically look at you differently without asking any questions. Be skeptical of your so called friend, partner that will offer you an immediate package(drugs) or lure into anything illegal rather than some money without strings attached or just positive advice.

Being on parole in the beginning was ok. I had a very understanding, not pushy parole officer. My problems with parole began when he got a promotion and I was assigned to a gun-ho, his own rules parole officer. He made every day of parole pure hell for me. He accomplished his goal by getting me to do something to violate and become incarcerated once again. Just remember that it's easier and more fun to deal with a parole officer once a week-once a month rather than a bunch of corrections officers 24/7.

My mother, the greatest woman to ever live was the most helpful person to me when I got out as well as the person who held me down my entire bid. Even though she is now amongst the Angels, she still continues to be instrumental in my everyday decisions and growth as a productive member of society. Don't ever turn your back on those who held your back.

The steps that I've taken to heal from the traumatic experience of being incarcerated is to reflect on the things that caused me to become incarcerated. For years I kept my prison identification card in the top of my sock drawer as a reminder before I left home and did something that could earn me a new prison id.

Many return to a life of crime because that's all they feel they know how to do. Many prisons fail to teach inmates marketable work skills in preparation for one's release. Most men feel they have to be providers by any means necessary and attempt to get money by any such means. To protect yourself you've got to have a viable and sensible plan prior to being released. Just like everything else always have a plan B and C on deck. Stay away from negative people doing negative things as well as any and all things that caused you to become incarcerated.

By the way, a few things that a person convicted of a felony can't do is hold certain jobs i.e. Policeman, Doctor, Nurse, Pharmacist, just to name a few. You can't own a firearm. In some states you can no longer vote or may have to petition the courts for your rights to be reinstated. If your conviction was of a sexual nature you may be required to register as a sex-offender for the rest of your life. It may be almost impossible to gain profitable legal, non-physical backbreaking employment i.e. Construction, Landscaping with a felony on your record. Very few make it out the game unscathed, don't think you're going to be the exception.

My final thoughts are to remind anyone thinking about entering into a life of crime is to be ready to get caught. You might get away once, twice maybe even 10 times, but getting caught is inevitable.

Lance "Butter" Pickett

Former Inmate

FACTS THEY DON'T TELL YOU ABOUT

Felony Disenfranchisement is when after you have a felony or get out of prison, you lose your right to vote. In one case, a lady with a felony conviction who was not off of her parole/supervision went to vote was given a 5 year prison sentence for voter fraud. She did not realize that the papers she signed with her Parole Officer said that she was not allowed to vote.

Did you know 1 in 13 African-Americans have lost their right to vote whereas 1 in 56 non-blacks have lost their right vote?[127]

What were Martin Luther King Jr. and the blacks in the South fighting for? Do we appreciate the struggle of our ancestors so future generations could vote?

Parole, Probation and Community Supervision. They are supposed to help you transition to a law abiding citizen when you come home. Some POs are cool and help you where they can, don't stress you and let you live your life. Others are on a power trip, give you early curfews, pop up wherever, make you quit your job you work after 7pm, yet provide no alternatives to support yourself or your family. In 2010 South Carolina, created a law for violent offenders and decided folks just coming home needed to be on paper (supervision), they retroactively created a rule that you must have 2 years Community Supervision after one's max out date, basically stating that you have to do an EXTRA two years after your sentence. AND you must pay the $50 monthly fee. These are <u>new rules</u> that were not even part of the original sentence.

Parole, Probation and Community Supervision. Many have heard about Meek Mills and how he was given a short sentence and 7 years of probation.[128] Because he did not "comply" and had "technical" violations the judge/parole sent him back to prison. One can argue that since he did not comply, fine, he should be punished. However he should have completed his whole sentence and have been a free man by 2015 or so. But instead, it was 2018 there he was back in prison with an additional 2 to 4 year prison term after the fact.

What the system does is add additional year(s) of supervision/prison after violations, so one may NEVER complete their sentence. Below are some reasons for parole/probation/supervision violations:

- Positive Drug/Alcohol test
- Non-payment of supervision fees
- Being late for curfew
- Traveling out of jurisdiction/state without permission
- Missing an appointment w/Parole Officer no matter the reason is (even if your mother/child is choking)

SOLUTIONS

FIRST THINGS FIRST

First Impressions are EVERYTHING!!!

Get a navy or black suit, with 2 nice ties and 2 shirts. Go to Goodwill or find a program that provides free suits, if you have limited funds. Also get a pair of black, navy or brown (if there is nothing else) shoes. Shine them up and make them look nice, even if they are old. Make sure your hair/edges are shaped up, even if it is long.

FOR PREVIOUSLY INCARCERATED (Felons).

The Doe Fund

Attend a 2 year or 4 year college. You most likely can get financial aid to help you with school fees and help offset your cost of living.

Organization and Job-training programs: Please email to provide us with your programs so that we can help ex-prisoners, especially those about to be or recently released, at info@imperial-imprint.com

461

BEFORE YOU GET INTO TROUBLE

G o into the military. Go to school/college. You CAN get financial aid/FREE money for school.

Get a trade! Licensed plumber, electrician, real estate professional, and tax preparer. (Go to your local unemployment office

Join Job Corps.

Move to a different state or city, but don't get caught up with those that are not doing anything for themselves.

Get your passport and a plane ticket and travel to a different country like Africa, Europe, and Asia. See how others live and you will appreciate being an American...No joke!

We at Imperial will start a webpage for different options for you to look at for help.

IF YOU ARE STILL IN SCHOOL

Get involved in school and afterschool activities. Let your principal, guidance counselor or and especially your parents know so they can help you.

If you are being bullied, get help. Try not to use physical means with a weapon to resolve the issue. Go to someone you trust. You do not want to wind up in prison.

Get involved with your YMCA, Police Athletic League, anything that has programs. Ask your school to assist you. It is THEIR DUTY to assist.

Or if you can, get an afterschool job! A legal one!

(I, Dawn, personally knew internationally famous rappers, before they became famous, who were in school, doing their rapping gigs and still working in McDonalds/minimum wage jobs…Why? Because it gave them a certain work ethic to be disciplined so when their chance of fame came about, they were ready…with a work history!)

People may say you are "soft" but you are still getting PAID, legally!

HOW TO HANDLE YOUR FRIENDS THAT ARE TROUBLE, OR GROUPS THAT WANT YOU TO BE WITH THEM & GET INTO TROUBLE

Bad friends (Just remember what the correctional staff person told you...EVIL HAS A FACE). If it don't feel right...RUN!

Talk to an older male who you respect. They can assist. If not, check out programs...use your cell phone or the internet...there will be someone...some program who can help you/talk to you even if they are in a different state.

Do NOT resort to violence if possible...and no matter what DON'T BREAK THE LAW!

Something to think about when you think about doing something illegal or hanging out with those not doing the right thing...

Support your church, community groups, go and be active in school. Join the Police Athletic Leagues so that you can be on the side of the law and know what and how to do things so that they can protect you and vouch for you should bad situations come up on the street.

Be a part of positive organization, sports, academic teams, youth groups with ex-offenders. Get a job if you can...or if you are finished with high school go to College (get financial aid and student loans...yes! You qualify) or go into the Military. Travel and work with Job Corps or programs that send you out of the United States to volunteer in 3rd world countries, Africa, Asia or Europe.

Be respectful of yourself & others and use that internet!

Be a part of something positive! Being a black male, or someone in a marginalized group, you will always have the police against you or stopping you for no reason...but if you have social networks, upstanding positive people who know you and can vouch for you... you will not find yourself in this horrible park where you cannot escape...called prison.

Please send comments to info@imperial-imprint.com if you want to share other ideas or have advice on how to handle this. We need your input to share with others so we can stop this cycle of crime and mass incarceration.

MAKING YOUR COMMUNITY LEADERS & POLITICIANS ACCOUNTABLE

Now, you may THINK that you do NOT have power, but alas, you do. As long as you can vote, you have family and friends that can vote...YOU HAVE POWER! Let your current politicians know that we need more Community Programs, Summer Youth Employment Programs, Ex-Offender Re-entry/Job programs in your neighborhoods. Let them know that people need jobs and positive programs for the youth, especially afterschool programs for the kids.

Politicians have NO EXCUSE not to get the job done. Call their offices, write letters and let them know your demands. If they will NOT listen to you, help you or your communities, let them know you will be VOTING THEM OUT and working with your friends and family to get someone else elected who will take care of the needs of the community. (Use that cell phone of yours to get their names and telephone number to their offices)

One website we found to help you find your elected officials is: https://www.usa.gov/elected-officials[129]

If you are eligible to vote then even YOU can run for office and take their seat away from them. USE YOUR VOTING POWER!!! If you are an American citizen then these are your rights! USE THEM!

If you are incarcerated or on parole, probation or community supervision, check to see if you are able to vote. Please do NOT vote until you are cleared to do so, as you do not want to get in trouble for voter fraud.

In Maine however, you can vote even while in prison, so please be sure to vote, if you are a Maine prisoner.

Below is an infographic created by the Community Coalition based in South Central Los Angeles (www.cocosouthla.org), as per their website, "Community Coalition empowers everyday people to transform their communities." Go to their website and see what they are doing. (They generously provided Imperial Imprint permission to use their infographics in this book to show their support in helping YOU!)

In the below infographic see how YOUR tax dollars can be spent to help people from even THINKING about going to prison. However, instead, money is being given to the prison system. The below infographic shows how placing one youthful offender in prison costs the same as giving 155 Summer Youth Employment Jobs to a community or sending 789 kids to Space camp.

Which do you think would be more effective in your neighborhood? How do you think that having a summer job or going to a space camp will change how you see the world? Incarceration or Prevention?

465

Also, many criminal justice laws are based upon people registering and voting for people who share their vision and their causes. It is imperative to vote, as mentioned earlier, Prison telephone companies are lobbying and giving money to politicians to make it difficult to see or speak to your loved ones unless you pay for their services. Stop politicians who are not helping you and trying to make the world a better place by getting involved and VOTING.

As per a New York Times article it states that the reason for high incarceration rates in the United States is due to democracy. The article further reads, "Most state court judges and prosecutors in the United States are elected and are therefore sensitive to a public that is, according to opinion polls, generally in favor of tough crime policies. In the rest of the world, criminal justice professionals tend to be civil servants who are insulated from popular demands for tough sentencing."[130]

Your vote is POWER! Use it! And if your community leaders and your politicians are not listening and helping you…Put someone else in office that will!

- *I see a lot of politicians talking/not talking about criminal justice reform. Ask them when was the last time they went to the prisons unannounced to see the true conditions and speak to those who are incarcerated? How many are doing something on the outside to create programs to STOP young people from entering the system.*
- *Ask your legislators to reinstate the rights for people who are formerly incarcerated to have the opportunity to have Federal Jobs, AND to remove the underlying and "hidden" restrictions that prevent one from obtaining state licenses (within reason). This is true criminal justice/prison re-entry reform. "Teaching a person to fish...not just giving them a piece of fish."*
- *Also ask those who feel that we do NOT need criminal justice reform. Are they adding or cutting funding to neighborhoods to create programs so the children have positive and healthy extracurricular activities? Demand answers from them or vote them OUT!*

Real Talk!

WHY CALIFORNIA SHOULD FULLY FUND PROP 47

THE COST OF INCARCERATION ⓋⓈ THE COST OF PREVENTION

The implementation of **PROP 47** reduced court costs and the need to pay private prisons to house California residents. It will save the state $135 million in 2015-2016. Unfortunately, Governor Brown plans to keep $100 million of those savings in the prison system.

These savings should be directed to the "Safe Neighborhoods and Schools Fund" to support prevention and treatment services. Here are a few ways the State can invest in communities instead of incarceration.

$62,300
PER YEAR

 **INCARCERATE 1 ADULT**

OR

SEND 9 ADULTS TO DRUG TREATMENT

SEND 15 KIDS TO PRE-SCHOOL

$233,000
PER YEAR

 INCARCERATE 1 YOUTH

OR

SEND 789 KIDS TO SPACE CAMP

SPONSOR 155 YOUTH JOBS

$100,000,000 CAN FUND *

50 YOUTH CENTERS   **500** INTERVENTION WORKERS   **25,000** YOUTH JOBS

Youth Justice Coalition 1% Campaign · Contact: www.youth4justice.org

Tell Governor Brown to FULLY FUND PROP 47! Sign the Petition!
cocosouthla.org/prop47petition

COMMUNITY COALITION

The above infographic was created by Community Coalition http://cocosouthla.org/inforgraphics/. The organization generously provided Imperial Imprint LLC permission to use this infographic for this book.

ADDITIONAL LETTERS
& END POEMS

ADDITIONAL LETTERS & END POEMS - *Table of Contents*

471

KEVIN WHITFIELD – POEM: CRYING OUT

I'm in Solitude, but I gotta give great gratitude, even though I'm in this hell, my mind is in full aptitude. When I think the hardest I'm inside this cell, I guess these four walls I'm living in have a story to tell. So bear with me, while I share what my crying eyes have seen and my mind has endured. All these things are true and exact not what my ears have heard. So as I lay here, these walls seem to be closing in on me, I try my best to keep my sanity. We've been locked down now for two weeks strong. I'm banging on the door asking, "How long?" But the only answer I get is shut up! And lay your ass down. But I know the answer to that is, two more weeks as I try not to frown. So I prepare myself, for the long and strenuous haul, but when I need an answer who do I call? The walls are sticky and the floors are sweaty and I'm screaming "Someone come get me."

My lil homey just got a LIFE sentence for a twenty piece rock, now he's walking around with anger still filled with shock. At twenty years old his society life is done. Never having the chance to raise a daughter or a son. Now that's stressful, because I can feel his pain, longing to hold my grandson is driving me insane., Now, no name, no blame, but it's a damn shame. How does a politician of the state get caught with a half brick and claims he's not in the game? No different, just like everybody else situation, while we receive LIFE sentences and he only gets probation.

Now it's sad to see teenagers come in here with 45 years on their back having to do 85%. Oh, did I mention they were (Black). Now, that's sad, because most don't have a high school education. Throw their asses in jail is their answer for our generation. But what saddens me more, I see it all the time, men trampling each other for that devil's love potion better known as the "Pill line." Some walk around like zombies without a care in the world, some don't know if they wanna be boy or girl. Yeah, homosexuality is what they seem to promote, you can't even order a swimsuit issue book, because they say that not for a man to look at. But you can order all the muscle man magazines for your eyes to see, who they think they fooling it sure ain't me.

Now, the 13th Amendment says, "You're a slave to the state if convicted of a crime," they just modified things from 150 years back in time. Now I ain't lying, a lot of peoples will to live is dying, some of the hardest dudes you know lay at night crying. So we drown our sorrows by smoking weed, and drinking fermented fruit, but when it all wears off we're still in this state suit. They say the Department of Correction is to correct your wrong. **"We want you to do better, and be ready for Society"** is their lame ass song. But with no constant education rehabilitation, to help you along, things will only get worse what the hell their doing wrong? But I know, it's a big business now (Prison Industries, and canteen purchases) they making millions WOW! You got to excuse me, because my vision is kinda blurry, I'm getting a lil teary eye thinking of my family, hoping today nobody tries to kill me.

The reason I wrote this is to express how I feel about mass incarceration and how the youth are being plucked away to live their young lives in prison, a place where no man wants to be. Now don't get me wrong we all may have done things, some worse than others, that may cause you to pay your debt to society. But when the system gets their hand on you they don't let go. Everyone deserves a second chance especially if they have worked hard for it.

It seems like you can earn a degree, never get in trouble and still, you get shot down at parole. But the man who just stabbed his roommate goes home without a fuss. Reason being, they don't want the man who's got himself together. Because if you know yourself for who you are and elevated then you are a threat. But if you still got that menace mentality they can say, "look we let him go, and look at what he has done...killed somebody." So let's keep them all in jail and live our lives. So youth, don't give in to the bullshit don't get caught in this web because its hell! And it's only going to get worse Peace!

We need y'all. Real talk.
Kevin Whitfield

473

BYRON SPIVEY - ADVICE TO THE YOUTH

D ecember 11, 2013 2:00pm ---The (Glory) of "Fathers" our Future. Every kindred, nation, people and tribe, tongues, I pen in hope to reach one. Reproofs of instruction is the way of life. The (path) chosen will be a legacy left to see also remember what goals was set; can a torch or baton be passed on generations to come, even in setbacks, delays. We are here, "born" to help (mankind) not decline, or follow the crowd, do as the majority.

Mandela is an example, of self-worth, the earth to share a lot, possessions, give in care. (Love) the (Key) free in mind, spirit and soul, break-strongholds. I warn you, via "Belly of the Beast" get out a (Bad-cycle) you think is swagg; Then you'll know you been had, regrets, if I can do it over again, time waits on no one, (be) the Guidance one.

December 16, 2013- #273097 is my name, state property, because I made decisions that landed me in prison. A single mother home, but my father never spoke nor taught me manhood. So the streets and peers became my teachers, school was deemed fashion show plus sex pool to try also act out codes of so called life cycles, what was the norm? Fit in. I had many give advice, saying to stop, slow down, and think. You have a purpose, talents, be someone! Give back to the community. Help others, lead, don't follow. Warnings, I regret, wishing to start over again, do right, be free.

I write, in hope that whoever reads these lines of my soul. Know that authority rules, and laws are part of our being moral citizens. Don't be a Government child. I knew better, chose to rebel, be a thug, now I pay the price— a Natural LIFE sentence. So make wise choices, don't be in denial or 'The Belly of the Beast is where you'll sleep.'

Byron Spivey # 273097
Perry Correctional Institution Q1B-201-T
430 Oaklawn Road
Pelzer, SC 29669

COREY WILLIAMS - "I SEEK REFUGE WITH GOD FROM THE ACCURSED SATAN"

In the name of God, the Beneficent, the Merciful "And that there should be among you a group who call (Mankind) unto virtue and enjoying what is good and forbid wrong; and these are they who will be successful" Holy Qur'an 3:104

Dear Stranger:

If you are able to read what I have quoted above then you are of age to understand what I am about to write you underneath this oppressive society that I am currently in. And hopefully through the word within this letter you may gain some mental insight and knowledge to help you overstand your outlook on life and the world you live in so that you will be able to stay above this oppressive society the world calls a prison.

Just think about how I started this letter: 'Dear Stranger.' Notice how I didn't call you son. To do that, some type of relationship has to be established in between. And let's always be honest with each other. You don't know me anymore than you know that there is a planet called Jupiter in space fifth from the sun. I know you are cognizant of me however, knowing me is an entirely different thing. And that's how I feel towards you. I also know that it is hard to love something, someone that you are just aware of. I blame nobody but myself, the choices I made in my life deprived me from knowing you and to become a successful man.

I once stood where you are standing now. I'm not talking about the same spot, but out in the world where every day I could move around and make conscious decisions. And again, I say and emphasize that because of the conscious decisions I made in my life. I missed out and still am missing out on yours.

Believe me when I say that I was very conscious of picking up bad habits from these friends and other people because I didn't want to be the odd ball out. I was conscious of not listening to the guidance of my mother as she tried her best to teach me to be a successful man in the world. I heard what she said; I just didn't cloak myself with her words. I guess it's a little too late to say that I should have listened, but it's not too late for me to warn you.

- Listen and cloak yourself with the advice of your mother
- To enjoin what is good and forbid wrong amongst others and yourself
- To always think before you act.

You best believe the choices you make in life will determine which road along your highway you will end up on, and each road leads somewhere. Some to failure, some to disaster, some to success. Try not to jump on the road I took that led me to a place where I will not get anything to eat if I have any peach fuzz on my face. A place where I get punished for someone else's actions. A place where the word "joy" does not exist. A place where it is highly possible that I can get served two boiled eggs, two biscuits, a slice of cheese for breakfast, and a bologna sandwich for lunch and dinner for days, weeks and months at a time.

This is a place where one's power to do as he pleases is stripped from him. For example, if an 18 year old correction officer tells a grown man maybe the age of 40 to go to his cell for no apparent reason that man will submit like a child to the C.O. or face what is to come and believe me it is not worth it. Here within this oppressive society there is no win.

Even though you are young, ask yourself, "Why would I want to succumb to something like that?"

I seriously hope that you don't travel the road I took. I am one who before my incarceration didn't realize that everything I was doing was negative: Associating myself with a negative crowd, drinking, smoking, flossin,' so called hustling, chasing girls, and clubbing. All of these things and more I was involved in, and now as I sit here and look back on my life, I now recognize that I've consumed a lot of negativity without giving the world something positive. Hold up!!!! Yeah I did leave something positive, that is YOU, stranger.

You have the potential, the ability, the chance right now to travel on your highway and end on a road to become successful in the world. Be able to envision success and activate it within your psyche so that your mind will show you the proper blueprint to achieve your goal. Become one who is on top and not on the bottom as I have ended. Please cogitate on this letter carefully, success has to start somewhere.

Before I end this letter, I want to tell you not to be afraid or ashamed to pick up a dictionary and look up any word within this letter you don't know. As a matter of fact I challenge you to pick up a dictionary and look up every four-letter word or more presented in this letter. And I will leave you with a few more word to look up and commit to your vocabulary.

- Celerity
- Esoteric
- Precept
- Sunna or Sunnah

Corey Williams, SCDC# 259070

RASHAUN THOMAS aka RASTA - ADVICE TO THE CHILDREN

Greetings to the Youth! Choices are very vital in life. No matter who you are, we live and learn from our choices. Our parents and elders always used to say, "A hard head makes a soft behind" and "you make your bed then you sleep in it." The outcome and struggles are up to the individual. No one really wants a rough life. The youth are our new leaders and the future. We the Afrikan American must continue our progress and not look down on your own kind. Each one, teach one. Unity is a force that cannot be stopped like water, it cannot be held down for long. Knowing our past is supposed to make us strong, we can do anything. But your mental has to stay focused, and you need experience strengthening the mental also.

Don't be afraid to say No! I am learning from my mistakes in prison the hard way, you see I was in them streets and the streets don't love no one. See them streets have two destinies: prison or the graveyard. So just think, do you want to be doing time, 20 or 40 years, or perhaps LIFE? All that can be avoided by finding a good mentor, plus keeping your circle with positive individuals. Take me for example and take heed to my mistakes. I wanted to be grown at an early age. Hang out with the older guys, not listening to my mother. Don't do none of that! There's nothing wrong with being by yourself or moving on your own decisions. Make your standards high, challenge yourself. Write down things you want to achieve and make them out as you accomplish that goal you wrote down. Then move to the next.

Respect God and don't be shy or afraid to pray (chant) and start meditating at a young age. And most of all READ, READ, READ truthful and educational books, then quiz yourself and another person too. Be their motivator. If they see you striving to learn, they may join you. Don't be another statistic. The penitentiary is packed with blacks." We must break that cycle. Have love in your heart which is the greatest commandment. It is hard to go wrong when you have respect and the concept of love and discipline pulling up the rear. Youth stand tall and strive to make good choices all through your life.

Hotep! One Luv, King Rasta

Rashaun Thomas, SCDC# 278371

477

ROBERT JOHNSON aka BROTHER NADIR - THE ROAD TO PRISON & THE LIFE INSIDE OF IT

Jan 14, 2014 --I am writing this letter to you because I wish had written it to me when I was younger, before I made certain choices and did certain things that would destroy my life. I realize that there is nothing that can be said to get you to understand what's at stake. I just hope that sharing my experience can someday serve as a reminder of where you don't want to be.

My name is Nadir. I'm a 34-year old black male doing a 35 year sentence for murder. I was born and raised in Milwaukee, Wisconsin, a city with high concentration of gang activity - Gangster Disciples, New Breed Black Gangsters, Latin Kings, Vice Lords, Black Peace Stones, Spanish Cobras– beside the stock supply of street gangs in any large city. My initiation into gang life began at the age of 11, and those choices that I made even then continue to affect me today.

I've currently been incarcerated for 16 years in a maximum-security prison in South Carolina. When you do the math you'll figure out that I was 18 years old when I started this life of imprisonment. Before I share with you the realities of prison life, I want you to get just a glimpse of where I come from prior to me committing the crime that got me making the same choices and seeing yourself in the same situations.

My childhood was a special time in my life. I came from a loving family with my mother grinding hard working two, sometimes three jobs to take care of me and my older sisters. I was far from spoiled, but Moms made sure that we had memorable birthdays, Christmases, and all our other family members were involved, always creating many good memories. My favorite part of childhood—besides being with family—was going outside and playing with the kids on my block. I was always able to meet friends and compete in any games that we played. I remember those summer days looking up at the sky and wanting to experience life as free as the open air of nature. As a young boy, I wondered what my life would bring. I had no idea how much control I would have over my life, assuming that when I "grew up" I would be able to do anything I ever wanted to do or be anything I wanted to be. Childhood is full of hope for the future of growing up.

I can remember sharing with my school teacher back in kindergarten when asked, "What do you want to be when you grow up?" I said, "I want to be a football player!" I was too young to know all my options or even know all the discipline, training and all the odds against me becoming a professional athlete. I had no clue. I was free to dream, free to be naive in my goal and aspirations. As I became a teenager, the picture of my future became more hazy, but because of my perception and life experience, more realistic. I can see now how various things influenced my perception about what I wanted out of life. I was exposed to gang violence in general at a young age. Violence was a common way of resolving conflict in my neighborhood. If you didn't know how to fight, you were at a loss to protect yourself from the taunting and teasing of other kids. My reputation for resolving conflict with my fists started back as early as I could remember and became part of a violent lifestyle and aggressive image as I approached my early teens. I fought in the neighborhood, at school, on the school bus. Wherever and whenever I felt I had to prove my toughness, it was going down. I looked up to the most intimidating guys in my neighborhood, hoping one day I would command the respect amongst my peers that they did amongst theirs.

Along with this image of toughness came a necessary air of confidence and coolness that I adopted from my older peers, what we refer to as "swag" nowadays. This person seems to attract the attention of everyone who had some significance in a young teen's life. It was a certain aura of power that came with "the image." I felt that I could have that power and influence. I could use it to become popular, get the girls, and get the respect that I thought was so essential to whom I was as seen by my peers. I use the word "peers" instead of "friends" because trying to impress people to win their acceptance and approval absent any other connection except for status comparison, is the basic function of peer relations. A friend is one who you should be able to be yourself with without regard for status. The connection is deeper and not just on the surface. At least that's how it should be in my opinion.

There are many images and roles in the media, pop culture, and society that influence us all. In my teenage years, hip hop culture and artists provided me with many images of how to live, what was cool, and what was lame. It also exposed me to risky, reckless and criminal behavior. Now don't get me wrong, all rap artists don't promote destructive lifestyle, but the majority of the artists I chose to give ear to were about that life. Scarface, MC Eiht, Spice 1, 2Pac, Mobb Deep, Kool G Rap, Snoop Dogg, and many others—they rapped about pimping, hustling, putting in work, robbery, and murder. You even had female gangster rappers like Boss putting it down. I flooded my mind with the music, the videos, and adopted the role. What I saw or heard in the videos and rap songs was not so dissimilar to what was real in my neighborhood. The artists just made it more alluring. I followed and mimicked the roles until I became what the rap stars rapped about, all to the approval of my peers who were under the same influences. That was the life I chose, which was a road paved for prison. And it's not like I wasn't told. I had much counseling from family members, professionals and O.G.s that had given me warnings. They saw the signs. A cellblock or a tombstone, they would tell me, promise me - even threaten me - if I chose to keep pressing down the same road. I heard but I didn't listen and chose what I felt was life for me, a "G."

Now let me be clear on this point. Everything I'd done leading up to my incarceration was based on choices I made. I had many options to do other things with my life, even though at times I felt trapped, felt like I could see no other direction for my life. I could have pursued my education and stayed focused in school rather cutting classes to get high and drink. I could have attended the local community center and gotten involved with after-school programs or constructive activities rather than hanging out in the streets with "my crew." and getting into things we had no business doing. I wasted a lot of time out there in the streets, driven by my choices of rap music to take risks that held dire consequences (i.e. prison and death). I could have relied on the support of those around me who loved me and cared for me enough to try to steer me in the right direction. If only I had chosen to listen and explore other options, maybe I could have built a better future for myself than the reality I find myself in today.

I have spent almost two decades behind bars—plenty of time to reflect on all that I could've done better with my life. Now I'm here where so many said I would be one of those two places (cellblock or tombstone). I often wonder why I could not see my future so clearly back then. I never thought that I could be convicted for the crime of murder and sentenced to spend all of my 20's, 30's and 40's in a prison. I would not graduate high school, nor get married, have children, attend my sister's wedding, my niece's and nephew's graduations. I would not attend high school reunions, or link up with old friends on Facebook to share our success. My life could have been so much more than what it is today. And what is my life today? A depressing life of confinement. The gangster's sojourn, the thug life rite of passage.

The reality of prison is grim, devoid of purpose and meaning. The prison system is in place to control and punish it's incarcerated by stripping away all power for us to rebuild our lives. Our lives consist of separation from family, isolation from society, deprivation from all forms of pleasure and joy. Prison is a hostile environment.

Many people in prison have been abused and struggle with mental health issues—realities which contribute to the high frequency of violence. Along with that, most prisoners have earned their stay in prison for committing some of the most heinous act while in society—murder, rape, kidnapping, armed robbery, criminal sexual conduct with minors. We're dealing with people with a warped moral compass, most of whom have a very callous view of life. Many don't value their own lives, let alone the lives of others.

In addition to the depressing mentality of the inmate population, there are the intense restrictions imposed on you by prison guards and officials that add extra pressure and tension to the whole atmosphere. This is not a happy place to be. You miss out on the simple things just as much as the most significant ones, like eating an orange or any fresh fruit for that matter, or a real hamburger. All the meat they serve in here is inferior grade made from the scraps (guts, bones, with a little meat) collected up in meat processing plants, ground up to make "turkey" or "chicken" patties. Most of us who've done enough time to see dozens of fellow prisoners develop stomach viruses and cancer forego the meat from our diet. Other than that you're forced to eat a high carb diet which can be bad for your health and can even produce diabetes. Your best bet is, to not eat much food at all if you have a long sentence.

You have very little privacy in this environment, and no rights to personal property, even property you purchase. Correctional Officers ("C.O.s") doing routine shakedowns can confiscate your radio, TV, hot pot, books, magazines, tennis shoes for virtually any excuse. Prisoners constantly have property taken from them that they purchased at exorbitant rates (e.g. a low-quality generic brand portable TV worth $60 in the electronics section at Wal-Mart costs you $200 in here—but when it burns out after only six months of use, trying to have it repaired will get you a disciplinary and get your TV confiscated.) I could go on and on about the conditions of confinement. The point is I know you don't want to be here. I didn't want this for my life then and I don't know, but it's too late for me to change that. I made a choice, needless to say, a very unwise and unintelligent choice, one that will cost me 35 years of my life.

I was given a number 16 years ago. When I came to prison, I noticed that we all had a number, nothing special. Everybody's number is different. The numbers reflect how long someone has been locked up. For instance, if your number starts with a '2' like mine, you could have served anywhere from 10 to 20 years. If it starts with a '1' that could be anywhere from 20-35 years, and a '0' usually indicates a person who's been down for more than four decades. The numbers keep adding up as more and more people are incarcerated for bad decisions they made in life— decisions that will hurt their families and wreck their futures. I hope you will choose life, freedom, and a better future than one offering a cellblock or a tombstone.

Peace,

Brother Nadir -Robert Johnson

#262974 – January 4, 2014

481

JIMMY WINDHAM - A COVENANT SEALED IN BLOOD

(This is letter is long, however we agreed with Mr. Windham, that this would move some of the people reading this book)

INTRODUCTION TO THE FOLLOWING ARTICLE WRITTEN BY JIMMY WINDHAM

Brother Jimmy Windham is a dear brother, who has come to know Christ after he was incarcerated in 1984. He sent the following article to be published in "The Testimony of Truth" and expressed in his letter to us that he had studied blood covenants a few years ago and felt to write concerning what a blood covenant means to believers. The particular blood covenant which he refers to here in this article is not one that was practiced exactly in every nation of ancient times but is similar and so relative. Each culture adopted blood covenant as a means of surety for agreements but they varied in numerous ways. Understanding the blood covenant should give those who have entered into the New Covenant with Jesus Christ great assurance and confidence in God and in His promises to His people as they consider foe covenant made between God and Abraham. Blood covenants were among the first and oldest of historical traditions.

In ancient times men were most often untrue to their word, and even covenants were no positive proof that one of the two parties in covenant would keep his part of foe agreement. Strife often broke out between the covenant parties, resulting in property loss, destruction and death. There was no positive way to enforce the covenant made. Although the seriousness of a covenant was taught and stress placed upon its obligations, when it became difficult or inconvenient to remain true to one's word and breaking the covenant had no seriously demanding consequences, it was easily broken. Even men with most noble intentions, at times found themselves in a strait to keep their commitments. Pressures of life or things unforeseen would often cause them to fold, leaving the other party, unfortunately, holding the bag. For this reason a covenant was sought which would be more binding and would have serious repercussions if broken, therefore making the agreement more sure.

As Brother Jimmy Windham wrote in his article, a blood covenant was signed in blood with a third party present in which death was the result of any who would break the covenant. Men would not thoughtlessly sign nor flippantly disregard a blood covenant, for the ramifications demanded his blood. May Brother Jimmy's article bless those who read it and encourage each one to claim the promises of God, provided in Christ Jesus.

A COVENANT SEALED IN BLOOD by Jimmy Windham

On a lonely mountain a teenage boy lay wonder-eyed on an altar as his elderly father stood over him with a sharp pointed knife in his hands. All his lather could say after he had bound his son's hands with a leather cord was, "Son, you know I love you, so trust me, for this is for the God I've always told you about" Isaac had absolute faith in his father's God and Who was now his God. Isaac obeyed his father even though he could have easily taken the knife from his aged father. But disobedience wasn't an option, for he knew his father was a godly man. The night before, when he asked his father where the sacrifice was to go with the wood he carried up the mountain, his sweet old father kindly told him, "God will provide" (Jehovah Jirah). From the time he sat on his father's knee as a child and throughout his teenage years, his father Abraham had meticulously and methodically taught and instilled every promise his eternal, all-creating God had given him. Isaac was very familiar with the events that surrounded the miracle of his birth and the natural impossibility of it. So Isaac knew very well that Jehovah was his father's God. He also understood the implications of God's promises as they applied to him. In order for God to king forth nations from his elderly father, God would also bless him and his seed. He grew up as a teenager trusting in his father's God. So, as he lay on this crude altar unsure of what was transpiring and how this act would affect God's promises, his childlike faith was strong in his father's words, "Trust me, son, God will provide." Abraham was a man of faith and never once doubted that God would not raise Isaac up if he indeed plunged that knife into his chest. The writer of Hebrews records: (Abraham) "Accounting that God was able to raise him up, even from the dead; from whence also he received him in a figure" (Heb, 11:19).

A covenant became a way to be certain that men would remain true to their word. A blood covenant involved an agreement between two people that was breakable only by the death of one of the two parties involved.

Men in Abraham's day and era were not known for keeping their word. Because of the dishonesty among men, a covenant became a way to be certain that men would remain true to their word. If either broke the covenant that was sworn in blood, it resulted in a death penalty to the one who broke the covenant by the executor of the covenant and who was the third party to the agreement. The example of one man's integrity of those days is seen in the dispute that developed between Abraham's herdsmen and Lot's. God blessed the flocks of both men and the land became too small for both herds and it resulted in contentions between Abraham's herdsmen and Lot's herdsmen over the land as well as the wells of water. Abraham, being a righteous man, gave Lot the greener, well-watered land in the valley while he moved his possessions and flocks to the more arid mountainous land away from Lot. There were many disputes between wealthy landowners whose agreements didn't turn out as well as that between Abraham and Lot and at times war would break out between one land owner and his neighbor. This always resulted in property damage and often produced loss of life in the families involved. The solution to this was to call for a truce in which a blood covenant was instituted. In elementary school, most of us studied the Indians of North America and read about the Indian "blood covenant" in which both parties would cut their hand with a knife and then shake, thereby making them blood brothers.

Among ancient men, the procedures and ceremonies involved in blood covenants varied in different cultures. I read a few years ago in one culture, where a blood covenant called the executor to bring both families to the boundary line of their properties. Both families brought a young lamb from their flocks, which lamb was to be spotless without blemish. The executor then slew both lambs and within a trail of twenty feet on the boundary line of the properties, he poured out the sacrificed lambs' blood. This was called, "the blood trail". The head of each family, standing at the end of the blood trail, was handed, by his oldest son (heir), his weapons and his coat. The elder for one family walked down the trail of blood and handed the elder of the other family his weapons and his coat. He would then walk back to the middle of the trail of blood where the executor stood. While his family, his servants, and the other family with their servants all looked on, he would swear as he stood in blood, that his weapons were now his neighbors and would never be used against him or his family, and his coat, representing his goods and necessities, were now his neighbors if he needed anything. He would complete the ceremony by walking over to the other family's side to be hugged and kissed by all, for now he took their name. In turn, the head of the other family followed the same ritual. As they all knelt, the executor would proclaim, "Today you've exchanged weapons, coats, and names as you stood in blood before both families and these witnesses. From henceforth, there will not be anything other than peace among you, for whosoever breaks this covenant will be put to death."

Like the American Indians, Abraham knew well what a blood covenant meant and the seriousness of this covenant. Although the procedures were somewhat different in his culture from feat written above, the principles were the same. The covenant made between God and Abram is found in Genesis 15. Reading in Genesis 15:9-10, "And he said unto him, Take me an heifer of three yew's old, and a she goat of three years old, and a ram of three years old, and a turtledove, and a young pigeon. And he took unto him all these, and divided them in the midst, and laid each piece one against another: but the birds divided he not" Once this was done, it left sort of an isle between the animal parts through, which we see in verse 17, the Spirit of the Lord passed between those parts establishing His covenant with Abram, whose name was then changed to Abraham.

Now, before Abraham stood on that hill ready to confirm the covenant, he had the gospel declared unto him. In Galatians 3:8, reading from the Amplified Version, "And the Scripture, foreseeing that God would justify (declare righteous, put in right standing with Himself) the Gentiles in consequence of faith, proclaimed the Gospel (foretelling the glad tidings of a Savior ling beforehand) to Abraham in the promise, saying, in pit shall all the nations of the earth fee blessed," Verse 9: "So then, those who are people of faith are blessed and made happy and favored by God (as partners in fellowship) with the believing and trusting Abraham." Abraham was given the gospel of a Savior coming to die for all his family. Abraham entered into a blood covenant with God and stood on that mountain with you, me and all his children in his loins, ready and willing to do his part in sacrificing his only Stilt of promise, because he had received the gospel and knew God would sacrifice His Son in fulfilling His part in a blood covenant with mankind. Now, the blood of God's only slain firstborn Son is shed and covers our hearts if we let God bring us to the blood trail of Calvary's hill. We all were God's enemies by nature of our flesh, but if we will stand in this shed blood and make our promises to God and His family, trade him our weapons for His weapons and our filthy (coat) rags for a robe of pure white (righteousness) His coat, we enter into this covenant with God. I promised God that if He'd save me and forgive me of all my terrible sins I would present my body to Him as a sacrifice. My father, Abraham's God, heard me as I knelt there and the Holy Spirit, who is the executor, heard my vows and sealed them in the blood covenant I have with God. But when it was God's turn, He spoke so many promises to you and me that they had to be written down in a Book that has 66 smaller books. His promises to you and me include eternal life. He knew we wouldn't keep our end of the covenant we made with Him which, if broken, was punishable by death; therefore He slew His firstborn Son in order that we might live. Now, what does that mean for you and me? We can go to any promise written in those 66 books and we can stand on it because God, Who cannot lie, sealed it in blood! His blood! He has given us His weapons; "Wherefore take unto you the whole armor of God" (Eph. 6:13). He's standing in foe trail of blood holding them out for us. Why? So we'll be able to withstand all the tricks and darts of the enemy. Our weapons can't defeat foe devil but His can and He has given them to us. Our weapons are carnal, but His are mighty, "the weapons of our warfare are not carnal but mighty through God" (Eph. 6:13-18). We also received His name as part of our blood covenant with God. Are you sick? In one of the books with promises, His covenant says (and remember it's sealed in blood), "He was wounded for our transgressions, he was bruised for our iniquities, the chastisement of our peace was upon him and with his stripes we are healed" (Isa. 53:5). Do you want to live forever and never die? He promised you in blood that if you'll "confess (repent with your whole heart) to the Lord Jesus and believe with your whole heart that God raised him from the dead, you'll be saved. (Rom. 10:9) In His scripture, He asked, "Why will you die?" For it is not God's will that any would perish but His will is that all will come to repentance (II Peter 3:9).

The blood of God's only slain firstborn Son is shed and covers our hearts if we let God bring us to the blood trail of Calvary's hill

I'm in prison doing a life sentence, incarcerated in 1984 until now, and I'm so unworthy of this blood covenant with God. But God wants us all to repent and turn to Him, for it was in love that He died and shed His blood, to guarantee you and me eternal life. Today is fee day feat He's speaking to your heart and asking you to find someone whom you are certain knows God and will pray with you, or get alone right now and pray and repent until you know God has forgiven you. It doesn't matter what you've done or what sins you have committed in the past, God will forgive you. If He had mercy on me He'll have mercy on anybody, for I know as Paul feat Jesus Christ came to save sinners of whom I was chief. You have opportunity today to enter into a covenant with the Almighty God, a covenant sealed in His own blood. God's own Son died for you so you can live. Time is running out on the earth, so make your peace with God today. I'm praying for you! Pray for me also. A Prisoner of Jesus Christ.

Note about Brother Jimmy Windham

Brother Jimmy is incarcerated in South Carolina and desires everyone's prayers. The Lord has recently blessed him by giving him a Christian roommate named Ralph. While having the option to move to the "Character Dorm," he chose to remain where he is to be a light to those who sit in the greatest darkness and because God gave him a Christian roommate. Recently the warden decided to make the unit where Jimmy is a faith based unit. They will be allowed access to the recreation field and have all the privileges of those in the "Character Dorm." God has blessed Brother Jimmy in many ways while he daily faces very difficult situations, so continue to pray for him. For others who are incarcerated and read "The Testimony of Truth," Brother Jimmy wants to encourage you to know that God loves you and will do for you exactly as He has done for him. God will forgive, save and give you freedom and eternal life. Just call upon Him and He will hear and answer. Praise God!

Mr. Windham has written a book with Christian based writing that can be bought for a small fee.

TERRIEL MACK aka MUKATA AMAZUU (ZAM ZAM)-'*BLACK CHILD*' RAP SONG FOR "LETTERS TO OUR SONS"

[HOOK] "BLACK CHILD, Keep the faith and Hold yo' Head Up"
"BLACK CHILD, Wit Jah blessings it's gone get better"
"BLACK CHILD, I know you fed up, BLACK CHILD"
"STRUGGLE ON NEVA LET UP!"

[Verse 1]

BLACK CHILD, If you fit that description listen with yo' wholehearted attention let yo' 3rd eye envision this benediction dat Mukata givin' you and don't misconstrue this with idle chatter coming from now a day rappers/

A BLACK CHILD myself with a duty to speak on truth regardless of repercussions these issues here need discussing and Imma say apologize ain't a part of the equation cuz a I do dis for the past present & future of my nation/

BLACK CHILD from a linage made for more that this peonage/

Outshining diamonds and gold although we were born penniless/

Our Black melanin skin can be traced back through da millennium/

And in this same Blackness creation found its beginning in the Black Genesis/

Toss contrary hypothesis in the Garbages/

They mis-educated us but they will never be smart as us/

That's why before we born through abortion clinics they target us/

Or they lock us in cages so our children can grow up fatherless/

The heart of us pump Kujichagulia marvelous/Promise if we unite they'll think twice before they war wit us/

The Almighty I in control in control of what to be in store for us/

This only the beginning, JahJah got even more for us BLACK CHILD

[HOOK] "BLACK CHILD, Keep the faith and Hold yo' Head Up"
"BLACK CHILD, Wit Jah blessings it's gone get better"
"BLACK CHILD, I know you fed up, BLACK CHILD"
"STRUGGLE ON NEVA LET UP!"

[Verse 2]

BLACK CHILD, open your eyes to reality/

Every day on the news police gun down Blacks randomly/

BLACK CHILD time behind these prison bars is really hard/

Everyday penitentiary living will leave yo mental scared, why?/

Da food is garbage CO's heartless, plus them strip searches annoying/

And all them shackles and chains rattle, ya brain/
And they call u by a number not ya name/
This place'll drive you insane/that's simple and plain/
Dope game only gonna lead you to prison or dead/
Don't be afraid to use your head, make better choice's instead/like go to school,
Don't be a fool dem books got lots of knowledge in 'em/
As I sit in this prison I think like "Man I shoulda listen"

"Man I shoulda listen"
"Man I shoulda listen"
"Man I shoulda listen"

As I sit in this prison I think back like "Man, I shoulda listened"
As I sit in this prison I think back like "Man, I shoulda listened"
As I sit in this prison I think back like "Man, I shoulda listened"
As I sit in this prison I think back like "Man, I shoulda listened"

EPILOGUE

Some of the participants of this project, have been fortunate enough to have made it home to their family and loved ones. They are with productive members of their communities. They can now put this experience behind them and move on with their lives. Some will one day be able to join them while others will never get to experience life on the other side of the fences ever again.

Though some of the letters within this book might depict a grim reality of prison life, this project was not intended as a scare tactic but was intended to be used as a vehicle to shed light on an ever growing problem that plagues our society, mass incarceration. Also to have those most affected by this problem share their experiences and knowledge. This provided an opportunity to share their pain and experiences with those who may not otherwise know what it is like to live behind prison walls.

Some chose to use the opportunity to speak to the youth of our nation other chose to address personal family issues while others took the opportunity to expose the living conditions along with the mental, emotional and physical damage that life within confinement causes. After reading this project one can no longer view Prisoners as people casted away or animals, but as living, breathing, caring, passionate, intelligent, creative, and loving human beings concerned about their personal families as well as the families of others. Who have been affected or may one day be affected by mass incarceration. If something isn't done to fix this problem mass incarceration is not just a Black, White, Hispanic, or any other ethnicity problem. It is an American problem; although the poor and disenfranchised are the most affected. In addition, The Sentencing Project report 'Mass Incarceration in Middle America' shows how in some suburbs and rural areas incarceration rates are growing.[131] The wealthy also find themselves in iron bracelets and shackles (Just ask Martha Stewart). At some point we as a nation must take a look in the mirror, and ask ourselves where are we going wrong? Though individuals commit crime social and environmental conditions also play a major part. When there are few jobs and limited opportunities along with peer pressure, and other life issues, one's survival instinct will kick in and cause him or her to sell drugs, rob, steal or cheat another out of their money. Does this mean they should be thrown in prison and given 30 or 40 years or should they be placed in institutions where they are provided an opportunity to learn a trade, placed in work programs and given jobs upon completion?

Unfortunately individuals with crimes such as these are the ones causing the nation's incarceration rate to rise to the numbers they are, and will continue to rise unless something is done to change. They are also taking up space that should be used for individuals committing violent crimes such as murder, rape and molestation. Jails across the country are overcrowded with sentenced criminals awaiting beds in prisons, but where there are none due to overcrowding. Especially in States with mandatory minimum sentencing and 85% laws these states are experiencing move overcrowding issues than others. Though the problem doesn't lie in the sentencing structures it lies in our capitalistic society. We have to start somewhere for if we continue down the path we are currently headed eventually almost half of our nation's people will either be in prison or on probation or parole.

**************End Comments from Dawn*************

I hope that the letters, infographics and interviews in this book gave you some insight of what prison is really like. What a life of crime will bring you and the fact that you are considered 'nothing' to some of those who work in the prison and to many in society as a whole.

When in prison you are still the same you with hopes, fears, dreams and needs of friendship, love, companionship, knowledge. Having the need to be heard, seen and respected as a man. All of those things are dead in prison.

On September 9, 2016 there was a work stoppage by prisoners to protest the treatment of how prisoners are being treated and working for little to no wages (Remember 'DID YOU KNOW? Convict Lease')…basically slavery. NO ONE KNEW…the press and the most major stations did not cover it and it went unheard. As per Wearechange.org, "The prison strike didn't merit a single mention in NYT, Washington Post, NPR, CNN or MSNBC"[132] Don't become a voiceless person. It was not until this year in 2018, two years later, that media attention was finally given to the 2018 strike and the fact that people in Louisiana are now making $0.04 per hour to work and inmates in California are firefighters making "$1 to $2 per hour for the work, but are not allowed to join the fire department when they get out of prison. I have personal experience as my loved one used to do this work in 1992-93 and he was not allowed firefighter employment upon release. Prisoners are still fighting and have given demands for more humane treatment, but few to no US news outlets are reporting on this despite the fact that Criminal Justice and Prison reform is a "hot" topic right now.

Cherish your freedom, your right to vote and your right to be you!"

You have only one life to live…live it to the fullest.

We have given you reasons why you should not take a gamble and commit crimes and wind up in prison like these men. Prisoners, ex-prisoners, law enforcement and the loved ones of these men have shared with you the life you will live should you wind up in prison. The flip side to this is that perhaps telling you what can happen to you is not enough. You are willing to take that chance of committing that crime.

In an article by the National Review it states, "The problem with deterrence, however, is that we overestimate prospective criminals' foresight and self-discipline. At its root, crime is generally a failure of self-discipline."[133] And furthermore there have been studies that suggest "Conservative criminologists such as the late James Q. Wilson and Richard Herrnstein pin primary blame for crime on criminals' impulsively satisfying their immediate desires. They are short-sighted gamblers; who else would risk getting shot or arrested in order to steal $300 and a six-pack of beer from a convenience store?"[134] So perhaps all of these letters mean nothing to some of you. The authors have wasted their time and energy trying to help you. So I leave you with this...

At the end of the day, after all the craziness in the world, you only have one mind and one body. Only you can truly protect it, nourish it, keep it safe and enjoy all that it has to offer. When living in prison, the system and the inmates will fight you every day to take your mind and your body away from you...why put yourself at risk to live like that? The choice is yours.

ACKNOWLEDGEMENTS

Heru and I would like to give a special thank you the Lord, Most High, for keeping us focused and carrying us through for this project to come to completion. I also would like to thank The Sentencing Project, Community Coalition and "In the Public Interest" for having acknowledged our requests and providing Imperial Imprint with permission to use their valuable and informative infographics. Sometimes a picture is worth a thousand words. We thank ThomsonReuters for allowing us to use "Civil Asset Forfeiture" from their website. I also want to give special thanks to Mr. & Mrs Lewis Fielder "Hearts For Inmates", Julian Ferguson, aka Wali Abdul Rahim, James "Yuk" Sigler (the young man on the cover of the book), Ronnie 'Atiba' Jordan, Kevin Whitfield, Bryan Attaway, Tyrone D. Tisdale, LA Bernsten and Matthew Radford for making the extra effort to write these letters after I asked them to do so personally. Thanks also to Andrew Lawrence who still participated and supported the book even after being released from prison. I also thank all of the men who took their time, effort and caring by writing these letters to make a positive difference in the world and to save our children. I also thank those who I do not know but from just hearing about the project they gave their time, such as Kenneth "Syncere Bullmaster" Rivera, Lumumba Incumaa (Theodore Harrison), Philip Copeland (these three guys were all in Solitary Confinement at the time), Paul Valdez and Torrance McCray.

I also thank all of my friends and family who believed in this project and provided additional ideas and support such as Heru's brother, Bashir Muhammad-Jordan aka Dr. Shajeem, Lisa Downing, reviewed and helped rewrite the Synopsis and my Introduction, King Justice, aka Streets for having the vision of Imperial Imprint through his writing of Mya Mafia--Rise of a Gangstress and someone we can always depend on to write anything that is needed. My Aunt Jill, who as a former social worker herself, reviewed the whole book, editing and providing guidance and suggestions to enhance the book. My dad Wiley & my beloved sister Noelle (May they rest in peace) and her husband, my brother (in-law) John and my nephew Jonathan and my mom Ruth, daughter Ruthie and cousin Valarie. My brother Rodney, Erik C (Guns Down/Life Up & NYC Health and Hospital), Bette W, Audrey D and those who cared for my children when I had to work on this project. We also thank Heru's mom, Ms. Wyonnie who has also been like a mom to me since I was 17 years old (and may she rest in peace as she passed January 2017) and of course Heru's cousin, Derrick, a correctional officer who participated in the book and Heru's dedicated partner Nikki, their two beautiful children and two grandsons. I thank our graphic designer who created the book cover Ernest

Kumi, from Kumasi, Ghana and our editor Intelligent Allah of KooziArts LLC. And Brian Scott Stapleton, (from Perry Correctional Institution's Character Based Unit) who did not know me or Heru but has been my dependable rock with editing, reviewing and obtaining additional letters to make this book complete. I also would like to thank Len "Petey" Rollock who participated just by Bashir asking him to assist and not knowing me, but having faith in me and this project as well as Wayne "Abkur" Pray and Millie.

And of course a big thank you to the Imperial Imprint LLC family and our intern Thomas Takyi who lives in Ghana. Those who are part of the company all went the extra mile as far as reaching out and sharing our vision so that others would write letters to make a difference in the world, Kobe Carter, Streets, Stanford "Saddiq" Tucker, Andre Cannon, James Hays, Michael Moore, Wayne Alexander, Anthony F. Martin & James "Yuk" Sigler who all stuck it out and did not give up even when it looked as if there was no end in sight. Thanks so much guys for having faith and keeping me going when I felt like giving up. I would also like to thank Paul B. the first person to pre-order our book on Amazon.com.

As a side note, although he does not want to be noted as one of the official "Author/Editors" King Justice/Streets ("KJ") was instrumental in writing most of the Factoids, promotional information as well as the original draft summary for the back of the book. KJ only has an 8th grade education, but his hard work, determination and the love of writing reflects as one with all of the education in the world. I have 2 Master's degrees, however whenever I need something written up, he is the person I go to. He is an extraordinary writer and person!

There are so many others that have supported us, I thank you all. As well the Department of Corrections by not trying to hinder or retaliate against the men, myself or our efforts to make a positive difference in the world. We hope that the DOCs throughout the country will continue to support our efforts. Most of all, again, we thank the Lord for giving us the vision and the fortitude to make this book a reality.

NEXT BOOK IN THE LETTERS TO OUR SONS SERIES

"BLINDSIDE DIARIES - LIFE BEHIND THE FENCES"
The Journal of Horace Abney aka Heru Mossiah Maat – October 2013

Welcome to my life behind the fences. What you are about to read, is a documentary into the lives of 14 different inmates. Who will be sharing the intimate details of their everyday lives? For thirty-one days we will be giving you a look into the prison experience through the eyes of the ones who count the most, the prisoners.

Since the very first prison was built there has been studies conducted by so called professional criminologist. Who feed society a bunch of bullshit about how we think and feel, and why we do the things we do. After reading *Blindside Diaries* the way you view the criminal element of our society should change, and if not at least you'll have a real understanding of how we think and what life is like behind the prison fences.

My name is Horace Abney inmate #316024. I am currently serving a 30 year sentence in the South Carolina Department of INcorrections for trafficking cocaine. I've been hostage for the last 10 years of my life for a crime that in God's eyes isn't even considered a crime, but the injustice system of our society sends us to prison by the boat loads. Serious crimes such as murderers, rapist, child molesters and armed robbers roam free, and when they are apprehended they receive less time than some individuals with drug charges. In my opinion this is the craziest thing in the world. There are some guys who are back here, who have truly done some heinous shit, and they have less time than I do, yet the people in power call this justice. Even when you prove to the courts that your rights have been violated and a judge agrees and grants you relief, they still don't wanna let you go. They file frivolous appeals stalling the inevitable, causing your stay to be drawn out for another one and a half to two years.

This is my current situation. I've been blessed to have been one of very few who went back to court and received a favourable ruling from a judge. In my P.C.R. hearing that was held close to a year ago on October 31 2012. The judge saw how my constitutional rights were violated because my appellate attorney that was assigned to my case failed to raise an obvious constitutional violation that was preserved on the record for review by my trial counsel. *(Updated September 2016: The high court in Columbia, SC overturned Heru's appeal and reinstated the 30 year sentence. At this point he will not be released until 2029)*

The judge ruled my appellate counsel ineffective and overturned my 30 year sentence vacating it and remanding me back to the lower courts for a new trial. There is no way that the attorney general's office could read the transcript in my case, and not see how my lawyer failed me as her client. But yet they still appealed the judge's ruling causing me to exert patience waiting for the higher courts to make their decision.

Some would've allowed this to break their spirits. Me on the other hand I thank our prison system for holding up my release. This last year of my incarceration has been the most productive in the entire 10 years since I've been doing time. Once my case was overturned I experienced a serious paradigm shift. A realization set in that I truly hadn't made any progress towards establishing a direction in which my life would head if I were to have been set free, and this saved me because I knew I couldn't go back out into society with my same frame of mind in which I came in with.

The majority of my incarceration was spent idly wasting time playing cards, board games, and shooting the shit about irrelevant things that would have no impact on my success in life upon my release. The C.A.C which stands for Cultural Awareness Committee (C.A.C), is a group of conscious-minded brothers that plan and arrange all of the cultural events that the prison, allows us to participate in such as Kwanza, Black history month, Black August, talent shows etc. Last February the members of the C.A.C convinced the warden to allow them to show educational black conscious inspired D.V.D's throughout the month of February. During this time they showed Powernomics by Dr. Claude Anderson, Hidden Colours which is a collaboration of multiple black scholars, Miafa 21 that dealt with the African slave trade, The reinstitution of slavery by Dr. Ray Haggins, Post Traumatic Slave Syndrome by Dr. Joy De Gruy Leary and a few other inspirational D.V.D's that impacted my psyche drastically.

The more I started to learn about myself and what was done to my people, and what is still being done to my people. The more I realized that I had to change my way of thinking and the way I was living. The first thing I did was enrol in school to get my G.E.D. Even though I already had passed it once before while I was in North Carolina. I decided to take it again just to reawaken my dormant brain cells. I attended school for all of three months just to freshen up on math which has always been my most despised subject. Soon as the test was made accessible for me to take, I was signed up. I passed with flying colors finishing in the top five percentile of the State.

During this time I also became an avid reader tackling books that only just a few months ago. I wouldn't have had the patience or the interest to read. Books such as the *Auto Biography of Malcolm X, The Destruction of black civilization, The Falsification of African Consciousness, The African Origin of Civilization, Christopher Columbus* and *The African Holocaust, The Isis Papers*, and much more literary mind-awakening material written by our African scholars. They taught me more about my history than any text book I ever read in school. On my journey of enlightenment, I also became familiar with the Black Panthers reading *Blood in My Eyes, Soledad Brother, Seize the Time, Ashata,* and *Last Man Standing*. These revolutionary-minded brothers and sisters taught me about the struggle and also sent me down a path of responsibility.

I joined the C.A.C and also signed up for any positive programme that was available on the yard. I started attending Rasta Class, Seven Habits of Highly Effective People, Re Entry, Man to Man and Lifer's Group. I started allowing my voice to be used in constructive conversations instead of frivolous ones. Brothers started to take notice and would comment on my transition into the world of the awakened.

I also started receiving certain perks that come along with respect and honor behind these institutions fences. Being from N.Y. and locked up around a bunch of brothers that consider you different from them just because you have a different accent and walk. It takes you awhile to start getting any love. Especially when the majority of them are jealous of you 'cause your family take care of you and makes sure you don't need for anything.

Anyway I was able to connect with an old family friend that I hadn't seen or spoken to since I was 11 or 12 years old. I was speaking with my mom and she mentioned that she had spoken to Dawn. I was shocked to hear that she was back in contact with the family and had been for the past few years. I asked my mom for her phone number and called as soon as I hung up from her. She answered and was elated once she heard over the recording that it was me who was calling.

She informed me that she'd been inquiring about me and was wondering how I was doing. She gave me all of her information and we started corresponding from that day forth.

Dawn is an old acquaintance of my older brother who took an extreme liking to my family while they were an item. She was always nice to me and treated me like a little brother, always encouraging me to stay in school and to get my education. We used to always pick on her saying she sounded like a valley white girl because she was highly educated and used proper English when she spoke. Whenever she had the time she would spend some of it with me and take me out to museums and fancy eateries exposing me to a more cultured way of life.

Due to certain chains of events that happened in our lives we lost contact with one another, and hadn't spoken until the day I was able to catch her on the phone. While corresponding back and forth in one of her letters she offered to pay for me to take college correspondence courses through Ohio University. With me now travelling down my path of awakening it would've been a wonderful opportunity. But my case had been overturned for about three or four months at this point and I was well wishing that the A.G.'s office wouldn't appeal and that I would be going home soon. Plus after seeing the prices there was no way I was going to allow her to pay for something that in my opinion the State should have been offering anyway. So I turned down her offer.

As time moved forward and we were becoming more and more reacquainted with one another. I remind you we hadn't spoken to one another since I was 11 or 12 and she was around 19 or 20. I'm 37 now so there was a lot of catching up we had to do. It took her awhile to remember that she was speaking to a grown man with two children and not the same 12 year old child that she remembered me as.

While we were reacquainting ourselves with one another through letters, I was continuing to contemplate about what I was going to do with my future once I was released from prison. Then one day a brother, King Justice aka Streets, brought me a book catalogue of the Sister Wahida Clark. She was show casing not only her own books but books written by other authors as well along with personalized greeting cards that were drawn by artist in prison. I could tell because brothers around me were also drawing the same type of cards and had been since I'd been locked up. She had just completed a ten year prison sentence herself, so I knew that was where they come from.

Then it hit me like a ton of bricks. This sister is helping brothers and sisters that are still in prison along with her own. So I started thinking, man that's it! You can start a publishing company and provide a venue for brothers around you to get their literary material out to the public. There were brothers who I always saw writing books, drawing, and reciting original poems and songs they had written, but I never gave it a second thought until I saw this catalogue.

So I approached the brother who showed me the catalogue and asked him how his book writing venture was going and was he making any leeway on getting his material published. He informed me that he was working with another brother on the yard but the dude was bullshitting him, and he asked me why. I told him that I was back in contact with a very business savoy sister who I might be able to convince to assist him in getting his work out there but first I'd have to read one of his books. So he gave me a book entitled *MYA MAFIA-The Rise of a Gangstress*, and a vision was formed.

After reading the book, I liked it so much that I immediately jumped on the phone and called my sister collect and had her do a three way call to connect me with Dawn. I ran the idea by her and told her that I'd like her to be my business partner on this venture. At first she wasn't that receptive of my idea so I told her to think about it and get back to me.

Soon as I got off the phone with her I shot back to my room and wrote her a letter going more into detail about my vision, and explained to her that if she was willing to pay for me to take correspondence courses, Which would be an investment that she'd have to wait awhile before she would've been able to receive any money back, and this was something that could benefit the both of us much quicker and could be way more lucrative and that I'd be able to pay for myself to go to college once I made it home.

After writing the letter I approached the brother again and told him that I was almost 100% sure that I could convince Dawn to assist us in getting his material out to the public by posting it on E-books, but that I'd like to rewrite his book and enhance some of the narration so the story would sound better. He agreed and for the next 30 days I spent from sun up to sun down rewriting MYA MAFIA. I almost felt like it was my own book that's how much efforts I put into making the story better.

When I received a response back from Dawn to my first letter she was still a bit skeptical about the idea, but said she was still looking into it and the answer wasn't yes but it also wasn't no. That was all I needed to hear. I sat back down and wrote her another letter emphasizing the point of how lucrative this business venture could be. I also explained to her about another idea I had about creating an Art website where we would sell artwork drawn and painted by prisoners and that there were some very talented brothers back here that all they need is someone who believes in them and their talent and they would go hard for them. I also explained to her that I was so serious about this that I was currently in the process of rewriting the brothers book because I felt as if I could make it better.

In her next letter her answer went from an "I don't know" to a full-fledged "Yes." She had made time to research the idea and run it by a few of her trusted colleagues and she said everyone told her it was a good idea and that she should seriously consider it. Hence, the birth of Imperial Imprint LLC, my baby.

After a few more weeks of research and more input from her colleagues, Dawn suggested that after I completed rewriting my partner Streets book that I should do a journal project with about four other inmates where we document our everyday lives behind these prison fences for one month then send her the journals and she would have one book made out of them. She said that a colleague of hers watches a reality show called "Lock Up" on CNBC where they film the lives of inmates in some prisons throughout the United States and that the show was extremely popular, and that she should try to convince me to do something similar only it would be in print and not film.

It didn't take much convincing soon as I heard the idea, I loved it and anyone I shared the idea with said it was a good one, some even volunteered to participate soon as they heard it. Hence, the idea for *Blindside Diaries* was born.

I hope you enjoy reading about our lives and that you gain a little more respect for individuals that are incarcerated, and come to understand that some of us are utilizing your tax dollars for more than three free meals and a place to sleep at night.

Sincerely,
Heru Mossiah Ma'at!

Tuesday, October 1, 2013, 4:45 A.M. Day One!

Awoke to the sound of the officers keys rattling and click clanking in and out of everyone's doors as he opened them. *A sound that will probably haunt me for the rest of my years on this earth.* I lay in my bunk for a few until my head cleared from last night's cloudiness. Once I gained my equilibrium, I rose and thanked the most high as I do every morning and prepared myself for another day in the belly of the beast.

Moving as quietly as my 6'2 245lb frame would allow, giving my cellmate respect and not trying to awaken him, I stood and adorned my pajamas/uniform. I say that because to me that's what our uniforms look like a set of tan pajamas with one back pocket on the pants, and one shirt pocket on a short sleeve collared shirt.

Once dressed, I made my way over to our bathroom which is about three short steps from my sleeping quarters. I got a good stretch in touching the cell walls from side to side in front of the sink, then held down the flush button on the toilet so the water could repeatedly flush as I urinated so that I nor my cellmate would have to hear my urine hitting the water in the toilet, which is another sound I've grown to despise. After washing my hands I brushed my teeth and washed my face. Then I grabbed my cup, spork (spoon/fork combined into one) and I.D. the three necessities you need for every meal in this place. I made my way out the cell door to await the call for breakfast and to do my job of sweeping and mopping the rock which is one big common area. I'm one of about 12 dorm janitors that they have assigned to keep the dorm clean. I choose to clean early because I've become a real morning person since I've been in this place. After cleaning, I finished my entry and awaited the call for chow.

6:25am.

500

I hate even having to go to the cafeteria to eat. It's such a harassing processes that if I had enough money on my books I would never go down there. It's about 40 yards away from the dorm I'm housed in, and from the time you step out the front door you're under constant scrutiny. An officer usually stands right in front of the dorm staring in your face to make sure you are clean shaven, because the grooming policy they have in this bullshit state requires it. If you are not clean shaven they send you back to the dorm without eating. They could care less if you have anything in your locker to eat. Then they make us line up until everyone from our side of the dorm is out of the building and in a straight line on the right side of some yellow lines they had inmates paint on the ground. On the way to the mess hall they expect you to stay on the right side the whole way down. I make it my business to walk on the left side of the line sometimes when my rebellious spirit has control of me.

They also want you to have your ID (which is also basically your bank card cause it's what you use whenever you go to the store) clipped on to your collar displayed for all officers to see. I also violate this rule because it makes me feel like a tagged dog. So I play like my clip is broke and just hold it in my hand whenever I pass by an officer. Once we finally make it into the café, officers are standing all over your back and making you sit at tables with guys you may not want to sit with, and then they only give you ten minutes to eat from the time your dorm is called. Which feels more like five minutes then when they decide time is up they walk around standing behind you screaming, "Time is up! Time is up!...Everybody out whether you are done eating or not!"

Many of the brothers get into confrontations with the officers during feeding times because they just can't take the harassment and a lot of them have no food in their lockers so they are trying to fill up as much as possible. So when a C.O. rushes them out before they are finished their meal they flip. Not because they are unruly but because they are hungry and a hungry convict is a dangerous convict. Fortunately this morning went smooth with no situations and no one being hauled off to lock up.

8:45 A.M.

Just woke up and shaved (which I hate doing) after taking a short nap. Waiting for them to call 9:00 traffic so I can head up to the education building and speak with the guys in the art programme about our potential business venture. Made sure to shave so I wouldn't be turned around and sent back mad at the officer about something I could prevent just by making sure I was in compliance.

The captain and lieutenant just walked in the dorm to do their daily sign in to the log book. I hate this particular captain's guts. He is a real arrogant, condescending, young, white prick who is gotten a real smart mouth and loves to harass people whenever he gets the chance. If I could, I'd beat his ass on

G.P. He seems to enjoy oppressing the people. The lieutenant is a chubby brother who is about my age he's not that bad but he is starting to change ever since he has been promoted. Just like most of them, the higher they climb in rank the more butt kissing assholes they become. Very few of them remain civil and treat us as human beings instead of as just another number they've been hired to count and tell what to do.

11:30 AM.

Returned to the dorm after having a productive conversation with the brothers in the art class. They are stoked, ready to get the venture up and going, and can't wait for Dawn to return from her trip to India. She had to go over to train people in her professional field because the company she works for is outsourcing to India. Which mean more jobs lost to the American People. We are spoiled and many large companies are ducking Obama care. Anyway, being she's over there our venture has been set back. But I know if she was willing to leave her daughter and go overseas for two months it has to be for something positive and extremely lucrative.

12:30pm.

Twelve O'clock traffic was called late and my dorm has a basketball game in the gym today against another dorm. It's their gym day, not ours, so I know the coach and the officer that works in the gym is gonna be tripping, not wanting to let people from our dorm that's not on the list in. So I grabbed my folder and journal so I could look professional like I was coming for something else other than to watch the game. Sure enough, rat boy and the officer was at the door with the road block checking names off as guys walked up. Once I got to the door the officer saw my folder in my hand and didn't even question me about what I was doing up there. I slid by like I had an EZ pass and walked straight over to the bleachers and fell in with the crowd. Rat Boy is my nick name for the coach cause to me that's what he looks like a big dark skinned rat. Plus his character is flawed when it comes to his people. Instead of doing certain things that's within his power to do he'd rather do the bare minimum and act like a white man with black skin. What we call a modern day house nigga.

3:30pm.

It's currently count time and my roommate and I are locked in our cell with one another until the count clears. They count us four times throughout the course of the day. During the weekdays and six times on the weekends because of visits. I think they feel we are just gonna get up and walk out with our visitors or something. I can't see no other reason for so many damn counts. During the week they count once at 7:15 am, then at 3:15 pm, then at 9:00 pm, and the last one is 11:30pm lock down. The worst part about count is when they assign a dick head officer to the dorm and every time he counts he feels he has to yell at the top of his or her lungs that its count time and we need to be standing with our lights on. Some officers go extremely hard about it, blaming on your door if they get to it and you are not standing with your lights on. Some are laid back and could care less as long as they can see in your room and can tell that you are alive.

The other thing I hate about count is being locked in the room with my roommate it almost seems as if every time it's count time he comes down with a bad case of gas and straight fucks the room up. The rooms we're housed in were intended to be one man cells so you can just imagine the size. Both of us are big men living in a room that is smaller than some people's bathroom. Other than his occasional bad gas he's a pretty good roommate. He gives me my respect and space when I need it, and I also do the same for him. Having a good roommate is probably the most important part of doing time, cause if you and him don't get along things can become extremely stressful.

9:45pm.

Just got out the shower feeling refreshed after cleansing my body of the day's grime and film of filth this place leaves on you. The showers are small stainless steel boxes about the size of an outside bathroom. If you move the wrong way you bump into the wall and I can't speak for other guys but when I do touch the walls I feel dirtier than when I got in. It's probably a psychological thing, but knowing that you share the showers with 97 other guys that use their time to have relations with themselves just has never sat well with me. In addition you even have some sick bastards who shit in the shower from time to time, and even though there is someone who scrubs them down every day sometimes twice you can never clean away the mental stain things like that leave on your mind.

11:30pm.

It's now lock down time and I'm tired of sharing my thoughts with y'all nosey motherfuckers so I'll get back at y'all later.

Wednesday, October 2, 2013, 4:30 AM. Day Two!

Good morning. Your back to hear more, huh! Well I'm anxious to tell you. This morning I awoke to my roommate standing about four inches away from my head. Holding the flush button down while he urinated. Next thing I know my nose is hit with a very unpleasant smell. Of course I cursed him out in my head like you stinking motherfucker. It's truly a shame that our bedroom is also our bathroom. Then to top it off my neck and back are aching from sleeping on uneven springs and a thin ass mattress with a pillow made out of a plastic material that fucks your neck up more than assist your sleep. I seriously need a good chiropractor which will be one of the first places I go when I get out of this hell hole.

5:45 A.M.

Just returned from breakfast and heard one of the most ignorant statements that I've heard in a long time. One of the most redneck nastiest officers that work here was running the yard. I am the treasurer over the community placing me in charge over the funds that we pool together to purchase D.V.D's, Books and any other educational material that we can get our hands on to awaken the masses. It's every member's duty to (for those that can afford it) donate $2.00 along with two envelopes every month and once it reaches a certain amount we use the funds to purchase materials we need. I'm the one who holds the funds and keeps track of who donated what I didn't want the position cause I don't like being over other people's money, but I accepted the responsibility.

8:45am.

For some reason with this officer, he has the tendency to call dorms to go eat back to back without allowing the line to die down some, so you won't be standing around backed up out the door. While I was walking by him I asked him why he does that dumb shit? His remark was, "You are all a bunch of cattle gotta move ya out and move ya in." He had my blood so hot that I felt like straight blasting on his red neck, pale face, cracker ass but I remained cool and just continued on to breakfast.

What I should of said was that's why you have a defective gene in you and produce stupid children....

Waiting for them to announce 9:00 traffic so I can go to a C.A.C. meeting. We meet every Wednesday to discuss upcoming events and to plan the set ups.

11:20 A.M.

Just got back to the dorm from the C.A.C meeting. Every time I sit amongst the brothers I smile within. It truly feels good to be in the presence of positive-minded men who look and think like me, and that's about making the best out of this fucked up situation that we are in.

We discussed the preparations for this year's Kwanzaa, and appointed which members would handle what. Concerning the music and speeches. We also discussed the treasury funds and I made everyone aware that the goods had been switched out for a green dot that was sent to an outside sponsor so she could come in and give us some much needed direction and guidance. Once the meeting was over we ended it with our pledge to the ancestors who paved the way for us to be here today.

Once I returned to the dorm I had to defecate something terrible. When I made my way up to my cell my roommate was taking a nap. I hated to have to wake him up but when you gotta go you gotta go.

3:30pm.

It's now count time. Wasn't anything all that interesting to talk about from my last entry to now. My brain is kind of exhausted so I'm gonna take a nap and get back at y'all in a couple of hours.

6:10pm.

On my way to Buddhist class to learn about the culture and practice of the Zen. In my opinion the more well-rounded an individual the better chance he or she has to succeed.

8:15pm.

Buddhist class was very informative. We covered the Noble Eightfold Path, which are eight virtuous views that if applied correctly to your life will lead you down a path of righteousness? They consist of Right View, Right Thinking, Right Speech, Right Action, Right Livelihood, Right Diligence, Right Mindfulness, and Right Concentration. The instructor of the class is a fellow comrade in the struggle by the name of Caesar Covington. explained that once one comes to terms with the true meanings of these livid ties and learn how to apply them to one's life, only then will they truly be set down the path of righteousness and in tune with one's higher self. I found the class liberating, at the end we meditated in darkness for about 10 minutes clearing our minds of all negativity. I never knew meditation could be so stress relieving. It seemed as if all my tension and uneasiness this place causes on the daily just lifted off of me and floated away.

11:30pm.

Just received an E-Mail from my business partner over the kiosk—a basic programming computer that allows us to send E-Mails to our loved ones. At first I didn't even want to look in the things direction, cause I was somewhat intimidated by it. Then my sister from another mother set up an account so we could communicate with one another while she was out of the country. After receiving my very first message, then having someone show me how to reply. I've straight fell in love with the damn thing. I see why people are so addicted to texting. It's straight up the shit. Anyway the E-Mail she sent me lifted my spirits so high, because she eased all of my concerns with her trust issues. For a minute she had me feeling like she was second guessing whether or not our business venture was a good one. After tonight's message I now know we are on the same page. Damn it feels like a ton of bricks has been lifted off my shoulders.

I can barely keep my eyes open so y'all gonna have to wait till tomorrow to read some more.

October 3, 2013, Thursday, Day Three!

4:10 A.M.

The C.O. opened the doors early for some reason this morning and announced that we were first for chow. So I had to jump up and get dressed quick. After dressing, washing my face, and brushing my teeth, I grabbed my three necessities and headed out the room. I started my daily routine of cleaning the rock and before I could finish sweeping they called us to go eat.

As I made my way down the walkway, I proceeded to walk on the left side of the yellow line. I was in one of my fuck the rules moods this morning, and for that mood I was rewarded with not being able to eat breakfast. The same asshole officer was working the yard as yesterday and he sent me back cause I wouldn't step back across the line when he told me to.

My locker was straight so I didn't argue and came back to the dorm and continued to do what I was doing before I left.

4:55 A.M.

The rest of the dorm started filing back in from breakfast. A brother who claims he's from N.Y., but who probably hadn't been up there since he was a teenager. Approached me while I was mopping and asked me had I seen someone pick up his radio and headphones from the table. I informed him that I hadn't and continued to mop.

This particular brother is a real cool older dude. All he does is sit at one of the tables on the rock and draw and make cards all day that he sells to support himself.

After he walked away from me he walked over to a few more brothers that had been turned around this morning and asked them the same question.

They responded the same way I did. I saw the brother walking around back and forth up and down the stairs to his room. Then he stood out in front of his room and yelled out "Attention on the rock, attention on the rock." This is what anyone does when they want everyone to stop what they are doing and listen to what they have to say. "I don't know which one of y'all grimy no good sonofabitches picked up my shit, but I'm gonna give you the opportunity to give it back. I'm going in my room for 10 minutes you can either slide it under my door or sit it back on the table and everything a be good."

No one said nothing and nor did the thief give him his shit back.

5:15 A.M.

About 15 min later he emerged from his room with a sheet around his neck and a white cable cord sticking out of his back pocket. He walked over to both garbage cans the one on the top tier and the one on the bottom. Dumping out the contents sifting through the trash checking to see if the thief had stashed his property in either one. Once he came up empty he started to address the rock again. "Listen all I want is my motherfuckin' shit back whichever one of y'all pussy motherfuckers took it just tell me and we can handle it like men. If you think I'm a pussy boy just try me, and all y'all other nosey motherfuckers in here, y'all see every motherfucking thing else I know one of y'all seen who got my shit. Come let me know and I'll keep this shit between us, but if my shit don't pop up or if don't nobody tell me shit I'm gonna make everybody suffer."

By this time I had finished mopping and called the brother over to me and tried to reason with him, but he was too vexed and had worked himself up to the point of no return. If I had enough money on my books I would of offered him my radio because I rarely listen to it, but my account was damn near on E and I didn't know when I was gonna get some more money, and he probably wouldn't of excepted it, anyway cause to him it's about the principle not the property.

He walked away from me and made his way up the stairs, and walked in the showers, and filled up two mop buckets with water then he addressed the rock again. "If I ain't got my shit back by shift change there won't be no more football being watched on them motherfucking T.V.'s If y'all don't want me to watch'em no body gonna watch 'em."

Somebody screamed out "I'm tired of hearing you wolfing if you gonna do something do it," antagonizing the brother instead of rationalizing with him being an instigator. You know there is always gotta be an ignorant, negative minded individual who would rather encourage stupidity instead of defuse it.

The brother said, "I'm gonna show you better than I can tell you and anybody that don't wanna get caught up in what I'm about to do I suggest you head to your room and lock in when the C.O. lock the doors for shift change." This was my cue cause I couldn't afford to get caught up in no bullshit especially not when Imperial was on the verge of becoming a reality. So I made my way to my room.

6:00 A.M.

The C.O. locked the doors about 15 minutes ago. I'd been well wishing the whole time that the brother would calm down and change his mind. My wish went unanswered. I was lying back on my bunk and the dorm had an eerie silence then I heard a big splash of water, as the brother lunged the first bucket of water over the rail of the top tier splashing one of the televisions then you heard another as he splashed a second one.

After hearing the water and the mop buckets come crashing down to the floor of the bottom tier, I jumped out my bunk just in time to see the brother walk pass my door with a crazed, determined look in his eyes. He made it down the stairs and over to the front entrance door of the wing and took the sheet (which I was wondering what he was gonna do with it) and laced it through the bars then tied it off, preventing the officers from being able to open the front door. He then walked over to the televisions and began smashing them with a long handled push broom (The televisions sit up above the rock in a metal cage that was built for them. Two of the televisions were flat screens and the other two which he threw the water on were the old model built to last forever kind. He was now pommelling the flat screens with the push broom)

After annihilating the televisions the brother was about to teach everyone in the dorm their next lesson in convict lol. He marched back up the steps and went to the first room door on the top tier. After reaching in his back pocket and retrieving the cable cord, he attached a lock to the end of it and yelled out "lock down bitches" then smashed the cell window with the lock and cable cord. He repeated the same action at every cell door repeatedly screaming out "lock down bitches, lock down bitches, lock down bitches!"

By the time he reached my door, which was the tenth cell on the row I had laid down on my bunk and covered my head up preparing for the glass to fly into my cell. Sure enough once he reached my door I heard, "lock down bitches," as glass flew all over my cell, and when I say all over I mean all over. The shit was everywhere.

About three or four doors down from mine the lock must've flew off the cable cord, and into someone's cell cause I could hear him yelling at them to kick his shit back under the door, and whoever it was wasn't complying. His answer to that was to march back down the stairs and grab two push broom attachments then he marched back up and continued to smash the windows swinging the broom heads like a drummer beating those large Congo drums, while continuing to call out "lock down bitches" at every cell door.

Once he finished with the top he started on the bottom only leaving about five cell windows unbroken, 'cause he had worn himself out and was tired by then. I stood at my cell door watching the whole thing shaking my head thinking, "Damn bruh all this over some fucking head phones and radio." He dropped the broom heads and calmly walked over to the front door and untied it, but the officers were making their way through the back door through the Rec field entrance. They approached the brother with their mace in hand. He told them "Y'all better not spray me I'm done doing what I wanted to do." And turned around and allowed them to handcuff him. Two officers hauled him off to lock up while three others ran the few inmates that had stayed out their cells to witness the events first hand, into their rooms securing all cell doors and placing both sides of the dorm on lock down just like the brother anticipated.

I went on and fell back and dozed off to sleep after the highly eventful morning and it was only 6:00 A.M. It was gonna be a long day.

10:00 A.M.

I was awoken from an unrestful sleep by the sound of radio chatter. I adorned my sneakers while stepping over the shards of broken glass scattered across our cell floor. I made my way over to the cell door and gazed out over the rock through the empty rectangular hole where the glass on the floor use to be standing around the officer station were numerous lieutenants, captains, and two associate wardens. They were looking around the rock, assessing the damage the brother had caused. The look on their faces was priceless, it look as if all of them were saying "What the fuck happened?" They were taking photos and writing incident reports.

I called over to another one of the dorm janitors and asked to pass me his broom so I could sweep the glass up from off the floor. Luckily his cell was two doors away from mine and I was able to reach my hand through the broken window frame and grab the broom. The windows were made of the same type of glass as a window shield so when the brother smashed it, he sent small beads of glass flying everywhere.

There was glass in the window ceil at the back of the cell all over the table top and on me and my roommates' beds. I told my roommate to stay on his bunk and I cleaned the room thoroughly from top to bottom getting up all of the glass I could.

2:00 P.M.

I ate a lunch of oatmeal and peanut butter on bread that I fixed myself 'cause I no longer eat the suicide meat they serve us in the lunch bags when we're on lock down. I sat back and watched a little bit of television that I was fortunate to be able to afford to due to the love of my family.

I heard some commotion out on the rock so I walked over to look out the door. It was the maintenance guys already working on repairing the windows. The Major and Warden were also walking around going door to door trying to get guys to write statements about the incident. Once the warden reached my door I called out from the bed, "It was an isolated incident warden only one man did all that and you already took him to lock up."

He responded saying, "Yeah but I heard that someone robbed him. What you know about that."

I answered "I don't know nothing about that but I do know it was the action of one person. So we shouldn't be locked down for long right?"

He said "We'll see gotta look into everything first." Then he walked off.

When the Major got to my door I asked the same thing. He didn't insult me by trying to get any information out of me. He only responded by saying that "These windows gotta get fixed before y'all come out and that will probably be finished today but look forward to being down tomorrow as well." I had figured as much and fell back and made a few more entries in my journal.

6:00 P.M

Shift just changed for the day. The maintenance crew finished fixing all of the windows about an hour and a half ago. I'm already tired of being on lock down. I've always been a people's person and hate having to be confined to a room all day having to listen to and smell my roommate pass gas. I swear sometimes it smells as if something has crawled up in his ass and died.

Plus I had to miss two of the self-improvement classes. I attend on Thursdays one is called Re-Entry the other is entitled Man to Man. Re-Entry is a class that's instructed by a very positive Muslim brother by the name of Nadir. This brother has about 15 years left to go on his sentence and he's already been down like 13 or 15. But by the way he carries himself you would never know it. He always has something positive to say and he has dedicated his life to assisting brothers in getting their life on the right track.

In Re-Entry he prepares brothers who are on the verge of being released back into society, by discussing what to expect once we get out there. We also have done mock interviews where we filled out job applications and took turns being the interviewer and the interviewee. Every week we discuss topics concerning growth and development and challenge one another with Q and A's about life and its obstacles.

Man to Man is another self-improvement class that the brother Nadir is the co-ordinator of along with another Muslim brother by the name of Qasib. In Man to Man we discuss the things in which define what it takes to be a real man. The theme for the class is 'A Man Doesn't Do What He Wants To Do He Does What Is Necessary.' I admire both of these brothers for their dedication to the struggle.

11:30 P.M

Lock down time couldn't of come fast enough I'm ready to get tomorrow over and done with cause more than likely they are not gonna let us off lock down until Saturday and boy am I ready. They even left all of the glass and water on the rock untouched just to let us know what time it is. Well my eyes are getting heavy. I'll get back at y'all tomorrow.

AUTHOR/EDITOR BIOGRAPHY

Dawn Simmons is an advocate for the civil rights and social services of people. She has many years of experience working voluntarily with children, those incarcerated, the elderly and disabled. In addition she has worked in Finance for over 20 years primarily in Derivatives Operations.

Ms. Simmons was born and raised in Harlem, New York where she attended The Brearley School and took dance and piano lessons from her family's dance and piano studio each Saturday in the South Bronx. Her parents separated and she, her mother and sister moved to Flushing Queens, where she graduated from Flushing High School. Upon graduation she attended Bryn Mawr College, a semester abroad at the Universite de Paris-IV Sorbonne and then graduated from the University of Southern California. Ms. Simmons holds a Master's Degree in Spiritual Psychology from the University of Santa Monica and a Master's Degree in Social Work from Columbia University.

Ms. Simmons has held many volunteer positions throughout her career. She worked as a volunteer for the Department of Juvenile Justice, New York City and Central Juvenile Hall in Los Angeles, California, a Catholic Eucharistic Minister, Office for Students with Disabilities where she was an office aide, and a peer counselor. She volunteered for Hospital Audiences, Inc. (HAI) which takes persons with disabilities to events such as the theater, the zoo, and other cultural activities. She also volunteered for the Urban Youth Bike Corps, an Injury Prevention Program through Columbia University at Harlem Hospital for young males 13-17 years of age. She volunteered with Habitat for Humanity, Ghana building houses and at that time created an English language school and breakfast program for children ages 5 – 16 years old that lasted about 3 years in Nkenkaasu-Ashanti, Ghana. Currently she is working with prisoners through her company, Imperial Imprint LLC, which publishes books and art by prisoners to give them a voice to help stop crime and mass incarceration. Ms. Simmons is on the Community Advisor Board of Harlem Hospital. She was a candidate for City Council in 2017 and is a District Leader for the 70 AD in Harlem. She also is a commentator for the podcast series www.fromwithinseries.comdiscussing current issues.

Professionally, Ms. Simmons has worked for Wall Street firms since 1993. She was also a Math teacher, flight attendant and interned at the Kings County District Attorney's Office in the Counseling Services Unit, as well as working at Columbia University Social Intervention Group. She was a Program facilitator for Project EBAN; a National Institute of Mental Health (NIMH) program aimed at reducing risk through sexual activity for HIV positive African-American sero-discordant couples while in school for her Social Work degree. Ms. Simmons has since returned to Wall Street where she works in Derivatives Operations in Fixed Income, Equities and Credit and has trained employees in both the United States and India.

Ms. Simmons is a firm believer in civil rights, criminal justice reform and a strong advocate for a robust and equal education for children and adults. Ms. Simmons is a firm believer in education through, experience and travel, as she has lived in England, France and Africa, and worked in India, and has traveled throughout the United States and Europe. With education, whether it is academic, vocational or otherwise, Ms. Simmons believes that one can do or be anything they dream to be.

Favorite Quote: "There are three (3) types of people, those that make things happen, those that watch things happen and those that wonder what happened... Which one are you?"

****

Heru Mossiah Maat also known as Horace Abney Jr. was born and raised in Queens, New York. He grew up in a loving household, the youngest of five children and was a good student. Due to circumstances out of his control, when he was 11 years old, his mother was arrested for a crime that she did not commit and put into jail for two months. During that time he went to live on the other side of town with his aunt, since they lost their apartment. Unfortunately the school system and the people were not the same and Heru got caught up in the lifestyle.

To make a positive change in his life, when he about 22 years old, he moved to North Carolina with his infant daughter. Unfortunately the life style was not much better there and he found himself involved in drugs. His girlfriend and his daughter lived with him, however he was arrested on drug trafficking charges (non-violent) and in 2003 was tried in abstensia in South Carolina, that resulted in a 30 year prison sentence, which they labeled as a violent crime, because the amount of drugs they say he had was considered drug trafficking.

Despite the troubles that Heru has had, he remains optimistic and has a thirst for learning. He believes in helping others and by co-founding Imperial Imprint LLC with Dawn Simmons, he has created a means for many of the prisoners to have a voice to help the children and adults both inside and outside of the prison walls to make the world a better place.

Heru hopes to get out of prison prior to his 2029 release date, as his long-term girlfriend, his two beautiful children and two grandsons are waiting for him to return to society to enjoy their lives together.

AUTHORS & WRITERS

INDEX

S

T

V

W

Y

BIBLIOGRAPHY

Alexander, M. (2011, October 13). *Michelle Alexander: More Black Men Are In Prison Today Than Were Enslaved In 1850.* Retrieved May 29, 2016, from The Huffington Post: http://www.huffingtonpost.com/2011/10/12/michelle-alexander-more-black-men-in-prison-slaves-1850_n_1007368.html

American Enterprise Institute. (2018, July 12). *Criminal justice reform in 2018: A conversation with Rep. Hakeem Jeffries (D-NY) and Rep. Doug Collins (R-GA).* Retrieved July 29, 2018, from American Enterprise Institute: http://www.aei.org/events/criminal-justice-reform-in-2018-a-conversation-with-rep-hakeem-jeffries-d-ny-and-rep-doug-collins-r-ga/

Bakeman, J. (2014, February 18). *Republicans rally against Cuomo's prison-college plan.* Retrieved December 2, 2015, from Politico: http://www.politico.com/states/new-york/albany/story/2014/02/republicans-rally-against-cuomos-prison-college-plan-011039

Basti, V., & Gotsch, K. (2018, August 2). *Capitalizing on Mass Incarceration: U.S. Growth in Private Prisons.* Retrieved August 13, 2018, from The Sentencing Project: https://www.sentencingproject.org/publications/capitalizing-on-mass-incarceration-u-s-growth-in-private-prisons/

Beitsch, R. (2015, July 30). *States Rethink Restrictions on Food Stamps, Welfare for Drug Felons.* Retrieved April 6, 2016, from Pewtrust.org: http://www.pewtrusts.org/en/research-and-analysis/blogs/stateline/2015/07/30/states-rethink-restrictions-on-food-stamps-welfare-for-drug-felons

Bibas, S. (2015, September 16). *The Truth about Mass Incarceration.* Retrieved October 5, 2016, from National Review: http://www.nationalreview.com/article/424059/mass-incarceration-prison-reform

Bolen, E., Cai, L., Dean, S., Keith-Jennings, B., Nchako, C., Rosenbaum, D., et al. (2018, July 30). *House Farm Bill Would Increase Food Insecurity and Hardship.* Retrieved August 5, 2018, from Center on Budget and Policy Priorities: https://www.cbpp.org/research/food-assistance/house-farm-bill-would-increase-food-insecurity-and-hardship

Browne, J. (2008). *Rooted in Slavery: Prison Labor Exploitation.* Retrieved October 12, 2016, from Race, Poverty & the Environment (Reprinted from RP&E Vol. 14, No. 2: Just Jobs? *Organizing for Economic Justice,* 2007): http://www.reimaginerpe.org/20years/browne

Bump, P. (2015, April 29). *Hillary Clinton hopes to undo the mass incarceration system Bill Clinton helped build.* Retrieved May 30, 2015, from The Washington Post: http://www.washingtonpost.com/blogs/the-fix/wp/2015/04/29/hillary-clinton-hopes-to-undo-the-mass-incarceration-system-bill-clinton-helped-build/

Burnett, G. M. (1988). A young Dakota wayfarer falls victim to a notorious penal system, but public outcry brings the system's abolition. In G. M. Burnett, *Florida's Past, People and Events That Shaped the State, Volume 3* (pp. 122-25). Sarasota, FL: Pineapple Press.

Capital and Main; Gary Cohn . (2014, October 23). *Newt Gingrich And Jay-Z Find Common Cause In A Prison Reform Proposition.* Retrieved May 30, 2015, from The Huffington Post: http://www.huffingtonpost.com/2014/10/23/proposition-47_n_6038310.html

Cassell, P. (2014, March 18). *Should a drug dealer acquitted of running a drug ring be sentenced for running a drug ring?* Retrieved October 18, 2018, from Washington Post: https://www.washingtonpost.com/news/volokh-conspiracy/wp/2014/03/18/should-a-drug-dealer-acquitted-of-running-a-drug-ring-be-sentenced-for-running-a-drug-ring/?noredirect=on&utm_term=.3d9b22f605ce

Center for Constitutional Rights. (2015, June 1). *Torture: The Use of Solitary Confinement in U.S. Prisons.* Retrieved August 28, 2016, from Center for Constitutional Rights: https://ccrjustice.org/home/get-involved/tools-resources/fact-sheets-and-faqs/torture-use-solitary-confinement-us-prisons

Cohen, S. (1985). *Visions of social control:Crime, punishment, and classification.* Cambridge, UK: Polity.

Community Coalition. (n.d.). *Are Our Children Being Pushed into Prison?* Retrieved September 3, 2016, from Community Coalition: The above infographic was created by Community Coalition http://cocosouthla.org/inforgraphics/

Community Coalition. (n.d.). *Why Are We Criminalizing Poverty?* Retrieved September 2, 2016, from Community Coalition: http://cocosouthla.org/inforgraphics/

Community Coalition. (n.d.). *Why California Should Fully Fund Prop 47.* Retrieved September 2, 2016, from Community Coalition: http://cocosouthla.org/inforgraphics/

Conaway, H. A.-C. (2018, August 3). *H.R. 2, AGRICULTURE AND NUTRITION ACT OF 2018.* Retrieved August 5, 2018, from FARMBILL-House

Agricultural Committee-Chairman K. Michael Conaway: https://agriculture.house.gov/farmbill/

Dargis, M. (2012, November 21). *Filmmakers Still Seek Lessons From a Case That Rocked a City - The Documentary 'The Central Park Five'*. Retrieved October 30, 2016, from New York Times.Com: http://www.nytimes.com/2012/11/22/movies/the-documentary-the-central-park-five.html

Davidson, A. (2014, June 23). *DONALD TRUMP AND THE CENTRAL PARK FIVE*. Retrieved September 16, 2016, from The New Yorker: http://www.newyorker.com/news/amy-davidson/donald-trump-and-the-central-park-five

Democracy Now! (2016, February 22). *Exclusive Interview: Albert Woodfox of Angola 3, Freed After 43 Years in Solitary Confinement*. Retrieved February 26, 2016, from Democracy Now!: http://www.democracynow.org/2016/2/22/exclusive_interview_albert_w oodfox_of_angola

Digital History. (2016). *Along the Color Line, Convict Lease System, Digital History ID 3179*. Retrieved October 16, 2016, from Digital History, http://www.digitalhistory.uh.edu/: http://www.digitalhistory.uh.edu/disp_textbook_print.cfm?smtid=2&psid =3179

Equal Justice Initiative. (2016, February 8). *Private Prison Phone Companies Lobbied for Criminalization of Cell Phones in Prisons*. Retrieved January 3, 2017, from Equal Justice Initiative: http://eji.org/news/private-companies-lobbied-to-criminalize-cell-phones-in-prisons

Erlich, R. (1995, Fall). *Prison Labor: Workin' For The Man*. Retrieved May 29, 2015, from umass.edu: http://people.umass.edu/kastor/private/prison-labor.html

Federal Bureau of Prisons. (2018, September 29). *Statistic - Inmate Race*. Retrieved October 14, 2018, from Federal Bureau of Prisons: https://www.bop.gov/about/statistics/statistics_inmate_race.jsp

Fields, G., & Emshwiller, J. R. (2011, July 23). *Many Failed Efforts to Count Nation's Federal Criminal Laws*. Retrieved August 28, 2016, from The Wall Street Journal: http://www.wsj.com/articles/SB10001424052702304319804576389601079728920

Frizel, S. (2015, April 29). *Hillary Clinton Calls for an End to 'Mass Incarceration'*. Retrieved May 30, 2015, from Time.com: http://time.com/3839892/hillary-clinton-calls-for-an-end-to-mass-incarceration/

527

Frumin, A. (2014, April 28). *The long, slow push to prison sentencing reform.* Retrieved May 30, 2015, from MSNBC.com: http://www.msnbc.com/msnbc/the-long-push-prison-sentencing-reform

Garland, D. E. (2001). Introduction: The meaning of mass imprisonment. In . In *Mass imprisonment: Social causes and consequences* (pp. 1–3). London: SAGE.

Gast, P., & Sutton, J. (2013, October 2). *Dying 'Angola 3' inmate is released in Louisiana.* Retrieved October 9, 2016, from CNN: http://www.cnn.com/2013/10/01/justice/angola-3-former-black-panther-ordered-released/index.html

Getlen, L. (2014, February 23). *Corrupt 'Kids for Cash' judge ruined more than 2,000 lives.* Retrieved February 1, 2016, from New York Post: http://nypost.com/2014/02/23/film-details-teens-struggles-in-state-detention-in-payoff-scandal/

Gotsch, K. (2018, April 24). *Families and Mass Incarceration.* Retrieved August 27, 2018, from The Sentencing Project: https://www.sentencingproject.org/publications/6148/

Hager, Eli; The Marshall Project and Guardian US. (2016, September 16). *Justice for Some: Real estate, tax lawyers forced to do public defenders' job in Louisiana.* Retrieved September 28, 2016, from The Times-Picayune Greater New Orleans, Nola.com: http://www.nola.com/crime/index.ssf/2016/09/justice_for_some_real_est ate_t.html

In the Public Interest. (2016, June). *How Private Prison Companies Increase Recidivism.* Retrieved October 24, 2016, from In the Public Interest: https://www.inthepublicinterest.org/wp-content/uploads/ITPI-Recidivism-ResearchBrief-June2016.pdf

In the Public Interest. (n.d.). *In the Public Interest.* Retrieved 11 2, 2016, from In the Public Interest: Democracy, shared prosperity, and the common good: https://www.inthepublicinterest.org/

In the Public Interest. (n.d.). *Programs Not Profits.* Retrieved 11 2, 2016, from In the Public Interest: https://www.inthepublicinterest.org/programs-not-profits/

Jacobs, A. (2004, January 22). *Student Sex Case in Georgia Stirs Claims of Old South Justice.* Retrieved September 14, 2016, from New York Times: http://www.nytimes.com/2004/01/22/us/student-sex-case-in-georgia-stirs-claims-of-old-south-justice.html?_r=0

Jacobs, S., & Annese, J. (2016, October 16). *Mom dies of 'broken heart' after son Kalief Browder killed himself last year.* Retrieved October 30, 2016, from New York Daily News.com: http://www.nydailynews.com/new-york/bronx/exclusive-mom-late-kalief-browder-dies-broken-heart-article-1.2833023

Johnson, A. (2016, September 16). *Did You Know We Are Having the Largest Prison Strike in History? Probably Not, Because Most of the Media Have Ignored It.* Retrieved October 5, 2016, from Alternet.org: http://www.alternet.org/media/did-you-know-we-are-having-largest-prison-strike-history-probably-not-because-most-media-have

Kearney, M. S., Harris, B. H., Jacome, E., & Parker, L. (2014, May). *Ten Economic Facts about Crime and.* Retrieved February 5, 2016, from Hamilton Project Policy Memo May 2014: http://www.hamiltonproject.org/assets/legacy/files/downloads_and_links/v8_THP_10CrimeFacts.pdf

Khalek, R. (2011, July 21). *21st-Century Slaves: How Corporations Exploit Prison Labor: In the eyes of the corporation, inmate labor is a brilliant strategy in the eternal quest to maximize profit.* Retrieved February 19, 2017, from Alternet.org: http://www.alternet.org/story/151732/21st-century_slaves%3A_how_corporations_exploit_prison_labor

Kincade, B., & Godard, T. (2016, March 23). *The Economics of the American Prison System.* Retrieved June 2, 2016, from smartasset.com: https://smartasset.com/insights/the-economics-of-the-american-prison-system

Kirby, H., Libal, B., Madison, P., Morris, J., & Quong Charles, K. (2013). *The Dirty Thirty: Nothing to Celebrate About 30 Years of Corrections Corporation of America.* Retrieved October 2, 2016, from http://grassrootsleadership.org/: http://grassrootsleadership.org/cca-dirty-30

Kittle, R. L. (2016, April 21). *Shorter Prison Term Supporters Pack SC House Hearing.* Retrieved September 18, 2016, from WSPA.org Channel 7 News: http://wspa.com/2016/04/21/shorter-prison-term-supporters-pack-sc-house-hearing/

La Vigne, N. G., Davies, E., & Brazzell, D. (2008, February). *Broken Bonds Understanding and Addressing the Needs of Children with Incarcerated Parents.* Washington D.C.: Urban Institute Justice Policy Center.

Lane, E. (2016, February 19). *Why has Albert Woodfox been in solitary for more than 40 years?* Retrieved September 30, 2016, from The Times-Picayune Greater New Orleans: http://www.nola.com/politics/index.ssf/2015/06/albert_woodfox_solitary_confin.html

Lee, T. H. (2014, June 3). *Not Separate, Not Equal: Feds Look at Native Kids in Public Schools.* Retrieved October 10, 2016, from Indian Country:

http://indiancountrytodaymedianetwork.com/2014/06/03/not-separate-not-equal-feds-look-native-kids-public-schools-155085

Lewis Jr., C. E. (2015, March 3). *Is Solitary Confinement Cruel and Unusual Punishment?* Retrieved August 28, 2016, from Social Justice Solutions: http://www.socialjusticesolutions.org/2015/03/03/solitary-confinement-cruel-unusual-punishment/

Library of Congress. (2016). *H.R.2646 - Helping Families in Mental Health Crisis Act of 2016*. Retrieved October 2, 2016, from Congress.gov: https://www.congress.gov/bill/114th-congress/house-bill/2646?q=%7B%22search%22%3A%5B%22h.r.2646%22%5D%7D&resultIndex=1

Liebergen, S. (2016, September 8). *Police admit first use of the 'Blue Lives Matter' law was a mistake*. Retrieved October 10, 2016, from AOL News: http://www.aol.com/article/2016/09/08/police-admit-first-use-of-the-blue-lives-matter-law-was-a-mist/21468611/

Liptak, A. (2008, April 23). *U.S. prison population dwarfs that of other nations*. Retrieved October 9, 2016, from New York Times: http://www.nytimes.com/2008/04/23/world/americas/23iht-23prison.12253738.html?_r=0

Luan, L. (2018, May 2). *Profiting from Enforcement: The Role of Private Prisons in U.S. Immigration Detention*. Retrieved August 26, 2018, from Migration Policy Institute: https://www.migrationpolicy.org/article/profiting-enforcement-role-private-prisons-us-immigration-detention

Maloney, E. T. (n.d.). *Rights Of Detainees and Prisoners in the United States*. Retrieved October 14, 2018, from University of Florida (UFL) Law: https://www.law.ufl.edu/_pdf/academics/centers/cgr/11th_conference/Tim_Maloney_Rights_of_Detainees.pdf

Martyris, N. (2017, February 17). *Frederick Douglass On How Slave Owners Used Food As A Weapon Of Control*. Retrieved February 24, 2017, from www.npr.org: http://www.npr.org/sections/thesalt/2017/02/10/514385071/frederick-douglass-on-how-slave-owners-used-food-as-a-weapon-of-control

McElhatton, J. (2008, June 29). *A $600 drug deal, 40 years in prison*. Retrieved October 18, 2018, from The Washington Times: https://www.washingtontimes.com/news/2008/jun/29/a-600-drug-deal-40-years-in-prison/

Melamed, S. (2018, January 25). *Father. Son.Cellmates. GENERATIONS OF PHILLY FAMILIES ARE INCARCERATED TOGETHER*. Retrieved August 25, 2018, from The Inquirer Daily News philly.com:

http://www.philly.com/philly/news/crime/prison-family-life-sentences-mass-incarceration-philadelphia-pennsylvania.html

Miller, C. (2016, September 8). *Louisiana Man Charged with Hate Crime for "Verbally Attacking" Cops (Updated)*. Retrieved October 8, 2016, from PINAC: http://photographyisnotacrime.com/2016/09/08/louisiana-man-charged-with-police-hate-crime-after-verbally-attacking-cops-during-drunken-arrest/

Morris, J. (2016, August 3). *America's blue dawn: How "Blue Lives Matter" bills might only raise tensions with police*. Retrieved October 9, 2016, from Salon: http://www.salon.com/2016/08/03/americas_blue_dawn_how_blue_lives_matter_bills_might_only_raise_tensions_with_police/

Mukherjee, K. (2016, July 8). *Congress Is on the Verge of Passing a Landmark Mental Health Bill*. Retrieved July 9, 2016, from Fortune.com: http://fortune.com/2016/07/08/congress-mental-health-bill/

NAACP. (2016). *CRIMINAL JUSTICE FACT SHEET - Incarceration Trends in America*. Retrieved May 2, 2016, from NAACP: http://www.naacp.org/criminal-justice-fact-sheet/

Neff, Joseph. (2018, July 23). *Punished for Crimes Not Proven - Brett Kavanaugh and the case of Gregory "Boy Boy" Bell*. Retrieved October 14, 2018, from The Marshall Project: https://www.themarshallproject.org/2018/07/23/punished-for-crimes-not-proven

Overby, S. (2010, May 27). *Prison Labor: Outsourcing's "Best Kept Secret"*. Retrieved June 2, 2015, from CIO.com: http://www.cio.com/article/2417888/outsourcing/prison-labor--outsourcing-s--best-kept-secret-.html

Oxford Bibliographies. (2012, April 24). *Mass Incarceration - Christopher Wildeman*. Retrieved May 28, 2015, from Oxford Bibliographies: http://www.oxfordbibliographies.com/view/document/obo-9780195396607/obo-9780195396607-0033.xml#obo-9780195396607-0033-bibItem-0014

PBS Channel Thirteen. (n.d.). *Slavery by Another Name*. Retrieved October 16, 2016, from The Public Broadcasting Service: http://www.pbs.org/tpt/slavery-by-another-name/themes/peonage/

Pelaez, V. (2016, August 28). *The Prison Industry in the United States: Big Business or a New Form of Slavery?* Retrieved October 2, 2016, from Global Research: http://www.globalresearch.ca/the-prison-industry-in-the-united-states-big-business-or-a-new-form-of-slavery/8289

Phelps, M. S. (2018, January 2018). *The Lesson of Meek Mill: A Probation System 'Set Up to Fail'*. Retrieved July 25, 2018, from The Crime Report:

https://thecrimereport.org/2018/01/31/the-enduring-lesson-of-meek-mill-a-probation-system-set-up-to-fail/

Porter, N. D. (2013, October). *Ending Mass Incarceration: Social Interventions That Work.* Retrieved October 2, 2016, from The Sentencing Project.org: http://www.sentencingproject.org/wp-content/uploads/2015/12/Ending-Mass-Incarceration-Social-Interventions-That-Work.pdf

Prison Fellowship. (2018). *FAQS ABOUT CHILDREN OF PRISONERS.* Retrieved August 15, 2018, from PrisonFellowship.org: https://www.prisonfellowship.org/resources/training-resources/family/ministry-basics/faqs-about-children-of-prisoners/

Prison Policy Initiative. (2010). *United States Incarceration Rate Rates by Race and Ethnicity, 2010 [Graph].* Retrieved May 30, 2015, from Prison Policy Initiative: http://www.prisonpolicy.org/graphs/raceinc.html

Quest. (2016, September 19). *The Largest Prison Strike in History Is Being Ignored By Major Media.* Retrieved September 22, 2016, from We Are Change: http://wearechange.org/largest-prison-strike-ignored/

Rios, E. (2016, April 11). *These Public Defenders Actually Want to Get Sued - Because the right to a lawyer doesn't count for much if nobody's willing to pay for it.* Retrieved October 9, 2016, from Mother Jones: http://www.motherjones.com/politics/2016/03/new-orleans-public-defenders-financial-crisis

Rodriguez, S. (2015). *FAQ.* Retrieved October 2, 2016, from SolitaryWatch.com: http://solitarywatch.com/facts/faq/

RT. (2016, September 8). *New Orleans man becomes first arrestee under new 'Blue Lives Matter' hate crime law.* Retrieved October 10, 2016, from RT: https://www.rt.com/usa/358731-man-arrested-blue-lives-matter-hate-crime/

Salaam, Y. (2016, October 27). *How 'affluenza' threatens to reach the presidency.* Retrieved October 31, 2016, from Amsterdam News.com: http://amsterdamnews.com/news/2016/oct/27/how-affluenza-threatens-reach-presidency/

Schenwar, M. (2016, September 29). *A Virtual Visit to a Relative in Jail.* Retrieved October 3, 2016, from New York Times: http://www.nytimes.com/2016/09/29/opinion/a-virtual-visit-to-a-relative-in-jail.html?mabReward=A3&moduleDetail=recommendations-1&action=click&contentCollection=Opinion&region=Footer&module=WhatsNext&version=WhatsNext&contentID=WhatsNext&src=recg&pgtype=ar

Sentencing Project. (2015, December). *Fact Sheet: Trends In U.S. Corrections - Drug Policy.* Retrieved March 3, 2016, from The Sentencing Project: http://www.sentencingproject.org/publications/trends-in-u-s-corrections/

Sentencing Project. (2015, November). *Fact Sheet: Trends In U.S. Corrections - Felony Disenfranchisement.* Retrieved March 3, 2016, from The Sentencing Project: http://www.sentencingproject.org/publications/trends-in-u-s-corrections/

Sentencing Project. (2015, November). *Fact Sheet: Trends In U.S. Corrections - Life Sentences.* Retrieved March 3, 2016, from The Sentencing Project: http://www.sentencingproject.org/publications/trends-in-u-s-corrections/

Sentencing Project. (2015, November). *Fact Sheet: Trends In U.S. Corrections - Racial Disparities.* Retrieved March 3, 2016, from The Sentencing Project: FACT SHEET: TRENDS IN U.S. CORRECTIONS

Simon, J. (1993). *Poor discipline: Parole and the social control of the underclass, 1890 - 1990.* Chicago: University of Chicago Press.

Sledge, M. (2018, August 24). *Judge grants class-action status to lawsuit against Louisiana public defender system.* Retrieved August 25, 2018, from The New Orleans Advocate: https://www.theadvocate.com/new_orleans/news/courts/article_3990da7a-a7e0-11e8-b394-63c6bf424ab6.html

Subramanian, R., & Delaney, R. (2014, February). *Playbook for Change? States Reconsider Mandatory Sentences Playbook for Change?* Retrieved May 30, 2015, from The Vera Institute of Justice: http://archive.vera.org/sites/default/files/resources/downloads/mandatory-sentences-policy-report-v2b.pdf

Taylor, D. (2018, August 15). *Parents in prison: The child health crisis no one is talking .* Retrieved August 15, 2018, from The Inquirer Daily News philly.com: http://www2.philly.com/philly/health/kids-families/parents-in-prison-the-child-health-crisis-no-one-is-talking-about-20180815.html

The Marshall Project . (2016, September 16). *Justice for Some: Real estate, tax lawyers forced to do public defenders' job in Louisiana.* Retrieved October 9, 2016, from Nola.org: http://www.nola.com/crime/index.ssf/2016/09/justice_for_some_real_estate_t.html

The Sentencing Project. (2012, September 27). *Parents In Prison.* Retrieved August 23, 2018, from The Sentencing Project: https://www.sentencingproject.org/publications/parents-in-prison/

The Sentencing Project. (2016, September 16). *Mass Incarceration in Middle America.* Retrieved October 3, 2016, from The Sentencing Project: http://www.sentencingproject.org/news/mass-incarceration-middle-america/

The Sentencing Project. (2018, July). *Felony Disenfranchisement: A Primer.* Retrieved August 25, 2018, from The Sentencing Project: https://www.sentencingproject.org/issues/felony-disenfranchisement/

The Sentencing Project. (n.d.). *The Sentencing Project*. Retrieved April 3, 2015, from The Sentencing Project: http://www.sentencingproject.org/template/page.cfm?id=107

The Sentencing Project; Source: Bureau of Justice Statistics Prisoners Series. (2018, June). *Trends in U.S. Corrections U.S. State and Federal Prison Population, 1925-2016*. Retrieved August 9, 2018, from The Sentencing Project: https://sentencingproject.org/wp-content/uploads/2016/01/Trends-in-US-Corrections.pdf

The White House Boys. (2008, March 22). *Martin Tabert's Story*. Retrieved October 16, 2016, from The White House Boys: http://www.thewhitehouseboys.com/tabert.html

Thomson Reuters. (n.d.). *What Is Civil Asset Forfeiture?* Retrieved June 14, 2018, from FindLaw.com: https://criminal.findlaw.com/criminal-rights/what-is-civil-asset-forfeiture.html

ThomsonReuters. (2018). *Asset Forfeiture Laws by State*. Retrieved June 4, 2018, from FindLaw: https://criminal.findlaw.com/criminal-rights/asset-forfeiture-laws-by-state.html

U.S. Department of Education Office for Civil Rights. (2014, March). *CIVIL RIGHTS DATA COLLECTION-Data Snapshot: School Discipline*. Retrieved October 10, 2016, from U.S. Department of Education Office for Civil Rights: http://ocrdata.ed.gov/Downloads/CRDC-School-Discipline-Snapshot.pdf

US Legal.com. (n.d.). *Hands-off Doctrine Law and Legal Definition*. Retrieved October 14, 2018, from USLegal.com: https://definitions.uslegal.com/h/hands-off-doctrine/

USA.gov. (2016). *How to Contact Your Elected Officials*. Retrieved October 2, 2016, from USA.gov: https://www.usa.gov/elected-officials

UTC. (2014, March 4). *Wife of murdered prison guard urges justice for man placed in solitary 42 years ago*. Retrieved October 9, 2016, from Amnesty International: https://www.amnesty.org/en/latest/news/2014/03/wife-murdered-prison-guard-urges-justice-man-placed-solitary-years-ago/

Vespa, M. (2015, June 6). *How Many Federal Laws Are There Again?* Retrieved January 14, 2016, from Townhall.com: http://townhall.com/tipsheet/mattvespa/2015/06/06/how-many-federal-laws-are-there-again-n2009184

Wagner, P. (2012, August 28). *Incarceration is not an equal opportunity punishment*. Retrieved September 16, 2018, from prisonpolicy.org: https://www.prisonpolicy.org/articles/notequal.html

Walker, G. (2016, May 7). *New Georgia law lifts food stamp ban for drug felons.* Retrieved July 15, 2016, from The Red & Black: http://www.redandblack.com/athensnews/new-georgia-law-lifts-food-stamp-ban-for-drug-felons/article_e047283c-1413-11e6-ad63-6767de912a3e.html

Walsh, D. (2016, June 2). *On the Defensive - The right to legal counsel has long been the gold standard of American justice under the Constitution. But what happens when a state refuses to budget for public defenders? Louisiana is finding out.* Retrieved October 9, 2016, from The Atlantic: http://www.theatlantic.com/politics/archive/2016/06/on-the-defensive/485165/

Weisburd, Kate; The Marshall Project. (2016, June 16). *Getting suspended or expelled in school should not keep people out of college.* Retrieved September 29, 2016, from The Times-Picayune, Greater New Orleans: http://www.nola.com/crime/index.ssf/2016/06/getting_suspended_or_exp elled.html

Weisenthal, J. (2012, March 12). *This Investor Presentation For A Private Prison Is One Of The Creepiest Presentations We've Ever Seen.* Retrieved September 2, 2016, from Business Insider: http://www.businessinsider.com/the-private-prison-business-2012-3

Weiser, B. (2014, June 19). *5 Exonerated in Central Park Jogger Case Agree to Settle Suit for $40 Million.* Retrieved September 16, 2016, from New York Times: http://www.nytimes.com/2014/06/20/nyregion/5-exonerated-in-central-park-jogger-case-are-to-settle-suit-for-40-million.html

Wells, I. B. (1893, August 30). *THE REASON WHY The Colored American is not in the World's Columbian Exposition. Lynch Law (From the reprint of the 1893 edition, Robert W. Rydell, ed., Urbana and Chicago: University of Illinois Press, 1999.).* Retrieved October 16, 2016, from University of Pennsylvania: http://digital.library.upenn.edu/women/wells/exposition/exposition.html# IV

Wells, Ida B. (1893, August 30). *The Reason Why the Colored American Is Not in the World's Columbian Exposition. The Convict Lease System (From the reprint of the 1893 edition, Robert W. Rydell, ed., Urbana and Chicago: University of Illinois Press, 1999.).* Retrieved October 16, 2016, from University of Pennsylvania: http://digital.library.upenn.edu/women/wells/exposition/exposition.html# note

Whiteside, L. (2015, July 29). *Obama to offer Pell grants to prisoners.* Retrieved December 2, 2015, from CNN Money: http://money.cnn.com/2015/07/29/news/inmates-pell-grants-obama/

Wikipedia. (2016, October 8). *Angola Three.* Retrieved October 9, 2016, from Wikipedia: https://en.wikipedia.org/wiki/Angola_Three

Wikipedia. (n.d.). *Convict lease.* Retrieved October 12, 2016, from Wikipedia: https://en.wikipedia.org/wiki/Convict_lease

Wikipedia. (n.d.). *Kids for cash scandal.* Retrieved February 1, 2016, from Wikipedia.org: https://en.wikipedia.org/wiki/Kids_for_cash_scandal

Wikipedia. (n.d.). *Marcus Dixon.* Retrieved September 14, 2016, from Wikipedia.org: https://en.wikipedia.org/wiki/Marcus_Dixon

Wildeman, C., & Western, B. (2010, Fall). *Incarceration in Fragile Families.* Retrieved May 29, 2015, from http://www.futureofchildren.org/: http://www.futureofchildren.org/futureofchildren/publications/docs/20_0 2_08.pdf

Wolfers, J., Leonhardt, D., & Quealy, K. (2015, April 20). *1.5 Million Missing Black Men.* Retrieved May 30, 2015, from New York Times, The Upshot: http://www.nytimes.com/interactive/2015/04/20/upshot/missing-black-men.html?_r=0&abt=0002&abg=0

Zanolli, L. (2016, May 13). *Louisiana's Public Defender Crisis Is Leaving Thousands Stuck in Jail With No Legal Help.* Retrieved June 2, 2016, from Vice News: https://news.vice.com/article/louisianas-public-defender-crisis-is-leaving-thousands-stuck-in-jail-with-no-legal-help

INDEX/ENDNOTES

[1] Garland, David. 2001. Introduction: The meaning of mass imprisonment. In *Mass imprisonment: Social causes and consequences*. Edited by David Garland, 1–3. London: SAGE

[2] The Sentencing Project. (n.d.). The Sentencing Project. Retrieved April 3, 2015, from The Sentencing Project: http://www.sentencingproject.org/template/page.cfm?id=107

[3] NAACP. (2016). CRIMINAL JUSTICE FACT SHEET - Incarceration Trends in America. Retrieved May 2, 2016, from NAACP: http://www.naacp.org/criminal-justice-fact-sheet/

[4] Kearney, M. S., Harris, B. H., Jacome, E., & Parker, L. (2014, May). Ten Economic Facts about Crime and. Retrieved February 5, 2016, from Hamilton Project Policy Memo May 2014: http://www.hamiltonproject.org/assets/legacy/files/downloads_and_links/v8_THP_10Crim eFacts.pdf

[5] Ibid, p 10

[6] Ibid, p 1

[7] Wolfers, J., Leonhardt, D., & Quealy, K. (2015, April 20). 1.5 Million Missing Black Men. Retrieved May 30, 2015, from New York Times, The Upshot: http://www.nytimes.com/interactive/2015/04/20/upshot/missing-black-men.html?_r=0&abt=0002&abg=0

[8] Bump, P. (2015, April 29). Hillary Clinton hopes to undo the mass incarceration system Bill Clinton helped build. Retrieved May 30, 2015, from The Washington Post: http://www.washingtonpost.com/blogs/the-fix/wp/2015/04/29/hillary-clinton-hopes-to-undo-the-mass-incarceration-system-bill-clinton-helped-build/

[9] Frizel, S. (2015, April 29). Hillary Clinton Calls for an End to 'Mass Incarceration'. Retrieved May 30, 2015, from Time.com: http://time.com/3839892/hillary-clinton-calls-for-an-end-to-mass-incarceration/

[10] American Enterprise Institute. (2018, July 12). Criminal justice reform in 2018: A conversation with Rep. Hakeem Jeffries (D-NY) and Rep. Doug Collins (R-GA). Retrieved July 29, 2018, from American Enterprise Institute: http://www.aei.org/events/criminal-justice-reform-in-2018-a-conversation-with-rep-hakeem-jeffries-d-ny-and-rep-doug-collins-r-ga/

[11] Capital and Main; Gary Cohn . (2014, October 23). Newt Gingrich And Jay-Z Find Common Cause In A Prison Reform Proposition. Retrieved May 30, 2015, from The Huffington Post: http://www.huffingtonpost.com/2014/10/23/proposition-47_n_6038310.html

[12] Frumin, A. (2014, April 28). The long, slow push to prison sentencing reform. Retrieved May 30, 2015, from MSNBC.com: http://www.msnbc.com/msnbc/the-long-push-prison-sentencing-reform

[13] Subramanian, R., & Delaney, R. (2014, February). Playbook for Change? States Reconsider Mandatory Sentences Playbook for Change? Retrieved May 30, 2015, from The Vera Institute of Justice:

http://archive.vera.org/sites/default/files/resources/downloads/mandatory-sentences-policy-report-v2b.pdf

[14] The Sentencing Project; Source: Bureau of Justice Statistics Prisoners Series. (2018, June). Fact Sheet: Trends in U.S. Corrections - U.S. State and Federal Prison Population, 1925-2016. Retrieved August 9, 2018, from The Sentencing Project: https://sentencingproject.org/wp-content/uploads/2016/01/Trends-in-US-Corrections.pdf

[15] Ibid

[16] Prison Policy Initiative. (2010). United States Incarceration Rate Rates by Race and Ethnicity, 2010 [Graph]. Retrieved May 30, 2015, from Prison Policy Initiative: http://www.prisonpolicy.org/graphs/raceinc.html

[17] Wagner, P. (2012, August 28). Incarceration is not an equal opportunity punishment. Retrieved September 16, 2018, from prisonpolicy.org: https://www.prisonpolicy.org/articles/notequal.html

[18] Federal Bureau of Prisons. (2018, September 29). Statistic - Inmate Race. Retrieved October 14, 2018, from Federal Bureau of Prisons: https://www.bop.gov/about/statistics/statistics_inmate_race.jsp

[19] Alexander, M. (2011, October 13). Michelle Alexander: More Black Men Are In Prison Today Than Were Enslaved In 1850. Retrieved May 29, 2016, from The Huffington Post: http://www.huffingtonpost.com/2011/10/12/michelle-alexander-more-black-men-in-prison-slaves-1850_n_1007368.html

[20] NAACP. (2016). CRIMINAL JUSTICE FACT SHEET - Incarceration Trends in America. Retrieved May 2, 2016, from NAACP: http://www.naacp.org/criminal-justice-fact-sheet/

[21] Ibid

[22] Ibid

[23] Fields, G., & Emshwiller, J. R. (2011, July 23). Many Failed Efforts to Count Nation's Federal Criminal Laws. Retrieved May 29, 2015, from The Wall Street Journal: http://www.wsj.com/articles/SB10001424052702304319804576389601079728920

[24] Ibid

[25] Vespa, M. (2015, June 6). How Many Federal Laws Are There Again? Retrieved January 14, 2016, from Townhall.com: http://townhall.com/tipsheet/mattvespa/2015/06/06/how-many-federal-laws-are-there-again-n2009184

[26] Ibid

[27] Ibid

[28] Cohen, S. (1985). Visions of social control: Crime, punishment, and classification. Cambridge, UK: Polity.

[29] Simon, J. (1993). Poor discipline: Parole and the social control of the underclass, 1890-1990. Chicago: University of Chicago Press.

[30] Wildeman, C., & Western, B. (2010, Fall). Incarceration in Fragile Families. Retrieved May 29, 2015, from http://www.futureofchildren.org/: http://www.futureofchildren.org/futureofchildren/publications/docs/20_02_08.pdf

[31] Oxford Bibliographies. (2012, April 24). Mass Incarceration - Christopher Wildeman. Retrieved May 28, 2015, from Oxford Bibliographies: http://www.oxfordbibliographies.com/view/document/obo-9780195396607/obo-9780195396607-0033.xml#obo-9780195396607-0033-bibItem-0014

[32] Kincade, B., & Godard, T. (2016, March 23). The Economics of the American Prison System. Retrieved June 2, 2016, from smartasset.com: https://smartasset.com/insights/the-economics-of-the-american-prison-system

[33] Kirby, H., Libal, B., Madison, P., Morris, J., & Quong Charles, K. (2013). The Dirty Thirty: Nothing to Celebrate About 30 Years of Corrections Corporation of America. Retrieved October 2, 2016, from http://grassrootsleadership.org/: http://grassrootsleadership.org/cca-dirty-30

[34] Weisenthal, J. (2012, March 12). This Investor Presentation For A Private Prison Is One Of The Creepiest Presentations We've Ever Seen. Retrieved September 2, 2016, from Business Insider: http://www.businessinsider.com/the-private-prison-business-2012-3

[35] Luan, L. (2018, May 2). Profiting from Enforcement: The Role of Private Prisons in U.S. Immigration Detention. Retrieved August 26, 2018, from Migration Policy Institute: https://www.migrationpolicy.org/article/profiting-enforcement-role-private-prisons-us-immigration-detention

[36] Basti, V., & Gotsch, K. (2018, August 2). Capitalizing on Mass Incarceration: U.S. Growth in Private Prisons. Retrieved August 13, 2018, from The Sentencing Project: https://www.sentencingproject.org/publications/capitalizing-on-mass-incarceration-u-s-growth-in-private-prisons/

[37] Erlich, R. (1995, Fall). Prison Labor: Workin' For The Man. Retrieved May 29, 2015, from umass.edu: http://people.umass.edu/kastor/private/prison-labor.html

[38] Overby, S. (2010, May 27). Prison Labor: Outsourcing's "Best Kept Secret". Retrieved June 2, 2015, from CIO.com: http://www.cio.com/article/2417888/outsourcing/prison-labor--outsourcing-s--best-kept-secret-.html

[39] Kearney, M. S., Harris, B. H., Jacome, E., & Parker, L. (2014, May). Ten Economic Facts about Crime and. Retrieved February 5, 2016, from Hamilton Project Policy Memo May 2014: p 11 http://www.hamiltonproject.org/assets/legacy/files/downloads_and_links/v8_THP_10Crim eFacts.pdf

[40] Porter, N. D. (2013, October). Ending Mass Incarceration: Social Interventions That Work. Retrieved October 2, 2016, from The Sentencing Project.org: http://www.sentencingproject.org/wp-content/uploads/2015/12/Ending-Mass-Incarceration-Social-Interventions-That-Work.pdf

[41] Pelaez, V. (2016, August 28). The Prison Industry in the United States: Big Business or a New Form of Slavery? Retrieved October 2, 2016, from Global Research: http://www.globalresearch.ca/the-prison-industry-in-the-united-states-big-business-or-a-new-form-of-slavery/8289

[42] Maloney, E. T. (n.d.). Rights of Detainees and Prisoners in the United States. Retrieved October 14, 2018, from University of Florida (UFL) Law: https://www.law.ufl.edu/_pdf/academics/centers/cgr/11th_conference/Tim_Maloney_Right s_of_Detainees.pdf

[43] US Legal.com. (n.d.). Hands-off Doctrine Law and Legal Definition. Retrieved October 14, 2018, from USLegal.com: https://definitions.uslegal.com/h/hands-off-doctrine/

[44] The Sentencing Project; Source: Bureau of Justice Statistics Prisoners Series. (2018, June). Fact Sheet: Trends in U.S. Corrections - Life Sentences. Retrieved August 9, 2018,

from The Sentencing Project: https://sentencingproject.org/wp-content/uploads/2016/01/Trends-in-US-Corrections.pdf

[45] Martyris, N. (2017, February 17). Frederick Douglass On How Slave Owners Used Food As A Weapon Of Control. Retrieved February 24, 2017, from www.npr.org: http://www.npr.org/sections/thesalt/2017/02/10/514385071/frederick-douglass-on-how-slave-owners-used-food-as-a-weapon-of-control

[46] Conaway, H. A.-C. (2018, August 3). H.R. 2, AGRICULTURE AND NUTRITION ACT OF 2018. Retrieved August 5, 2018, from FARMBILL-House Agricultural Committee-Chairman K. Michael Conaway: https://agriculture.house.gov/farmbill/

[47] Bolen, E., Cai, L., Dean, S., Keith-Jennings, B., Nchako, C., Rosenbaum, D., et al. (2018, July 30). House Farm Bill Would Increase Food Insecurity and Hardship. Retrieved August 5, 2018, from Center on Budget and Policy Priorities: https://www.cbpp.org/research/food-assistance/house-farm-bill-would-increase-food-insecurity-and-hardship

[48] Rodriguez, S. (2015). FAQ. Retrieved October 2, 2016, from SolitaryWatch.com: http://solitarywatch.com/facts/faq/

[49] Center for Constitutional Rights. (2015, June 1). Torture: The Use of Solitary Confinementin U.S. Prisons. Retrieved August 28, 2016, from Center for Constitutional Rights: https://ccrjustice.org/home/get-involved/tools-resources/fact-sheets-and-faqs/torture-use-solitary-confinement-us-prisons

[50] Lewis Jr., C. E. (2015, March 3). Is Solitary Confinement Cruel and Unusual Punishment? Retrieved August 28, 2016, from Social Justice Solutions: http://www.socialjusticesolutions.org/2015/03/03/solitary-confinement-cruel-unusual-punishment/

[51] In the Public Interest. (2016, June). How Private Prison Companies Increase Recidivism. Retrieved October 24, 2016, from In the Public Interest: https://www.inthepublicinterest.org/wp-content/uploads/ITPI-Recidivism-ResearchBrief-June2016.pdf

[52] Equal Justice Initiative. (2016, February 8). Private Prison Phone Companies Lobbied for Criminalization of Cell Phones in Prisons. Retrieved January 3, 2017, from Equal Justice Initiative: http://eji.org/news/private-companies-lobbied-to-criminalize-cell-phones-in-prisons

[53] Walker, G. (2016, May 7). New Georgia law lifts food stamp ban for drug felons. Retrieved July 15, 2016, from The Red & Black: http://www.redandblack.com/athensnews/new-georgia-law-lifts-food-stamp-ban-for-drug-felons/article_e047283c-1413-11e6-ad63-6767de912a3e.html

[54] Beitsch, R. (2015, July 30). States Rethink Restrictions on Food Stamps, Welfare for Drug Felons. Retrieved April 6, 2016, from Pewtrust.org: http://www.pewtrusts.org/en/research-and-analysis/blogs/stateline/2015/07/30/states-rethink-restrictions-on-food-stamps-welfare-for-drug-felons

[55] Community Coalition. (n.d.). Are Our Children Being Pushed into Prison? Retrieved September 3, 2016, from Community Coalition: The above infographic was created by Community Coalition http://cocosouthla.org/inforgraphics/

[56] U.S. Department of Education Office for Civil Rights. (2014, March). CIVIL RIGHTS DATA COLLECTION-Data Snapshot: School Discipline. Retrieved October 10, 2016,

from U.S. Department of Education Office for Civil Rights:
http://ocrdata.ed.gov/Downloads/CRDC-School-Discipline-Snapshot.pdf
[57] Lee, T. H. (2014, June 3). Not Separate, Not Equal: Feds Look at Native Kids in Public
Schools. Retrieved October 10, 2016, from Indian Country:
http://indiancountrytodaymedianetwork.com/2014/06/03/not-separate-not-equal-feds-look-
native-kids-public-schools-15508
[58] Whiteside, L. (2015, July 29). Obama to offer Pell grants to prisoners. Retrieved
December 2, 2015, from CNN Money: http://money.cnn.com/2015/07/29/news/inmates-
pell-grants-obama/
[59] Bakeman, J. (2014, February 18). Republicans rally against Cuomo's prison-college plan.
Retrieved December 2, 2015, from Politico: http://www.politico.com/states/new-
york/albany/story/2014/02/republicans-rally-against-cuomos-prison-college-plan-011039
[60] Getlen, L. (2014, February 23). Corrupt 'Kids for Cash' judge ruined more than 2,000
lives. Retrieved February 1, 2016, from New York Post:
http://nypost.com/2014/02/23/film-details-teens-struggles-in-state-detention-in-payoff-
scandal/
[61] Wikimedia Foundation, Inc. (n.d.). Kids for cash scandal. Retrieved February 1, 2016,
from Wikipedia.org: https://en.wikipedia.org/wiki/Kids_for_cash_scandal
[62] http://www.nydailynews.com/sports/football/jets/marcus-dixon-overcomes-molestation-
conviction-high-school-racism-long-journey-nfl-ny-jets-article-1.982917
[63] Wikipedia.org. (2016). Marcus Dixon. Retrieved September 14, 2016, from
Wikipedia.org: https://en.wikipedia.org/wiki/Marcus_Dixon
[64] Jacobs, A. (2004, January 22). Student Sex Case in Georgia Stirs Claims of Old South
Justice. Retrieved September 14, 2016, from New York Times:
http://www.nytimes.com/2004/01/22/us/student-sex-case-in-georgia-stirs-claims-of-old-
south-justice.html?_r=0
[65] The Sentencing Project; Source: Bureau of Justice Statistics Prisoners Series. (2018,
June). Trends in U.S. Corrections - Racial Disparities. Retrieved August 9, 2018, from The
Sentencing Project: https://sentencingproject.org/wp-content/uploads/2016/01/Trends-in-
US-Corrections.pdf
[66] Liebergen, S. (2016, September 8). Police admit first use of the 'Blue Lives Matter' law
was a mistake. Retrieved October 10, 2016, from AOL News:
http://www.aol.com/article/2016/09/08/police-admit-first-use-of-the-blue-lives-matter-law-
was-a-mist/21468611/
[67] Morris, J. (2016, August 3). America's blue dawn: How "Blue Lives Matter" bills might
only raise tensions with police. Retrieved October 9, 2016, from Salon:
http://www.salon.com/2016/08/03/americas_blue_dawn_how_blue_lives_matter_bills_mig
ht_only_raise_tensions_with_police/
[68] RT. (2016, September 8). New Orleans man becomes first arrestee under new 'Blue
Lives Matter' hate crime law. Retrieved October 10, 2016, from RT:
https://www.rt.com/usa/358731-man-arrested-blue-lives-matter-hate-crime/
[69] Wells, Ida B. (1893, August 30). The Reason Why the Colored American Is Not in the
World's Columbian Exposition. The Convict LeaseSystem (From the reprint of the 1893
edition, Robert W. Rydell, ed., Urbana and Chicago: University of Illinois Press, 1999.).
Retrieved October 16, 2016, from University of Pennsylvania:
http://digital.library.upenn.edu/women/wells/exposition/exposition.html#notehttp://digital.l
ibrary.upenn.edu/women/wells/exposition/exposition.html#note

[70] Wikipedia. (n.d.). Convict lease. Retrieved October 12, 2016, from Wikipedia: https://en.wikipedia.org/wiki/Convict_lease

[71] Digital History. (2016). Along the Color Line, Convict Lease System, Digital History ID 3179. Retrieved October 16, 2016, from Digital History, http://www.digitalhistory.uh.edu/: http://www.digitalhistory.uh.edu/disp_textbook_print.cfm?smtid=2&psid=3179

[72] Wikipedia. (n.d.). Convict lease. Retrieved October 12, 2016, from Wikipedia: https://en.wikipedia.org/wiki/Convict_lease

[73] Wells, I. B. (1893, August 30). THE REASON WHY The Colored American is not in the World's Columbian Exposition. Lynch Law (From the reprint of the 1893 edition, Robert W. Rydell, ed., Urbana and Chicago: University of Illinois Press, 1999.). Retrieved October 16, 2016, from University of Pennsylvania: http://digital.library.upenn.edu/women/wells/exposition/exposition.html#IV

[74] Browne, J. (2008). Rooted in Slavery: Prison Labor Exploitation. Retrieved October 12, 2016, from Race, Poverty & the Environment (Reprinted from RP&E Vol. 14, No. 2: Just Jobs? Organizing for Economic Justice, 2007): http://www.reimaginerpe.org/20years/browne

[75] Digital History. (2016). Along the Color Line, Convict Lease System, Digital History ID 3179. Retrieved October 16, 2016, from Digital History, http://www.digitalhistory.uh.edu/: http://www.digitalhistory.uh.edu/disp_textbook_print.cfm?smtid=2&psid=3179

[76] Ibid

[77] Wells, Ida B. (1893, August 30). The Reason Why the Colored American Is Not in the World's Columbian Exposition. The Convict Lease System (From the reprint of the 1893 edition, Robert W. Rydell, ed., Urbana and Chicago: University of Illinois Press, 1999.). Retrieved October 16, 2016, from University of Pennsylvania: http://digital.library.upenn.edu/women/wells/exposition/exposition.html#note

[78] Ibid

[79] PBS Channel Thirteen. (n.d.). Slavery by Another Name. Retrieved October 16, 2016, from The Public Broadcasting Service: http://www.pbs.org/tpt/slavery-by-another-name/themes/peonage/

[80] The White House Boys. (2008, March 22). Martin Tabert's Story. Retrieved October 16, 2016, from The White House Boys: http://www.thewhitehouseboys.com/tabert.html

[81] Ibid

[82] Burnett, G. M. (1988). A young Dakota wayfarer falls victim to a notorious penal system, but public outcry brings the system's abolition. In G. M. Burnett, Florida's Past, People and Events That Shaped the State, Volume 3 (pp. 122-25). Sarasota, FL: Pineapple Press.

[83] Ibid

[84] The White House Boys. (2008, March 22). Martin Tabert's Story. Retrieved October 16, 2016, from The White House Boys: http://www.thewhitehouseboys.com/tabert.html

[85] Browne, J. (2008). Rooted in Slavery: Prison Labor Exploitation. Retrieved October 12, 2016, from Race, Poverty & the Environment (Reprinted from RP&E Vol. 14, No. 2: Just Jobs? Organizing for Economic Justice, 2007): http://www.reimaginerpe.org/20years/browne

[86] Community Coalition. (n.d.). Why Are We Criminalizing Poverty? Retrieved September 2, 2016, from Community Coalition: http://cocosouthla.org/inforgraphics/

[87] Zanolli, L. (2016, May 13). Louisiana's Public Defender Crisis Is Leaving Thousands Stuck in Jail With No Legal Help. Retrieved June 2, 2016, from Vice News:

https://news.vice.com/article/louisianas-public-defender-crisis-is-leaving-thousands-stuck-in-jail-with-no-legal-help

[88] Ibid

[89] Rios, E. (2016, April 11). These Public Defenders Actually Want to Get Sued - Because the right to a lawyer doesn't count for much if nobody's willing to pay for it. Retrieved October 9, 2016, from Mother Jones: http://www.motherjones.com/politics/2016/03/new-orleans-public-defenders-financial-crisis

[90] Hager, Eli; The Marshall Project and Guardian US. (2016, September 16). Justice for Some: Real estate, tax lawyers forced to do public defenders' job in Louisiana. Retrieved September 28, 2016, from The Times-Picayune Greater New Orleans, Nola.com: http://www.nola.com/crime/index.ssf/2016/09/justice_for_some_real_estate_t.html

[91] Sledge, M. (2018, August 24). Judge grants class-action status to lawsuit against Louisiana public defender system. Retrieved August 25, 2018, from The New Orleans Advocate: https://www.theadvocate.com/new_orleans/news/courts/article_3990da7a-a7e0-11e8-b394-63c6bf424ab6.html

[92] In the Public Interest. (n.d.). Programs Not Profits. Retrieved 11 2, 2016, from In the Public Interest: https://www.inthepublicinterest.org/programs-not-profits/

[93] In the Public Interest. (n.d.). In the Public Interest. Retrieved 11 2, 2016, from In the Public Interest: Democracy, shared prosperity, and the common good: https://www.inthepublicinterest.org/

[94] Thomson Reuters. (n.d.). What Is Civil Asset Forfeiture? Retrieved June 14, 2018, from FindLaw.com:https://criminal.findlaw.com/criminal-rights/what-is-civil-asset-forfeiture.html

[95] Thomson Reuters. (2018). Asset Forfeiture Laws by State. Retrieved June 4, 2018, from FindLaw: https://criminal.findlaw.com/criminal-rights/asset-forfeiture-laws-by-state.html

[96] Jacobs, S., & Annese, J. (2016, October 16). Mom dies of 'broken heart' after son Kalief Browder killed himself last year. Retrieved October 30, 2016, from New York Daily News.com: http://www.nydailynews.com/new-york/bronx/exclusive-mom-late-kalief-browder-dies-broken-heart-article-1.2833023

[97] UTC. (2014, March 4). Wife of murdered prison guard urges justice for man placed in solitary 42 years ago. Retrieved October 9, 2016, from Amnesty International: https://www.amnesty.org/en/latest/news/2014/03/wife-murdered-prison-guard-urges-justice-man-placed-solitary-years-ago/

[98] Gast, P., & Sutton, J. (2013, October 2). Dying 'Angola 3' inmate is released in Louisiana. Retrieved October 9, 2016, from CNN: http://www.cnn.com/2013/10/01/justice/angola-3-former-black-panther-ordered-released/index.html

[99] Lane, Emily; NOLA.com; The Times-Picayune. (2016, February 19). Why has Albert Woodfox been in solitary for more than 40 years? Retrieved September 30, 2016 , from NOLA.com: http://www.nola.com/politics/index.ssf/2015/06/albert_woodfox_solitary_confin.html

[100] Ibid

[101] Dargis, M. (2012, November 21). Filmmakers Still Seek Lessons From a Case That Rocked a City - The Documentary 'The Central Park Five'. Retrieved October 30, 2016,

from New York Times.Com: http://www.nytimes.com/2012/11/22/movies/the-documentary-the-central-park-five.html

[102] Weiser, B. (2014, June 19). 5 Exonerated in Central Park Jogger Case Agree to Settle Suit for $40 Million. Retrieved September 16, 2016, from New York Times: http://www.nytimes.com/2014/06/20/nyregion/5-exonerated-in-central-park-jogger-case-are-to-settle-suit-for-40-million.html

[103] Salaam, Y. (2016, October 27). How 'affluenza' threatens to reach the presidency. Retrieved October 31, 2016, from Amsterdam News.com: http://amsterdamnews.com/news/2016/oct/27/how-affluenza-threatens-reach-presidency/

[104] Weiser, B. (2014, June 19). 5 Exonerated in Central Park Jogger Case Agree to Settle Suit for $40 Million. Retrieved September 16, 2016, from New York Times: http://www.nytimes.com/2014/06/20/nyregion/5-exonerated-in-central-park-jogger-case-are-to-settle-suit-for-40-million.html

[105] Dargis, M. (2012, November 21). Filmmakers Still Seek Lessons From a Case That Rocked a City - The Documentary 'The Central Park Five'. Retrieved October 30, 2016, from New York Times.Com: http://www.nytimes.com/2012/11/22/movies/the-documentary-the-central-park-five.html

[106] Davidson, A. (2014, June 23). DONALD TRUMP AND THE CENTRAL PARK FIVE. Retrieved September 16, 2016, from The New Yorker: http://www.newyorker.com/news/amy-davidson/donald-trump-and-the-central-park-five

[107] Dargis, M. (2012, November 21). Filmmakers Still Seek Lessons From a Case That Rocked a City - The Documentary 'The Central Park Five'. Retrieved October 30, 2016, from New York Times.Com: http://www.nytimes.com/2012/11/22/movies/the-documentary-the-central-park-five.html

[108] Davidson, A. (2014, June 23). DONALD TRUMP AND THE CENTRAL PARK FIVE. Retrieved September 16, 2016, from The New Yorker: http://www.newyorker.com/news/amy-davidson/donald-trump-and-the-central-park-five

[109] Weiser, B. (2014, June 19). 5 Exonerated in Central Park Jogger Case Agree to Settle Suit for $40 Million. Retrieved September 16, 2016, from New York Times: http://www.nytimes.com/2014/06/20/nyregion/5-exonerated-in-central-park-jogger-case-are-to-settle-suit-for-40-million.html

[110] Neff, Joseph. (2018, July 23). Punished for Crimes Not Proven - Brett Kavanaugh and the case of Gregory "Boy Boy" Bell. Retrieved October 14, 2018, from The Marshall Project: https://www.themarshallproject.org/2018/07/23/punished-for-crimes-not-proven

[111] McElhatton, J. (2008, June 29). A $600 drug deal, 40 years in prison. Retrieved October 18, 2018, from The Washington Times: https://www.washingtontimes.com/news/2008/jun/29/a-600-drug-deal-40-years-in-prison/

[112] Cassell, P. (2014, March 18). Should a drug dealer acquitted of running a drug ring be sentenced for running a drug ring? Retrieved October 18, 2018, from Washington Post: https://www.washingtonpost.com/news/volokh-conspiracy/wp/2014/03/18/should-a-drug-dealer-acquitted-of-running-a-drug-ring-be-sentenced-for-running-a-drug-ring/?noredirect=on&utm_term=.3d9b22f605ce

[113] Kittle, R. L. (2016, April 21). Shorter Prison Term Supporters Pack SC House Hearing. Retrieved September 18, 2016, from WSPA.org Channel 7 News: http://wspa.com/2016/04/21/shorter-prison-term-supporters-pack-sc-house-hearing/

[114] Bibas, S. (2015, September 16). The Truth about Mass Incarceration. Retrieved October 5, 2016, from National Review: http://www.nationalreview.com/article/424059/mass-incarceration-prison-reform

[115] Schenwar, M. (2016, September 29). A Virtual Visit to a Relative in Jail. Retrieved October 3, 2016, from New York Times: http://www.nytimes.com/2016/09/29/opinion/a-virtual-visit-to-a-relative-in-jail.html?mabReward=A3&moduleDetail=recommendations-1&action=click&contentCollection=Opinion&region=Footer&module=WhatsNext&versio n=WhatsNext&contentID=WhatsNext&src=recg&pgtype=ar

[116] The Sentencing Project; Source: Bureau of Justice Statistics Prisoners Series. (2018, June). Fact Sheet: Trends in U.S. Corrections- Drug Policy. Retrieved August 9, 2018, from The Sentencing Project: https://sentencingproject.org/wp-content/uploads/2016/01/Trends-in-US-Corrections.pdf

[117] Mukherjee, K. (2016, July 8). Congress Is on the Verge of Passing a Landmark Mental Health Bill. Retrieved July 9, 2016, from Fortune.com: http://fortune.com/2016/07/08/congress-mental-health-bill/

[118] Library of Congress. (2016). H.R.2646 - Helping Families in Mental Health Crisis Act of 2016. Retrieved October 2, 2016, from Congress.gov: https://www.congress.gov/bill/114th-congress/house-bill/2646?q=%7B%22search%22%3A%5B%22h.r.2646%22%5D%7D&resultIndex=1

[119] Melamed, S. (2018, January 25). Father. Son.Cellmates. GENERATIONS OF PHILLY FAMILIES ARE INCARCERATED TOGETHER. Retrieved August 25, 2018, from The Inquirer Daily News philly.com: http://www.philly.com/philly/news/crime/prison-family-life-sentences-mass-incarceration-philadelphia-pennsylvania.html

[120] Prison Fellowship. (2018). FAQS ABOUT CHILDREN OF PRISONERS. Retrieved August 15, 2018, from PrisonFellowship.org: https://www.prisonfellowship.org/resources/training-resources/family/ministry-basics/faqs-about-children-of-prisoners/

[121] Taylor, D. (2018, August 15). Parents in prison: The child health crisis no one is talking . Retrieved August 15, 2018, from The Inquirer Daily News philly.com: http://www2.philly.com/philly/health/kids-families/parents-in-prison-the-child-health-crisis-no-one-is-talking-about-20180815.html

[122] Ibid

[123] Ibid

[124] Melamed, S. (2018, January 25). Father. Son.Cellmates. GENERATIONS OF PHILLY FAMILIES ARE INCARCERATED TOGETHER. Retrieved August 25, 2018, from The Inquirer Daily News philly.com: http://www.philly.com/philly/news/crime/prison-family-life-sentences-mass-incarceration-philadelphia-pennsylvania.html

[125] Prison Fellowship. (2018). FAQS ABOUT CHILDREN OF PRISONERS. Retrieved August 15, 2018, from PrisonFellowship.org: https://www.prisonfellowship.org/resources/training-resources/family/ministry-basics/faqs-about-children-of-prisoners/

[126] The Sentencing Project. (2012, September 27). Parents In Prison. Retrieved August 23, 2018, from The Sentencing Project: https://www.sentencingproject.org/publications/parents-in-prison/

[127] The Sentencing Project. (2018, July). Felony Disenfranchisement: A Primer. Retrieved August 25, 2018, from The Sentencing Project: https://www.sentencingproject.org/issues/felony-disenfranchisement/

[128] Phelps, M. S. (2018, January 2018). The Lesson of Meek Mill: A Probation System 'Set Up to Fail'. Retrieved July 25, 2018, from The Crime Report: https://thecrimereport.org/2018/01/31/the-enduring-lesson-of-meek-mill-a-probation-system-set-up-to-fail/

[129] USA.gov. (2016). How to Contact Your Elected Officials. Retrieved October 2, 2016, from USA.gov: https://www.usa.gov/elected-officials

[130] Liptak, A. (2008, April 23). U.S. prison population dwarfs that of other nations. Retrieved October 9, 2016, from New York Times: http://www.nytimes.com/2008/04/23/world/americas/23iht-23prison.12253738.html?_r=0

[131] The Sentencing Project. (2016, September 16). Mass Incarceration in Middle America. Retrieved October 3, 2016, from The Sentencing Project: http://www.sentencingproject.org/news/mass-incarceration-middle-america/

[132] Johnson, A. (2016, September 16). Did You Know We Are Having the Largest Prison Strike in History? Probably Not, Because Most of the Media Have Ignored It. Retrieved October 5, 2016, from Alternet.org: http://www.alternet.org/media/did-you-know-we-are-having-largest-prison-strike-history-probably-not-because-most-media-have

[133] Bibas, S. (2015, September 16). The Truth about Mass Incarceration. Retrieved October 5, 2016, from National Review: http://www.nationalreview.com/article/424059/mass-incarceration-prison-reform

[134] Ibid

Made in the USA
Columbia, SC
29 January 2019